ALSO BY DAVID BURNHAM

The Rise of the Computer State

A Law Unto Itself

David Burnham

A LAW UNTO ITSELF

Power, Politics, and the IRS

RANDOM HOUSE NEW YORK

Library of Congress Cataloging-in-Publication Data
Burnham, David
A law unto itself: power, politics, and the IRS / by David Burnham.
Bibliography: p.
Includes index.
ISBN 0-394-56097-3
1. United States. Internal Revenue Service. 2. Tax administration and procedure—United States—Corrupt practices. I. Title.
HJ5018.B87   1990   353.0072'4—dc20   89-42778

To Molly, Sarah, and Joanne

Acknowledgments

Sometimes the genesis of a book becomes somewhat vague to an author. But this is not the present case. About five years ago Steve Engelberg, a friend and young reporter in the Washington Bureau of *The New York Times,* looked up from his desk in the newsroom and suggested I write an investigative book about the IRS. Almost immediately I realized Steve had hit upon a terrific idea, one that followed naturally from my long-standing interest in law enforcement and privacy issues.

To thank all the others who have contributed to the writing of this book is not possible. The Alicia Patterson Foundation, a wonderful organization that supports independent writing projects, selected me to be one of its 1987 fellows. The J. Roderick MacArthur Foundation and the Deer Creek Foundation provided additional essential support. Jerry Berman and Morton Halperin of the American Civil Liberties Union generously offered me a year of office space. Then Michael Pertschuk and David Cohen suggested I take up residence within their small organization, the Advocacy Institute.

The IRS has not always been so cordial. Former Commissioner Lawrence Gibbs and several other officials, for example, refused to be interviewed. Their separate decisions contrasted with the actions of the IRS's public affairs office, which courteously answered hundreds of my large and small questions. Most of the day-to-day burden of my endless inquiries fell on the shoulders of Wilson Fadley and Johnnell Hunter.

This is the second book I have written with the expert and supportive editorial advice of Bob Loomis of Random House. I am grateful to him. Once again, my agent Robin Straus has been a wonderful friend and counselor.

Contents

A Law Unto Itself

Thinking About Taxes and the Taxman

It was Benjamin Franklin, of course, who two hundred years ago told us that nothing was certain in this world except death and taxes.

This worn sample of Franklin's elegant knack for stating big truths in simple ways came to mind a while ago as I began reading a stack of government reports on the Internal Revenue Service, nuclear war, and taxes. More specifically, the reports tell how the IRS and its parent agency, the Treasury Department, plan to go on collecting taxes from us after two hundred nuclear bombs have dropped on the United States and killed 100 million Americans, destroyed incalculable amounts of property, and incinerated a substantial part of the records that document the wealth of the nation.

Here, memorialized in the turgid prose of long-forgotten bureaucrats, was stated the absolute first rule of all governments: Nothing, not even the incredible destruction of nuclear war, is more important to any government than the collection of taxes.

Considering the awful mess these federal planners had been asked to resolve, the relentless optimism of their reports is both bizarre and touching. The title chosen by a midlevel Treasury Department technician for his February 1966 analytic report on tax policy in the postattack period tells it all: *Fiscal Planning for Chaos.* One has to be truly upbeat to develop a tax plan for chaos.

This 1966 study also reflected the perversely self-centered perspective common to all government bureaucrats. In one section, for example, the official indicated that his primary concern about a possible nuclear attack was the disorder that such a strike would bring to *government* rather than the unimaginable horror it would wreak on *society.* "Because the post-attack period would be one of chaos and disorganization of the revenue service," the official warned, "emergency tax proposals for individuals, corporations and bank and nonbank financial institutions should be required to meet two standards. They are (1) revenue yield adequate for defense, short-term emergency needs and rehabilitation, and the quick restoration of services and damaged industrial facilities essential to national survival, and (2) simplicity of administration even to the exclusion of considerations of equity."[1]

The collected doomsday papers of the Treasury Department and its tax collection arm, the IRS, indicate that revenue collection after a nuclear attack remained a nagging concern throughout most of the cold war. A few months after the 1966 report, on the day after Christmas 1967, for example, Treasury Secretary Henry H. Fowler sent a confidential memo to Price Daniel, director of the Office of Emergency Planning. In ironic keeping with the seasonal tradition that it is better to give than to receive, Fowler informed Daniel of the department's current thinking about how the nation's taxpayers could go on paying taxes after a catastrophic nuclear attack and some of the working assumptions behind the project.

"For emergency planning purposes," the Treasury Department statement began, "the estimate is widely used that a nuclear attack on U.S. metropolitan areas could result in 100 million casualties. Property damage would be incalculable in monetary values. That such devastation is considered a serious possibility forces us to the conclusion that no matter what form of tax system is adopted, one basic problem will be simplifying tax administration."

Because Treasury believed it was likely that a nuclear attack would cause different levels of devastation in different parts of the United States, the department concluded that there would be some regions where "a tax system would not be necessary" and other areas where some kind of formal tax system could be maintained.

In the regions of catastrophic damage, where no tax collection would be feasible, the government would declare martial law and commandeer all available resources to meet emergency needs. In those areas, the government would confiscate all food stores to supply free "soup kitchens" and order healthy survivors to work in hospitals and other essential facilities. "Money payments could be suspended and tax collection could be suspended. Simply stated, everybody would be in the Army."

But after the initial phases of the emergency in even the most hard-hit regions, Treasury predicted that a limited market economy and monetary exchange system would begin to emerge. In this second stage, the Treasury Department concluded, the actual collection of taxes would be required if the government was going to begin acquiring significant amounts of food, medicine, and other supplies by the payment of money. "A flat rate gross receipts tax would be simple to administer and fully adequate to economic requirements."

The experts concluded that, as the American people began to rebuild during the post-attack period, "problems arising out of wide income differentials would not exist and the refinement of an income tax would not be necessary.

"Nevertheless," they continued, "it would be desirable to have on the books a personal income tax at the outset of the emergency. The reasons for the very early establishment of a personal income tax even though the private economic sector may have ceased to function, are that (1) the Revenue Service should have time to plan the administration of the tax . . . and (2) liability should be established at the earliest phases of the emergency to tax illegal gains made by speculators and black market operators."

One interesting little Treasury Department paper focused on the problems the IRS would face when it tried to measure wealth after a nuclear attack. "Consider a firm whose principal assets consist of a professional football team valued, pre-attack, at $15 million," the study said. "Suppose that the players survived the attack and that all the debts of the team were fully paid up. Any plan to levy a net-worth tax post attack must face up to the fact that this firm's relative worth in real terms is certainly not going to be the same as pre-attack."

Once they had completed their deliberations, the Treasury Department and the IRS decided the time had come to ask Congress to grant the agency vast standby powers that might be needed should nuclear war actually commence. On October 31, 1977, IRS Commissioner Jerome Kurtz said the "basic purpose of the [proposed] legislation is to provide maximum flexibility and decentralization of authority in order that the Internal Revenue Service may effectively carry on operations in areas that have been subjected to an enemy attack."

But even after Congress had approved the emergency powers legislation, the Treasury Department continued to worry about whether or not in the post-attack confusion the IRS would actually be able to collect taxes based on individual income. "If there is sufficient damage to the records normally required to document and determine income, it would be necessary to scrap the income tax system as we know it," concluded a 1981 policy paper, *Design of an Emergency Tax System.*

"Instead of an income tax, one could design a general sales tax which would raise the revenue required. Such a tax should be implemented in this situation with as few as possible exemptions from the tax base. This has the dual feature of simple administration and the encouragement of savings to aid in the rebuilding of capital stock since with a consumption base, savings is exempted from the tax."

The 1981 Treasury study concluded that the general sales tax "on final sales would have to be approximately 20 percent in order to replace current individual and corporate taxes, social security taxes and estate and gift taxes." (In a subsequent paper, it was decided that the sales tax would have to be upped to 24 percent.)

The continuing trickle of policy papers and legislative proposals demonstrates that the top officials of the federal government of the United States were determined, come the hell of nuclear war or, implicitly, the high water of any natural disaster, to continue to collect taxes. In a most concrete way, the unswerving determination of these officials to complete their mission no matter how desperate the nation's condition confirms the wisdom of the death-and-taxes observation of the sage of Philadelphia.

History, of course, is very much on Franklin's side. No major civilization has shrunk from the essential and often unpleasant business of collecting taxes. In fact, one of the world's first written references to taxes is a complaint about how the government in question had continued collecting a special war tax long after the war that had prompted it had ended. The Sumerian civilization began to flourish about 4000 B.C. on the fertile plain that lies between the Tigris and Euphrates rivers. On clay cones excavated near the ancient Sumerian city of Lagash, about 150 miles southeast of Baghdad, an unknown scribe told how the government had instituted a period of heavy taxation during a war but then refused to give up its taxing powers with the return of peace. The scribe wrote that from one end of the land to the other, even in the absence of fighting, "there were tax collectors." Everything was taxed. Much to the outrage of the people, even the dead could not be buried without official tribute.

This period of intense taxation many thousands of years ago left its historical mark with the birth of a proverb that in various forms has continued to echo through the ages. "You can have a lord, you can have a king, but the man to fear is the tax collector."[2]

The connection between burdensome taxes and war has since remained a subject of interest to both taxpayers and scholars. In the thirteenth century, for example, Thomas Aquinas noted that under normal conditions of peace the king should "live on his own." But in time of war, when the king's revenues might not be adequate, his subjects could be taxed to enable him "to provide for the common good from the common goods."[3]

The ticklish problem of defining the common good almost always has been the troublesome stumbling block. In 1966, the most successful musical group of that period offered its negative view of the whole process in "The Tax Man":

> If you drive a car, I'll tax the street
> If you try to sit, I'll tax your seat
> If you get too cold, I'll tax your heat
> If you take a walk, I'll tax your feet
> Cause I'm the tax man
> Yeah I'm the tax man.

Thus did the four young millionaires collectively known as the Beatles render their jaundiced view of the English tax collector.

Adam Smith, the great eighteenth-century economist, offered something far more constructive than tired complaints when he outlined the principles of fair taxation that to this day seem a model of good sense. The four key points, Smith contended, should be equality (proportional taxation), certainty, convenience of payment, and economy of collection. "The tax which each individual is bound to pay ought to be certain, and not arbitrary," he wrote. "The time of payment, the manner of payment, the quantity paid, ought to be clear and plain to the contributor, and to every other person, so the tax payer is not put in the power of the tax gatherer."

Smith's words strike the contemporary American ear as an acute comment about the problems that continue to plague today's Internal Revenue Service. "By subjecting the people to frequent visits and odious examination of the tax gatherers, it may expose them to much unnecessary trouble, vexation and oppression; and though vexation is not, strictly speaking, an expense, it is certainly equivalent to the expense that every man would be willing to redeem himself from it."[4]

At about the same time that Smith was developing his sensible rules, Edmund Burke, a British statesman and historian, in an essay on the

French Revolution of his time, mused on the absolute core connection of taxes and tax collection to the existence of the nation. As we shall see, this connection probably is the best single explanation why the Internal Revenue Service has been granted a unique set of powers. "The revenue of the state is the state," Burke said.[5]

Since the beginning of recorded history, the power to tax, or not to tax, has been used for both good and ill. The application of this power often has a surprisingly modern ring. In the Old Testament Book of Ezra (7:24), for example, we are instructed about the tax exemption provided the established religion of that period. "It shall not be lawful to impose toll, tribute or customs" upon "any of the priests and Levites, singers, porters, Nethinium or ministers of this House of God."

More recently, two Supreme Court justices, John Marshall and Robert Jackson, also offered up lessons about the far-reaching impact of taxes and tax collectors. "An unlimited power to tax involves, necessarily, a power to destroy; because there is a limit beyond which no institution and no property can bear taxation," Chief Justice John Marshall wrote in 1819.[6] More than one hundred years later, Associate Justice Robert Jackson, musing on the power of taxation, but from a slightly different perspective, wrote, "No other branch of the law touches human activities at so many points."[7]

Over and over again, taxes and tax collectors have served as the engines of historical change. In the early days of the white settlement of North America, for example, opposition to the imposition of taxes was the motivating force behind two of the most significant events of American history.

In the first instance, the forces that ultimately led to the drafting of the Declaration of Independence in 1776 were set in motion eleven years before when the British Parliament passed the Stamp Act. In the second instance, the first serious exercise of power by the government of the United States came when the just-elected president, George Washington, marshaled an army to suppress the violent opposition of frontier farmers to a tax on whiskey. The single element common to these two events was what then and now is called the excise tax, sometimes a fee paid for a license to carry on certain occupations, sometimes a tax on the manufacture, sale, or consumption of such various commodities as liquor or tobacco.

The strong opposition of the North American colonies to the Stamp Act, Lord George Grenville's 1765 excise tax, had many precedents in the mother country. As early as 1610, members of Parliament had denounced plans for the collection of what are also sometimes called interior or inland tax duties. And it was not until the outbreak of the Civil War in 1642 that the government was able to win Parliament's reluctant consent for the first excise tax on the British people. Almost a century later, Sir Robert Walpole created a hurricane of opposition to the few excise taxes then on the books by calling for tougher collection procedures. Walpole's plan generated the largest deluge of petitions and instructions from outraged constituents that up to that time had flooded Parliament. Members denounced the proposal on the grounds that it would create "swarms of tax gatherers," standing armies, and "arbitrary laws of excise." The Right Honorable William Pulteney, for example, argued that Walpole's proposal "breathes nothing but the principles of the most arbitrary and most tyrannical governments that have been established in Europe." He denounced the excise as "a badge of slavery."[8]

Given Great Britain's long history of opposition to the principle of the excise tax, Grenville's 1765 request that Parliament impose the Stamp Act tax on the colonies to offset the expenses of defending them during the French and Indian War is somewhat surprising. Even more curious was Parliament's professed difficulty in understanding the strong American objections to the tax. As argued in London by Franklin and others, winning the consent of the people through their chosen representatives was an essential precondition for the just collection of internal taxes, another name for the hated excise taxes. The strong feelings of the colonials generated so many protests and demonstrations that Grenville had second thoughts about the political wisdom of the Stamp Act tax, and it was withdrawn about a year after its imposition. But a germ of revolution had been planted in the body politic of the American people. It should also be noted that the legislation accomplishing Grenville's tactical withdrawal from the political brier patch of the Stamp Act included strategic language asserting the broad power of Parliament to pass laws binding on the colonies. In 1767 Parliament acted on this general assertion when it approved the Townshend Act, which established a set of colonial duties on a number of items, including tea. Six years later, in 1773, a small group of outraged colonials dressed as Indians dumped cargoes of tea into Boston Harbor. Then, in April 1775, the long political debate about Britain's right to impose excise taxes on the colonies changed character during a violent confrontation at Lexington and Concord. America's Revolutionary War had began.

The subsequent victory of George Washington's Continental Army over the British forces, however, did not resolve the dispute over who had the power to decide the taxes that would be paid by the American people. It just changed the locus of the debate. In 1781, the thirteen states approved the short-lived Articles of Confederation, reserving to their separate selves the power to tax. Seven years later, partly because of the major diplomatic and political problems created by the inability of the Confederation to collect taxes, a small band of men gathered in Philadelphia, ostensibly to devise ways to improve the Articles of Confederation. Very soon, however, merchants, politicians, and lawyers at the convention began to consider a revolutionary new plan of government for the former colonies. The constitution they drafted in 1787 called upon this new federal government to exercise the essential power of any real governing body. This was, of course, the "power to lay and collect taxes, duties, imposts and excises." The taxing power granted the new government when the constitution was officially adopted in 1788 was far more extensive than Parliament had dreamed of assuming in the decades before the War of Independence. And many Americans were as opposed to the federal claims as they had been to those of the Crown. William Goudy of North Carolina, for example, argued that the tax clause in the new Constitution "will totally destroy our liberties." In 1788 and 1789, a sizable number of citizens still believed that internal taxes were no business of the central government and should be left to local representatives who lived among their constituents and were intimately familiar with their wants and needs.

But George Washington, who became president in 1789, very definitely did not belong to this camp. Neither did Treasury Secretary Alexander Hamilton. Establishing the constitutional principle of centralized taxation, however, was a long way from persuading Congress to approve a tax law and even further from actually collecting taxes. The first step was accomplished in March 1791, when the House and Senate approved a bill establishing a tariff system that included duties on selected imports and an internal excise tax on distilled whiskey.

The section of the new law mandating the whiskey excise tax was of great significance because it almost immediately sparked the first outbreak of violent opposition to the brand-new government. A second provision of the law, however, would have far more long-term importance to the people of the United States. For it was under this second provision, granting the Treasury Department the power to collect taxes, that Hamilton in 1792 first established the Office of the Commissioner of Revenue, the predecessor of what is today known as the Internal Revenue Service.

Although the tax critics of that era were clearly wrong when they predicted that the Constitution's tax provision would lead to the development of a tyrannical federal government which ultimately would destroy itself, they were right when they said that attempts to collect the excise tax on whiskey would lead to the outbreak of what many historians regard as the first civil war of the United States.

In fact, the opposition to the new whiskey tax became the largest single instance of armed resistance against the authority of the federal government between the year the Constitution was adopted and the beginning of the second Civil War, in 1861. The Whiskey Rebellion peaked in a march of about seven thousand armed frontiersmen on Pittsburgh, then a small river town on the edge of the frontier, and in the refusal of virtually every farmer living on the western slope of the Appalachian chain to abide by the hated law. In the successful effort to put down this genuine rebellion and to establish the principle of federal taxation, a determined President Washington ultimately was forced to nationalize 12,950 state militiamen, an army that came close to matching the number of "Continentals" who followed him through the key battles of the Revolutionary War.

The protest against George Washington's whiskey tax came in several shapes. First there were speeches and demonstrations and organizing meetings. Then in September 1791 sixteen frontiersmen disguised in women's clothing assaulted an excise tax collector named Robert Johnson. They stole his horse, cut his hair, tarred and feathered him, and left him in a "mortifying and painful situation."[9]

After several more years of scattered acts of violence, the federal government began to lose patience. In the summer of 1794 U.S. Marshal David Lenox headed west from Philadelphia armed with subpoenas ordering the appearance of over sixty distillers before the federal district court in Philadelphia. John Neville, a retired military commander who was one of the first agents hired by the new commissioner of revenue, became his local guide.

The federal marshal and the tax collector began serving the subpoenas on July 15. On the next day, the local militia surrounded the house where Neville was staying, a battle broke out, and one militiaman was mortally wounded.

The line had been drawn in the frontier dust. As news of the outrage flowed back to Philadelphia, then the capital of the nation, President Washington and Secretary Hamilton decided that an overwhelming response was required. On August 4, 1794, Supreme Court Justice James Wilson sent Washington an official ruling that "from the evidence which has been laid before me I hereby notify you that in the counties of Washington and Allegheny, the laws of the United States are opposed, and the execution thereof obstructed by combinations too powerful to be suppressed by the ordinary course of judicial proceedings, or by the powers vested in the marshall of that district."[10]

Justice Wilson's ruling was required before Washington could federalize the militias of Pennsylvania, New Jersey, Virginia, and Maryland. On September 30, accompanied by this ragtag army of thirteen thousand, Washington, Hamilton, and Secretary of War Henry Knox headed west to meet with two emissaries of the rebels. At the meeting, Washington told the Westerners that he regarded "the support of the laws an object of first magnitude" and that nothing short of "unequivocal proofs of absolute submission" would suffice. Now convinced that the rebellion could be contained, Washington turned command over to General Light-Horse Harry Lee.

"The most substantial roundup of suspects in western Pennsylvania occurred on November 13. Mounted troops struck in the dead of night, in some cases literally dragging men from bed and without permitting the prisoners to dress themselves for the journey ahead. About 150 half-naked frontiersmen, some of them with bare feet, were then 'driven before a troop of horse at the trot through muddy roads seven miles from Pittsburgh.' "[11]

Eventually, about twenty of the tax protestors, mostly obscure frontier farmers, were dragged to Philadelphia and tried for treason. In the end, the juries acquitted all but two of the prisoners.

With the absolute right of the federal government to collect taxes firmly established, Washington chose to act in a magnanimous way. The president pardoned the two convicted felons. Thus ended what to this day remains the most widespread and violent resistance to federal taxes in the history of the United States.

In 1801 Thomas Jefferson and other anti-Federalists were elected and the tax dispute that had been so important to Washington, Hamilton, and the establishment of federal authority was pushed aside. The Jeffersonians could afford to abandon the hated internal tax because the limited federal government of that day could be largely financed by customs duties. Most of the four hundred tax collectors who had been hired by the revenue commissioner during the Washington administration were fired. Thus, while the federal government's lawful authority to collect internal taxes had been firmly established, the government found it did not need them.

But six decades later, the voracious demands of what we now call national defense dramatically altered the needs of the government.

It was the Civil War that created the modern tax collection apparatus we now know as the Internal Revenue Service. Abraham Lincoln was inaugurated president in March 1861 and immediately faced a genuine budget crisis. There was no way the massive demands of the impending war with the South could be financed by customs duties. On July 1, 1862, Congress approved revolutionary legislation that included the nation's first real income tax. The fever of war blinded Congress to the fact that its decision to collect a federal tax on the incomes of individuals almost certainly violated the Constitution's mandate that "direct taxes shall be apportioned among the several states." The military demands implicit in the North's decision to preserve the Union at any cost required that Lincoln and his Republican Congress create a far-reaching tax system. Although the Civil War version of the income tax was comparatively modest, the July 1862 legislation also established death duties and a broad excise tax on all manufactured goods.

To take on the difficult job of collecting these needed taxes, Congress re-created the Office of the Commissioner of Revenue.[12] And within a few days of Congress's approval of the broad new tax law, George S. Boutwell of Massachusetts, now considered the nation's first tax commissioner, went to work with the help of three clerks in a single room in the Treasury Department. By January 1863, the commissioner commanded a small army of four thousand tax collectors.

In terms of revenue collection, the new agency was quite successful. Just four years after its creation, for example, revenues from the federal excise, income, and inheritance taxes totaled $311 million. This compared with $28.5 million the government collected during one year just before the start of the war.

From the beginning, however, there were a number of problems that will sound familiar to the modern taxpayer. The four-page Civil War income tax form was far simpler than today's. But the Civil War version was sufficiently complicated that even a very shrewd Illinois lawyer named Lincoln was unable to understand all of its provisions. This is proven by the fact that eight years after Lincoln's assassination it was discovered that in 1864 the president had overpaid his taxes by $1,250. The money was returned to the Lincoln estate. To this day, critics charge that the tax agency is possessed with an unholy desire to confuse the public with obscurely written, hard-to-understand forms.

There were other early manifestations of administrative difficulties that have continued to plague the agency. At first, revenue collectors were paid a percentage of the collections they extracted from taxpayers. It soon became apparent that this explicit cash incentive could lead to serious abuse and it was abolished. But substitute techniques to encourage the tax collectors to pursue their unpleasant tasks had to be found. Thus it is that at least for the last fifty years top officials of the agency have repeatedly denied the existence of the formal quota systems that they routinely have used to energize revenue officers.

The Civil War tax collectors also were subject to improper political influence from above and bribes from below. Joseph J. Lewis, the second head of the tax agency and a friend of Lincoln, hired "private collectors for delinquent accounts [who earned] commissions ranging up to 50 percent, an arrangement tailor made for some unscrupulous collectors, who, after effecting the collection, simply continued westward with both their own and the government's money."[13] A special commission, created by Congress at the end of the war, reported finding other problems that sound familiar to the modern student of the IRS. "Pay scales were lower than those prevailing in private industry, appointments were made on the basis of political patronage and efforts were made to secure the discharge of service personnel who, in carrying out their duties, had interfered with the private interests of influential persons."[14]

With the end of the Civil War, customs receipts on imported goods and excise taxes on tobacco and alcohol once again became adequate to meet the relatively modest needs of the peacetime federal government. The nation's first inheritance tax left the scene in 1870 and the modest income tax was repealed in 1872. While the reach of the federal tax collectors thus was greatly reduced and the number of collectors dwindled, Congress this time chose to maintain the Office of the Commissioner of Internal Revenue.

The increasing support for a number of populist notions and the rising industrialism of the late nineteenth century gradually led to a profound change in the public's thinking about the proper role of the federal government and the need for additional revenue. In 1894 Congress once again established a modest income tax. But this time, without the pressing demands of the Civil War, the Supreme Court quickly ruled the new tax unconstitutional on the grounds that it violated the apportionment provision of the 1787 Constitution. But pressure for the income tax was irresistible and on February 13, 1913, the Constitution's Sixteenth Amendment was ratified.[15] The language and its intent were direct: "The Congress shall have power to lay and collect taxes on incomes, from whatever source derived, without apportionment among the several States, and without regard to any census or enumeration."

That same year, just eight months after ratification of the Sixteenth Amendment, Congress approved legislation reestablishing the federal income tax. This time the powerful pump that has provided the fuel required for the operation of an expansive federal government became a permanent part of the nation's tax structure.

The creation of the Office of the Commissioner of Revenue in 1862, followed in 1913 by the permanent establishment of the income tax, are two of the three great legs that support today's federal tax system. The third essential leg was created in the middle of World War II, when Congress approved legislation requiring employers to withhold from salaries and wages taxes owed by individuals. Although the withholding statute traditionally receives only passing attention from most tax scholars, its importance in increasing the basic power of the IRS cannot be overstated.[16] From the foundation established by the widely separated actions of Congress in 1862, 1913, and 1943 has grown today's massive and highly computerized Internal Revenue Service.

While almost all Americans wish their federal taxes could be lower, and millions harbor various grudges against the way the IRS goes about the job of tax collection, the agency enjoys astonishingly wide support. Despite the multitude of specific objections, an overwhelming number of Americans agree with the general principle that federal taxes are an absolutely essential part of our civilization. A huge consensus supports federal programs to build highways, conduct medical research, provide assistance to the elderly and disabled, and look out for this country's national security interests. Although promises not to increase taxes are a part of the reelection kits of most politicians, this consensus further understands that taxes are essential if these widely agreed upon programs are to flourish.

It is in support of these generally popular goals that Congress has gradually built a massive and intricate body of tax law that imposes four specific requirements on the American people, private businesses, government agencies, and other institutions. While complex in detail, these four obligations can be easily summarized.

First, all taxpayers, individual and corporate, are required to *file* timely statements about their income.

Second, the income tax returns of these individuals and corporations must correctly *report* the taxes they owe.

Third, all taxpayers must *pay* their taxes according to a precisely determined schedule.

The fourth basic requirement applies only to employers: Any institution with hired hands must regularly *deduct* the taxes owed by their employees and immediately forward these withheld funds to the government.[17]

That's it. Very simple. But to make sure that most taxpayers abide by these four clear and widely accepted tax obligations, the Congress, the courts, and the agency itself have over the years passed hundreds of laws, handed down thousands of decisions, and issued uncounted numbers of regulations that together have molded the IRS into a genuinely formidable organization.

In fact, with the probable exception of a handful of agencies in the Soviet Union and China, there is little question that the IRS today is the single most powerful bureaucracy in the world. As a corollary to this astonishing ranking in the olympics of organizational authority, I believe that the IRS has become the single most powerful instrument of social control in the United States.

The power of the IRS in contemporary America rests on a number of distinct but sometimes overlapping factors that seldom are considered as a whole. They include the following.

SIZE. At last count, the IRS had about 123,000 employees. This makes it without question the largest law enforcement agency in the United States. The IRS, for example, has five times more employees than the Federal Bureau of Investigation and four times more than the New York Police Department. The number of Central Intelligence Agency employees is secret. But it currently is estimated that there are about twenty thousand managers, analysts, and clerks in the CIA's Washington office. Guesses about the number of CIA covert agents working outside the United States range from a low of six thousand to a high of forty-eight thousand. The law establishing the CIA gives the agency no traditional law enforcement powers and includes a provision specifically prohibiting it from conducting most of its activities in the United States. The Social Security Administration, which again has no general law enforcement authority, has about sixty thousand employees.

LEGAL AUTHORITY. Over the years, the IRS's quiver has been stuffed with a much larger number of very sharp enforcement arrows than have been granted to any other law enforcement agency in the United States.

One unique IRS arrow is its independent authority to impose massive civil penalties. If either the IRS or the FBI decides a suspect has committed a *crime,* a lot of hurdles must be leaped before that individual is put in prison. The agents must gather evidence, persuade an independent prosecutor to present the evidence to a grand jury, make sure the evidence is convincing enough so that the grand jury will indict the suspect, and then present the evidence to a regular jury that decides whether the suspect is innocent or guilty. During the last step a judge, who belongs to a separate branch of government, the judiciary, will try to guarantee a fair trial, and a defense lawyer will challenge at least some of the government's assertions. So the FBI and the IRS are roughly equal in the checks and balances department when it comes to bringing criminal charges.

But the IRS, unlike the FBI, has a second route for punishing alleged malefactors. It can charge taxpayers with one or more of the 150 *civil violations* that have been established by Congress during the last seventy years. In a recent year, for example, without any independent review, the agency assessed almost 27 million penalties that called for the payment of over $14 billion in fines.[18] If a taxpayer feels the penalty is not justified, there are sometimes expensive ways the penalty can be challenged either within the IRS or before the courts. But because of the special nature of civil tax law, the legal burden almost always rests with the taxpayer to prove his or her innocence. This contrasts with criminal cases, of course, where the burden of proving the suspect's guilt is placed on the government.

An entirely different kind of power exercised by the IRS—and by no other law enforcement agency in the United States—concerns its lawful authority to grant or refuse tax-exempt status to various kinds of educational and charitable organizations. Because of the important role such organizations play in almost every aspect of American life, the IRS's decisions can either advance or retard an amazingly broad range of social activities, including the practice of religion, the role of private schools, the availability of birth-control counseling, and the right of political parties to present their sometimes unpopular views.

INFORMATION. Other things being equal, the institution with the most information has the most power. Unlike the FBI, which by law and tradition focuses almost all of its attention on criminals and suspected criminals, the IRS has a lawful interest in virtually every American. One of the most vivid examples of this interest is the basic legal requirement that all taxpayers file tax returns with the agency, which often include the most intimate details of their lives. Individuals, corporations, and other institutions provided the IRS with 194 million tax returns in 1988.

But the IRS has many other sources of information. In recent years Congress has rapidly increased the number and kind of institutions that are required to provide the agency a notice of any payment they make to an individual. According to the latest available estimates, the IRS now receives just under 1 billion such third-party reports a year.

With the help of high-speed computers, most of the hundreds of billions of bits of detailed information given to the IRS by the nation's employers, banks, corporations, universities, car dealers, state tax agencies, real-estate agents, and other assorted record keepers are compared with information presented by taxpayers on their income tax returns. This astonishing feat of information collection and matching has been deemed essential for the collection of federal taxes. But it also provides the IRS with the raw material of a computerized national data base unmatched by any other agency in the United States.

A 1976 law established the general principle that tax return information, a major component of this data base, is confidential. But the same law now includes more than sixty specific exceptions to that rule. One is the requirement that the IRS share all the information it obtains about the nation's millions of taxpayers with the fifty states and New York City. The reciprocal of this requirement is that the fifty state tax agencies and New York City are required to share with the IRS all the information they collect about the taxpayers living in their separate jurisdictions.

Another aspect of the IRS's unique legal authority to collect information is its power to order banks, employers, and other institutions to provide information about a taxpayer without obtaining a warrant from a judge. This contrasts with the FBI and all other federal, state, and local police forces, which in such situations are required to obtain a judicial warrant.

The IRS also has been granted authority to seize summarily the assets of any taxpayer it believes might be contemplating flight. Once again, the law empowers the IRS to make a "jeopardy assessment" without the prior approval of a judge. Furthermore, another law called the anti-injunction statute makes it extremely difficult for federal judges to enjoin the agency from making such a seizure. No other federal, state, or local agency in the United States has such power.

THE POLITICAL AND SOCIAL ENVIRONMENT. So far we have been considering the size of the IRS, the information the agency collects, and its various enforcement powers. But gauging the overall authority of an army requires more than simply compiling a list of weapons in its arsenal. An equally important, but often overlooked, determinant of power is the terrain in which the army maneuvers.

In the case of the IRS, three political or social elements outside the immediate control of the agency work to magnify its already formidable strength. The first is the sheer reach and confused ambiguity of the tax laws written by Congress. While the broad requirements of the current law—timely reporting, accurate assessments, and timely payments—are simple, the detailed obligations are overwhelming. One small indicator: A recent count found that the Revenue Code of the United States is now printed on 2,200 pages, not including the 7,600 pages of regulations, which also have the force of law.

From the very first, the requirements of the income tax have engendered confusion. In 1913, Senator Elihu Root of New York replied to a friend who had written to him to complain about the complexity of the brand-new income tax law: "I guess you will have to go to jail. If that is the result of not understanding the Income Tax Law I will meet you there. We shall have a merry, merry time for all our friends will be there. It will be an intellectual center, for no one understands the Income Tax Law except persons who have not sufficient intelligence to understand the questions that arise under it."[19]

The continuing reality of this general confusion is supported by a large number of surveys showing that neither the taxpayers, the tax practitioners on whom the public relies for expert advice, nor the IRS itself actually understands many of the provisions of the tax law. It has become a chestnut of good financial reporting, for example, to ask a sample of tax preparers to work out the taxes owed by a hypothetical family. Almost every time this experiment is done, the practitioners are unable to agree on "the right answer." In 1988, *Money* magazine asked fifty tax preparers to complete the tax return of a hypothetical couple who earned a combined salary of $100,000 and had three children. The hypothetical situation was moderately complex because the make-believe family's investments included stocks, mutual funds, and corporate and municipal bonds and because Mom and Dad owned a second home that they occasionally rented out.

The fifty tax pros chosen by *Money* magazine came up with fifty different tax bills, ranging from a low of $7,202 all the way up to $11,881. Clearly there was no right answer. When the magazine conducted the same survey with fifty more tax preparers in 1989, the confusion was even worse than the previous year.[20]

But the tax preparers of the United States, who now earn $3.5 billion a year in return for their somewhat shaky advice, are not alone in their confusion about the meaning of the murky tax laws.[21] They share this uncertainty about the law they are trying to obey with the IRS agents who are trying to enforce it.

The IRS and the General Accounting Office (GAO), an investigative arm of Congress, have done a series of studies in which IRS employees assigned to answering taxpayer questions about the tax law was tested in their knowledge. In 1975, the GAO cited an IRS study in which a sample of more than one thousand telephone assisters was asked a series of nineteen questions over an eleven-week period shortly before April 15. The IRS found that one out of five of their answers to the public was not correct.[22]

Twelve years later, the GAO did another in this continuing series of studies. Again it was found that one out of five of the answers provided the public by the IRS was incorrect. The 1987 report added, however, that an additional 17 percent of the IRS responses were not complete. In other words, one third of the answers provided the public by specially trained IRS employees were either incorrect or incomplete.[23]

The inability of the taxpayers, the tax preparers, and the IRS to understand the tax law is a shocking commentary on the poor quality of this legislation. It is hard to overstate the consequences that flow from a set of laws that the public is unable to comprehend. Testifying on February 27, 1974, before a Senate subcommittee, Thomas F. Field, then the director of a citizens' group called Tax Analysts and Advocates, offered a broad judgment of the problem: "A tax system is unsuitable for a democracy if it can't be understood by the taxpayers themselves."

Field's general assessment points to two specific questions. How can there be meaningful due process, the lawyer's phrase for fair government, in a Kafkaesque world where neither the enforcers nor the citizens understand the law? And from the perspective of the IRS, can it not be asserted that the more ambiguous the law, the more powerful the enforcing agency?

Here, an analogy might help. A driver and a police officer are usually very clear about the meaning of a red light. In most cases, both parties also know when the mandate of the light has been violated. In the same way, almost everyone understands it is a violation of law to snatch a purse or to shoplift.

But when it comes to the IRS and a possible tax violation, there frequently are no glaring red lights to either warn the taxpayers when they are violating the law or signal the enforcers when a law has been violated. Thus it is that the ambiguous, hard-to-understand tax laws of the nation give IRS investigators far more latitude about when and where to crack the whip than the criminal law gives the average police officer.

The second important, and partially related, empowering element in the IRS's social environment is that the complex requirements of the tax law mean that a determined revenue officer can find questionable or illegal entries in the tax returns of a huge number of taxpayers. The potential reach of the tax laws is truly astonishing. An instructor at an IRS school for training tax examiners probably was slightly exaggerating the case a few years ago when he told Susan B. Long, a leading tax expert, that agents could find "errors" in 99.9 percent of all tax returns. Still, this means that it is not just the crooked business executive, the drug dealer, and the right-wing tax protestor who suddenly can find themselves facing civil or criminal tax charges. Almost all of us can.

The reality that so many are somehow in violation of a supremely murky law gives the agency and the individual agent an astonishingly free hand to pick and choose their targets.

The third seldom noticed component of the IRS's environment that contributes to the agency's independent power is the congressional imperative that *nothing* must stop the collection of taxes. Federal cash payments to the nation's highway builders, welfare mothers, defense contractors, and Social Security recipients are the essential lifeblood of congressional politics. To guarantee their reelection, incumbent members of Congress must deliver the goods to their constituents. But Congress cannot continue to give away federal money unless the U.S. Treasury, the source of its largess, is continually replenished. Thus it is that the political imperative of not messing with the IRS comes close to being a law of nature almost as unbending as the force of gravity.

The effect of this rule is that rarely are the operations of the single most powerful law enforcement agency in the United States examined by Congress, the only body that has a clear and continuous responsibility to make sure that the IRS is working in a fair and effective manner. While aggressive congressional oversight of the executive branch is a key element of the American notion of checks and balances, the House and Senate have almost always given it short shrift. The historical failure of Congress's tax committees to show any real interest in examining the performance of the IRS except when it is totally awash in scandal is a shocking and important failure that further enhances the authority of the agency.

Thus it has come to pass that the IRS has developed into the largest, most computerized, and least examined law enforcement agency in America. History tells us that the agency's vast power has led to many kinds of abusive and arbitrary acts. But history also tells us that the IRS, with a mighty assist from the withholding laws, has been astonishingly effective in carrying out what may well be one of the most difficult tasks assigned to any government agency.

The current official mission statement of the IRS defines its job this way: "The purpose of the Internal Revenue Service is to collect the proper amount of tax revenues at the least cost to the public, and in a manner that warrants the highest degree of public confidence in our integrity, efficiency and fairness."

There is concrete proof that the IRS in many ways does an excellent job executing the first part of its mission: bringing in revenue. In 1988, for example, the agency collected nearly one thousand billion dollars—that's $1,000,000,000,000—an incomprehensible sum that sometimes is referred to as one trillion dollars. Looking at the process a couple of years ago, the IRS calculated that the taxpayers of America actually owed the government $877 billion, $95 billion more than they reported. Because of the current budget problems, it has been fashionable to express astonished concern about this $95 billion tax gap. The cries of outrage, however, miss the key point: American taxpayers provide the government almost $9 out of every $10 that the government estimated the taxpayers were required to pay. Given the complexity of the tax laws, this must be considered an amazing accomplishment.

In the unending pursuit of tax dollars, the agency has splintered itself into hundreds of different units with widely varied responsibilities. Because the work of the agency must be divided by the demands of both function and geography, the organizational plan of the IRS is confusing.

At the very top of the IRS, sitting in a large office in Washington, is the commissioner. He and his chief counsel are the only two agency officials actually appointed by the president and confirmed by the Senate. Congress's 1952 decision to eliminate almost completely the politically appointed jobs in this massive agency came in the wake of a major corruption scandal. The intent was to reduce the chance of improper political influence. But it is hard to reduce the opportunity for improper influence without at the same time reducing the accountability needed to assure the proper functioning of any agency.

Throughout the long history of the IRS, very few commissioners have remained in office long enough to understand and lead the agency. Since the end of World War II, the average tenure at the top position has been only thirty-seven months. During this period, fat offers from leading law and accounting firms interested in capitalizing on the expertise and cachet of former commissioners have contributed to the rapid pace with which most of them have left the agency.

The comparatively brief reign of most IRS commissioners has both advantages and disadvantages. On the plus side, it has prevented the IRS from ever becoming the personal kingdom of, say, a J. Edgar Hoover, the brilliant bureaucrat who came to dominate the FBI and, in the end, ordered it to engage in a large number of illegal and improper actions. This lack of a single, highly visible executive is one of the major reasons that the IRS has remained less a focus of liberal concern than has the FBI.

On the other hand, the rapid turnover at the top has guaranteed that few of the agency's forty commissioners ever gained sufficient knowledge so that they could fairly be held accountable for either its successes or its failures.

The view that many IRS commissioners have been irrelevant is widely shared by experienced employees of the agency. Mitchell Rogovin now is a top Washington lawyer. During the Kennedy and Johnson years he held three high-level federal tax jobs: special assistant to the commissioner, general counsel of the IRS, and assistant attorney general for tax matters. "It's the master sergeants who run the IRS," he said. "I was in the Marine Corps when I was a kid and the IRS and the Corps are just the same. Both are run by the master sergeants." A second IRS official, a member of the agency's permanent cadre, agreed with Rogovin: "If you ask IRS people around the country about the changes that occurred in the agency under Cohen or Caplin or Alexander or Gibbs, they wouldn't understand the question. They know that all changes in the IRS come very very slowly and that the service is run by the sergeants."

The partial leadership vacuum at the very top has guaranteed that, to the limited extent to which IRS operations are directed from Washington, the directions come from a small unknown cadre of senior civil servants who have spent their entire careers slowly inching up the agency's promotion ladder. Not surprisingly, most of the longtime career officials who are admitted to the upper echelons of the priesthood are cautious men who have mostly adopted its genuinely conservative view of the world. The suspicious, almost paranoid, mind-set of many of these senior executives may help explain why the agency has repeatedly challenged the development of social organizations not planted firmly in the middle of the road.

Also contributing to the agency's lack of centralized direction is the organizational structure deliberately chosen by Congress in the early 1950s after a major corruption scandal had swept through the agency. In an effort to reduce the improper political influences that had contributed to the scandal, Congress decided to increase the independent authority of the agency's regional commissioners and district directors and to eliminate all but two of the massive agency's political appointees.

The long-term effect of this sweeping reorganization has been that, although the assistant commissioners who surround the commissioner in Washington are free to issue policy memos, testify before congressional committees, prepare charts, and hold meetings, they have little real authority over the tens of thousands of investigators, auditors, and clerks who actually go about the job of collecting taxes.

The relatively weak authority of the in-and-out commissioners and their terminally cautious assistant commissioners in Washington guarantees that the seven regional commissioners in charge of the North Atlantic, Mid-Atlantic, Southeast, Central, Midwest, Southwest, and Western regions and the sixty-three district directors below them have more independent power than might be expected.

It is widely and, I think, incorrectly believed that the actions taken by government agencies mostly are the products of rational and conscious decisions made by leaders on the basis of their values, interests, and experiences. Television news, which must have a talking head to speak for the White House, the State Department, or any other agency, strongly reinforces this misleading view of how government bureaucracies actually function. But as shown by the analysis of Graham T. Allison and a handful of other scholars, the actions of government probably can be better understood as the output of a lumbering bureaucracy that acts more out of habit than thought, making most of its decisions according to previously established operating procedures.[24]

Christopher Pyle, a professor of political science at Mount Holyoke College in Massachusetts, recently summarized this view of government. "Agencies, like individuals, have priorities, perceptions, goals, and past stands," he explained. "Like individuals, the agencies engage in negotiations, mutual adjustments, compromises, and anticipatory reactions to perceptions of adverse power elsewhere. But the first rule in predicting what an agency will do is to assume that it will behave much as it has in similar circumstances in the past."

There are many aspects of the IRS that make this bureaucratic explanation of how government agencies work ring unusually true. Sometimes, of course, in the case of the IRS, a determined individual like Franklin Roosevelt or Richard Nixon can push the agency slightly out of its predetermined rut. But the rapid turnover at the very top of the IRS, the recruitment of most of its top administrators from within, and the almost complete lack of outside review make the agency astonishingly consistent in the often erratic and hard-nosed way it deals with the American people.

CHAPTER 2

First Encounters
with the IRS

Every year, millions of Americans take part in a complex ritual marking one of the great ceremonial days of the United States: the April 15 deadline for filing the dreaded federal income tax return.* Many of the

---

*It is not easy to measure the work product of the IRS. Consider the apparently simple question of how many individual Americans are taxpayers. Surprisingly, this is a number the IRS itself cannot calculate. The latest annual report states that in 1988 a total of 194,305,000 tax returns were filed with the agency. Of these, 152 million were income tax returns. Of the income tax returns, 107 million were filed by individuals, 4 million by corporations, and 1.8 million by partnerships, with the balance falling into several other categories. But a significant number of individual income tax returns cover the income and taxes of more than one person. The IRS reports that in 1988, 48 million of the 107 million individual income tax returns were joint returns. Thus, the 107 million individual income tax returns are estimated to cover about 155 million taxpayers. Further complicating this calculation, however, is the fact that in some families filing a joint income tax return, only one partner is actually earning any income and paying taxes, although both partners signing a joint return are liable and thus in a legal sense are taxpayers.

There are many other reasons why even the simplest IRS statistics must be handled with care. For example, the grand total of 194 million returns filed in 1988 includes 28.2 million

natives actually devote several frenzied weeks preparing themselves for the final rite—normally celebrated during the closing hours of Tax Day.

Unlike most other major civic and religious ceremonies, which have developed their own distinct images, April 15 remains something of a visual wasteland. The Pilgrim families and their bountiful harvest dinner of wild turkeys, corn pudding, and other vegetables of course remind us of Thanksgiving Day. But what image springs to mind when you think of April 15?

The first somewhat dated candidate that occurs to me is an illustration that Norman Rockwell painted for the cover of the old *Saturday Evening Post* in 1945. The painting shows Dad sitting at his desk, a stubby pencil in his hand, surrounded by a small blizzard of tattered pay stubs, receipts, and other small pieces of paper. Dad is in a swivet as he fills in the numbers on the Smith family's good old 1040 form. On the wall calendar just behind Dad's head the day that taxes were then due, March 15, has been circled in red.

In my town at least, this Norman Rockwell painting has been brought into the electronic age in a somewhat modified form by one of our local television stations. Every April 15, as the midnight deadline approaches, Channel 5's mobile television crew descends on the post office to capture pictures of the good-humored postal workers as they accept the last-minute returns from obviously relieved taxpayers. All is well! The deadline has been met! Our civic responsibilities are fulfilled!

But just as Rockwell's wonderfully folksy paintings largely ignored the painful truths of the Great Depression, World War II, and McCarthyism, so most of the television and print stories that blossom each spring shortly before April 15 miss the real story of tax collection in the United States.

This is because the filing of the dreaded 1040 tax return, while eventually important to the government's bookkeepers, actually has very little to do with the extraordinarily complex and quite efficient process by which the United States each year extracts one trillion dollars ($1,000,000,000,-000) from the American people. In fact, the tax return and the April 15 deadline are in many ways irrelevant to the government's essential task of assuring the steady flow of dollars into the federal coffers.

---

that were prepared by institutions paying employment taxes. Because most employment returns are filed on a quarterly rather than an annual basis, however, the 28.2 million employment tax returns actually represent about 7 million organizations. Yet another complicating factor is that many institutions each year file several different kinds of tax returns. This means that in a single year one corporation might file a corporate income tax return, an excise tax return, and four employment tax returns.

The first fact about tax collection that we all know and most of us forget is the ferocious bite of withholding. The underlying truth is that only a small fraction of the money owed each year by individual taxpayers actually is lifted from their pockets on April 15. This is because since the middle of World War II, the government has required almost all employers to skim off the Treasury's share of the cream *before* they pay to the individual taxpayers what most of us think of as our salary.

The self-congratulatory claims by federal tax officials that most of the people of the United States pay their taxes on a voluntary basis is thus extremely misleading. The supposed wonder of "voluntary compliance," the favored catchphrase of generations of congressmen and IRS officials, makes for nice speeches. But it has very little to do with how federal taxes are collected.

This withholding process is so efficient that four out of five of all tax dollars paid by individual Americans in 1988 were handed to the government without the money ever passing through the hands of the taxpayers. The principal explanation for the effectiveness of withholding lies in the way work is organized in the United States. According to the latest count, nine out of ten of America's 126 million workers were employed by about 6.3 million organizations, such as corporations, schools, law firms, television stations, police departments, and even the IRS itself. Because the basic tax law since 1943 has required all of these organizations to withhold federal taxes and instantly forward them to the government, a substantial chunk of the IRS's reputation for efficient tax collection actually should be credited to the administrative efforts of the 6.3 million employers in the United States, and not to the agency.

The widespread withholding of individual income taxes is of major importance to the government for obvious, and some not so obvious, reasons. The single most obvious plus involves the steady, almost instantaneous flow of tax dollars into the federal coffers.

Paradoxically, the less obvious effects of withholding may be more important to the government than the speedy collection of billions of dollars of revenues. Systematic withholding, which by definition avoids the requirement of large lump-sum payments to the government, has a major impact on the way many Americans think about taxes in general and the tax collector in particular. First, taxes that are deducted before the paycheck is handed to the worker are almost invisible. It's very hard to get excited about the government seizing something you never actually had in your physical possession.

Second, the habit of large numbers of taxpayers to arrange for their employers to withhold more for taxes than they will owe has meant that for the last few decades a majority of the American people have received an annual refund check. During a single recent year, for example, the IRS dispatched refund checks averaging more than $800 apiece to four out of five of the nation's individual taxpayers.

Because the withholding process is almost invisible, and the refund check so visible, many accountants and tax lawyers say that a substantial number of taxpayers gradually have abandoned the essentially correct picture of the agency as a hard-nosed tax collector and have adopted the false view that the IRS is a benevolent bureaucracy that gives away money to the needy middle class. For many Americans, the IRS has become the agency that each spring *sends out* millions of refund checks totaling almost $100 billion rather than the agency that each year *collects* about one thousand times more in taxes than it gives away.

Byron Good is an old friend. He also is a brilliant anthropologist who teaches at the Harvard Medical School. One morning a year or so ago we were idly talking about my work on this book. "You know," he mused, "I believe I'm like a lot of people in that, when I think of the IRS at all, it is mostly positive. I hardly notice the deductions marked on the stub of my regular paycheck because I never had the money in the first place. And then, every spring, my IRS refund check seems to arrive just when I need a little money to pay an unexpected bill."

In fact, national surveys have determined that, while many Americans remember the size of their refund checks and whether they were larger or smaller than the previous year, a much smaller number of taxpayers recall their total tax obligation.

These widely shared misperceptions about the IRS, about taxes, and about the yearly refund are of major importance to the government because they work to undermine potentially revolutionary thoughts that federal taxes are unacceptably high. "I don't think there is any question there would be a national revolt against current federal taxes if the public paid them all on April 15," said Andrew Levine, once a lawyer in the IRS's national office. "Withholding provides the key illusion which allows our tax system to function. That's okay by me because I happen to support most of the federal spending programs."

At a less cosmic level, the basically false public understanding of tax collection also has proven politically useful to the IRS. The public relations payoff to the tax agency begins with the dynamic that it is the dramatic arrival of the comparatively small refund check, and not the steady trickle of withholding, that dominates the public attitude toward the IRS. Given the image created in the minds of millions of Americans by the prompt arrival of the yearly refund check, it is hardly surprising that many taxpayers tend to support the IRS when critics raise valid questions about the agency's frequently arbitrary and sometimes political tactics.

Thus it is that regular withholding and the soothing refund check serve the important, perhaps essential, political function of making bearable what might be regarded as exorbitant if the American people were forced to pay their total tax bill on a single day.

But fiddling with withholding policy and refund practice also can serve narrower political ends. During the last months of the 1960 presidential campaign, a mild economic recession occurred that probably helped John F. Kennedy win his narrow victory over Richard Nixon, the responsible incumbent in the sense that he was vice president when the recession occurred. But once Kennedy was in office, the recession became a drag on the family's ambitious political plans. One of the first items of business, therefore, was the drafting of a broad plan to speed up the economy. Shortly after Kennedy took the oath of office, the president received a two-page memo from Frederick G. Dutton, one of his top lieutenants, describing the various parts of this economic counterattack. The second item on Dutton's February 15, 1961, memo to JFK concerned an IRS effort to inject the economy with a quick dose of money: "Four billion dollars in *income tax refunds* are to be speeded."[1]

Although a trifle manipulative, the Kennedy administration's clever and politically useful decision to lean on the IRS bureaucracy as part of its program to reverse a recession was neither illegal nor improper. A decade later, the same judgment probably can be applied to a second effort to influence withholding policy, this time by the men around President Nixon. But the ability of both the Kennedy and the Nixon teams to modify IRS withholding and refund policies without any changes in the tax laws, for what can be regarded as political purposes, demonstrates a seldom examined aspect of the IRS's hidden impact on the moods of the American people.

The Nixon administration's interest in the nuances of withholding policy was first noted in a November 16, 1971, memorandum from Ken Cole, a political strategist on John Ehrlichman's staff, to Peter M. Flanigan, a White House economic coordinator. Cole complained that during the previous year the Treasury Department and the IRS had "screwed up" politically by allowing widespread underwithholding of taxes.[2] Underwithholding has a negative impact on the national mood, Cole observed, because it causes "many people come tax submission time to have to delve into their savings to pay taxes owed."

Cole's memo of concern was not ignored by the Nixon administration.

Four months after receiving it, Flanigan, the White House aide, dispatched a detailed follow-up note to Treasury Secretary John Connally; George Shultz, then director of the Office of Management and Budget; and two obscure White House figures who would later gain considerable notoriety during the Senate Watergate hearings, John Dean and Charles Colson. Flanigan's memo described how the Nixon team that year planned to avoid the negative political fallout caused by the underreporting of the previous year.

Flanigan's note began by quoting Bill Greener, then the IRS public affairs officer, as agreeing with the proposition that "the political situation is worse during an under-withholding period, which we experienced last year." He then outlined an eight-point public relations program the White House had devised. Its purpose was to make sure the Nixon administration's political capital was not again depleted by the general public irritation felt by taxpayers when they discovered they owed a larger than usual portion of their federal taxes on April 15. The answer, of course, was to encourage taxpayers to overwithhold and thus make sure they would be eligible for the fat and politically soothing refund checks.

The first item on Flanigan's list described a request for assistance that the Nixon administration already had dispatched to a large group of its natural allies. "IRS Commissioner Johnnie Walters sent all major corporate executives a personal letter six weeks ago urging them to assist their employees to the maximum degree in filling out the new W–4 [withholding] forms."

But the actual withholding of taxes is not the only part of the IRS's enforcement apparatus that makes the annual April 15 filing somewhat less important to the government than the anxious taxpayer might think. A massive and entirely separate IRS program guarantees that, long before the taxpayer's tax return arrives on the agency's doorstep, the government already has been handed a good deal of information about that individual's financial activities.

This second and largely invisible aspect of the IRS's information collection process centers on the broad legal requirement that large categories of people and organizations that give money or something of value to someone else are supposed to tell the government about it. Almost all Americans are familiar with the W2 form, the granddaddy of this particular kind of obligation. The W2, of course, is the annual form your employer uses to inform the IRS exactly how much he, she, or it paid you during the previous year. It also reveals how much your employer withheld from your salary for federal taxes, state taxes, and Social Security.

But in recent years, three developments have occurred that have fundamentally altered the reach of this particular IRS information-gathering program. First, Congress has vastly expanded the different kinds of institutions and individuals who are required to send third-party reports to the IRS. Second, Congress substantially increased the penalties for failing to obey the new reporting requirements. Finally, technological changes have given the IRS a low-cost way to use the information.

The range of income information now flowing into the IRS is truly amazing. Institutions that provide pensions and annuities to elderly persons must let the government know about the transactions on form W–2P. Casinos and racetracks must report the winnings of lucky gamblers on form W–2G. Restaurants are required to inform the IRS about the estimated tips earned by their employees on form 8027. All interest payments and dividends paid by a bank or corporation must be reported on forms 1099–INT or 1099–DIV. When a broker arranges a sale or a barter exchange sets up a swap of property, the middleman must send the details of the transaction to the IRS on 1099–B. When you sell your house, the real-estate agent who closes the deal is required to report the property's actual closing price on form 1099–S. When a government agency such as the Veterans Administration loans an individual money that is secured by property, the agency is required to report the loan on form 1099–A. When an out-of-work individual receives an unemployment check or a taxpayer gets a tax refund from a state or city, the agencies administering these programs must report the payments to the IRS on form 1099–G.

The ultimate reach of the IRS's rapidly expanding information collection program, however, is best illustrated by the requirements associated with the agency's all-purpose form, 1099–MISC. Among those now obligated to send in 1099–MISCs are publishers who pay their writers $10 or more in royalties, organizations that give prizes worth $600 or more, professional fishermen who pay their crews from the sale of the catch or part of the catch, corporations or associations that pay honoraria, lawyers who give a colleague a finder's fee for referring a case, and insurance companies that pay a body repair shop to replace your crumpled fender or a doctor to mend your ailing body.

The IRS booklet explaining the amazing scope of the agency's information return system provides dozens of hypothetical examples of other situations where 1099–MISCs must be filed. One such hypothetical concerned a Mr. Black, a real-estate agent who collected $1,000 in rent, deducted his $100 commission, and passed on the $900 balance to the owner of the building. "Mr. Black must report the gross amount of $1,000 on Form 1099–MISC," the IRS said.

To back up all these reporting requirements, Congress has given the IRS permission to impose impressive fines. A bank, broker, employer, or real-estate agency, for example, can be fined up to $100,000 for not filing the required information returns or for not supplying the taxpayer's identification number. This upper limit does not apply, however, in situations where the IRS decides an institution failed to exercise "due diligence" in reporting interest and dividend payments or intentionally disregarded other requirements.

In this case, at least, the penalties have worked wonders, and the IRS now receives more than 1 billion (1,000,000,000) such third-party reports each year. In 1987, for example, employers sent the IRS 181,962,639 W2 forms. In the same year, gambling casinos and racetracks dispatched 872,475 W–2Gs concerning the earnings of their winners. Banks and other interest-paying institutions sent 299,170,352 form 1099–INTs. And a mixed bag of other individuals and organizations coughed up a grand total of 27,070,974 form 1099–MISCs.

Just a few years ago, these 1 billion reports would have served almost no purpose except to fill up a few very large government warehouses. But because of the swift spread of computers within government and into almost every other nook and cranny of American life, the IRS reports that more than 90 percent of the reports are now submitted to the agency in electronic form rather than on bits of paper. This fact means that machines, rather than people, can actually look for inconsistencies between the numbers provided by the millions of employers, insurance companies, banks, corporations, real-estate agents, and lawyers and the numbers provided by the individual taxpayer. The process has become so fast and so cheap, in fact, that the IRS claims it is able to match essentially all of the 1 billion W2s, 1099s, and 8027s with all of the 100 million plus individual income tax returns now being filed each year. The effect of this nearly universal match is that an information-collecting process that for many years had functioned only as a psychological weapon against the taxpayer now has been transformed into a genuine enforcement tool.

But let's go back to Norman Rockwell's father figure, sitting in the kitchen as he completes the family 1040, and the latter-day television news feature showing the anxious but jubilant families as they drive up to the post office to mail their returns just before the midnight deadline. Both familiar images imply that the nation's tax laws are sufficiently understandable so that most American taxpayers feel confident that they are able to fill out their annual tax return without the assistance of paid experts.

Once again, however, this comforting picture of the informed self-sufficiency of the American people is somewhat off the mark. Remember that in fact about half of the nation's taxpayers now turn to professional tax preparers each year either because they feel they do not understand the tax law or because they do not have the time to prepare their return. Although the precise cost of these special services is not known, two surveys provide strong evidence that professional advice costs taxpayers a lot of money. One study, based on a survey of Minnesota taxpayers, estimated that in 1982 the people of the United States handed tax preparers between $3 billion and $3.4 billion to help them complete their federal and state income tax returns. A more recent survey of Syracuse taxpayers found that in 1987 an individual with a complex tax return gave his or her tax preparer an average of $364, a substantial increase from the $184 such services cost in 1986. The average spent for professional help to prepare the simplest federal return, the 1040EZ, was $51 for the 1987 return and $45 for the previous year. Partly because of the complexity of the law, a number of surveys have found that a good deal of this costly advice is not correct.[3]

With the help of the neighborhood H & R Block, a prestigious accounting firm, or perhaps all alone, April 15 finally arrives and the taxpayer's return is sent to the government, usually courtesy of the U.S. Postal Service. What is the procedural path taken by the return as it moves through this vast agency? How does the IRS make the decision about whether or not a particular return will be examined?

WHAT HAPPENS TO YOUR RETURN?

The first stop for most of the 100 million plus individual tax returns is one of the IRS's ten regional processing centers. During the busiest periods in March, April, and May, these massive information factories hire a large number of part-time employees and go to work on an around-the-clock schedule as they attempt to cope with an astonishing flood of paper. In a recent year, for example, one IRS processing center located in Fresno, California, received more than 32 million pieces of mail. This is a lot of mail, well over 100,000 pieces a day during the peak periods. Because the law requires the IRS to pay interest on all the refunds it has not processed forty-five days after April 15—assuming the taxpayer has filed a proper return—the agency during this period is under enormous pressure.

Every day, loaded Postal Service trucks back into the loading docks of the regional service centers where the millions of envelopes are shoved into the receiving ends of special fifty-foot-long machines that begin the

IRS's high-speed processing procedure. The machines have three distinct functions. First, they mechanically open all the envelopes. Second, they quickly read the bar codes on the preaddressed envelopes that the IRS tries to persuade taxpayers to always use. Third, depending on the information supplied by the bar codes, the machines shoot the letters into one of thirty-six different metal buckets. (Uncoded envelopes go to a thirty-seventh location for manual sorting.)

Loaded onto large handcarts, the now-opened envelopes are trundled to another part of the center where different groups of "extractors" go to work. One of the first steps is to separate the returns that include payments from those that don't. After the amount of the payment has been recorded according to the taxpayer's identification number, the remittances are immediately deposited at a bank.

Next a "transcriber" swiftly eyeballs the returns, mostly to make sure the taxpayer has filled in all the necessary blanks. If everything appears to be in order, the transcriber types a small portion of the information reported on the tax return into a computer terminal. After several checks designed to reduce clerical errors, the key information extracted from each return is analyzed for validity, consistency, and mathematical accuracy by a computer located at the regional center. If the return passes the initial field tests, the transcribed information is transferred to computer tape. The ten regional service centers ship these transactional tapes daily to the IRS's National Computer Center in Martinsburg, West Virginia. During a study completed several years ago for Congress, the General Accounting Office found that, on the average, 3,500 tapes a week flowed between the regional and national centers. (After the selected tax information has been transferred to the tapes, the paper returns are placed in storage in the service centers for six weeks and then retired to federal record centers. The tax returns of individuals are maintained for seven years. Corporate returns are held longer, some forever.)

Once the regional computer tapes have arrived at the high-security Martinsburg facility, the tax return information contained on them is sorted into account number sequence and posted to the IRS's master file, where it is stored along with the information that has already been collected about each taxpayer during the previous two years.

The IRS's master file is a summary account showing what every taxpayer in the nation has paid to the government and what was assessed in taxes, interest, and penalties. At least in theory, the goal for each taxpayer is a zero balance.

It only requires about one fifth of an inch of magnetic tape to store three years' worth of financial data about the average taxpayer. (As information about a taxpayer is removed from the three-year master file, it is archived on tape. Although the storage system has serious flaws, the goal is to create a perfect institutional memory.)

Every year, the initial run of computers at the national center in West Virginia calculates that about 15 percent of these individual and corporate accounts are not in balance, most frequently that the selected taxpayers owe the government some additional taxes. This finding automatically triggers the center's high-speed printers to prepare notices requesting the taxpayers to pay up.

These initial computerized notices fingering the taxpayers whose national accounts indicate they owe the government money serve a second function: They trigger a process whereby the detailed account information about these taxpayers is sent back to the appropriate regional center and placed in a separate computerized network called the Integrated Data Retrieval System (IDRS). This on-line system provides field agents in each region instantaneous access to the summary tax information about the taxpayers in their area whose accounts were found not to balance. At the present time, IDRS information about taxpayers can be examined by agents sitting in front of fifteen thousand terminals located in IRS offices all over the United States.

With selected information about the millions of individual and corporate taxpayers lifted from the tax returns and transferred to the national and regional computer systems, and the first notices dispatched, the IRS is ready to launch a broad range of efforts to assure itself that the taxpayers of the nation have paid the taxes they owe.

The importance of the check you write on April 15 is the first big myth about tax collection in the United States. Probably the second big myth concerns the significance of an IRS audit, that dreaded moment when an agent challenges some claimed deduction and asks to see your supporting financial documents. The IRS audit, a gaudy nightmare for most taxpayers, is widely misunderstood. Many Americans, for example, believe that the formal IRS tax audit is the principal method the agency uses to contact and identify those taxpayers who owe additional taxes. This is not correct. Beginning in the early 1960s, the IRS slowly began to develop what it calls its Information Returns Program (IRP). In this program, the agency's computers compare the information recorded on individual tax returns with the information provided by employers, banks, and corporations about the wages, dividends, interest, and other kinds of payments they have made. If the computers find a discrepancy, a notice of inquiry is sent to the taxpayer. In 1988, for example, the IRP generated 3.9 million notices that ultimately led to an assessment of $1.8 billion in additional taxes from Americans who filed returns but somehow failed to report some portion of their total income. In addition, IRP enabled the IRS to identify 3 million individuals who had failed to file any tax return at all.

Because a taxpayer may get more than one IRP notice in a year, it is not known exactly how many individuals were contacted this way by the IRS. It is reasonable to assume, however, that three or four times more taxpayers are now being confronted about potential tax problems through the IRP than as a result of an audit. Despite this disparity, the old-fashioned audit still has an important impact on the behavior of taxpayers, in part because of the many years of IRS publicity about audits.

Within the IRS the lead player in the job of auditing tax returns is the Examination Division, one of the three major operating arms of the IRS. The two other principal IRS units are the Collection Division and the Criminal Investigation Division, whose work will be described in the next two chapters. The functions of all three divisions are implied by their names. The task of the Examination Division is to examine returns, identify the taxpayers who apparently have failed to meet their tax obligations, and notify them what they owe. The Collection Division is the IRS's dunning arm. With various levels of intensity, it muscles reluctant taxpayers into coughing up the money they owe. The Criminal Investigation Division, while much smaller than the other two, conducts the more glamorous kinds of tax investigations where criminal, rather than civil, violations are suspected.

DECIDING WHO GETS AUDITED

A surprising reality about the Examination Division is that in recent years it has audited only about 1 million returns a year, roughly 1 percent of all those filed by individual taxpayers in the United States. The tiny fraction of Americans who can realistically expect to be placed under the IRS microscope each year means that the agency's task of selecting the right candidates for this particular honor is a critical one.

The first step in the IRS's complicated selection process is the responsibility of Thomas Andretta, head of the Examination Division's research and planning office. "What we try to do is select for audit the most noncompliant returns," Andretta explained in an interview.

One source of information for Andretta as he goes about his difficult job is the Taxpayers Compliance Measurement Program (TCMP). The heart of the TCMP is a national survey of fifty thousand randomly selected taxpayers. These lucky people have been scientifically selected to represent all of the millions of Americans who file a tax return each year. As their reward, this sample of fiscal guinea pigs is subjected to a highly intensive audit that requires them to document the claims made on every item on their return. The special answer sheet used by IRS agents when conducting a TCMP audit is twelve pages long and has 367 questions. The detailed results of the TCMP audits, which have been conducted every three years since 1976, are then fed into a special IRS computer. The primary goal here is not to catch the people the IRS feels have not paid sufficient taxes. Rather, the goal is to use the results of these special audits to develop a statistically valid portrait of the tax-reporting habits of the American people. Who is making the errors or doing the chiseling? Where do the errors and chiseling occur? How many tax dollars are being lost in each area? How much can the government recover?

To present all this data in an understandable way, the IRS divides the fifty thousand taxpayers into twelve different classes. For individual taxpayers, the different classes are divided by primary source of income (salary, business, or farm) and amount of income. Thus, the final product of the TCMP is a kind of numerical road map that the IRS uses to estimate the proportion of Americans in each of these twelve different groupings who by accident or design can be expected to shortchange the government, the various ways they will go about doing it, and how much the government would recover in each class if the full amount was paid.

The statistical profiles created by the TCMP give the IRS a strategic overview of how the tax system is working and where its problems are. But the survey data serve another purpose. Combined with detailed information drawn from the agency's master file, they help the agency develop what is called the Discriminant Function (DIF) methodology. DIF is one of a large number of statistical techniques that government agencies and industry have been using for many years to make predictions. With DIF, a set of variables is developed that, at least in theory, predicts the behavior of the group that is being examined. Outside the IRS, for example, the credit industry has used the DIF methodology to evaluate the behavior of potential customers.

The main reason why the IRS initiated the search for an automated scoring system was that the sharp increase in tax returns filed by the American people meant that its agents were no longer able to screen them manually and decide which should be audited. From 1936 to 1956, for example, the number of returns filed increased from one return for every

4.7 Americans to one return for every 1.9 Americans. An automated system to select the returns that were most likely to need an audit thus became essential to tax administration.

The DIF system, however, has had some important ancillary advantages for the IRS. Ever since its development, for example, DIF has been heavily publicized by the agency on the grounds that this magic machine guarantees that tax returns are selected for audit on a scientific basis and never for political or other nontax reasons.

There are many reasons why the agency's promotion of DIF is misleading. Since the system was first adopted, for example, the cutoff points have been set at levels that mean far more returns are placed in the "need for audit" category than can ever be audited. Partly because DIF is not a perfect scoring system, it certainly would not make any sense to use the system to select every return that the IRS would audit. At the same time, however, the high cutoff points have meant that the final decision about which returns will be audited is actually made not by the machine but by the sometimes sound and sometimes whimsical judgment of a large number of IRS personnel.

Another reason IRS publicity about DIF is misleading is that the agency has developed at least ten other methods for selecting returns for possible examination, some of which are also computerized. One special program, for example, is designed to rank returns that claim tax shelters. Although DIF at one time accounted for 70 percent of the initial screening decisions, IRS documents have recently indicated that DIF-scored returns now make up less than 50 percent of the first cut.

Finally, IRS audits are also triggered by tips from former spouses, business competitors, other kinds of whistle-blowers, newspaper stories about an opulent life-style, and even IRS agents' personal grudges against individual taxpayers. This is not to say that acting on the basis of most of these leads is inappropriate, only that a good number of audits are not selected by an unbiased, nonpolitical, evenhanded machine.

EQUAL TREATMENT UNDER THE LAW?

The sometimes quirky quality of the IRS examination process does not end with a highly subjective selection system. Actual production statistics from the IRS suggest that taxpayers in different parts of the United States do not receive equal treatment from the agency. Some of the regional disparities are extensive. While 14 out of 1,000 income tax returns were audited in 1988 in the IRS's San Francisco district, only 5 out of 1,000 faced the same difficult process in New Jersey.

The tables in the appendix of this book, based partly on information published in the agency's annual report and partly on additional data provided by the IRS, appear to indicate many similar aberrations.

Consider the column of table 1 describing the agency's 1988 audit rate in each of its districts. Why did the IRS audit only 9 out of 1,000 returns in Chicago, when 14 out of 1,000 were audited in Manhattan? Why were the returns of 7 out of 1,000 Iowans examined when 11 out of 1,000 North Dakotans were asked to defend their financial claims? Does it make sense that Dallas taxpayers were twice as likely to face audits as those living in Philadelphia?

Now look at the last column. The geographic variations in the percentage of returns being audited by the IRS appear even more curious when economic factors are considered. Why, for example, does the North Atlantic region, the section of the country with the highest adjusted gross income, have the lowest audit rate in 1988? Why are the taxpayers of Wyoming, who have an average adjusted gross income of $22,951, nearly twice as likely to face an audit as the taxpayers of Maryland, who have an average adjusted gross income of $29,186?

Tom Andretta, in charge of developing the division's annual auditing plan, contends that the anomalies are extremely misleading and largely disappear when the different mix of taxpayers living in each of the agency's sixty-three districts is taken into account. But the contrasting numbers are extremely vivid. Doesn't the fact that taxpayers living in the San Francisco area are far more likely to be audited than those in New Jersey prove that the agency's front-line troops are not following the national plan?

"No," Andretta replied. "Your table smushes up a lot of numbers that should not be jumbled together. Each district has its own economic complexion, its own distinct mix of taxpayers. Regardless of where they live we try to treat similar classes of taxpayers the same way."

"Are you saying that a San Francisco taxpayer with a $50,000 income and a little tax shelter will be treated in exactly the same way as a person with the same income and tax shelter who happens to live in Newark?" I asked.

"As close as we can come," he replied.

Robert Miller is an experienced revenue agent now assigned to the IRS office in Wheaton, Maryland, a suburb close to Washington, D.C. He has also worked for the agency in Chicago and Long Island. "Districts can have very different characteristics," he explained. "When I worked in Chicago, the director there was very aggressive and statistics-minded. He pushed production very hard. In the Brooklyn district, which takes in Long Island, the whole office worked differently. In my view, it was much more prudent, much more professional, and much more willing to look at each situation on a case-by-case basis. Maybe this goes with the live-and-let-live attitude of New York, the original melting-pot city."

Andretta agreed with Miller that there can be some district-to-district variations but argued that the overall impact was minimal. He pointed out, however, that the annual examination guideline developed each year in Washington did specifically authorize district directors to launch their own examination projects. In the IRS's general guidelines for fiscal 1988, for example, seven priorities are established to guide the managers in deciding where to point their guns. The first item in the national priority list was the returns that had been selected for examination under the Taxpayer Compliance Measurement Program. The second priority was the returns that had been put on the top of the heap by the tax shelter selection process. The sixth priority was "locally initiated work."

This is the way Andretta described the sixth priority. "Mr. District Director, if you find areas of noncompliance that you think are deeper than those indicated by the plan, then by all means deviate from the plan. So the director in Boston, for example, might decide there is a special problem among the fishermen in his district, identify who they are, and undertake a large number of examinations of them."

Could such locally initiated projects destroy the goal of evenhanded enforcement? "That depends on how you define evenhanded," Andretta said. "I define it as auditing the most abusive returns wherever they are filed."

Another important factor that can get in the way of auditing the most noncompliant returns throughout the country involves having sufficient numbers of trained auditors to undertake the work. One senior IRS official, for example, told me that the primary reason why the audit rate was low in Massachusetts was that the Boston District Office was having trouble hiring auditors because of the competitive job market in the booming New England economy.

Andretta confirmed that local economic conditions sometimes created obstacles to hiring the correct number of trained people. "Right now," he said, "the IRS is very big in Texas, where the economy is having some trouble. We have lots of employees in Texas and lots of returns are being examined. Boston is tough. New York City is tougher. In fact, we're trying to get salary supplementals from the Office of Personnel Management to make us more competitive up there."

The planning official said he believed such hiring problems caused some minor and generally short-term variations in the examination levels of different districts. "There can be all kinds of reality that intervene. Say one district has a lot of older agents who all retire at about the same time. That means we will have to hire a large group of young and relatively inexperienced people. The result: For the first couple of years in that district we won't have the folks we need to audit the most complex returns that are filed there. But within a year or two our training programs correct the problem."

Each year, IRS headquarters in Washington decides how many returns that it expects each of the seven regions to audit. Then the regions pass on the production requirements to the sixty-three districts. At least since World War I, the precisely defined output statistics contained in the national plan have been criticized as encouraging the use of arbitrary quota systems. For just as long, the IRS has denied these criticisms.

The subtle nuances of this continuing debate were nicely captured in a wonderful report on the IRS prepared in 1975 for the Administrative Conference of the United States, a small organization that seeks to improve federal administrative practices.[4] The principal author was Charles Davenport, now a law professor at Rutgers University in New Jersey.

"It is clear that the Internal Revenue Service has not devised the audit plan as some type of diabolical method for the subtle application of production pressures on line personnel," Davenport and his team of researchers observed. "Nevertheless, in an effort to direct its employees toward the accomplishment of its established objectives, it has developed a tool to measure and monitor progress toward their achievement."

These well-intended pressures from above, Davenport observed, lead the examiners "to close cases as quickly as possible with some tax change. Of course, this type of perceived pressure can cut both ways. As expressed in numerous letters written to us and others made available to us, agents may assert non-existent or questionable issues, or they may drop or trade viable issues, both actions for the purpose of closing cases or justifying time spent on a case."

While Davenport saw the audit plan as harmful to the IRS and the goal of evenhanded tax collection, he and his fellow consultants concluded in a tongue-in-cheek way that the plan also offered some advantages. "It satisfies Congress," they said. "It permits (perhaps encourages?) the feeling of productivity apparently necessary to even government workers in a private, profit-and-growth-oriented society. It also permits the objective, even if perhaps erroneous, measurement of abstract concepts and offers rocks to cling to in a sea of otherwise subjective quicksand."

Late each spring, with the annual audit plan at hand and huge stacks of returns from which to choose, the men and women of the Examination Division go to work. Given the vast size of the agency, the number of returns that actually are formally audited each year may strike the average citizen as extraordinarily small. It should be remembered that during all of 1988 IRS agents only managed to examine 1.06 million of the 107 million returns filed by individual taxpayers.

THE VIEW FROM FORT APACHE

It is a harmful but understandable reality that most examination officers begin each day firm in the conviction that the taxpayer who comes to their attention is wrong. A second widely held conviction of many examination officers relates to their perceived duty to assert and maintain the IRS's position on all issues.

Opposing the typical IRS agent's negative view of the taxpayer, on the other hand, is the equally hostile view of some taxpayers toward the IRS. Many taxpayers, for example, strongly resent being considered tax cheats when, in their view, the problem involves an inadvertent error or innocent misinterpretation of the law.

The mutually hostile views held by tax collectors and taxpayers contribute to the development of an adversary atmosphere that in turn tends to reinforce the already existing negative beliefs. Not that both parties don't have some evidence to support their views.

On one side, the agency has long contended that taxpayer "errors" somehow end up favoring the taxpayer more frequently than they favor the government. In an IRS report on tax compliance written twenty-five years ago, for example, the agency noted that to the extent that taxpayers have room for maneuvering they avail themselves of this opportunity. "Five percent of the tax returns contain math errors and such errors are predominantly in the taxpayer's favor. Moreover, the size of the error favoring the taxpayer is about 1½ times as large as the error favoring the government. Also, there is evidence indicating that 2 out of every 5 individual tax returns filed contain errors (other than math errors) and that in 85 out of every 100 cases the error is in the taxpayer's favor."[5]

Although the IRS's findings were somewhat exaggerated by the pro-government assumptions of the researchers, the skeptical view of the taxpayer supported by this and other such studies routinely is reinforced by the agency. The examiner is repeatedly informed, for example, that the computerized process by which returns are initially scored is highly scientific and therefore, by definition, must be correct. The examiner also knows that the computer-scored returns have been screened by experienced supervisors who have been instructed to select returns that are most likely to have errors that will require correction. Finally, the examiner knows that a failure to find a problem in the returns that have been selected will lead management to question the agent's competence.

"Thus the examining officer enters an audit with the expectation of finding errors and assessing a deficiency against a taxpayer whom he suspects as being dishonest, careless or unknowledgeable, but probably not correct," Davenport observed.

Given the growing budget deficit pressures on the IRS to collect every tax dollar the agency possibly can, it is not surprising that more recent observers find little change in the basic relationship between the tax agency and the taxpayer. One such expert is Karyl Kinsey, who for the last few years has been studying the administration of the tax laws for the American Bar Foundation. In 1987 the researcher completed a study on the social dynamics of tax encounters based on open-ended interviews she conducted with forty-three tax practitioners and twenty-five IRS employees in the Chicago metropolitan area.[6]

Kinsey observed that a key factor in most tax encounters is that one of the adversaries, the IRS agent, "also functions as a judge with legal authority to make decisions about the disposition of the case and to apply penalties, not only against the taxpayer, but against the tax practitioner as well." In tax matters, she added, "it is actually more the exception than the rule that neutral third parties hear the case."

Kinsey further found that very few tax practitioners believe the IRS is entirely neutral in how it writes the tax regulations interpreting the broad language of Congress's tax laws or how it then goes about interpreting the regulations it has written. In support of this point, the researcher quoted one of the forty-three tax practitioners interviewed for her study. "As a tax attorney, I know that regulations are not law. I'm willing to say, in certain instances, that the IRS is just plain wrong in interpreting what they [the laws] said. Their goal is to raise revenue."

In summarizing this lawyer's observations, Kinsey drew upon her own research and a number of studies of other administrative agencies somewhat similar to the IRS. "In this instance," she said, "the lawyer is articulating the view that IRS interpretations are driven by organizational incentives to raise money. Bureaucracies are by no means neutral interpreters of the law—they tend to define the law in light of what helps them achieve valued organizational goals, and tend to resist efforts of external control agents to correct their interpretations."

And in a substantial number of cases, the men and women of the IRS act on their organizational beliefs. In 1988, for example, the agency's examiners decided that individual taxpayers owed additional taxes in 746,549, or 74.2 percent, of the 1,060,000 cases that were selected for examination.[7]

There is truly shocking evidence, however, that a significant proportion of IRS claims against the taxpayer is not correct. The only known audit of the quality of IRS audits ever undertaken by an independent organization was completed by the General Accounting Office in 1979.[8] During the tax year covered by the GAO study, the IRS audited just under 2 million returns and assessed $1.8 billion in additional tax and penalties. After examining a sample of IRS audits, the GAO reported the following conclusions:

- In slightly more than one third of the sample cases, IRS agents "assessed an incorrect tax because of technical errors, computational errors or failure to make automatic adjustments."
- In about half the audits, the agents "overlooked significant audit issues."
- In more than 60 percent of the cases, the agents did not follow agency procedures and ask taxpayers about unreported income they may have earned.

In a very general way, an earlier study by the IRS itself confirmed the GAO's harsh conclusions. The 1973 agency study, reluctantly made public some years later as the result of a suit under the Freedom of Information Act, examined the quality of the special audits done in connection with the Taxpayer Compliance Measurement Program. Because of the importance placed on the compliance program by top officials of the IRS, these audits are thought to be more accurate than audits done in the normal course of agency business. Despite these pressures, however, the Internal Audit section of the Inspections Division of the IRS found that 23 percent of the TCMP audits showed procedural or technical errors and 13 percent had line items on a check sheet incorrectly filled out.[9]

Because current tax law is far more complex than it was in the 1970s and because the quality of agents attracted to the IRS has declined since that period, the proportion of inaccurate and incomplete audits has almost certainly increased.

Whatever the number of wrongful IRS audits, 12 percent of the 814,000 taxpayers who in 1987 were accused of owing the government additional taxes after a formal audit appealed their rulings. This is not to say, of course, that all those who appealed had valid grievances. On the other hand, numerous surveys have found that many taxpayers wronged by the IRS do not bother to appeal because the law is murky, the chances of winning slim, and the cost of appeal sometimes high.

THE AUDIT

For whatever reason, frequently valid, sometimes not, the tax returns of those who have been selected for a formal audit are segregated from those returns that have passed muster.

There are two basic kinds of audits. For those in the first category, the taxpayer is notified by mail that certain questions have been raised about one or more specific matters and asked to come into the IRS office with the necessary books or records to resolve the identified problems. For example, the letter might indicate that the agency has questions about an individual's medical deductions. Office audits usually involve relatively simple issues and comparatively little money. In the hierarchy of IRS agents who audit returns, the men and women conducting the office audits have the least training and experience in tax matters.

The auditor handling an office audit typically will have very little knowledge of the taxpayer whose case has been assigned to him or her. This means that the auditor normally limits the inquiry to the specific matter that was discussed in the IRS's first letter. In most circumstances, the auditor is not given time to collect any special information. It is not unusual for an auditor to handle six or seven cases a day.

More complicated matters are assigned to revenue agents, who mostly conduct field examinations, auditing the taxpayer's returns and supporting documents at the taxpayer's home or office. Revenue agents hold accounting degrees and have undergone further training by the IRS. According to IRS procedures, the revenue agent is supposed to prepare a written plan prior to commencing a field audit. The plan spells out the documents, books, and records that will be required to resolve all the outstanding issues. After contacting the taxpayer, usually by telephone, an appointment is scheduled and then confirmed by letter. The determination that a particular case will be handled as a field audit is dictated by the probable need of the revenue agent to have complete access to the taxpayer's books and records. Partly because the revenue agents are supposed to probe for problems in addition to those that were discovered during the IRS's initial study of the tax return in question, field audits usually will require days, weeks, and even months to complete.

In 1988, 533,000 of the agency's 1 million audits were conducted in IRS offices and 352,000 in the field. (The balance consisted of service center audits, which involve cases where taxpayers have made claims that are clearly not allowed by law—such as deducting the costs of a funeral—and that are disallowed by a letter without any kind of formal audit.)

Even assuming the best intentions, the highest intelligence, and the most expert training of the government's tax agents, the judgments they regularly are required to make often are extraordinarily difficult. Tax avoidance, the arrangement of the taxpayer's affairs to minimize the taxes that must be paid, is legal. Tax evasion, which the IRS handbook defines as an act involving deceit, subterfuge, and concealment, is illegal.

Concerning just the small number of tax cases that might be handled as a formal criminal matter, the judgments are equally difficult. "The question of whether a particular action is tax avoidance or tax evasion tends to boil down to the question of whether there has been 'intent' to defraud the government and 'wilfulness' in incorrectly reporting one's tax liability," observed one recent manual on dealing with the IRS.[10] "Here, obviously, we move into the realm of mind-reading."

Because so few Americans ever face criminal tax charges, however, the actual impact of the ambiguities that divide civil from criminal tax investigations is limited. After all, in 1988, only 2,769 taxpayers actually were indicted on criminal tax charges. During the same year, the IRS concluded that about 746,549 of the 1,060,000 individual taxpayers it formally audited were liable for additional taxes and penalties.

But the legal shadow cast by this tiny handful of criminal cases is considerable. This is because all revenue agents conducting theoretically routine audits for the Examination Division have been instructed to be alert for indications of fraud that could be referred to the Criminal Investigation Division.

In theory and under IRS administrative procedures, revenue agents who discover what appears to be tax fraud are supposed to suspend the civil investigation and refer the case to the criminal side. At this point, the IRS's criminal investigators, who will be discussed in a later chapter, are supposed to deliver a *Miranda*-like warning explaining the taxpayer's legal rights. According to critics, however, revenue agents sometimes use their special status as investigators of civil cases to camouflage the gathering of evidence for the far more serious business of pursuing indictment on criminal charges.

After the civil audit has been completed, the examiner can come to one of four conclusions. The first and favored option is for the examiner to conclude that the taxpayer owes the government additional taxes. As already noted, this is the decision reached in about three out of every four examinations. A second choice, less favored by the IRS, is for the examiner to decide that the government owes the taxpayer money. The third option is for the examiner to declare a draw: Nobody owes nobody nothing. The fourth possibility is for the auditor to decide that even though some adjustments are required on the taxpayer's return no additional taxes are due.

Many social and bureaucratic pressures push agents to act. Almost every year, for example, the commissioner troops to Capitol Hill to brag about how the agency has once again met the numerical requirements of the audit plan. And every year, he tells Congress that, if you will only give us another few million dollars for extra agents, we will give you many more hundreds of millions of dollars in additional taxes. These promises by the chiefs inevitably are translated into marching orders for the Indians. The resulting pressure may well be the single best explanation why, as documented by the GAO, IRS agents either assessed an incorrect tax or overlooked important audit issues in more than half of the cases selected for study.

A second major factor shaping the final outcome of an audit goes to the underlying legal authority of the agent in relation to the taxpayer. Under the law, in most disputes with the IRS, it is the taxpayer who is required to provide the government with documentary substantiation that the items that have been challenged are in fact allowable. The obligation on the taxpayer to support the statements on his or her tax return exists in civil proceedings in both the IRS and the federal Tax Court. When the government brings criminal tax charges in federal district court, however, the burden is on the government to prove its case. This reality means that IRS auditors spend most of their time only looking for an income deduction that can be challenged. Although the first goal of auditors theoretically is to determine how much the taxpayers owe the government, the claimed deductions are in fact the central concern. This focus leads auditors to concentrate their attention on the books and papers presented by the taxpayer rather than worrying about other possible enforcement areas such as unreported income.

While searching for grounds to challenge a deduction, auditors obviously consider the relevant tax laws and regulations. It is at this point, after the available factual evidence has been considered in the context of the examiner's understanding of the law, that the IRS agent presents the taxpayer with the government's claim.

(Historically, the IRS has viewed the audit as serving only one purpose: It is an excellent stick by which the agency can beat the taxpayer. We have become so accustomed to this approach that other possible uses of the audit seem naive. In fact, however, a few state tax agencies have decided that more tax dollars would be gained if the audit was used to educate taxpayers, as well as to punish them.)

If the taxpayer does not agree with the IRS claim, the law provides an elaborate system by which the claim can be appealed.* Within the agency itself, taxpayers have long had the right to appeal an agent's decision to his or her supervisor or to take the matter to the IRS's Appeals Division. The 1988 Taxpayers' Bill of Rights also expanded the authority of the Taxpayer Ombudsmen, agency employees who administer the IRS's Problem Resolution Program. Under the new law the ombudsmen may now issue a "taxpayer assistance order" (TAO) to a taxpayer who is suffering or is about to suffer "a significant hardship" at the hands of the IRS. The TAO, however, is mostly limited to collection actions by the agency and may not be used to enjoin a criminal investigation or contest the merits of an assessment of tax liability. Appeals also can be taken to a special federal court established by Congress only to consider tax mat-

---

*The proportion of American taxpayers with poor knowledge about appealing IRS tax claims has been documented by several surveys conducted for the IRS. The most recent was undertaken in July and August of 1987 by Louis Harris and Associates, Inc. Question 38d asked a national sample of 2,003 taxpayers about their awareness of a number of services offered by the IRS and whether they thought the services were of good or poor quality. Eighty percent of the taxpayers were aware of the telephone assistance program operated by the IRS; 70 percent knew they could obtain tax assistance if they walked into a field office; and 45 percent understood that the IRS would actually compute the tax owed for those filing on Form 1040A or 1040EZ.

Only 32 percent of the respondents, however, were aware of an "administrative Appeals System (if disagree with IRS about amount of tax owed)." This answer indicated, of course, that 68 percent of the respondents were not aware of such an administrative system.

A second question asked by Harris indicated that when the question was asked in terms of a general principle—rather than a specific appeals system—a much larger proportion of taxpayers seem to know that they have a broad right to challenge an IRS assessment. "As far as you know, can taxpayers appeal IRS decisions or actions when they think that IRS has made a mistake or is no appeal possible?" Eighty-one percent of the respondents answered yes, 5 percent no, 4 percent "depends," and 10 percent not sure.

ters. The filing of an appeal in either of these forums automatically halts IRS demands for payment until the dispute has been resolved.

Finally, in most circumstances, taxpayers can take their challenges to either a federal district court or the federal court of claims. Taking an appeal to either of these two courts, however, has a disadvantage. Before filing, a taxpayer first has to pay the back taxes and penalties claimed by the government and request a refund. If the refund is denied, the taxpayer then can file with one of the two federal courts.

Of the 814,007 taxpayers who IRS examiners found wanting in 1987, 49,000 initiated administrative appeals within the IRS, 40,491 appealed to the Tax Court, 181 went to federal district court, and 902 went to the court of claims.

While several ways are available to challenge an IRS claim, appeals are complex, time-consuming, and difficult to pursue in an effective way without expensive professional advice. Over the years, a number of studies have shown that taxpayers who press their challenges through several levels of appeal within the IRS fare better than those who only take their protest to the first stage. In one sample year, for example, IRS conferees at the district level settled for requiring the taxpayer to pay forty-two cents of every dollar that had originally been assessed. Those that took their cases to the highest agency appeals board, on the other hand, only paid thirty cents on the dollar.

These statistics suggest that the settlement process can work very well for those taxpayers with the means to hire skillful and persistent advocates but that it presents great difficulties to those with modest means.

CHAPTER 3

Collecting Taxes

Let's get down to serious business. How does the IRS actually extract hard dollars from the ambitious businessmen, economic dropouts, greedy movie stars, famous writers, criminal entrepreneurs, hungry waiters, and plain citizens the agency claims have failed to pay the taxes they owe?

Although forcing the unwilling, the mistaken, or the forgetful to pay their fair share of taxes involves scores of different laws, thousands of pages of regulations, 150 separate penalties, several hundred computer programs, and the work of tens of thousands of IRS agents, the overall process is quite simple. The IRS begins by identifying the individuals and businesses it believes are delinquent. Then the agency applies the authority it feels is required to get the money.

The IRS's collection efforts focus on two major categories of delinquent taxpayers. First, there are those who have filed an income tax return. They usually have paid some of their taxes. Second, there are those who have not filed a return. Sometimes they have not paid any taxes, sometimes they have. An individual working for a company, for example, may not file a return even though the company withholds taxes in his or her name.

When it comes to calculating the taxes that the agency claims are owed by the individuals and businesses who have indeed submitted a return, the IRS has four distinct approaches. The first approach comes very early in the tax year, immediately after the taxpayer's return has reached one of the agency's ten regional service centers. It involves a series of mathematical and clerical tests that check such matters as the accuracy of the addition and subtraction reported on the return.

The legal definition of mathematical or clerical errors, however, is very broad. It includes the incorrect use of IRS tables, tax return entries that on their face are inconsistent with other data on the return, the omission of required information, and the claiming of a deduction or credit that exceeds a statutory limit. From the point of view of the agency, one of the interesting points about the accuracy tests and clerical tests is that the taxpayer does not have the right to appeal any correction.

In 1988, these computer checks resulted in the identification of 18 million faulty returns with a claimed liability of $737 million in additional taxes and penalties. Once the IRS computers have spotted the errors, printed notices are automatically dispatched to errant taxpayers.[1]

The IRS's second approach for determining whether or not more taxes are due is also based at the ten regional service centers. In this program, IRS examiners assigned to the centers send computerized notices to taxpayers about obvious kinds of problems that they have spotted during a cursory review of selected returns. In 1988, service center examiners identified 560,000 problem returns that they said called for the payment of $750 million in extra taxes and penalties.

The third approach for determining whether or not additional taxes are due comes a good deal later in the tax year, after the IRS has transferred to its own computers at the National Computer Center in Martinsburg, West Virginia, all the reports that employers, banks, brokers, and other distributors of income have submitted about the payments they made during the previous year to individual taxpayers. When the IRS discovers a discrepancy between the information provided by the organizations making the payments and the information included on the tax returns of the people who received them, a notice is generated stating that it appears to the IRS that the taxpayer may owe some additional taxes. Because discovering this kind of discrepancy involves matching the information contained on 107 million individual tax returns with the information contained on about 1 billion W2s, 1099s, and other kinds of income statements, the process is totally computerized.

In 1988, this particular matching program led the IRS to send out 3.8 million discrepancy notices claiming $1.8 billion in additional taxes and penalties. (Because there were legitimate explanations for many of these apparent discrepancies, the actual assessments were significantly less than the original claims.)

Finally, of course, collection actions are triggered after an IRS agent has conducted a formal audit and found a deficiency, and the individual or business has failed to meet the IRS's demands. Although the IRS's computerized programs to spot mathematical errors and the underreporting of income identify *far more* problem returns than those picked up by the traditional audit program, the back taxes and penalties claimed as a result of formal audits amount to the *largest share* of revenue brought in by the IRS's various enforcement efforts. The IRS conducts a relatively small number of audits because they are so expensive. These audits raise the most revenue, however, because the IRS makes a considerable effort to select returns for examination that are most likely to have serious problems.

In 1988, the IRS reported conducting only 1 million field or office audits of individual tax returns. As a result of these comparatively intensive sessions, however, the agency informed taxpayers they owed $19.1 billion in additional taxes and penalties and were due $636 million in refunds.

As a result of successful taxpayer challenges, the IRS in the end collects only about $2 out of every $3 that it initially claims. One study found that as a result of the appeals process, whether within the IRS or at the Tax Court, 15 percent of the taxpayers had their original assessments reduced to zero and 69 percent had their assessments reduced between 1 percent and 99 percent. The remaining 16 percent had their original assessments sustained in full or increased.[2]

For those who have not bothered to file a tax return at all, the IRS has other tricks up its sleeve. Some "nonfilers," for example, are identified by comparing the computerized list of this year's taxpayers with the list of last year's taxpayers. A large number of additional nonfilers come to the attention of the IRS when the list of all the individuals who were identified by employers, banks, and other organizations as having received payments is matched with the list of all those who filed income tax returns. If you appear on the first list but not on the second, you are likely to become a target of the Collection Division. In 1988, the IRS identified a total of 3 million nonfilers this way. Far less frequently, nonfilers may become collection targets as a result of intelligence from the IRS's Criminal Investigation Division or tips from informants.

Thus, working with billions and billions of bits of financial information drawn from hundreds of millions of reports and income tax returns, the

IRS searches for individuals and businesses that in one way or another have not paid the taxes they owe. The absolute essential key to the low-cost handling of this truly gigantic mass of information is an identifying number for every single taxpayer. The 1961 law requiring all individuals and businesses to adopt a permanent Taxpayer Identification Number, known to everyone in the business as a TIN, was a major milestone in the collection of taxes. For individuals, the TIN is their Social Security number. (In 1986, Congress amended the original Kennedy-era law when it required parents to obtain Social Security numbers for their children if they wished to claim them as personal deductions. In the first years of the law, it applied to all children five and older. Now, it applies to children two and older.)

With the help of these different approaches, the agency each year identifies tens of millions of filers and nonfilers who it believes owe the government additional taxes. Over the years, the resulting actions by the Collection Division have enabled the government to collect a great deal of money. In 1988 alone, the haul, including penalties and interest, was $23.3 billion.

It should be remembered, however, that because of the overwhelming success of the withholding process and the general willingness of Americans to pay the balance of their taxes on April 15, the dollars extracted from taxpayers as a result of formal collection actions actually amount to only a very small fraction of all federal revenue. In 1988, for example, the enforcement projects of the IRS brought in about 2.8 percent of all federal taxes.

Nevertheless, the IRS has always been convinced that its hard-nosed enforcement activities are essential to its overall mission. The agency's theory is that the show of aggressive collection moves against the small number of malingerers is the threat that convinces the rest of us to "voluntarily comply" with the tax laws.

Regardless of how the delinquent taxpayer is identified, the agency's computers generate a notice claiming the additional taxes. Usually, the first notice is a polite but firmly worded request. If there is no response to the first inquiry, the computer is programmed to dispatch a second somewhat more firmly worded version. If necessary, the second notice is followed by a third and a fourth.

IRS statistics show that individual taxpayers in some parts of the country are far more likely to receive a first notice than are those living in other parts of the country. For every 1,000 individual tax returns filed in the Central Region in 1988, for example, the IRS mailed out 54 first notices. The Central Region includes Michigan, Indiana, Ohio, Kentucky, and

West Virginia. In the Western Region, however, the area covering California, Nevada, Oregon, Washington, Idaho, Alaska, and Hawaii, the IRS dispatched 95 first notices for every 1,000 tax returns. (See Appendix, table 2).

Does this considerable variation in first-notice rates reflect poor management on the part of the IRS, fundamental differences in the honesty of the taxpayers living in the two regions, or the existence of some unknown factor? Two IRS Collection Division officials, who agreed to be interviewed only if they were not identified by name, said they were not able to provide a sure-fire answer. But because the notices are generated by computers that are set to operate on a uniform national standard, the officials rejected the idea that the variation might be accounted for by differences in the enforcement demands of the two regional commissioners. More likely, they thought, was the explanation that for some unknown reason the taxpayers in the Western Region are somewhat less law-abiding than are those in the Central Region.

A different perspective is provided by examining over a period of time the number of first notices sent out by the IRS. During the last few years, for example, the total volume of first notices has slowly declined while the total number of individual returns filed has gradually increased. During the same period, IRS statistics show that except for the last two years the average amount of back taxes that the IRS claimed on each first notice has made a substantial jump. In 1977, the average first-notice claim was $952; in 1983, it was $1,722.

Does the absolute decline in first notices suggest that American taxpayers are becoming more lawful? And does the abrupt increase in the average claim mean that those who are shortchanging the government have become more ambitious? Almost certainly not. The IRS officials said they believed both changes were the product of shifts in official policy and the law. "Partly as a result of amendments in the law, a large number of lower income taxpayers have been removed from the tax rolls," one of the agency collection executives said. "So this has meant that a fair number of the smaller dollar accounts are no longer being issued first notices."

The notices are effective. Of $23.3 billion secured by the Collection Division in 1988, for example, $10 billion came into the government as a result of first notices sent to taxpayers. Subsequent notices yielded an additional $5.4 billion.

But for taxpayers who have chosen to ignore the flurry of computer-generated dunning notices, the service center computers take the next prearranged step. This occurs when the computers at the ten regional service centers designate the cases of the remaining taxpayers as either a tax delinquent account (TDA) or a tax delinquent investigation (TDI).

Within the IRS, the TDA or TDI designation generally means that the name and related tax information about the person or business who has ignored the demands of the written notices are transferred from the regional service center to one of twenty-one specialized offices that the IRS has located around the country to undertake a more intensive kind of dunning, this time by telephone. These twenty-one offices make up what is called the Automated Collection System (ACS).

(The TDA designation is reserved for taxpayers who have filed a return; the TDI is for those who have not. Because the TDIs, the nonfilers, often represent a more serious challenge to the IRS, some are sent not to the twenty-one ACS offices but directly to one of the IRS's sixty-three district offices for assignment to a revenue agent.)

In 1988, the IRS initiated a total of about 3 million tax delinquent accounts and 1.7 million tax delinquent investigations.

DUNNING TAXPAYERS

Each of the twenty-one Automated Collection System offices has a lot of telephones and video-display terminals, a computer, and about three hundred IRS employees, including the manager, contact specialists, researchers, and other support personnel. The computer in each office stores the TDAs and TDIs that have been sent to it, decides the priority of each case, displays all the account information about an individual taxpayer on a video screen when the contact specialist is ready to make a call, automatically dials the telephone number, and reschedules future calls if there is no answer or if the line is busy.[3]

The tracking operation of ACS offices is quite sophisticated. Although there is some variation from office to office, many of the twenty-one locations have established computer links giving them direct access to individual files maintained by such state and local offices as departments of motor vehicles and organizations filing federal unemployment insurance. Most unemployed workers, licensed drivers, and automobile owners in each state do not owe the IRS any back taxes. But computerized state lists are very useful when the contact specialist at the ACS is trying to locate a particular taxpayer. Voter registration lists are another handy tool. State and local files containing the names and addresses of doctors, lawyers, plumbers, and a variety of other licensed workers also provide useful tips about an individual's possible income. Even more helpful in this regard are state tax records. To eliminate the tedious business of thumbing through stacks of telephone books, some IRS collection offices have established direct electronic ties to the telephone company's information computer. Like the old reverse directories that listed the names of individuals by the addresses where they live, rather than by their names, the new computerized information system makes it easy for the IRS to identify quickly the names and telephone numbers of the neighbors of a particular target. Neighbors, of course, can be useful sources of gossip and other kinds of information.

Researchers and other support people in the center help the contact specialist by gathering information from IRS files; handling incoming calls; processing taxpayer correspondence; and tracking down the names, telephone numbers, and assets of the more reluctant taxpayers who either deliberately or unconsciously avoid the IRS.

After the home address, place of employment, banking arrangements, relevant tax information, and other intelligence have been collated about the delinquent taxpayer, the contact specialist calls the individual to discuss the payment of the problem tax or the filing of the missing return.

IRS experience shows that once telephone contact is made by the IRS, most taxpayers choose to pay, often exactly what the IRS says they owe. But in a fair number of cases, especially for upper-income taxpayers, there are negotiations, and the government agrees to accept a portion of the taxes, penalties, and interest that it initially had claimed was owed the Treasury.

In 1987, the IRS's Internal Audit Division completed a confidential report about how the IRS was using installment agreements to collect taxes. Because many aspects of the collection process require several years to unfold, the inspectors focused on the 4.5 million taxpayers who had been nominated for TDA or TDI status in 1984. When looked at three years later, the investigators found that 978,390 of the 4.5 million taxpayers—almost one out of five—had signed installment agreements covering $1.2 billion in owed taxes. By early 1986, the same study discovered, 60 percent of the debt covered by these agreements, or $724 million, already had been paid.

Despite the overall apparent success of the program, however, the investigators determined that the installment agreements were not being administered in an effective and equitable manner. The agreements the Collection Division had reached with upper-income and business taxpayers, for example, were less successful than those it made with lower- and middle-income taxpayers. Considering the results of the installment agreements worked out between the IRS and a sample of the upper-income and business taxpayers during the recent four-year period, the investigators determined that for every 85 cents that was collected, $1 was defaulted. For installment agreements worked out with lower- and middle-income taxpayers, on the other hand, the investigators discovered that for every $2.37 collected, $1 was defaulted. In other words, the effort to collect money from the less well-off was three times more effective than the effort aimed at the well-to-do.

The substantially higher failure rate among upper-income and business taxpayers occurred even though the IRS apparently gave them more favorable terms. For example, the average payback period for the sample of businesses in hock to the government was fifty-three months, more than twice the twenty-four months the IRS granted individual taxpayers.

Another serious problem with the installment agreements concerned the living expenses for food, rent, and other necessities that the agency allowed taxpayers while they were paying off their government debts under the agreements. Sometimes the terms of the expense agreements were extremely generous; other times they were very harsh. "In two of three regions, for example, questionable expenses such as karate lessons and cable television were allowed for 13 percent of the taxpayers in our sample," the auditors said. Even within a single IRS district some inconsistencies were hard to explain. "For example, one family of six was allowed $650 per month for groceries while another family of six in the same state was allowed only $250 per month for groceries," the report said.

An even more fundamental question about the IRS's ability to administer the tax collection process in an evenhanded way is raised, once again, by the district-to-district variation found in the agency's own performance statistics.

During 1988 only 22 out of every 1,000 taxpayers who had received tax delinquent account notices in New Hampshire were able to work out an arrangement to pay their tax debt over a period of time. This contrasted with Indiana, where 227 out of every 1,000 entered into such arrangements. Similar variations were even found among IRS districts located in the same state. Among Texas taxpayers living in the Austin district, for example, only 53 out of every 1,000 of those placed in the TDA category signed agreements; in the Houston district, it was 190. Among California taxpayers, there was a sharp contrast between those living in the IRS's Sacramento and San Francisco districts. In the former, 68 of every 1,000 of those with TDAs signed an agreement; in the latter, 166 signed agreements.

The IRS's own procedures frequently led the agency to handle taxpayers who had defaulted on their agreements in an inefficient and unfair manner. The report cited one situation where a forceful collection action was taken against an individual who had paid off almost all of the $558 he owed while no action was taken against another taxpayer who had only paid a small percentage of the $413 he owed. "In this particular example, the Service's arbitrary criteria for taking action on defaulted agreements resulted in harsher treatment of the taxpayer who was far more successful in reducing the delinquent account balance."

The report went on: "Taking enforcement action on accounts of nominal value while deferring significantly larger accounts is not an efficient utilization of resources and is not compatible with the Service's policy of equitable treatment of taxpayers."

The success of the IRS's massive system of dunning—first by mail, then by telephone, and finally by a living, breathing agent—is not entirely surprising, given the economic and legal resources that the government devotes to the job.

Ever since George Washington's army captured a small group of tax protestors in the forest of western Pennsylvania and dragged them back to Philadelphia for trial, the federal government has asserted its absolute right to penalize those who fail to pay their taxes. But during the last three or four decades, Congress has approved a series of laws vastly expanding the authority of the IRS to punish the American people for a growing number of tax-related violations. In the beginning, the tax agency was pretty much limited to penalizing those who did not pay their taxes when they were due. Now, the IRS has been granted the authority to penalize almost anyone who does not provide the agency with a wide range of information that Congress has determined is necessary for the administration of the tax laws. There are additional penalties if the required information is inaccurate or is not delivered at the scheduled time.[4]

The increase in the penalties the IRS can impose on taxpayers has been truly mind-numbing. In 1954, the federal tax code included a grand total of thirteen penalties. The IRS of course had the right to charge taxpayers who understated their incomes with either fraud or negligence. In addition, the agency could penalize those who failed to file a return, failed to pay an estimated tax, or, in the case of businesses, failed to pay withholding taxes.

By 1987, there had been an elevenfold increase in the number of penalties authorized by Congress. The scope of the 150 mostly new penalties gave the IRS unprecedented power over many aspects of American life.

No longer were a citizen's responsibilities limited to filing an annual tax return and paying the correct tax. In 1986, for example, the IRS was authorized to impose a penalty on taxpayers who failed to estimate correctly their taxes in the current tax year. Vice President Dan Quayle and his wife, Marilyn, were hit with a $254 penalty in 1989 because the couple underestimated their 1988 income and thus failed to withhold sufficient taxes.

In 1976, Congress gave the IRS power to penalize tax preparers who failed to enter their own taxpayer identification number on a return they had prepared, who cashed taxpayer refund checks, or who negligently or intentionally disregarded the law when preparing a return. This last part has caused considerable controversy because of the murkiness of the 1976 tax law. The problem: Can the IRS serve as a neutral referee when it comes to drawing the line between tax advice that aggressively seeks to minimize taxes and tax advice that disregards the law?

More recently, penalties have been added to punish many different kinds of business organizations that fail to provide the IRS with accurate and timely information about the interest and dividends they are paying to taxpayers.

And in June 1988, the Ninth Circuit Court of Appeals further strengthened the hand of the IRS to penalize taxpayers who in the agency's opinion have filed a "frivolous return." In this case a taxpayer from Billings, Montana, named Donna Todd wrote a brief comment on her tax return in a way that did not obscure any of the information required by the IRS. Her message: "Signed involuntarily under penalty of statutory punishment." The IRS, citing the frivolous-return provision of the law, fined Todd $500. Todd refused to pay the fine on the grounds that the penalty violated her constitutionally guaranteed right to free speech. The federal district court agreed with Todd. But when the IRS took the matter to the Ninth Circuit, the agency's action against Todd was upheld.

The increase in IRS authority to impose more and more penalties has been dramatic. But it has been easily matched by the agency's actual willingness to apply its new administrative tools. In 1978, for example, the IRS imposed 15.4 million penalties totaling $1.3 billion. Ten years later, it assessed 27 million penalties amounting to $14 billion.

Even the IRS has some doubts about all these penalties. "Over the past decade, it has been my concern and the concern of the IRS that the rapid expansion of civil sanctions in the Internal Revenue Code was occurring on an ad hoc basis without a consistent rationale as to the purpose or role of civil penalties in the tax administration process," IRS Commissioner Lawrence B. Gibbs told the House Ways and Means committee on

February 21, 1989. Taken together, he said, "they sometimes produce unintended results and have a combined impact that can be too severe."

DRACONIAN MEASURES:
LEVIES, LIENS, AND SEIZURES

While the increase in the application of civil penalties is truly impressive, it does not get to the heart of the extraordinary powers granted by Congress to assure the collection of the nation's taxes. Although some Americans do feel the delegation of authority to the IRS has gone too far, Congress may be correct in its view of what is necessary to maintain the flow of tax dollars into the federal Treasury.

But because IRS supervisors have little time to review the actual day-to-day decisions of revenue officers, and because the legal guidelines laid down by Congress are almost never precise, and because judicial approval is not required before the IRS acts, and because Congress has sharply limited the right of the courts to review IRS enforcement actions after the fact, there is significant room for abuse in how the IRS exercises these powers.

The IRS's basic arsenal does indeed contain some impressive weapons: levies, liens, and seizures. And the agency exercises these weapons with some frequency. In 1988, for example, IRS agents filed 838,000 liens and 2,153,000 levies and made 14,000 seizures.

The law authorizes the IRS to create a lien when the taxpayer, after a demand by the IRS, refuses or neglects to pay the tax. The filing of a lien provides public notice that the taxpayer is in economic trouble. Although the law does not state when a lien should be filed, the IRS manual says that this power should not be mobilized until "reasonable efforts" have been made to contact the taxpayer personally to seek the prescribed payment. If no payment is forthcoming, the regulations add, the lien may then be filed if it appears the collection of an account might be jeopardized. No definition of "reasonable efforts" or "jeopardy" is provided the revenue officer in the field. The overall effect of the manual's directive is that revenue officers file liens when they decide such action is necessary to protect the interest of the United States.

A tax lien is a document designed to inform an individual's creditors that the IRS now has a first claim on any assets that might be realized from the sale of the individual's holdings. If an IRS lien has been placed on a taxpayer's house, for example, the IRS is entitled to satisfy its claim first if the house is sold. Liens usually are filed with the county office where the deed of property is maintained. Because such files are considered public records, they are regularly checked by credit-reporting companies that want to obtain the latest information about the credit status of every individual living in each county.

As was the case with first notices and installment agreements, there is considerable variation in the IRS's use of liens in different parts of the United States. In 1988, IRS agents operating in the North Atlantic Region were least likely to issue a lien, 262 of them for every 1,000 tax delinquents. Most active were the agents working in the Midwest Region, where 321 liens were issued for every 1,000 TDAs. The numbers for the other regions were 265 in the Central, 274 in the Southwest, 282 in the Southeast, 289 in the Mid-Atlantic, and 313 in the Western regions.

The IRS contended that the different state and local laws strongly influence the number of liens it issued in different parts of the United States. "Some states require us to make multiple filings, one at the county courthouse, another with the state," one agency bureaucrat said. "Certain other states require us to file with a city court as well as the county. Obviously these multiple filings can affect the lien rate."

Could the policy preference of the individual director influence the chances that an average taxpayer might find a lien placed on his house? "I wouldn't think so," the IRS bureaucrat said. "You know the requirements in the agency manual are the same for everyone all the way across the country. And there are regional review programs that look at such programs to make sure they are in conformance with what is in the manual."

A levy is a document the IRS files with third parties such as employers, banks, credit unions, and stockbrokers who maintain the assets of a particular taxpayer. The levy in effect gives the IRS control over these assets.

The region-to-region variation in the IRS's use of levies was somewhat more pronounced than it was for liens. Here are the 1988 numbers. For every 1,000 tax delinquent accounts, 892 levies in the Western Region; 860 in the Mid-Atlantic; 735 in the Southwest; 714 in the North Atlantic and the Central; 708 in the Midwest; and 532 for the Southeast.

IRS collection officials again denied that poor administrative controls were in any way connected to the uneven application of levies. Instead, they said, variations probably were the result of different regional economic conditions.

During the last fifteen years, the total number of levies and liens issued by the IRS per 1,000 TDAs has nearly tripled. In 1972, there were 346 such actions for every 1,000 TDAs. In 1988, there were 997. This substantial increase in one of the basic enforcement techniques of the IRS, according to Collection Division officials, is largely the product of the computer. "Changes in the law and the availability of the computer mean we are able to collect and use a great deal more information about who is providing income to the individual taxpayer," one of the Collection Division officials explained. "This means that when we decide a particular taxpayer owes us back taxes, we have many more organizations that we can hit with a levy." The official was referring to the fact that the increased reporting requirements now enable the IRS to identify more sources of income than before.

This major increase in the ability of the IRS to comprehend the financial network surrounding every individual taxpayer is one of the most significant changes that has occurred in American regulatory life in the last quarter of a century. In recent years, efforts to further enhance the agency's ability to collect, store, and utilize more and more detailed information concerning all taxpayers has become a major policy objective. This goal was formally adopted in the spring of 1984, when the IRS completed a strategic plan for tax administration in the 1990s and beyond. Over and over again, in the euphemistic language of all bureaucracies, the 204-page planning document called upon the agency to "seek additional ways to create and maintain a sense of presence and improve our ability to detect sophisticated noncompliance."

But it is the physical seizure of property that has come to be regarded as the ultimate weapon of the IRS. The tax code gives the IRS the right to seize the property of any person who neglects or refuses to pay "any tax" thirty days after it mails a "notice and demand." With certain limited exceptions, all property and rights to property belonging to the delinquent taxpayer may be taken to satisfy the tax debt.

In the obscure words of the law, any kind of seizure intended to secure a debt is called a distraint. But over the years, the IRS has developed two distinct forms of distraint. One, which we have already discussed, is called a levy. The other is called a seizure.

In IRS usage, a levy refers to distraints upon assets (usually liquid) that are held by third parties such as an individual's employer or bank. A seizure, on the other hand, is a distraint of nonliquid property such as an individual's house or car. Because seizures are often events where the agent and the taxpayer are likely to meet and neighbors may well be able to watch, the potential for real confrontation is high. Under law and IRS regulations, the individual revenue officer has been granted great discretion in the issuing of levies or the seizing of property. As noted earlier, the IRS agent need not seek an independent judgment or court order before lowering either of these booms.

Once again, there is considerable variation in how IRS agents use these powers in different parts of the United States. During tax year 1988, for example, the IRS made six seizures for every 1,000 TDAs in the Southwestern Region, but only 4 in the Mid-Atlantic and North Atlantic regions.

The differences in the rates of seizures in the sixty-three IRS districts were more dramatic. In 1988, the six districts reporting the most seizures were Austin, 41 per 1,000 TDAs; Oklahoma, 33; San Jose, California, 31; Richmond, Virginia, 29; Fort Lauderdale, Florida, 27; and Louisville, Kentucky, 27.

Among the districts with the lowest rates were Nashville, 1; and Baltimore, Newark, Philadelphia, Buffalo, and San Francisco, all at 2 seizures per 1,000 TDAs.

Here are the 1988 rates for several big city districts: Manhattan was 2; Chicago, 4; Dallas, 4; and Los Angeles, 24.

The seizure rates in the most active districts thus were thirty to forty times higher than the rates in the districts with the least. The IRS has no explanation for the variations. "I really don't know how to explain it," one official said. "What we emphasize, of course, is adherence to the procedures spelled out in the manual. Reviews by the regional offices are designed to assure that the appropriate actions are taken at the appropriate time."

All of these complicated processes and procedures; all of these computerized notices; all of these levies, liens, and seizures turn out to be quite effective. In fact, despite the widespread impression to the contrary, the two Collection Division bureaucrats agreed that the number of Americans who were shortchanging the government probably had not fluctuated in recent years. "My sense of it is that compliance has remained fairly stable in collections, that there might even have been a slight improvement," one of the officials said.

At the end of 1987, there were 2,847,000 unresolved TDAs and TDIs that the IRS had initiated between 1982 and 1987. (After the sixth year, most are removed from the books because of the statute of limitations.)

The IRS calculated that the taxes, penalties, and interest owed by these 2,847,000 deadbeats were a bit more than $14 billion. Upon first consideration, this looks like an awful lot of taxpayers and an awful lot of unpaid taxes. But given the fact that the nation's taxpayers filed a total of more than 600 million tax returns during this six-year period and the IRS collected more than $4.3 trillion, the delinquencies actually are minuscule. One study found that a few years ago the IRS allowed less than one half of 1 percent of its final assessments to go stale and that all but 2.5

percent of its delinquent accounts were collected. (In the last few years, there has been an increase in the IRS's inventory of taxpayers who owe the government back taxes. The IRS contends, however, that this increase reflects the agency's improved ability to spot such taxpayers rather than an actual increase in noncompliance.)

Many months, and sometimes even years, can pass between the time when a return is filed and the moment an IRS agent decides to impose a levy or lien or actually seize the physical property of a taxpayer. Almost all IRS enforcement actions are preceded by a long string of notices. At any point in this process, the taxpayer may challenge the IRS's assessment by requesting an appeal. In addition, before the IRS issues a levy or a lien, the revenue officer is supposed to provide the target a warning notice. (Experienced IRS employees say that in actual practice this final warning requirement is sometimes ignored.)

But the IRS has several additional collection procedures up its sleeve where advance notice of an action and the right to appeal it before the trap is sprung are explicitly not provided. These procedures are for situations where the IRS believes the various normal warning notices might permit the taxpayer to place assets beyond the reach of the government. Thus, when a revenue agent thinks that collection might be jeopardized by the normal routine, the tax may be assessed and immediately collected without any kind of advance notice.

Since jeopardy assessments are made in emergency situations, there frequently is not time to collect reliable information about the tax dollars that are owed. Furthermore, because jeopardy assessments are designed to secure all the taxes that possibly might be owed, they frequently are on the high side. Sometimes astonishingly so.

TROUBLE IN MIAMI

One example of how this emergency procedure can go wrong involved Sharon Willits, an attractive Florida divorcée.[5] The case began at 7:30 P.M. on May 24, 1973, when two Miami police officers stopped Willits in the vicinity of the 79th Street Causeway. The two officers, members of the Miami Police Department's narcotics squad, had stopped Willits because they believed she was the companion of Rick Cravero, a man they suspected was a drug dealer.

Willits was taken to the station house, where she was asked to open her purse. The officers spotted a pistol. Willits was then arrested for carrying a concealed weapon, advised of her constitutional rights, and given a more complete search. Several white pills, $4,400 in cash, and a scrap of paper with some notes were found in her purse. The notes said: "Ceon—3000, Ron 1500, Slt 2000, P 500, C 400, ME 5900." Because of the presence of the pills, which Willits said were doctor-prescribed barbiturates, the police added the charge of possession of narcotic drugs. Later that night she was released on a $2,000 bond that was posted by a friend.

The police officers were aware that the IRS recently had been ordered to try to use its tax enforcement powers to curtail drug trafficking. So the next morning, they called John Zahurak, a special agent of the IRS, and informed him of the Willits arrest. Zahurak was told that Willits had said she was unemployed. He then determined she had not filed a return during the past four years.

On the basis of the police intelligence that Willits had been dating a suspected drug dealer, the pills in her purse, and the notes on the scrap of paper, Zahurak reached a startling conclusion: During the first five months of 1973, he calculated, Willits had earned commission income of $60,000 on the sale of $240,000 worth of cocaine.

At 3:20 that afternoon, with the approval of the IRS's district director, a special notice was sent to Willits by certified mail stating that, on the basis of her alleged $60,000 income so far in 1973, she now owed the government $25,549 in taxes. The jaws of the jeopardy assessment procedure snapped closed several days later, when the IRS served notices of levy for all of her assets.

Willits' lawyers asked the court to enjoin the IRS seizure. As later explained in an opinion of the Fifth Circuit Court of Appeals, Willits was divorced in 1972. The settlement with her former husband gave her alimony of $67.50 a month. This was terminated after five months for a cash payment of $400. The child support granted under the settlement to her two children did not stop. It too was for $67.50 a month. In early 1973, she had sold a house she had won during the divorce proceedings for $2,000 cash, with the purchaser assuming her mortgage.

The Court of Appeals decision noted that during a court hearing at the district level IRS agent Zahurak had been unable to cite any specific evidence to support his assumptions that Willits had sold cocaine, had earned a commission of $60,000 on the alleged activity, and thus had owed the government slightly more than $25,000 in taxes. The four pills found in her purse, for example, turned out to be barbiturates that had in fact been prescribed by her doctor.

On July 18, 1974, a little more than a year after the seizure, the Court of Appeals lowered the boom on the IRS. It said that the IRS seizure of Willits's property was based on "the altogether fictitious assessment" that agent Zahurak implemented on the basis of the untested speculation of the two Miami police officers. The court added that "a taxpayer under a jeopardy assessment is entitled to an injunction against collection of the tax if the Internal Revenue Service's assessment is entirely excessive, arbitrary, capricious, and without factual foundation."

In addition to denouncing the IRS for the specific actions it had taken against Willits, the Court of Appeals decision also challenged the IRS for marshaling its most ferocious powers for purposes not directly related to collecting taxes.

The decision noted that Congress had granted the IRS broad powers to seize property without normal due process protections for the explicit purpose of preventing the loss of tax revenues. It thus was essential, the judges added, that the federal courts not permit the IRS to mobilize these special powers as instruments of "summary punishment to supplement or complement regular criminal procedures."

THE COURTS GIVETH
AND THE COURTS TAKETH AWAY

In Sharon Willits's case, the court ruled that the IRS had arbitrarily abused its vast legal authority to make jeopardy assessments. More frequently, however, the courts are reluctant to second-guess the agency in the application of its unique collection powers. Two citizens who learned this lesson the hard way were Thomas L. Treadway and Shirley Lojeski. In the summer of 1982, Treadway was a prosperous Pennsylvania businessman and Lojeski, his live-in companion, was the owner of a successful riding stable.[6]

The case began in the fall of 1979, when an IRS revenue officer named Richard Boandl was asked by his supervisor to add Treadway to the portfolio of tax cases he was examining. Initially, Boandl concentrated on Treadway's 1977 tax return. Then he started looking at tax years 1978, 1979, and 1980.

In February 1982, more than two years after beginning his audit, Boandl decided that Treadway owed the government $247,000 in back taxes, penalties, and interest. The taxpayer was astonished and filed an appropriate notice appealing the assessment.

But Boandl was in no mood to play games. After a discussion with his supervisor, the revenue officer decided to institute a jeopardy and termination assessment against Treadway.

Given Treadway's lawful appeal, Boandl's decision to institute the emergency seizure process was unusual. But in August 1982, the agent made an even more surprising move by initiating separate assessment actions against Lojeski, who had been living with Treadway since 1980. Boandl took summary action against Lojeski on the theory that Treadway might be transferring his assets to her to thwart the IRS. Because Lojeski was never the subject of a tax investigation and had never been found to have not paid her taxes, the absolute first notice that she was in serious trouble came when the IRS filed a lien against her farm and seized her bank accounts, acts which made it impossible for her to use her money to pay her outstanding bills or to obtain an emergency loan.

Some months later, an IRS appeals officer ruled that Boandl's tax evasion charges against Treadway had been wrong, that the Pennsylvania businessman only owed a fraction of the $247,000 in back taxes and penalties that had been claimed by the government. The favorable tax ruling, however, did not compensate for the serious losses Treadway suffered. During the course of his battle with the IRS, Treadway had lost his job and had been forced to dispose of many of his assets to pay the necessary legal and accounting fees, which came to more than $75,000.

Boandl was not some rogue agent who had operated outside the normal bureaucratic procedures of the IRS. In fact, before the jeopardy assessments against Treadway and Lojeski could go forward, they had been approved by a grand total of nine different supervisors, up to and including the Philadelphia district director. Despite this massed array of approvals, however, evidence gathered at a later federal hearing proved that Boandl's theory that Treadway was transferring assets to Lojeski was based on his personal hunch rather than on any specific evidence. Finally, Boandl's hunch turned out to be dead wrong. Treadway had never sought to hide his money from the IRS by giving it to Lojeski.

Although Treadway's appeal against the IRS assessment was mostly successful, for a variety of legal reasons the Pennsylvania businessman had no grounds for suing either Boandl or the IRS for damages, nor could he recover all the legal and accounting expenses required to defend himself against what the IRS itself ultimately determined were generally incorrect charges. It was at about this time that the IRS reversed its actions against Lojeski, releasing the lien on her farm and the hold it had placed on her bank account.

Lojeski, however, felt she had a serious grievance. On July 24, 1984, she filed a suit in federal court claiming that the IRS's seizure of her assets had violated her rights under the Fourth and Fifth amendments. The

Fourth Amendment prohibits government agencies from making unreasonable searches and seizures; the Fifth Amendment guarantees citizens the right to due process.

After a lengthy trial, District Court Judge Charles R. Weiner decided in Lojeski's favor, holding that the seizure of her assets had been unreasonable and made without due process. He further ruled that the IRS actions had caused Lojeski actual damages. "She was threatened with foreclosure of her real estate because she didn't have funds to make her mortgage payment. She was sued by one supplier because she did not have money to pay her bill. She was humiliated, degraded and withdrawn."

Judge Weiner ordered the government to pay Lojeski compensatory damages of $67,000 and legal fees of $6,600. Lojeski and Treadway were elated. But their victory was short-lived. One year later, a panel of the federal Court of Appeals in Philadelphia decided that Lojeski's rights had not been violated. The compensatory award was invalidated.

In the summer of 1987, an understandably bitter Thomas Treadway testified before the Oversight Subcommittee of the Senate Finance Committee: "I am now broke, I have no job, no insurance policies and no car. We did nothing wrong, nothing illegal. We are the victims of an IRS mentality that believes that all taxpayers are criminals who should be punished."

Treadway said a second lesson he had learned was that lawyers as well as the IRS sometimes gouge taxpayers. His personal legal and accounting fees, he said, amounted to $75,000. The cost of Lojeski's suit was an additional $30,000.

But the loss of employment and a good deal of money seems to have been only part of the pain. More serious, it seems, was the damage to their reputations. "After years in this nightmare we have lost many of our acquaintances, family, and friends. Everyone assumes that the IRS *must* have had some basis for what it did. They refuse to believe that our great country with its constitutional protections could have allowed government agents to go berserk."

Why do agents sometimes go berserk? What drove agent Richard Boandl to pursue Thomas Treadway and Shirley Lojeski with such savage ferocity? Part of the answer, as Treadway himself suggested, is that many of the citizens with whom IRS agents deal are, in fact, violating the law or the rules of this unusually powerful bureaucracy.

This point requires emphasis and analysis. The IRS has sensible and elaborate procedures designed to target its employees' attention on taxpayers who are trying to avoid their civic responsibilities. This focusing effort means that in fact most of the taxpayers an agent sees each day are not complying with the frequently confusing laws. The problem develops when agents start to make the natural but incorrect assumption that, because most of their clients are not complying with the law, most Americans are lawbreakers. Good IRS agents try to resist adopting this attitude toward the public. But the misleading reality of their daily work makes the effort difficult. The astounding fact is that an overwhelming proportion of the American people try to pay the taxes they owe. In the face of an extraordinarily complicated and ambiguous tax law, this effort is heroic.

A second fundamental force shaping the generally negative attitude of most IRS agents toward the public is the basic premise of the tax law that permeates many of its regulations and procedures: Taxpayers suspected of not complying with the tax laws are considered guilty until they, the taxpayers, prove themselves innocent. It of course is obvious that the assumption of the civil tax law—guilty until proven innocent—stands in stark contrast with the key constitutional principle in all criminal trials that the burden of proof lies with the state, that citizens are innocent until the government proves their guilt.

The powerful attitudes generated by the day-to-day experience of the agents and the tax law's assumption of guilt are dramatically illustrated by the recollection of an IRS agent working in the agency's Collection Division in one southwestern state.

"For me, the genuinely shocking and destructive part of my job is the way we all started thinking about the public," she recalled in an interview. "This incredible attitude is best caught in the single word we often use when referring to the public. That word is 'slime.'"

Other agents, in other parts of the country, reported that "slime" did not have widespread usage. "I've heard it but I think 'deadbeat' was the usual term for the public during my wanderings," said an agent who has worked in IRS offices in Illinois, Maryland, and New York.

In a congressional appearance noted earlier in this chapter, Lawrence B. Gibbs, then the commissioner of the IRS, told the House Ways and Means Committee about the subtle conflicts that face every IRS employee as a result of the often ambiguous demands of the nation's laws and tax regulations.

IRS agents, he told the committee, are supposed to approach their jobs with the objective of protecting the government's interest. But the "true interest of the government is the impartial enforcement of the tax laws, and this requires that the treatment of taxpayers not be biased in the government's favor."

CHAPTER 4

Nailing the Tax Criminals

Special Agent William J. Haslinger was sure he had a major case. With the written approval of his boss, Haslinger and fourteen other IRS agents spent four days in April 1981 secretly tracking Michael Kuzma as he moved around the upstate New York city of Buffalo. Except for the deletion of a few names, the official IRS summary of the surveillance activity tells it all, moment by dramatic moment. Here are a few of the highlights.

At 8:22 A.M. on Wednesday, April 8, 1981, "a woman (allegedly the subject's mother) left the residence and boarded a bus (19A Main) which headed north on Bailey."

At 11:20 P.M. that night an IRS gumshoe observed Kuzma sitting at the back of Marvino's Pizzeria "looking through pornographic magazines."

At 7:00 A.M. the next day, "a woman believed to be the suspect's mother left the residence and boarded #4 on Broadway." An undercover IRS agent got on the bus too. The agent followed the mother when she "changed buses and boarded Elmwood 20A at the corner of Court and Franklin Street."

Later that morning, at 11:45 A.M., the "subject came out of his residence, spoke with the mailman and went back inside."

At 2:23 P.M. the IRS spies had a little setback. "Mechanical difficulty developed with surveillance van and it was taken out of operation."

At 3:36 P.M. the "subject left the Radio Shack Store with [name deleted in original]. They then drove across Union Road to Burger King, 4199 Union Road, Cheektowaga."

At 9:07 A.M. on Friday, "the subject left the post office carrying mail in his hand. He was photographed coming out of the post office by [name deleted in original]."

At midnight on Saturday, the log shows that Special Agent Haslinger, the initiator of the round-the-clock surveillance plan, walked into the entryway of the apartment building occupied by the suspect and recorded the names of all the residents displayed on the directory. Forty-five minutes later, another IRS agent followed Kuzma as he "left Sambo's restaurant and drove back to the apartment complex."

At 1:00 A.M. Sunday, April 12, Haslinger noted, "surveillance was terminated."

Four days of surveillance by fifteen of the district's forty-two highly trained special agents. It was a significant commitment of investigative power for an office responsible for making sure that the 1.5 million taxpayers within the Buffalo district's borders paid the taxes they owed the government. What had triggered the IRS's suspicions about Kuzma? Why had the agency mounted this elaborate and time-consuming domestic spy operation?

IRS documents show that Michael Kuzma had first come to the agency's attention three years before, in 1978. The suspicious act? Kuzma had written a letter to the editor of the *Buffalo Courier-Express* arguing that the Sixteenth Amendment authorizing the federal income tax was not constitutional. The letter was clipped from the newspaper as an IRS "information item," IRS Form 3949, and placed in a file that suggested that the writer "appears to be an illegal tax protestor."

One year later, in the spring of 1979, the IRS learned that Kuzma had rented a post office box. This raised flags in the minds of the agency's investigators because some tax protestors, to prevent the IRS from discovering where they lived, had adopted the tactic of having their mail sent to post office boxes controlled by third parties. The suspicions that had begun with Kuzma's letter to the editor, which then were reinforced with the discovery of his post office box, became even stronger when the agency checked its own records and discovered that he had never filed a tax return. To the investigators, the nonexistence of tax returns suggested that Kuzma almost certainly was a tax protestor.

Kuzma, in fact, had been only seventeen when he wrote the letter to the editor that had first triggered the IRS's interest in him. He lived with his mother, who claimed him as a dependent on her income tax return. The agents apparently did not ask themselves whether Kuzma's failure to file might be related to his age.

The agency's slowly developing suspicions came to a head in August 1980, when Haslinger was informed by the IRS's service center in Andover, Massachusetts, that a taxpayer named Dale Area had used Kuzma's post office box as the return address for a Fifth Amendment protest tax return.

The detailed story of the IRS's round-the-clock surveillance of Michael Kuzma is documented in a set of records that Kuzma later obtained from the agency under the Freedom of Information Act. In one of the documents that the IRS was forced to disclose, Special Agent Haslinger informed his supervisor that Kuzma "has been identified as a possible member" of "an organized group of individuals who seek to disrupt effective tax administration by their willful failure to comply with the tax statutes."

The evidence that Haslinger presented to his supervisor in his formal request for full-time surveillance of Kuzma provided no proof of such a sweeping allegation, consisting only of brief references to the rented post office box and the lack of an income tax return.

After Kuzma became aware of the surveillance activities and complained to IRS Commissioner Roscoe L. Egger, Jr., and Senator Daniel Patrick Moynihan, the Buffalo district director was ordered to investigate Haslinger's apparently obsessive interest in the young Buffalo businessman. In his report, District Director Marshall P. Cappelli acknowledged that the official IRS surveillance of Kuzma had "failed to disclose information to warrant initiation of a criminal case" and that the matter had then been dropped.

Cappelli, however, who previously had approved the fifteen-agent Kuzma project and had authorized up to $200 in expenses for "bus fares, parking fees, magazines, newspapers, food and beverages" while his troops were tracking Kuzma and his mom, could not bring himself to fault the investigation. "In my view, the Criminal Investigation Division has acted within the scope of its authority and I have no concern that there has been any impropriety by service employees in this matter."

The IRS, however, failed to require Cappelli to answer the right questions. Of course IRS Special Agent Haslinger had the legal authority to investigate Michael Kuzma.

But what about the glaring question of Cappelli's ability to manage his office? Should a cheeky letter to the editor and the separate findings that its teenage author had failed to file a tax return and had rented a post office box be sufficient to launch an extensive and time-consuming IRS investigation? What serious tax cases had Haslinger and his fourteen-agent posse failed to pursue while wasting their time trailing the Kuzmas around the streets of Buffalo? In a world where IRS agents are overwhelmingly outnumbered by serious tax cheats, isn't it essential that the IRS choose its targets with enormous care? Beyond the narrow but still difficult job of selecting truly significant cases for investigation, what is the core purpose of the Criminal Investigation Division of the IRS?

These questions have plagued the IRS for a long time, ever since that moment in 1922 when a remarkably good investigator named Elmer L. Irey was named as the first head of what was then called the Special Intelligence Unit. Over and over again, sometimes in the courts, sometimes in Congress, and sometimes within the meeting rooms of the top managers of the IRS, the debate has flared up: In a world of hundreds of thousands of potential targets, where should the Criminal Investigation Division focus its very limited force?

SMART COOKIES

The IRS criminal investigators who tracked the Kuzmas through the streets and fast-food joints of Buffalo were the direct descendants of the IRS team that fifty years before had locked up the nation's number-one criminal, Alphonse Capone. Partly because of the persistent memory of the genuine skill and integrity of the investigating team that captured this pathologically brutal gangster, the Criminal Investigation Division to this day is regarded as one of the smartest and most ingenious federal investigative agencies. In a more recent era, connoisseurs of smart law enforcement fondly recall the meticulous IRS investigation that ultimately forced a disgraced Vice President Spiro Agnew to resign his office for taking bribes. Although the Criminal Investigation Division has been the home for many intelligent and determined investigators, John P. Daley, an IRS special agent in Los Angeles from 1961 until a heart attack forced him to retire in 1975, has long been regarded as one of the very best.

"I never was a great street man," Daley said in an interview in the living room of his ranch house in West Covina, California. "But I always was pretty good at collecting bits and pieces of information and then making the right connections. The newspapers said I had something like 475,000 names in the indexes of my files and I guess that was fairly accurate."

Of course, as Daley acknowledged, IRS agents do have several legal and tactical advantages over their rivals in the Federal Bureau of Investigation and the Drug Enforcement Administration. IRS agents, for example, have considerably more independent authority to seize the papers of an subject under investigation than do the agents of the FBI.

"I would go into a bank and ask for the records concerning a particular person or company," Daley explained. "Sometimes, the bank would say no. They would refuse me even though they knew that my request did not violate any law or regulation. So I would pull out a blank subpoena and start filling it out. 'Okay,' I'd tell the reluctant banker, 'your lawyers can talk it over with my lawyers when I subpoena every single record you have in your files.' The reality that I could easily force a bank to produce many truckloads of records almost always meant the bank executive decided to help me locate the particular file I wanted. The FBI didn't have the same subpoena power."

Daley said the underlying threat of a tax investigation was the second bit of leverage that gave the IRS a secret advantage. "When an FBI agent walks into a businessman's office and announces he would like to talk about some sensitive matter, the businessman can choose to keep his mouth shut," he explained. "After all, most businessmen aren't criminal suspects. But when a businessman got cagey with me, I would just ask for his Social Security number and he would start wondering about a possible audit. Because questions can be raised about virtually any tax return, the executive almost always would change his mind."

Despite their special skills, unique tactical advantages, and vast data bases of tax information, a number of current and former Criminal Investigation agents agreed that the IRS wastes a large part of its time pursuing unimportant matters, what they often refer to as "junk cases." Independent studies, conducted by the General Accounting Office and the IRS's Internal Audit Division, confirm this view.[1]

There are many different reasons why so many of the IRS's criminal tax cases are insignificant. Probably the agency's single most serious handicap is that over the years government leaders have been unclear about what problems they wanted the agency's criminal investigators to tackle. This confusion about the division's long-term goals has left it vulnerable to the shifting whims of each new administration.

One aspect of this problem is that for at least the last fifty years a hard-to-measure portion of investigative time has been wasted on matters having very little to do with taxes and an awful lot to do with politics.

On October 2, 1975, Donald Alexander, then head of the IRS, told the Senate's Select Committee on Intelligence about a recent trip he had made to the IRS's Brooklyn office, where he found twenty-seven of the agency's criminal investigators collecting intelligence "and a far smaller number engaged in actually working cases." Alexander testified that he was concerned "about whether our sense of priorities was a sound one."

A second troublesome problem that has long nagged the Criminal Investigation Division involves a somewhat surprising debate over what kinds of tax criminals should be selected for investigation and prosecution. Over the years, various presidents, treasury secretaries, IRS commissioners, and attorneys general have tended to adopt one of two basic positions.

Some have held to the seemingly obvious position that the division should concentrate most of its enforcement efforts against the most serious kinds of tax cheating by the most serious tax cheats. Their major argument has been a simple one: Federal law makes tax collecting the IRS's central responsibility. Giving the IRS other assignments diverts it from the essential business of bringing in revenue.

But many other officials, including Robert Kennedy, Richard Nixon, and Ronald Reagan, have argued that the special legal powers granted the IRS for the purpose of investigating criminal tax offenses should be marshaled to deal with broader social problems, such as drug addiction and organized crime. They pushed Criminal Investigation to give heavy emphasis to organized crime suspects who also have violated the tax laws.

At first glance the debate seems a little silly, a useless scholarly exercise in legal semantics. And clearly, most of the emotional weight favors the Kennedy–Nixon side of the argument. After all, the Mafiosi and drug dealers are in fact genuine bad guys who frequently fail to pay taxes. What possible objection can there be to using the tax laws to nail these vermin to the wall?

If the IRS genuinely investigates a drug dealer because it believes the dealer is a tax cheat, there is, in fact, little room for objection. But when the IRS aims its arsenal of tax enforcement powers at an individual because the Drug Enforcement Agency or the intelligence unit of a local police department *believes* he may be a dealer, serious problems frequently have arisen. A fair reading of IRS history suggests that when the IRS has taken on such social ills as illegal drugs by going after the dealers, several distinct kinds of problems have been created.

The first is a practical one. Going after criminals has proven to be a poor way to raise revenue. Because criminals usually try very hard to hide the money they make from their various illegal activities and because such activities often seem to be less lucrative than estimated by official sources, IRS projects to raise revenue from organized crime suspects have always failed to meet their collection goals.

Another problem is legal in nature and grows out of the fact that the IRS was created by Congress to collect taxes. Ordering the agency to prosecute individuals because they are suspected drug dealers bends the tax laws in a subtle but important way. By administrative fiat, rather than by congressionally approved law, a special class of taxpayer is targeted for a special kind of tax enforcement. Because in this particular case the chosen targets are uniquely loathsome, the special IRS drug projects ordered by several recent presidents have won the support of many Americans.

But the decision to direct the IRS to concentrate its criminal enforcement powers on one, sometimes hard-to-define group has had an addictive quality of its own. If it's okay to order the IRS to go after an amorphous group called "organized crime," surely other "undesirable" kinds of people need special attention. Among other "undesirables" who in the recent past have been the targets of special and questionable tax enforcement programs are conservative Protestant ministers, civil rights activists, antiwar activists, and a host of other individuals outside the boundaries of mainstream American thought.

Critics of the special enforcement projects also worry that the partial diversion of the tax police from the business of collecting taxes ultimately may weaken the ability of the agency to complete its central mission. Supreme Court Justice Robert Jackson addressed this second concern in an eloquent concurring opinion he wrote in 1952. "The United States has a system of taxation by confession. That a people so numerous, scattered and individualistic annually assesses itself with a tax liability . . . is a reassuring sign of the stability and vitality of our system of government. . . . It will be a sad day for the revenues if the good will of the people toward their taxing system is frittered away in efforts to accomplish by taxation moral reforms that cannot be accomplished by direct legislation."[2]

Finally, the special enforcement programs also lead, almost inevitably, to violations of the constitutional promise that law enforcement agents will operate under the special set of rules contained in the Bill of Rights when they are pursuing a criminal suspect.

Here a little background is helpful. Traditional law enforcement agencies, such as the FBI and state and local police departments, have been authorized by law to make arrests that can result in the loss of liberty and, in some circumstances, in the use of deadly force. Because imprisoning or killing an individual is a highly serious act, the constitutional fathers established very special rules to assure that law enforcement officials did not abuse their powers in carrying out their jobs. These rules, which have been repeatedly interpreted and modified by the courts, were set down in several of the first ten amendments to the Constitution.

The mission of the IRS, of course, is to collect taxes. Because of the overwhelming importance of this unique task, and because IRS actions almost never deprive an individual of life or liberty, Congress and the courts have granted tax collectors special powers that have been specifically denied the traditional enforcement agencies.

In other words, when the Criminal Investigation Division of the IRS is pressed into using its special investigative powers for the purposes of enforcing the drug laws rather than gathering taxes, it is walking on the edge, and sometimes over the edge, of a constitutional precipice.

The proper line is extraordinarily difficult to draw and is obviously subject to widely varying interpretations. Precisely because it is so difficult to separate the appropriate from the inappropriate, specific abusive actions by the criminal investigating arm of the IRS routinely spill into the courts. But the cost of the confusion goes beyond the small stream of taxpayers who have proved in federal court that their rights have been abridged. The confusion also means that some parts of the IRS have grown comfortable conducting operations that often skirt the law.

One startling example of such illicit activities occurred during the Kennedy years, when Attorney General Robert F. Kennedy secretly pressured agents of the Criminal Investigation Division to install hundreds of electronic eavesdropping devices even though the taps and bugs violated federal policy established by previous presidents and the specific regulations of the IRS.

According to a subsequent report by the IRS itself and the testimony of dozens of IRS agents, between 1958 and 1965 the agency installed at least 287 "improper" or "questionable" electronic eavesdropping devices, most of them during the Kennedy administration. In addition, the IRS operated a secret wiretap school for selected agents and used government funds to buy eavesdropping equipment. On several occasions, for example, telephone company trucks were purchased so that IRS agents could pose as regular employees of the telephone company while installing taps, in one case in a city where electronic eavesdropping was flatly prohibited by state law.

Finally, with the approval of several senior officials in what is now known as the Criminal Investigation Division, a wiretap expert was sent out from Washington to undertake such chores as installing wiretaps in Wheeling, West Virginia, and teaching wiretapping techniques to IRS agents in Pittsburgh.[3]

During a July 13, 1965, hearing on the IRS's eavesdropping, Senator Edward V. Long said the evidence showed that the IRS was placing wiretaps all over the country. Long added that just four months before, however, Treasury Secretary Douglas Dillon had "sat in my office and assured me that wiretapping was absolutely banned in the Internal Revenue Service. He said that he and his colleagues at the national office knew of no cases of wiretapping. I am sure he was telling me the truth. Unfortunately, department and agency heads often do not have the means to know of such activities."

The use of IRS agents and funds for electronic eavesdropping aimed at selected organized crime figures directly violated a national policy established when President Franklin Roosevelt authorized the Federal Bureau of Investigation to use wiretaps only in national security cases involving such matters as international espionage. The secret spying by the tax agency also violated specific IRS regulations. The eavesdropping arguably did not violate the federal law of the period, which prohibited the interception and disclosure of telephone conversations, because the Justice Department had prepared a secret memorandum holding that the FBI could legally conduct its national security taps if it did not disclose the contents to Congress or to the courts. The effect of the federal law thus had been neatly subverted. As noted, however, at least some of the IRS taps were in direct violation of state statutes.[4]

Mortimer Caplin was IRS commissioner from February 1961 to July 1964. He was the official who, at least in theory, was directly in charge of the Criminal Investigation Division during the period when it was heavily involved in improper electronic surveillance. In an interview in 1989, Caplin insisted that he had never authorized such activities and that he was totally unaware of any occasions when IRS agents had used either taps or bugs to gather information. "Now, in that massive organization, if some people stepped over the line, it was done without authorization from my office, directly or indirectly, winks or no winks," he said. A senior partner in one of Washington's most respected law firms, Caplin maintained his position even when reminded of a sentence he had written in a directive issued to all senior officials of the IRS shortly after he was named commissioner. The directive was a rousing demand that the IRS greatly increase its enforcement efforts against organized crime. "In conducting such investigations, full use will be made of available electronic equipment and other technical aids, as well as such investigative techniques as surveillance, undercover work, etc.," the commissioner told his agency.[5]

If Caplin's assertion that he did not know about the hundreds of bugs and wiretaps of the IRS is correct, the widespread eavesdropping raises persistent questions about the agency's management that are in some ways more troubling than if the surveillance had been conducted with the commissioner's specific knowledge. Was the official legally responsible for directing the agency incompetent? Or was there some kind of official conspiracy within the agency to keep him uninformed? Was the extensive eavesdropping undertaken during those years evidence that the agency was out of control or that Attorney General Kennedy had secretly taken command of a powerful instrument of government for his political gain? If it happened once, will it happen again? Given the extremely small size of the commissioner's immediate staff in relation to the size of the IRS, is it ever possible for any commissioner actually to control the activities of the agency?

THE UNBALANCED ARCHITECTURE OF THE IRS

Because of its unusual legal powers and the highly sensitive nature of some of its investigations, the Criminal Investigation Division has played a role in the history of the agency that is way out of proportion to its size. The division has 4,000 of the IRS's 123,000 employees. This compares with about 30,000 in the Examination and 16,500 in the Collection divisions. (The balance of IRS employees are assigned to support, technical, and management units.)

The Examination and Collection people, of course, are limited to imposing *civil* penalties. When the suspicion of *criminal* fraud arises, the case is referred to the Criminal Investigation Division. One simple way to distinguish between civil and criminal matters is to remember that in criminal cases prison is a possibility. In all but a very few civil situations, the only possible punishment is a fine.

The small number of troops assigned to Criminal Investigation and the long period of time required to prepare almost any criminal case mean that only a tiny fraction of all tax penalties are criminal in nature.

Here are the numbers. In 1988, the IRS imposed a total of 23 million civil penalties. In the same year, as a result of the division's investigations, the Justice Department obtained 2,769 tax fraud indictments, winning convictions in 2,491 cases. In that year, then, criminal actions represented something less than one tenth of 1 percent of all IRS penalties. Expressed another way, one criminal tax conviction was obtained for every 9,200 civil penalties.

The extraordinarily small number of criminal tax actions in relation to the total tax penalties might suggest that the agency carefully targets only the most serious kinds of tax cases for criminal prosecution, its most serious sanction. IRS agents and tax lawyers, however, acknowledge that this is not the case, that a large number of IRS criminal prosecutions have little real significance. In the vernacular of the trade, they say the IRS brings far too many "junk cases" against "mom and pop" operations whose prime value to the agency is that they will quickly plead guilty because they don't have the resources to defend themselves.

TAX COPS IN NEW YORK CITY

It usually is quite easy to keep track of the quantity of work produced by a law enforcement agency like the IRS: Count the number of investigations that the agency initiates, the number of criminal tax indictments that the Justice Department obtains, and the number of taxpayers who plead guilty or are convicted of tax crimes.

But determining the quality of such work is much harder. In an effort to solve this problem, I decided to examine the total annual work product of the IRS criminal investigators assigned to one of the agency's sixty-three districts, in this case Manhattan.

Manhattan, of course, is not a typical district, but as the financial center of the United States, it could be expected to have a large proportion of genuinely important criminal tax cases. In 1987, somewhat more than one hundred special agents were assigned to the Criminal Investigation Division of the IRS's Manhattan District. In response to a request, Neil O'Keefe, the district's public affairs officer, provided a list of all of the criminal cases that had been resolved in 1986 as a result of IRS investigations.

With the help of this list, I attempted to locate and examine the records of every one of the eighty criminal cases that had been presented to the judges of what is called the Southern District of New York. (O'Keefe's list showed that investigations by the Manhattan-based special agents that year led to the indictments of an additional twenty individuals who were not located in the Southern District. These cases were heard by judges in other federal courts.) Because the files of some of the eighty cases could not be located at all or contained only a portion of the basic documents that should have been there, it is not possible to render a statistically valid judgment about the quality of the IRS cases in this particular district.*

Nevertheless, the lesson drawn from these files was not reassuring. The record suggested that, although the IRS had successfully prosecuted a number of apparently significant cases, many others appeared to involve situations of little importance.

Among the relatively small number of major criminal tax cases were four that involved million-dollar financial swindles and a fifth case brought against six individuals who were found guilty of massive tax fraud in connection with their operation of a popular religious organization.

The target of one of the largest of these four tax cases, for example, was David J. Heuwetter, the chief trader at a Wall Street company. Heuwetter's manipulations led to the collapse of his firm and to the loss of more than $300 million for the Chase Manhattan Bank and other traders in government securities. Heuwetter was sentenced to three years in prison after pleading guilty to conspiracy, securities fraud, and failing to file personal income tax returns.

A second major case involved Michael Senft, a general partner in another Wall Street firm. Senft was one of four men convicted of conspiring to supply investors with more than $130 million in phony income tax deductions through fraudulent securities trades. He was sentenced to fifteen years in prison and a $70,000 fine.

The focus of a third important tax case was Milton Davids, a garment district executive who was charged with illegally avoiding the payment of over $150,000 in taxes.

In a sentencing memo to the federal judge who heard the case, Assistant U.S. Attorney David M. Zornow explained why the government believed the charges were significant and why Davids should be sent to prison:

"As the court undoubtedly knows, tax evasion schemes have been pervasive in the garment center, and the Internal Revenue Service and this office have been investigating and prosecuting these schemes for

*The clerk of the federal court for the Southern District of New York graciously provided me with the court number for each of the individuals on the IRS list. Some of the associated case files were still physically stored in the federal courthouse at Foley Square in Manhattan. A larger number had been transferred to the federal document center in Bayonne, New Jersey. A number of case files could not be located at either location. Equally disturbing, most of the files did not appear to contain anywhere near a complete set of papers. Several persons associated with the Southern District, including one judge, indicated that the poor quality of the files is due to the fact that so many different offices handle them during the processing of each case.

years. Nonetheless this criminal activity prevails at flagrant levels in the garment district. Indeed, it is like an underground economy operating on an entirely different tax structure, and the attitude of the innumerable companies and individuals profiting from it can only be termed arrogant, no doubt because of the obvious difficulty in detecting and proving these crimes and the lenient treatment frequently afforded the few offenders who are actually convicted."

Zornow said that many executives deliberately and greedily chose to violate the nation's tax laws because they "know the odds are with them: the risks of getting caught are small, and the risks of incarceration are even smaller." He added that the enormous public resources required to win convictions in even the handful of prosecutions brought by the government will "have little value if the sentences imposed do not serve to deter the masses of those similarly motivated to commit these crimes of greed."

After considering the prosecutor's recommendation, District Judge Leonard B. Sand sentenced the garment district executive to two months in prison and thirty-four months on probation and ordered him to pay court expenses, a $15,000 fine, and the back taxes and interest he owed the government.

The investigation and prosecution of Davids, an important figure in one of New York's major industries, is an excellent example of how the IRS's criminal investigators should be spending their time. Unfortunately, however, many of the cases on O'Keefe's list involved insignificant small fry who had cheated the government out of relatively small amounts of money and, in some cases, no money at all. Remember, criminal tax cases are extremely costly and the IRS almost always can punish wrongdoers by imposing civil penalties.

Kirby Holmes was a bank clerk. The IRS charged him with failing to file a currency transaction report with the agency when one of the bank's customers deposited over $10,000 in currency with the bank. The filing of the report is required by law. Holmes pleaded guilty to the technical charge and was sentenced to one year of probation.

Margarita Baez was an unemployed mother who lived in the Bronx. The IRS brought criminal charges against her for filing a false W2 form claiming she had earned $5,444 in one year and was due a refund of $956.84. Baez pleaded guilty and was sentenced to two years' probation.

Utris Y. King was a private-duty nurse who was earning about $27,000 a year. The IRS brought criminal charges against her for filing a false income tax return. The agency said she was shortchanging the government by about $3,000 a year. King was sentenced to three years' probation.

Clevie A. Stewart was the sole officer and director of Precision Combustion Consultant, Inc. He was a small-business man who lived with his daughter in a two-bedroom apartment in Yonkers. According to the government, his actual income averaged about $32,000 a year during the three-year period investigated by the IRS. After his indictment, Stewart pleaded guilty to avoiding about $8,400 a year in taxes. All that remained to be decided was Stewart's sentence. On June 25, 1985, Bernard Wincig, his lawyer, wrote the presiding judge: "It is respectfully submitted that Mr. Stewart was not and is not a systematic tax evader or the mastermind of a fraudulent scheme, but rather a business man whose ill thought out business affairs snowballed in a relatively short period of time." Wincig's plea appears to have been successful. Stewart was sentenced to twenty-four months on probation, given no fine, and ordered to settle his case with the IRS.

Two years after the sentencing, I asked Wincig why the IRS had bothered to bring criminal charges against Stewart. "The government doesn't have time to undertake general investigations of small-business men like Clevie," he replied. "The usual explanation for this kind of case is that a former girlfriend or business associate dropped a dime, or now a quarter, on him," Wincig explained. (The phrase "to drop a dime" is an old New York colloquialism for tipping off a government agency anonymously, usually by telephone.) "Once a case gets into the system this way, it almost inevitably will be prosecuted to the end," the lawyer added.

The court record of another of the IRS's eighty defendants in Manhattan explicitly mentioned the role of a secret informant. The file said the IRS had prosecuted Flerida Serranno, a mother and divorced owner of a small grocery store in the slums of the South Bronx, because an anonymous tipster had sent the agency Serranno's secret account books. Serranno, whom the government charged with understating her income by tens of thousands of dollars a year for three years, was one of the few defendants who was convicted after an actual trial. The judge sentenced her to six months in prison and three years on probation.

The question here does not concern the guilt or innocence of Kirby Holmes, Margarita Baez, Utris King, Clevie Stewart, or Flerida Serranno. Almost certainly they all were guilty. The question concerns IRS priorities. Given the fact that the IRS only indicts about three thousand tax criminals each year for the entire United States, can the agency seriously argue that any of the five should have been on the list of America's most dangerous tax criminals? Does it make sense that some of the smartest and highest-paid investigators in the U.S. government spend their time making such cases when civil penalties can be imposed at far less cost? Why was the division that is responsible for investigating tax crimes in the world's richest city wasting a single moment of its time on the owner of a tiny grocery store in the slums of the Bronx? Who is being taught what lessons by these costly prosecutions?

It is hard to understand. However, the lawyer who represented Clevie Stewart, the small-business man from Yonkers, put his finger on one factor that helps to explain this craziness. There are great bureaucratic pressures on the Criminal Investigation Division to investigate every case that is brought to its attention by disgruntled employees, angry business partners, jilted lovers, and former spouses. The division is acutely afraid of the criticism that certainly would develop if Congress or the press learned that it had failed to follow a significant tip.

While this fear is understandable, and in some ways beneficial, it also means that the disgruntled employees and jilted lovers of America have a substantial voice in setting the investigative agenda of the IRS. No law enforcement agency should hand over control of its operations to its informants. Here, it might be helpful to consider a parallel situation in the New York Police Department. Some years ago, the anticorruption unit proudly boasted that it investigated every single corruption complaint it received from the public. When this apparently sensible practice was examined by a special commission headed by New York lawyer Whitman Knapp, however, it was discovered that the concentration on public complaints had a major unwanted effect. Because New Yorkers tend to speak their minds, the anticorruption unit always had enough cases to investigate. But because the tipsters were aware of only the most obvious kinds of corruption, the anticorruption unit concentrated most of its time on the least important matters. Very few citizens ever see a heroin dealer handing a narcotics detective a $5,000 bribe or a big-time pimp paying off the police captain who commands the vice squad. It is far more likely that the corruption they witness will involve a patrol officer taking a small monthly bribe from the liquor store owner who has trouble with drunks or the construction foreman who wants to park his trucks illegally.

The old Police Department policy of allowing citizen complaints to set the agenda for the anticorruption unit thus guaranteed that thousands of hours would be spent investigating relatively small cases and very little time on organized crime's massive and destructive efforts to subvert the department. For many years the criminal investigators of the IRS have fallen into the same kind of trap.

Another reason that IRS agents often spend a large part of their time investigating less important cases is that small-business men, bank clerks, and bodega owners in the Bronx seldom have the legal or political resources that can make the prosecution of powerful corporate officials a bureaucratic headache. Every so often, of course, a particularly determined special agent will persuade his or her supervisors to bring criminal tax charges against individuals with power and position. This happened in the case of Harry and Leona Helmsley, the New York millionaires. But such prosecutions are the exception, a bureaucratic reality of IRS life vividly attested to by an agency aphorism known to every experienced investigator. I heard it first from Richard Jaffe, a Miami agent who for many years before retiring in 1982 fought with the IRS managers about their timid ways.

"You know the old IRS rule," Jaffe said with a grim smile. "Big cases, big problems. Small cases, small problems. No cases, no problems."

CLEVER TRICKS

Despite the tired cynicism of many special agents, Criminal Investigation from time to time can be extremely inventive in its pursuit of a taxpayer or group of taxpayers it decides is violating the criminal tax laws. One New Yorker who failed to appreciate the occasional brilliance of the IRS was Jackson D. Leonard. Until his brush with the law, Leonard was a successful chemical engineer. But the hard part of his education came in 1972 when a Manhattan jury convicted him of omitting $72,852.51 from his income tax returns.

The IRS first became interested in Leonard's finances in 1969, when he was spotted as a potential suspect by one of the most ingenious surveillance projects in the agency's history. The unusual tracking project had been initiated by special agents in New York after they became convinced that an increasing number of taxpayers were using secret bank accounts in Switzerland to avoid paying taxes on significant parts of their income.

The tax agency was sufficiently worried about this lost revenue that it decided to identify all the probable customers of Swiss banks living in the New York area. The banks, of course, were extremely secretive. So the IRS arranged with the Postal Service to have its agents screen all of the business mail entering the United States from Switzerland and lift the names and addresses of all those who received a letter in an envelope bearing the return address of one of the banks. Pretty soon, however, the

IRS's time-consuming and somewhat obvious initial plan was thwarted when the banks learned about the agency's game and stripped the corporate logos from the envelopes sent to their customers in the United States.

First round to the banks.

By employing a version of the Trojan horse tactic, however, the IRS turned the tables on the banks. The agency's successful counterattack was wonderfully devious. First, a number of agents were instructed to write to the Swiss banks asking for information about how to establish an account. The agents wrote their inquiries on personal stationery so the banks had no way of guessing their identity. The banks, always on the lookout for new business, quickly responded to the inquiries. The logos of the banks of course had been deleted from the return envelopes. But because the banks used mechanical postage meters rather then stamps, all of the envelopes to their bogus customers in the United States bore the unique identifying number that is assigned to each purchaser of a postage meter. Once the IRS had prepared a list of the meter numbers used by each of the banks, the agency asked the Postal Service for permission to conduct a mail cover during the first four months of 1969.

"On the evenings of about 60 days during this period, a Postal Inspector and IRS Special Agents, working at the Main New York Post Office, photostated with high speed copiers the faces of all air mail envelopes without return addresses mailed from Switzerland to New York," Judge Henry J. Friendly later wrote in a decision for the U.S. Court of Appeals, Second Circuit. "Thereafter," Judge Friendly continued, "the postage meter numbers on these photostats were examined to see if they matched those known to be used by Swiss banks. This group was converted into a printout containing the recipients' names, addresses, dates of envelopes and the identities of banks. From the several hundred names on the printout, B. H. Morris, a senior regional analyst in the office of the Assistant Regional Commissioner of Audit, and Special Agent Boller selected a group of 100 in the Manhattan and about 50 in the Brooklyn District."

Leonard was among the chosen few. After his conviction for tax evasion, the engineer appealed. Among other defenses he contended that the scope of the IRS mail cover was an unreasonable violation of his Fourth Amendment rights against a general search.

The Court of Appeals rejected Leonard's objections, and the IRS's clever use of the tiny postage meter numbers was upheld as an appropriate investigative technique.

THE READING PUBLIC

A second ingenious IRS surveillance project of about the same period proved, after it was disclosed in the press, to be highly embarrassing for the agency and was quickly abandoned. On April 15, 1970, an IRS investigator checked with the Cleveland Public Library to determine whether any of three specific men suspected of planting a bomb in the Shaker Heights Police Department had checked out books on bombing. At that time, the Alcohol, Tobacco, and Firearms Unit was part of the IRS.

The investigator learned that Martin Birns, who the IRS believed had killed himself while rigging a bomb, had previously obtained such books from the library.

Two weeks later in Milwaukee, two IRS investigators asked city librarians for the names and addresses of all persons who had checked out books on explosives that were shelved in a restricted area of the library. The director of the library refused the request until the city attorney ruled the records were public and the information was provided. The Treasury Department later said the purpose of the request was to collect corroborating information about several specific individuals who were suspected of planting bombs in the Midwest. On May 8, agents in Richmond, California, acting on a tip that a particular group was making bombs, asked to examine library records. The request was rejected.

Then, during the last week of June 1970, three IRS agents asked twenty-seven libraries in the Atlanta area for the circulation records for books on explosives and, in the case of one agent, the names of all persons who had requested "militant and subversive" books.

On July 9, shortly after an article about the IRS visits was published in the *Washington Post,* Senator Sam J. Ervin, Jr., then chairman of the Senate Subcommittee on Constitutional Rights, attacked the practice in a letter to Treasury Secretary David M. Kennedy: "[T]hroughout history, official surveillance of the reading habits of the public has been the litmus test of tyranny."

Treasury Secretary Kennedy and the IRS were deeply embarrassed by the disclosures of the library sweeps and Ervin's well-publicized denunciation of them. With no valid defense possible, Kennedy tried to wrap his retreat in foggy generalities. "No agency of the Treasury Department is undertaking any general investigation of readers of books," Kennedy stated. "Treasury strongly opposes any of its law enforcement agents surveying or engaging in a general search of any body of records to determine which citizens may have read a particular publication, listened to a particular recording or viewed specific pictorial matter."

Despite the windy denial, however, Kennedy confirmed that the unit in the IRS's Atlanta office that had approached the twenty-seven libraries had been conducting a survey "to determine the advisability of the use of library records as an investigative technique to assist in quelling bombings. That survey, which was not directed by the national office, has terminated and will not be repeated." He also confirmed that IRS agents in Milwaukee, Cleveland, and Richmond, California, had indeed visited libraries to obtain information about specific persons suspected of being involved in several bombing incidents and "a militant group" allegedly considering the construction of bombs.

About a week later, IRS Commissioner Randolph W. Thrower and David H. Clift, executive director of the American Library Association, met to develop guidelines intended to give government investigators access to library records in certain narrowly focused conditions, but to prohibit "fishing expeditions."

ELECTRONIC TRACKS

The ultimate fate of a third, and apparently massive, IRS surveillance project called Operation Mercury is not known. But a single memorandum from the national director of the Criminal Investigation Division to the chief investigator in the Midwest Region provides insight into the division's constant search for investigative leads. The memorandum, dated August 11, 1971, also illustrates the cozy relations the IRS then enjoyed with one of the nation's important communications companies, Western Union.

The Washington official had reminded the regional investigator that he and top Criminal Investigation Division agents from other parts of the country had been sent rolls of microfilm that contained the names, addresses, and other information about every person in the country who had sent or received a Western Union money order in excess of $1,000.

"This phase of the operation was completed and punch cards were prepared from the transcription sheets," the official wrote. "The enclosed listings were processed. The information is arranged by state, and payee names are in alpha order by city. The data elements are: payee, to city, state, sender or purchaser, from city, state, amount, date and reel number."

The national director apologized that the information was somewhat dated and that its use for civil purposes soon would be impossible because of the three-year statute of limitations. "Therefore, the chiefs should make every effort to utilize this information in such a fashion to achieve maximum benefits. We suggest that this information be matched against open case files, and those names showing substantial activity should be matched against background files."

He also warned the regional official that the information about the senders and receivers of the money orders had been obtained from Western Union and that it therefore was necessary to take part in a little charade to protect the reputation of the company. "The source of this information is confidential," he said. "The documents were made available to us with the understanding that before we used them for investigative purposes Western Union would be served with a summons, in usual form, describing the documents needed. This procedure must be followed." Western Union apparently was willing to give the IRS any information it desired, but the company wanted the customers to believe incorrectly that it would surrender the data only when required to by a lawful subpoena.

SHEETS IN THE WIND

Sometimes in their pursuit of tax evaders the IRS gumshoes get down to the fundamental basics of life. Harry, Philip, and Joseph Dushey were in the sex business. For about ten years they had operated two whorehouses in New York City. One was called the Taj Mahal and was located at 10 West 46th Street. The Taj Mahal provided sex for anyone who walked in the door. The fee for each engagement ran between $30 and $80.

The Dushey brothers' second establishment, the Gramercy East, was located at 122 East 22nd Street. A far more exclusive joint than the Taj Mahal, it was a private club with annual membership dues of $81. Each time a member visited the Gramercy there was a $10 entrance fee. In addition to the dues and entrance fees, the customers also paid the club an additional service charge ranging from $60 to $150, depending on the service they desired. The prostitutes at the Gramercy East did not receive a salary, but were allowed to keep their tips, which the IRS determined could range from $60 to $600 a night. The Gramercy management took a 10 percent slice from the tips paid by credit card.

The Dushey brothers were extremely methodical. They kept detailed records of every aspect of their business. Their books showed the money spent by each customer, the length of time required for each transaction, and the manner of payment—cash, check, or credit card. The books also showed the income of each prostitute and the return on each eight-hour shift.

Despite the millions of dollars of income generated by the two sex centers, the Dushey brothers did not file a single income tax return from 1977 to 1982.

That was bad enough. But Martin Perschetz, the assistant U.S. attorney who prosecuted the case, added that as part of the conspiracy the Dusheys went to unusual lengths to protect themselves against IRS investigators. The brothers, he said, "would and did seek to assure that hostesses and other employees of the Taj Mahal and the Gramercy East would not cooperate with and provide information to the Internal Revenue Service by, among other things, requiring that all hostesses and other employees submit to polygraph examinations during which they would be asked whether they had cooperated with or were employed by the Internal Revenue Service."

Perschetz charged that the Dushey brothers owed substantially more than $500,000 in back taxes and had managed to conceal millions of dollars of income from their two sex factories.

But the record-keeping requirements of their substantial business—at one time the brothers employed more than sixty prostitutes—took precedence over their demonstrated fear of the IRS. Among the documents seized by the IRS, for example, were the laundry receipts charged against the two brothels. These receipts gave special agents an exact count of the number of sheets that were being sent out for washing each week. From this curious indicator, the agents were able to project the turnover rate and the annual revenues of the two houses.

After pleading guilty to tax evasion, Harry Dushey was sentenced to eighteen months in prison, Philip to one year, and Joseph to six months. All were ordered to file new tax returns and pay their back taxes. But in the violent and corrupt world of New York City, the successful prosecution of the owners of two busy whorehouses for tax fraud was barely noticed by either the public or the press. To this day, however, its role in jailing Al Capone, a far more sinister criminal, remains the Criminal Investigation Division's best-known accomplishment.

CHAPTER 5

Organized Crime
Is an Enemy in Our Midst

Al "Scarface" Capone was a genuinely evil man. He was born near the Brooklyn Navy Yard in 1899, and his first real job was as a bouncer and bartender at the Harvard Inn in New York City. Although he would later falsely claim he was wounded while in the army during World War I, a dance hall knife fight during that period left him with a scar along his left cheek and a memorable nickname. In 1918, he married Mae Coughlin, who one year later bore their only child, Albert Francis Capone. It was also about this time that the family moved to Chicago and Capone became a bodyguard and the bouncer at a bar and gambling establishment called the Four Deuces.[1]

Prohibition came to the United States on January 17, 1920. In Chicago, a large number of vicious gangs began a murderous ten-year war to control the illegal booze gurgling down the hypocritical throats of the American people who had supported the Volstead Act. There were hundreds of millions of dollars to be made and young Capone turned out to be a totally ruthless and extraordinarily skillful gangster. For example, it is known that on one occasion he personally beat to death three men whom he had invited to dinner. The chosen instrument was a baseball bat. His corruption of the police and most of Chicago's leading political figures, including Mayor Big Bill Thompson, was masterful. It is estimated that by 1928 Capone's control of the supply of illegal liquor and a string of whorehouses and gambling joints was bringing in more than $100 million a year.

It was indeed outrageous. And the upright president of the United States was outraged. Herbert Hoover liked to begin the day with a touch of exercise. Before breakfast he would meet on the White House lawn with his cabinet to toss the medicine ball.

"Have you got that fellow Capone yet?" Hoover asked Secretary of the Treasury Andrew Mellon, tossing the medicine ball in his direction. "Remember, I want that man in jail."

Although Elmer Irey understood that presidents rarely are denied their whims, he raised the right question about Hoover's order when looking back on his career some years later. "I couldn't help wondering," he wrote, "why a Treasury Department Unit charged with fighting tax, customs and narcotics frauds should be assigned to nab a murderer, a gambler, a whore monger and a bootlegger."[2]

But Irey and his specially assigned team went to work. Although a Justice Department team headed by Elliot Ness would later gain a great deal of attention for its attack on Chicago's gangsters with a self-promoting book and a television series called "The Untouchables," it was in fact the IRS that collected the evidence that eventually sent Capone, Case Jacket SI–7085–F, to federal prison.

The story of the investigation and prosecution is dramatic. Working on the inside was a secret IRS agent who in some accounts is called Michael F. Malone and in other accounts Pat O'Rourke. Whatever his real name, a colleague some years later would say that Malone "was the greatest natural undercover worker the Service has ever had. Five feet eight inches tall, a barrel chested, powerful two hundred pounds, with jet black hair, sharp brown eyes underscored with heavy dark circles and a brilliant friendly smile, Mike could easily pass for Italian, Jew, Greek, or whomever the occasion demanded. He was actually 'black Irish' from Jersey City." Malone went to Philadelphia and developed the undercover persona of one Michael Lepito. Some weeks later Malone turned up at the Lexington Hotel in Chicago. He was wearing a white snap-brim hat, a checked overcoat, and a purple shirt, all with labels from a well-known Philadelphia department store, and he spoke with an Italian accent.

Capone and his gang of bodyguards and henchmen occupied several lavishly decorated floors of the Lexington. Capone's sentinels were wary. They ran a check on the stranger. They intercepted his mail, which bore Philadelphia postmarks and consisted of letters carefully sprinkled with the slang phrases then favored by gangsters in the City of Brotherly Love.

Finally, one of the Capone gang approached him and asked his business. "Keeping quiet," Malone replied. A few days later Malone and the goon had a drink and the IRS undercover agent confided he was wanted for a burglary in Philadelphia. The mole had burrowed his way into the Capone organization and in the next two years would be an invaluable source of information.

On the outside was a special five-man IRS investigative team headed by Frank Wilson of Baltimore. Just before the team had been established to nail Al Capone, several of its members had been involved in a successful effort to convict his brother Ralph. The key break in the investigation of Scarface himself came after months of investigation. It was the summer of 1930. For many weeks, Wilson had been combing through the mountains of paper that had been seized during earlier fruitless raids on Capone establishments. The team already had examined more than a million items. But no evidence had been found to document the gangster's income.

As Capone's biographer recounted it, one hot August night well after midnight Wilson was exhausted and discouraged as he continued his seemingly fruitless search. While returning one batch of documents to the file, the IRS supervisor accidentally bumped into the cabinet; the drawer snapped shut and automatically locked. Wilson searched his pockets but couldn't find the key. In the hallway behind him there was another row of dusty old file cabinets. Wilson thought this would be a good place to stash the documents he had been working on until he could get a key the next morning. As he opened a drawer to temporarily stow the unwanted file, he spotted a package containing material that he had not previously examined.

"He broke the string. Out tumbled three black ledgers with red corners. They were dated 1924–26. Leafing through them, he stopped, electrified, at a page in the second ledger. The columns were headed BIRD CAGE, 21, CRAPS, FARO, ROULETTE, HORSE BETS."[3]

Wilson was no longer exhausted. He returned to his office with the miraculously discovered books, which four years before had been seized during a raid by local police. The books showed that the single operation they covered had made net profits of over $500,000 in one eighteen-month period. "Every few pages a balance had been taken and divided among 'A' (for Al Capone, Wilson surmised), 'R' (Ralph Capone), 'J' (Jake Guzik), etc." A balance of $36,687 on December 2, 1924, showed that A and J received $5,720.22 and R got $1,634.35.

Wilson was ecstatic. The handwriting in the ledgers was checked against those of hundreds of known gangsters collected from automobile registration records, the courts, banks, bail bondsmen, and others. Eventually a bank deposit slip was found with writing matching that in the ledgers. The name of the bookkeeper was Leslie Adelburt Shumway. Here was the key, the man who could bring down Capone. But first he had to be found and persuaded to cooperate.

Four months later, in February 1931, Wilson got a tip that Shumway was working as a cashier at a racetrack in Miami. With this lead, the bookkeeper was soon discovered in one of the cages of the Biscayne Kennel Club. Wilson approached Shumway and told him he had two choices. He could go on pretending ignorance about the Capone operations. If this was Shumway's choice, Wilson was prepared to hand him a subpoena in a very public way, thereby pretty well assuring that one of Capone's assassins would kill him. Or he could cooperate with the IRS investigators without a subpoena.

Given the options, Shumway agreed to testify before a grand jury. Buttressed by some other evidence collected by Wilson's team, the government indicted Capone for failing to pay $32,488.81 in taxes during 1924. His net income that year was estimated to have been $123,102.89. The indictment was kept secret while Wilson and his team continued to collect evidence. In June 1931, the grand jury voted to indict Capone for his tax liabilities from 1925 to 1929. Although the IRS knew it had documented only a fraction of his actual income during this four-year period, Capone was charged with earning more than $1 million and with owing $383,705.21 in back taxes and penalties.

Five days before the trial was to begin, the undercover agent, Malone, managed to call Wilson's boss, Irey, with critical information. "They got the jury list, chief," he said. "The boys are out talking with jurors with a wad of dough in one hand and a gun in the other. So long."[4]

Irey, worried that Capone would once again corrupt the law, contacted the judge hearing the case, James H. Wilkerson. The judge told Irey not to worry. On the first day of the trial the reason became clear. Early that morning, Wilkerson had ordered that the regular panel of jurists available to the other judges replace those on the list that Capone's thugs had been working on for the previous two weeks.

The trial began on October 6, 1931. After an IRS clerk testified that

Capone had filed no tax returns for the years from 1924 to 1929, the first substantive witness was Shumway.

Eleven days later, the jury found Capone guilty. On October 24, 1931, Judge James H. Wilkerson sentenced America's most powerful hoodlum to eleven years in jail, fines of $50,000, and court costs of $30,000. At the time, it was the stiffest penalty ever given to a tax evader.

Because of his extraordinary reputation, Capone was ordered held in jail pending his appeal. After both the court of appeals and the Supreme Court rejected the arguments of his lawyer, the gangster was taken to the federal penitentiary in Atlanta. He arrived on May 4, 1932, and was assigned number 40822. Two years later, Capone was transferred to a new federal prison just established for the "more dangerous, intractable prisoners."

Alcatraz, located on a small island in San Francisco Bay, was to be Capone's home until January 6, 1939, when, partially paralyzed with syphilis, he was returned to the mainland. After his release, Capone, his mother, wife, son, and brothers retired to a small estate in Miami. Capone died on January 25, 1947.

Given the corruption of local police agencies and prosecutors of the time, Herbert Hoover's decision to order the tax police to put Capone in jail may have been justified. To this day most Americans applaud the IRS prosecution of this most powerful criminal czar.

But President Hoover's decision also established a precedent that the IRS could be mobilized for a cause, in this case a worthy one, not directly related to the enforcement of the tax laws.

GETTING THE GAMBLERS?

In the Capone case, it was the president who established the IRS's enforcement policy. Frequently, however, forces outside the White House or the Treasury Department have weighed into the battle. An important outsider in the early 1950s was Senator Estes Kefauver, Democrat of Tennessee. In 1950 and 1951 Kefauver held a widely publicized series of hearings on the growing power of organized crime. Eventually, his committee issued a report sharply criticizing the IRS for failing to enforce the tax laws against gamblers and loan sharks.

Another key outside player during the early 1950s was Colin F. Stam, staff director of the House Ways and Means Committee. In late 1952, he managed to persuade Congress to pass a law requiring professional gamblers to register with the IRS, pay an annual $50 "occupational" tax, and provide monthly payments of 10 percent of their gross take to the government.

The new law presented gamblers with a catch-22. The penalty for not complying was up to five years in prison and a $5,000 fine. The penalty for complying with it, on the other hand, was that local law enforcement officials were provided with the names, addresses, employees, and gross takes of any gambler silly enough to register.

The IRS at first resisted the gambling proposal on the grounds that it would be difficult if not impossible to enforce. Surprisingly enough, Senator Kefauver also opposed the legislation, arguing that it would give local police officials the impression that the federal government condoned gambling.

Once Congress approved the law, however, John B. Dunlop, then the IRS commissioner, became an enthusiastic supporter, and the agency grandly announced that a force of five thousand investigators had been put to work enforcing it. (In those days, the agency had a total of 56,000 employees.)

Given all the other demands of the tax collection business, of course, the IRS did not actually have anywhere near five thousand agents who could be diverted from their normal duties. But even if it had been able to mobilize that number, the project was inherently ridiculous in relation to the vast size of the nation's illegal gambling industry. In 1951, for example, Dunlop traveled to New York City and announced that the IRS had initiated an intensive drive against 2,850 "known racketeers" and corrupt public officials in the New York region. He estimated that the tapping of racket and graft incomes should yield $258 million in back taxes and penalties.

It didn't take long for the squishy quality of Dunlop's prediction to reveal itself. One year after the commissioner's ambitious promise, James J. Guthrie, the assistant director of the agency in charge of the drive, announced that his agents had assessed a grand total of $15 million throughout the United States. It should always be remembered that announcing an inflated tax assessment is a lot easier than forcing the assessed to cough up the money.

The special IRS project aimed at racketeers and corrupt local officials was launched at about the same time that the agency itself was awash in a massive wave of corruption. These serious problems led to extensive congressional hearings, indictments of a number of senior tax officials including the assistant attorney general in charge of tax matters, the sudden resignations of many more officials, and eventually a major reorganization of the agency. One casualty of the restructuring of the IRS was apparently its highly touted but extraordinarily shallow drive to round up all of the nation's gangsters.

Organized crime dropped from the headlines of the American press and the consciousness of the American people. But then came the 1957 Apalachin meeting of senior Mafia leaders in upstate New York and the subsequent Senate hearings about the mob's infiltration of several major labor unions. Significantly, the labor racketeering hearings were organized by the younger brother of an ambitious Massachusetts senator named John Fitzgerald Kennedy.

CRIME FIGHTING DURING THE KENNEDY YEARS

In November 1960, with Robert Kennedy acting as his campaign manager, John Kennedy was elected the thirty-fifth president of the United States. The young president-elect swiftly decided he wanted his younger brother as attorney general. At the time, Robert Kennedy retained a fascination with organized crime that had been kindled by his intense involvement as chief counsel in the earlier labor racketeering hearings of the Senate.

Victor S. Navasky described the genesis of the new IRS drive against crime in his book *Kennedy Justice.* The Kennedy brothers had pretty well decided that they wanted their commissioner of internal revenue to be Mortimer Caplin, who had taught Robert when he was a student at the University of Virginia Law School. Robert Kennedy and Caplin had a final meeting a few weeks before the inauguration. "I saw Bob in December," Caplin told Navasky.[5]

"He asked me my views on tax and organized crime and whether I wanted to join the administration. He asked me to write a letter telling how I felt about IRS working closely with Justice in organized crime. I hadn't thought much about it, but I said sure. Then I went back and saw Dean Ribble and concluded, after much thought, that as long as we were making real tax investigations—not sham ones—there was nothing objectionable. I wrote him a long letter, five or six pages, spelling out my philosophy."

Caplin was appointed on January 24, 1961, and a special IRS organized crime squad was immediately detached to work with the Justice Department. Robert Kennedy proclaimed himself a true believer of the theory that the IRS should play a lead role in battling a variety of social ills. In an interview shortly after he became attorney general, he seemed to be echoing IRS Commissioner Dunlop's words a decade before. "We are going to take a new look at the income tax returns of these people to spot the flow of crooked money. I have been criticized on the ground that tax laws are here to raise money for the government and should not be used to punish the underworld. I think the argument is specious. I do recognize that tax returns must remain confidential. But I also recognize we must deal with corruption, crime and dishonesty."

The Kennedy brothers were certainly not the first to order the IRS into the war on corruption and dishonesty. And they would not be the last. The questions about the policy, however, have not changed. First, even assuming that the Kennedy-led war on organized crime actually resulted in less corruption and fewer heroin addicts—and that case certainly has never been proved—the more investigators who are assigned to a fairly small number of Cosa Nostra hoodlums, the fewer will be available to investigate the far larger and richer universe of white-collar criminals who infest what is considered legitimate business.

The second problem, of selective enforcement, was articulated by Howard Glickstein, a lawyer who worked in the Justice Department's Civil Rights Division at the time Kennedy was mounting his war on organized crime. "This time it's the Mafiosi, but the next time it could be the Black Panthers or Goldwater supporters."

A colleague of Glickstein's in the Justice Department's Tax Division put the problem of the Kennedy crusade in slightly different terms. "The purpose of the tax laws is to collect revenue. Once you bend them to catch criminals, you undermine the tax laws and ultimately destroy confidence in them. Justice has to be evenhanded. It can't be personal."[6]

Many years later, an experienced Washington tax lawyer named Donald Alexander offered a more partisan interpretation of Robert Kennedy and Caplin's decision to create Justice Department–IRS task forces to investigate leading organized-crime figures. At the time he spoke, Alexander himself had served as an IRS commissioner and had become a leading advocate of the theory that the IRS should concentrate on tax criminals rather than on organized crime figures.

Alexander said he thought Robert Kennedy had a hidden motive in creating the joint strike forces, one effect of which was to increase his personal control over the Criminal Investigation agents assigned to them.

"Bobby Kennedy didn't get along with J. Edgar Hoover and the FBI wasn't under Bobby's thumb," Alexander observed during a 1988 interview. "Bobby wanted his own investigative unit. So the attorney general called on the IRS and one of my predecessors as commissioner gratefully gave him what he wanted. It was terrible. I don't think the IRS should be taking orders about who it will investigate and who it will not investigate and how the investigation will be conducted from the political people in the Justice Department. These decisions only should be made by the professionals of the IRS."

Despite the doubts expressed by Howard Glickstein and other Justice Department officials, however, the department and the IRS greatly increased the number of investigations and prosecutions of organized crime figures. In 1960, the Justice Department counted nineteen organized crime indictments; four years later, it reported 687. The important role of the IRS in this campaign is suggested by Navasky's estimate that 60 percent of all organized crime figures who were prosecuted during the Kennedy years were indicted on tax charges.

The Kennedy crusade against organized crime generated critics outside the handful of quiet nay-sayers within the Justice Department. Chief among them was Senator Edward Long, a wealthy country banker and Democratic politician from Missouri who also had political ties to Teamster President Jimmy Hoffa. On March 26, 1963, Long was named chairman of the Senate Judiciary Subcommittee on Administrative Practice and Procedure.

With the help of an aggressive staff, Long's subcommittee held a series of critical hearings on the widespread use of mail covers, wiretaps, and bugging devices by a number of federal agencies, most especially the IRS. The hearings won Long the praise of leading civil libertarians. The hearings, however, also earned the senator the deep animosity of many Justice Department and IRS officials who eventually found a way to even the score. Because counterattacks on political critics are an important, unfortunate, and integral part of IRS history, details of the Long affair are described in chapter 12, on the failure of Congress and other institutions to maintain effective supervision of the tax agency.

After the November 1963 assassination of President Kennedy and the departure of his brother from the Justice Department, the joint IRS–Justice campaign against organized crime was greatly reduced. With urban riots and massive antiwar demonstrations sweeping the country, it is not entirely surprising that Nicholas deB. Katzenbach and Ramsey Clark, President Lyndon Johnson's attorneys general, had other things on their minds. In 1967, a group of House Republicans reported that two years after Robert Kennedy had left Justice the number of man-days in the field of agents from the Organized Crime and Racketeering Section of the Justice Department had decreased by over 48 percent.

THE PENDULUM SWINGS AGAIN

The IRS's first publicized effort to confront the general forces of evil had been focused on the gamblers. Of course it had failed. Robert Kennedy had led the IRS on its second broad crusade. This time the crusade was against organized crime. According to at least some of these crusaders, it too had a negligible impact. The third campaign was precipitated by a demand that the administration in power act on drugs. Campaigns to educate young people about the menace of drugs take a lot of time. Programs to provide clinics to wean young people from their destructive habits are costly. The fastest, cheapest, and possibly least effective route is enforcement. Once again, it was time to call in the IRS.

During the second half of the 1960s, marijuana became the drug of choice of a swiftly growing number of young Americans. Although marijuana was strongly associated with students at Berkeley, Columbia, and other universities who were mounting impassioned protests against their administrators, and with others who opposed the Johnson administration's Vietnam policy, polls showed its use to be a far broader phenomenon. July and August 1967 became known as the summer of love. The Woodstock festival came in 1969. To the politicians, bankers, bureaucrats, and police chiefs who ran the country, the clouds of smoke rising up from the massed protestors were almost as upsetting as the protests themselves. Sipping their bourbon or scotch, the men in power wondered whether the world was catching fire.

Something had to be done. And in January 1969, after Richard Nixon was sworn in as president, senior officials in the White House and Treasury Department began to push the IRS to mount a major program to suppress narcotics. Within the IRS, however, some worried that the new program might distract the agency from its prime mission: collecting taxes.

The Nixon administration figure most enthusiastic about turning the IRS into a drug enforcement agency was Eugene Rossides, an assistant secretary of the treasury. His nemesis within the agency was Randolph Thrower, the commissioner of internal revenue. Although the IRS is a part of Treasury, Rossides did not have direct authority over Thrower.

Rossides marched with Robert Kennedy in the vision that the IRS should enforce the laws against the corrupt and the wicked as well as against the tax cheats. Thrower, in contrast, held the view that the IRS's mandate was to collect taxes. With new players, the fascinating battle of wills between Rossides and Thrower over IRS involvement in narcotics enforcement, which of course echoed the earlier fights concerning the war on gambling and organized crime in the Truman and Kennedy years, would continue through the Bush administration.[7]

The exchanges in the Rossides-Thrower battle frequently reeked of animosity. "Your memorandum of March 5 expresses deep concern about the evils of narcotics trafficking and I can assure you we all share that concern," Thrower wrote Rossides on March 26, 1971. "We agree, too, that all available forces should be brought to bear against those who profit from this insidious traffic."

But Thrower went on to argue that the special demands on the IRS's authority had to be somewhat limited or collection of taxes from the public would suffer. "Our manpower is now spread over so many diversified activities that we cannot make sufficient audits and investigations in the general tax area to maintain and assure an acceptable level of general compliance with our tax laws. A breakdown in compliance is as great a threat to the welfare of our country as is the narcotics problem which we all abhor."

In a second memo in June, Thrower continued to resist the pressure from Rossides. "The service has not had sufficient experience in investigating narcotics subjects to assure that intensive tax investigation of major narcotics dealers would have a substantial deterrent effect on narcotics traffic."

In December 1971, an aide to Assistant Secretary Rossides charged that the top management of the IRS was "a reluctant bride" of the Nixon administration project to launch a coordinated attack on major narcotics dealers, even though the agency's street-level investigators were gung ho about busting druggies. Several years later, this deep split within the IRS broke out into open warfare.

Despite the resistance of IRS senior managers, Rossides would not be dissuaded. On January 4, 1972, for example, apparently without bothering to consult with the IRS commissioner, he sent a letter to the chiefs of police and sheriffs of virtually every police agency in the country trumpeting the start of "a major new action program to disrupt narcotics distribution by using the Internal Revenue laws." The Treasury official told the local law enforcement officials that the purpose of the drive "is to seriously disrupt the narcotics distribution system not only by prosecuting those guilty of criminal tax violations, but also by reducing drastically the profits of the narcotics traffic by reaching income not previously reported on tax returns."

Then came the key request to the police chiefs. The stated targets of the project were middle- and upper-echelon dealers and financiers involved in the narcotics business. "It is in this connection that I am seeking your assistance to provide us with a list of potential targets in your jurisdiction meeting the criteria outlined above as well as supporting intelligence information." The supporting intelligence included Social Security numbers; activities in the narcotics business; and all available information about a suspect's standard of living, income, and known assets.

Although senior IRS figures remained opposed to the agency's heavy involvement in narcotics enforcement, they had trouble controlling their special agents in the field, who found the shoot-'em-up world of narcotics investigations far more fun than the less glamorous business of tracking down everyday corporate tax cheats. The troops went their own way.

But when the size of the nation and the extent of the drug use are taken into account, the results of the intervention appear to have been negligible.

On November 6, 1972, John F. Hanem, head of the Criminal Investigation Division, sent Rossides a thirty-two-page progress report. "The accomplishments by the Service continue to be generally above expectations," he boasted. Although the report's charts and graphs all projected dramatic gains in the coming months of the drug war, the actual numbers were far from impressive.

Since the program's initiation fifteen months before, Hanem reported, 1,011 potential targets had been selected for investigation. Given the difficulty of collecting usable evidence in such cases, it is not surprising that this step of selecting possible targets was the high point of his report. During the same fifteen-month period, Hanem continued, IRS investigators actually had completed 238 investigations. Of this total, the special agents had recommended eighty-two prosecutions. Federal grand juries, however, had indicted only forty-three alleged drug traffickers. Hanem saved the worst for last: The special IRS project, which cost a total of $12 million, had resulted in convictions of fifteen dealers or 1.5 percent of the original IRS targets, obviously only a tiny portion of the nation's serious drug dealers.

In fairness, however, there was another aspect of the IRS's narcotics project. At the same time the criminal division was conducting the investigations that led to the fifteen convictions, the agency's Examination Division completed 384 sometimes overlapping audits of suspected dealers. During July, August, and September 1972, these audits resulted in civil assessments of $11.3 million in taxes from 356 individuals. A comparison of the number of drug dealers indicted over a fifteen-month period with those found to owe back taxes during a single quarter suggests that the application of the IRS's civil authority might have been somewhat more effective than the exercise of its criminal powers. But given the official estimates that the nation was then spending billions of dollars a year on marijuana, heroin, cocaine, and other illegal drugs, the total impact of the IRS effort seems negligible.

The Hanem report said that an unspecified number of civil assessments made against drug dealers were brought under an emergency procedure that allows the IRS to seize preemptively the assets of a suspect in situations where investigators believe the taxpayer may be about to flee the country or otherwise escape.

Hanem described this "jeopardy assessment" process in glowing terms. "There probably is no single procedure available to the Internal Revenue Service that will reduce the working capital and thus disrupt the drug trafficking as suddenly or dramatically as the jeopardy assessment," he claimed. "Termination of taxable income usually originates with arrests by the Bureau of Narcotics and Dangerous Drugs, or state or local police authorities where the individual is found in possession of large amounts of cash or other assets which the IRS may seize."

But as described in chapter 3, on collections, the improper use of the jeopardy assessment procedure by IRS agents in Florida eventually proved extremely damaging. It was the 1974 Court of Appeals decision denouncing the IRS's treatment of Sharon Willits that provided agency critics with the ammunition they needed to argue that the Wild West antics of the Criminal Investigation Division were seriously undermining the basic tax collection mission of the IRS.

The slashing court decision, however, was only one of several factors that in the early 1970s prompted the IRS once again to contemplate the hazards of using its enforcement powers for purposes other than tax collection. In July 1969, under pressure from the Democratic Congress and the Nixon White House, the IRS secretly created a small surveillance organization that later became known as the Special Service Staff (SSS). Its purpose was to focus the agency's various enforcement powers on civil rights and anti–Vietnam War activists. In early 1973, however, an anonymous citizen provided the Senate Subcommittee on Constitutional Rights with an IRS memorandum describing the SSS. Six months later, the brand-new head of the IRS, Donald C. Alexander, disbanded the SSS, stating that "political or social views, 'extremist' or otherwise, are irrelevant to taxation."

Although directed at a separate problem, Alexander's August 1973 announcement abolishing the SSS clearly indicated his concern about using the IRS for purposes other than collecting taxes. Shortly thereafter, in January 1974, Alexander seemed to anticipate the concern that would be expressed by the court in the forthcoming Willits decision. The occasion was a private letter to a senior official of the Treasury Department.

Disrupting the flow of narcotics, he said, might be a good by-product of IRS enforcement efforts. "It is not, however, the purpose of the tax system nor of the tax enforcement system. Tax laws, as I have said before, are an imperfect weapon to strike at the evils in our society—other than the evils of tax evasion."

Even as Alexander was attempting to deal with newspaper headlines generated by Congress's disclosure of the political surveillance activities encouraged by the SSS and the sharp criticism of agency narcotics efforts by the court of appeals, IRS agents in Florida were secretly conducting two other entirely separate intelligence-gathering projects that soon would create even greater political problems for the IRS and its commissioner.

One of these intelligence projects, Operation Leprechaun, had been initiated in the early 1970s by Special Agent John T. Harrison to gather information about prominent Miami residents, including judges and politicians. One of the nontax matters that had reached Harrison's ear concerned a judge who allegedly delighted in providing sexual services to the defendants who came before the court.

In early 1975, the *Miami Daily News* published a series of articles charging that the paid informants working with Harrison had gone completely off the track by collecting unverified gossip about the sex and drinking habits of scores of Miami taxpayers. The news accounts, which later were criticized by a grand jury as being considerably exaggerated, prompted embarrassing investigations of the IRS by two House subcommittees. (The waves created by Project Leprechaun took a long time to subside. As is told in Chapter 7, one dispute connected with the project came before the federal courts in the mid-1980s.)

The second intelligence project that eventually created a national storm of controversy had been initiated in 1965 by Special Agent Dick Jaffe, who had first told me about the IRS aphorism concerning big cases leading to big problems. The aim of Jaffe's project, which he called Operation Tradewinds, was to learn the identities of American citizens who had turned to illegal shelters in the Caribbean to lessen their tax burdens.

In September 1975, information about the secret Miami-based operation began to leak to newsmen in Washington after Alexander had disclosed its existence to a House subcommittee.

Jaffe was furious with Alexander for the handling of his case because the effect of the disclosure was to abruptly halt his undercover operation and thus curtail what he and many others in the agency viewed as an important investigation of wealthy and powerful tax cheats. Alexander, however, contends that his concern about Operation Tradewinds went only to the procedural question of whether it was proper and lawful.

As a result of the Court of Appeals decision lambasting the IRS for the jeopardy assessment against Sharon Willits and the negative publicity generated by the disclosure of the political investigations of the Special Service Staff during the early Nixon years, Alexander had become extremely sensitive to any situation that might be interpreted as questionable. Thus, when word of the latest chapter in Jaffe's extended investigation reached Washington, Alexander ran to Congress with a possibly premature mea culpa intended to head off what he feared might be another legal and public relations nightmare for the IRS.

The focus of Alexander's worry was a deliciously devious undercover operation that had provided Jaffe with a secret list of all the Americans who had deposited money with a small Bahamian bank to avoid paying millions of dollars in taxes. Jaffe had recruited a former police trainee named Sybol Kennedy as bait to lure a senior executive of the Bahamian bank to Miami.

The smitten banker walked blindly into Jaffe's trap. While Kennedy and the executive were enjoying a three-hour dinner at the Sandbar Restaurant in Key Biscayne, an IRS undercover agent named Norman Casper entered her apartment, forced open the executive's briefcase, and rushed the contents to a nearby location where Jaffe photographed all the revealing documents. The undercover agent then quickly returned the material to the briefcase before Kennedy and the unsuspecting executive returned from dinner. Kennedy, of course, had given the agent permission to enter her apartment.

Jaffe's highly successful spy operation, and the commissioner's immediate reaction to it, eventually created a situation in which a small group of angry and outspoken Criminal Investigation Division agents almost succeeded in driving Alexander from office.

Jaffe, one of the agency's smartest and most dogged investigators, was not a rogue cop. In fact, the whole operation, which came to be known as the briefcase caper, had been approved in advance by Jaffe's supervisors.

Despite these approvals, however, the raid was in fact of dubious legality. The Justice Department held that the search did not violate the constitutional prohibition against illegal searches. A federal district court judge ruled that the secret photographic mission was illegal and dismissed the criminal tax charges that had been brought against a midwestern businessman as a result of the evidence obtained by Jaffe. In the end, the

Supreme Court decided that the tax charges should stand. But the Supreme Court's decision was based on a technicality and did not rule one way or the other on the appropriateness of Jaffe's tactics.

Confronted with highly embarrassing headlines concerning Operation Leprechaun, the Willits case, and the Nixon administration's misuse of the IRS, and imbued with the natural distaste of most tax lawyers toward handling tax cases in the criminal courts, Alexander was furious. Tradewinds was halted. In addition to trying to disarm Congress by informing it of his problems, the embattled commissioner also attempted to impose a range of tough new controls over the Criminal Investigation Division and how and when it went about collecting information.

At least in the beginning, Democratic liberals in Congress supported Alexander's drive to curb the powers of the Criminal Investigation Division. But a large group of rebellious IRS field agents, silently backed by many of their senior supervisors, strenuously resisted the new restrictions.

The anger of these rebellious agents was so intense that it spawned a highly unusual bureaucratic revolution, a full-blown attempt to destroy Alexander's reputation. Their tactics included challenging the commissioner's leadership in both Congress and the federal court. Jaffe was a lead player, openly testifying against Alexander in House hearings and joining a legal action challenging his leadership that had been filed in federal court by the Federal Criminal Investigation Association. The association's lawyer, Jack B. Solerwitz, also spoke at the congressional hearings. He said the suit had been brought because the agency's criminal investigators "feel there was an alleged conspiracy to wreck the intelligence community in the IRS" and "destroy any effectiveness that the Division could have."

While the attacks were unusual, they at least were stated in a way that allowed the commissioner to identify his enemies and to respond to their criticisms. Far more vicious was a series of anonymous leaks to the press, apparently from current and former IRS agents, suggesting that Alexander was fundamentally dishonest. One such false rumor claimed that Alexander had closed down the Tradewinds investigation because one of his former law clients had been identified as a potential target. These leaks generated so many hostile stories that they ultimately led the attorney general and the secretary of the treasury to announce that they were investigating the commissioner. By late 1975, in fact, so many critical stories had been published in such papers as the *Los Angeles Times,* the *Washington Post,* and *The New York Times* that officials in the Ford administration's White House considered suspending Alexander from his post until the various investigations were completed.

Ultimately, however, the grand juries cleared Alexander of any wrong-doing, and the anger of the criminal investigators slowly began to dissipate. With the election of President Carter, Alexander retired, bruised but unbowed.

But bureaucracies do not take lightly to challenges from front-line troops, even if, as in this case, the bureaucracy itself mostly agrees with the challengers. Gradually, life in the IRS became very hard for Jaffe. Several years later, the IRS ordered Jaffe's immediate supervisor to bar him from investigating any major criminal tax cases. At first, Jaffe disputed the order. But finally, in 1982, he decided to retire. To this day, Richard Jaffe remains a bitter man. He is convinced that a number of subtle conspiracies within the higher reaches of the IRS and the Justice Department improperly blocked the prosecution of scores of major tax criminals, including those identified by his own lengthy investigation, Operation Tradewinds.

The best available evidence suggests that the successful prosecution of Al Capone was something of an aberration in the long chaotic history of the Criminal Investigation Division. But because legitimate privacy concerns make it improper for outsiders to look through the agency's files, it is difficult to judge the overall performance of the IRS's criminal enforcement efforts.

Over the years, however, two government organizations have conducted a number of independent studies. The General Accounting Office, the research arm of Congress, is one such organization. Its collective judgment is not flattering. In 1977, the GAO issued a report charging that the IRS's use of paid informants was seriously flawed. Two years later, the same office reported that the Criminal Investigation Division had no long-range plan to guide its agents and had inadequate information to measure their effectiveness. In the same year, it completed a report on the IRS narcotics efforts. "Relatively few criminal investigations of drug traffickers have been initiated and most cases have not led to prosecution recommendations, let alone convictions," it concluded. In 1982, the GAO examined the quality of an $8 million investigation by the IRS and the Labor Department of the massive pension funds controlled by the Teamsters Union. The joint investigation, it reported, "had significant shortcomings, left numerous problems unresolved and failed to gain lasting reforms in the Fund's operations."

Then there was a 1988 GAO study of the Reagan administration's effort to mobilize the IRS for the investigation and prosecution of "major criminals," drug traffickers, and organized crime figures who violate the tax laws. Given the heavy emphasis President Reagan and his vice president assigned to the war on drugs, the findings of the congressional investigators were surprising.

According to long-standing IRS policy, intensified once again by President and Mrs. Reagan's commitment to fight illegal drugs, the objective of the agency's special enforcement program was to identify, investigate, and prosecute major criminals. But when questioned by the GAO, the officials who headed the Criminal Investigation Division acknowledged that they had never sought to determine whether or not the targets selected by the field agents were in fact significant figures. So the GAO selected a random sample of special enforcement cases and asked the special agents who had conducted the investigations to assess their importance. After restudying the case files, the agents themselves acknowledged that two out of three "did not involve major criminals as defined by the IRS and other agencies."

The GAO also found that of all the major criminal cases referred by the Criminal Investigation Division to the Examination Division, only 50 percent resulted in the assessment of additional taxes. Furthermore, the IRS actually managed to collect only 30 percent of the taxes it had assessed.

There were other serious failings. The GAO found, for example, that the IRS had sometimes provided Congress with misleading information about the success of the special enforcement program. In one case, for example, a former assistant commissioner (Criminal Investigation) had passed information to the House and Senate that claimed that the average prison sentence imposed as a result of a special enforcement program conviction was fifty-three months. "However, our review of U.S. District Court docket sheets disclosed that the average jail sentence imposed for a SEP conviction was 28 months," the congressional investigators said.

The GAO is not the only skeptic when it comes to the Criminal Investigation Division. Sometimes, doubts are expressed by the IRS's own management experts. In 1970, Congress approved a law requiring all banks to report to the IRS every cash deposit or withdrawal exceeding $10,000. The law was intended to help the government prosecute organized crime figures and narcotics violations. For many years, neither the IRS nor Treasury sought to enforce this requirement. In 1981, for example, a little more than ten years after the passage of the law, the banks submitted reports on only 226,000 such transactions. But finally, after a series of Senate hearings criticizing the government for failing to enforce the reporting requirement, the banks began to comply. By 1985, in fact,

1.7 million "currency transaction reports" poured into the IRS. In 1988, the IRS received more than 5 million. Certainly a lot of reports. But what did the IRS's criminal investigators do with them?

A 1986 analysis by the agency's own Internal Audit Division found that, at the time of its investigation, the currency transaction reports sitting in IRS computers were mostly ignored.

Criminal Division's Office of Intelligence had developed procedures to give the district criminal offices access to the transaction reports. But an internal audit completed in May 1985 revealed that, in a survey of sample districts, six "used this capability infrequently or did not use it at all." (This was not the first time criminal investigators had been told they were ignoring valuable data. Seven years before, a report by the General Accounting Office had made the same point: The division wasn't using the currency information.)

Bruce Milburn is an assistant IRS commissioner, the man in charge of the Criminal Investigation Division. By all accounts, Milburn is a hard-working and intelligent man who has dedicated his entire working life to the difficult job of enforcing the tax laws. "Our goal," he told me, "is to develop and conduct investigations that result in successful convictions yielding a maximum deterrent value for achieving voluntary compliance. That's it. That's our overall mission in life." But the record suggests that Milburn may be pursuing a mission impossible.

What about the GAO finding that the IRS was grossly exaggerating the prison sentences of convicted tax cheats? "That was a problem in how we track those cases and we're trying to correct that now." Wasn't this a situation where the district offices were trying to puff the results of their investigations? "No, not at all. I have no concern about that. It's just a statistical flaw." Why did federal court records indicate that a significant portion of the criminal cases brought by the IRS in New York City appear to involve small amounts of tax cheating by relatively obscure individuals? "A few years ago, we might have had some questionable cases. But a lot has changed over the last five years. We are no longer looking for easy cases. We are pursuing complex and compliance-yielding cases. That is our job in life and that's what we're doing."

Why were the IRS criminal investigators in the field not using the currency transaction reports available in Washington? "A lot of improvements have been made since that report. Back then, we had fallen behind in placing the information in our computers. We now are current."

What was the significance of the GAO finding that only one third of the persons indicted for tax crimes under the special enforcement program aimed at major criminals were judged to be major criminals by the special agents who had investigated them? "You must realize that this record represents a significant success," Milburn replied. "In organized crime and narcotics cases, many of the people we prosecute are accountants, attorneys, airline pilots, and bankers who cannot be classified as major criminals but who nevertheless are of major importance."

The GAO's investigation supports the belief that a good number of Criminal Investigation Division cases have genuine merit. In a recent report, for example, the agency pointed to one case in Pennsylvania where conviction on drug and tax charges resulted in a sentence of forty-five years in prison and a $100,000 fine. A second case resulted in a twenty-five-year prison sentence for a major drug dealer in Detroit on charges that included tax evasion and ten criminal tax charges against bank officials who had assisted the dealer in laundering his illicit funds. In yet another case, a former bank investment officer in San Diego was sentenced to five years in prison and a $250,000 fine for her part in conspiring to launder $36 million through San Diego banks and a currency exchange.

While fully acknowledging the important criminal cases brought by the Criminal Investigation Division each year, however, the fact remains that every independent examination of the division has found a substantial portion were insignificant.

How, for example, can the IRS justify the four-day surveillance of Michael Kuzma, the Buffalo teenager? "From the way you describe the case, it sounds like a waste of time," Milburn replied. "But I would have to believe there was a sound reason for the operation. We don't willfully squander our resources. That's why it would take the approval of senior management officials to get that kind of surveillance going."

CHAPTER 6

New Math at the IRS:
2+2=3

Gina L. Husby was a senior vice president with the Bank of America in San Francisco; her husband, Paul, was a retired San Francisco police official. On March 11, 1986, the computer at the IRS's Service Center in Ogden, Utah, sent the Husbys a notice claiming they owed the government some additional taxes.

Although the California couple did not know it, they were about to be unlawfully defamed by one of the IRS's many poorly designed and badly managed computer systems.

The fiscal and psychic costs imposed on the Husbys by the IRS proved to be considerable. The costs imposed on all the other millions of taxpayers who over the years have been wrongfully damaged by the IRS are incalculable.

It is of course a given that Congress has assigned the IRS an extraordinarily difficult job. It also must be asserted that a large number of dedicated, intelligent, and honest IRS managers and employees are desperately trying to make their bureaucracy work. Finally, it is freely conceded that in some ways the IRS works: Collected revenues are now running about $1 trillion a year.

But these acknowledgments do not eliminate other truths. First, the agency's managers are responsible for the design and operation of a series of tax collection systems, many of them computerized, that often causes serious harm to honorable and well-intentioned taxpayers. Second, on many occasions these same managers have allowed their imperfect systems to go on harming innocent taxpayers long after their inadequacies were fully known to them.

Shortly after the California couple received the initial IRS demand for additional taxes, they met with their lawyer and decided the government's claim against them was not valid. On June 9, 1986, they formally asked the U.S. Tax Court for a hearing to resolve their disagreement with the agency. Under federal law and IRS regulations, when a taxpayer files such a petition, the agency is required to halt all of its collection activities until the dispute has been resolved.[1]

A few weeks after the Husbys had requested the hearing and had given the IRS written notice of this action, however, something unusual happened: The Ogden office sent a second computerized note demanding prompt payment of their alleged debt.

The Husbys' lawyer immediately filed a written complaint with the agency pointing out that because the couple had petitioned the Tax Court, the second demand for back taxes was illegal and improper. He also noted that should the IRS continue the collection process to the point where the agency moved to seize the assets of the Husbys, it would then be violating a section of the tax law prohibiting the government from the "knowing or negligent" disclosure of tax return information except in certain prescribed situations.

A third demand came from the IRS on November 10. The Husbys' lawyer fired off another written protest. Shortly thereafter, Debra K. Estrem, a San Francisco–based attorney for the IRS, acknowledged the mistake and promised that the collection action would be halted.

But somehow Estrem and her IRS colleagues in San Francisco were not able to transmit the news of their promise to the agency's Ogden computer. On December 15, 1986, and January 19, 1987—despite further protests from the Husbys—it dispatched two more personal dunning notices.

So far all the IRS notices had been sent directly to the Husbys. But that was about to change. On March 23, just one year after the collection process had begun, the IRS sent a notice of levy to the credit union of the San Francisco Police Department, seizing $3,789.53 held in an account by Paul Husby. On April 3, a second levy notice was served on the couple's stockbroker.

In total frustration, the Husbys and their lawyer turned to Federal District Court Judge Stanley A. Weigel, who immediately enjoined the IRS from issuing any more liens and levies on the couple's holdings. On April 13, 1987, however, despite the provisions of tax law, the agency's regulations, Estrem's official promises to stop the collection action, and the judge's injunction, the IRS computer dispatched a notice of lien to Marin County, where it was placed in the county's public files.

As always happens in such situations, the lien on the Husbys' house was soon spotted by credit company clerks who monitor county real-estate records. Shortly thereafter, the news of the lien was broadcast to the entire world by an item that was added to the record of their credit rating maintained by several companies. It also was picked up by a newsletter sent to area real-estate agents.

Judge Weigel, the Husbys, and the couple's lawyer were outraged and a hearing was scheduled. Speaking for the IRS at this session was Jay R. Weill, an assistant U.S. attorney in San Francisco.

Weill's attempt to defend what the system had done to the Husbys makes no sense. Weill informed Judge Weigel that the computerized system designed and operated by the IRS was "very effective and efficient in finding sources of assets from which to collect tax liability." He added, however, that once the process got started, it "sometimes was very hard to stop."

Despite the admission that the computerized dunning process had a systemwide problem and that incorrect claims against the Husbys had been generated by a faulty computer, Weill contended that the government was not liable for the mistakes. "There is no IRS agent here who has purposely and with bad faith improperly disclosed return information about the plaintiffs," Weill told the judge.

In a later interview with me, Weill did not mention the general problem of the hard-to-stop computer that he had cited in court. "We're talking here about a computer glitch, not a purposeful error," the federal prosecutor said. "This is a system that is spitting out tens of thousands of notices each day and I don't think Congress intended that the agency be penalized every time there is a little error."

Weill's maddening argument is familiar to anyone who has ever been victimized by any of the nation's large public or private organizations that regulate consumer credit, sell health insurance, license cars, provide Social Security, or take on dozens of other chores. "We didn't do it; the computer did it," the managers argue, magically excusing themselves from the responsibility of designing, purchasing, and operating the faulty computer systems that they have chosen to blame.

Although Weill may not have known it when he appeared before the court, IRS officials in Washington had long understood that the discrete bureaucratic atrocity that the agency committed on the Husbys was, in fact, not a little computer glitch, but a general problem that, to this day, continues to affect an unknown number of other taxpayers.

One bit of evidence indicating that IRS Commissioner Lawrence B. Gibbs and other senior agency officials knew about their flawed system emerged during a special briefing they received on March 16, 1988. The occasion was one of the regularly scheduled meetings of the commissioner's advisory group, a collection of tax lawyers, accountants, and state tax administrators who in theory serve as a policy sounding board for the agency.

A few minutes after eight on that March morning, Hank Philcox, the assistant IRS commissioner, Information Systems Development, began the first presentation of the advisory group's spring meeting. His subject was a massive new computer system the agency had begun planning in 1985. In his effort to justify the IRS's proposed expenditure of billions of dollars, however, the official felt compelled to describe the flaws in the fifteen-year-old system that the agency still employs. The current system, Philcox said, requires constant maintenance, is expensive to operate, and takes far too long to retrieve information needed by the agents.

Then Philcox turned to the issue of direct concern to individual taxpayers such as the Husbys. "Our inability to turn off the third or fourth notice is something we are concerned about," he told the commissioner's advisory group.

What happened to the Husbys was not an accident. What happened to them was the product of flawed choices made by officials of a flawed agency. In this particular case, the IRS many years before had selected a poorly designed system that caused this couple and thousands of other taxpayers to be treated in an abusive, arbitrary, and even coercive manner.

The poor management endemic to the IRS, however, imposes other kinds of major penalties on the taxpayers of America. A second such penalty relates directly to the amount of taxes paid by ordinary wage earners. As a result of a range of faulty management decisions, the IRS routinely fails to collect billions of dollars in taxes that are lawfully owed by individual and corporate taxpayers. This failure to properly target IRS enforcement and collection procedures on those who owe taxes necessarily means that the tax bills of more diligent taxpayers are unfairly inflated. A third kind of unnecessary cost imposed on the taxpaying public by incompetent managers manifests itself in the agency's purchase of hundreds of millions of dollars' worth of overpriced equipment, some of which is unneeded, some of which does not work.

Given the fundamental importance of taxes to the government, both Congress and the courts have always been cautious about acting on the complaints of taxpayers against the agency. But in the Husby case, Judge Weigel rejected the IRS's "computer glitch" defense and held the agency liable for its mistreatment of the couple. As the judge put it in his decision, he simply would not accept the argument that "this unfortunate incident was really nobody's fault, that a computer is to blame." The evidence was strong, his decision clear, and the IRS decided against an appeal. After weeks of negotiations, the government agreed to pay the Husbys $22,000 in damages and court fees.

(In 1988, Senator David Pryor persuaded Congress to pass the Taxpayer's Bill of Rights. According to Jeff Trinca, the senator's staff expert on tax matters, this new law is not expected to have an immediate impact on the massive system that damaged the Husbys. Under its provisions, however, Trinca believes that future Husbys may find it somewhat easier to hold the agency accountable. One section of the new law, for example, expands the authority of the IRS's Taxpayer Ombudsmen to issue a "taxpayer assistance order" to protect couples like Gina and Paul Husby who are suffering or are about to suffer a "significant hardship" at the hands of the agency.)

Judge Weigel's decision was an important development. A great victory for abused taxpayers everywhere. A strong restatement of the ground principle of government accountability. Maybe.

Maybe not. It is true, of course, that the judge awarded damages to Paul and Gina Husby. But the Husbys are just two of an unknown number of taxpayers who each year are mistreated by the same IRS process. What did Judge Weigel's decision do for all of these other uncounted victims? Remember that the judge did not order the IRS to fix its dunning system, to make it less susceptible to the systematic errors that were admitted by the assistant U.S. attorney in San Francisco and Hank Philcox in Washington. Remember also that the judge made no effort to identify the official who originally had authorized the flawed system to be installed. Remember, finally, that the computer system that wronged the Husbys in 1986 and 1987 is still churning out the same kinds of notices, levies, and liens.

To this day, no one knows how many other taxpayers have their assets frozen and their credit records damaged because of wrongful notices spewed out by the IRS computers in Ogden and other locations around the country. While stories about similar mix-ups appear in the press from time to time, the evidence is anecdotal and, it should surprise no one, the IRS does not collect statistics on the problem.

But Weill's statement to the court that the computerized process "sometimes was hard to stop" and Philcox's admission that turning off the "third or fourth notice" was a worry prove the existence of a systemic problem. I assume that Weill, Philcox, and Judge Weigel knew what they were talking about and that the Husbys were damaged by a recurring flaw built into the IRS's collection machinery. The next question is obvious: How many taxpayers were and are being kicked around?

Obvious questions, however, sometimes can produce misleading answers. This is because the scale of IRS operations is so vast that even when a tiny percentage is incorrectly handled the absolute number of abused taxpayers can be surprisingly large.

Here is the arithmetic. During the year the IRS made what it admits was an improper move against the Husbys, the agency sent out 2.7 million other notices informing taxpayers that they owed back taxes. As an outgrowth of these assessments, the IRS dispatched a total of 1.6 million levies to the banks, employers, and credit unions of the Husbys and all the other taxpayers whom the IRS felt had not paid their taxes. (Levies assert the government's control over the assets in the levied accounts.) During the same year, the agency filed 767,000 tax liens on the property of targeted taxpayers. (Liens give the IRS first claim on any assets realized by the sale of the liened property. Even in those situations where a taxpayer has no intention of selling his or her house, the lien can have a major impact on the taxpayer's financial situation. As we already know, this is because commercial credit companies such as TRW carefully monitor county property records specifically to pick up the names of individuals who are having trouble paying their taxes to the government.)

For the sake of this discussion, consider the possibility that for one reason or another the systematic computer problem referred to by Weill and the others meant that a tiny fraction—let's say only one half of 1 percent—of all the liens and levies filed by the IRS was improper. One half of 1 percent of 1.6 million is 8,000. One half of 1 percent of 767,000 is 3,835. From the perspective of the commissioner and his lieutenants, a system that works 99.5 percent of the time must look pretty good, maybe even a cause for celebration. But from the perspective of the 11,835 taxpayers who in our hypothetical case were wrongfully and illegally defamed, the unnecessary expense and pain loom very large.

It is not only individual taxpayers like the Husbys who are victimized by the bad management of the IRS. Sometimes, the agency's hapless harassment falls on the shoulders of businesses. As explained previously, the system by which the nation's millions of employers withhold the taxes owed by individual taxpayers is the single most important channel of revenue flowing into the coffers of the federal government. The role of employers in the tax collection process is truly gigantic. In one recent year, for example, over 5 million businesses and other employers made 66 million withholding tax payments to thirty-four thousand federal depositories (usually banks), which accounted for 80 percent of all IRS collections.

It is an amazing money machine that the IRS keeps trying to improve. Despite these efforts, however, the bureaucratic machinery set up to receive the withholding payments and credit them to the correct employer and the correct employee sometimes breaks down. In June 1986, one Kerry R. Kilpatrick, an official in the agency's own Internal Audit Division, completed a confidential report on some of these administrative shortcomings.[2]

Kilpatrick said that by the time the twelve months of 1986 were over the IRS system somehow would misplace about 1.1 percent of the withholding deposits. Although 98.9 percent of them would reach the right cubbyhole at the right time, he said, the 1.1 percent that somehow would take the wrong turn would lead the IRS to send employers 721,000 erroneous bills, penalties, refunds, and inquiries about withholding payments they had actually sent to the government. He estimated that in that year alone the withholding taxes covered by these improperly recorded deposits would total $6.5 billion.

"These problems will continue because of the inability of Internal Revenue Service control systems to timely identify and resolve employee and taxpayer errors," the auditor calmly observed. He then suggested a series of small fixes that might somewhat reduce the problem.

The Kilpatrick report dramatically illustrates how, in an agency as large and complicated as the IRS, a series of tiny administrative mistakes can cause serious mischief to thousands upon thousands of individuals and corporations. This was serious business. Erroneous bills, penalties, and refunds—nearly three quarters of a million of them—concerning $6.5 billion that the IRS could not immediately account for.

While the Kilpatrick report was bad enough, it failed to explore a broad range of questions that, if properly answered, would make clear that the underlying impact of the IRS accounting failures was indeed far-reaching. Kilpatrick, for example, did not determine the extent to which the mislaid withholding funds affected the tax accounts of individual taxpayers. Neither did he attempt to calculate the interest the federal government did not receive during the time the $6.5 billion was missing in action. He also failed to estimate how much it cost the government to send out the incorrect notices. Nor did he consider how much money the falsely accused employers spent trying to straighten out the record.

The Kilpatrick report, however, did include a disclosure about another very big problem caused by poor management. During 1985, Kilpatrick recalled in a historical footnote, the IRS had adopted a new system to collect withholding taxes that required employers to include a special numbered coupon with each payment they made. But somehow, an IRS bureaucrat somewhere in the middle reaches of the agency had failed to order the printing of a sufficient number of coupons.

The resulting coupon shortage made it difficult for the legitimate businesses that wanted to deposit their withholding payments in a proper fashion to get the funds credited to correct accounts. More significantly, the coupon shortage made it almost impossible for IRS sleuths to sort out the legitimate businesses that were trying to meet their obligations from the unscrupulous cash-short companies that knowingly were trying to rip off their employees and their government by not sending in the required withholding payments.

To the average citizen, the missing coupons might not sound very important. In fact, however, they prompted a significant collapse in one of the IRS's major enforcement areas. "One direct result of the inventory problem," Kilpatrick related, "was the [IRS] management decision to reduce the number of federal tax deposit penalties assessed, at an estimated dollar loss of over $100 million, and an unmeasurable long-range loss of compliance."

One tiny management failure by one IRS bureaucrat, and the federal government is out $100 million. But remember, in the end, the penalties that were not properly assessed against all those lawbreaking employers meant millions of dollars less in general tax revenues and increased demands on the ordinary taxpayer.

Sometimes the unnecessary expenses generated by poor management are more obvious than those described by Kilpatrick. A month after his investigation of the agency's withholding problems was completed, Gail A. Burns, another Internal Audit Division official, published her study of how the IRS had gone about the business of procuring some additional terminals for its central national information network. Burns said the IRS division in charge of this particular procurement had purchased two thousand more terminals than an agency study had found were needed and then proceeded to request funds for five thousand additional terminals. She reported that the cost of the unnecessary terminals was $25 million.

To document her allegation that at least some of the thousands of new terminals were not needed, Burns conducted a survey in a sample of IRS locations: three regional centers and ten district offices. The new terminals installed in the three regional centers, she acknowledged, were fully utilized. But in the ten district offices, Burns discovered so many unneeded terminals that, on the average, each one was humming less than 3.5 hours per a day, even though the network they were hooked into was in service for more than sixteen hours a day. "In one office," the official found, "22 Integrated Data Retrieval System terminals were delivered, although only five persons performed Integrated Data Retrieval System research."

The IRS often creates task forces to study its nagging problems. In 1986, for example, such a group was formed because the IRS found its filing system was collapsing. The specific problem was that agency employees frequently were unable to locate an individual tax return when they needed it for an audit or other agency action. Sometimes the returns were lost forever. Sometimes they turned up so long after they had been requested that they were useless. After a two-year study, the task force confirmed there was indeed a problem.

During the year ending in October 1987, IRS employees made 41 million requests for tax returns and other documents that had previously been provided the agency under the requirements of law. Because of faulty filing procedures and poorly trained personnel, however, the agency was unable to locate 2 million of the requested documents. Even where the documents were located, the searches often required an inordinate time to complete. In more than one third of the cases, IRS employees had not received the documents forty-five days after making their initial request.

Because missing or delayed documents seriously damage the ability of the agency to collect taxes and to treat taxpayers in an efficient and fair manner, one might expect the IRS to make every effort to maintain an effective retrieval system. The task force's 1988 report, however, concluded that this was not the case. "Unfortunately, over the years, the diligence directed [by the agency] towards the proper handling of tax documents has diminished." To support this judgment, the group pointed to the facts that the locations of stored documents had been moved to less desirable sites, the budgets and staff for document storage had been cut, and the grade level of managers and clerks assigned to the area had been downgraded.

The Husbys' credit rating was impeached because IRS managers were unable to stop the Ogden computer from generating false information. Hundreds of thousands of incorrect payment demands were sent to businesses because the computerized system for recording withholding payments did not function properly. Tens of millions of dollars in fines were not collected because a manager forgot to order enough necessary coupons. Millions of dollars were wasted on overpriced and unneeded computer equipment. The ability of the IRS to retrieve documents has been eroded.

Each of these complex situations is an example of bad management. IRS bureaucrats, of course, challenge this interpretation. They earnestly argue that the IRS's failures should be regarded as normal administrative problems that almost all large institutions encountered as they moved into the computer age. They contend that the IRS's past record—primarily its steady collection of billions of dollars a year in taxes—proves that the agency remains a good manager. They assert that the IRS effectively accomplishes its central mission: the collection of taxes in an efficient and equitable fashion.

There are times, it must be admitted, when you are sitting across the desk from a confident IRS official in a comfortable Washington office, when these arguments appear to be partly valid. But then you recall yet another administrative horror story and the IRS's smooth talk seems a good deal less persuasive.

In 1982, for example, senior officials of the IRS decided to close down a small staff organization explicitly created to oversee the design and installation of a new computer system in the agency's ten regional service centers. Unfortunately for taxpayers all over the United States, the managers ordered that this oversight group be abolished several years before the new computers were scheduled to go on-line. The lack of a central monitor meant that the same IRS managers were not informed during 1983 and 1984 that the installation of the new computers was falling farther and farther behind schedule. This, in turn, meant that the managers made no effort to head off what in 1985 would develop into the most disastrous year in the recent history of the IRS.

The vast scale of IRS operations makes it very hard to describe and comprehend the administrative chaos that almost swamped the agency during the 1985 tax year because of the incompetence of the agency's bosses. At one point, for example, the IRS lost fifty-eight computer tapes containing detailed information about millions of interest and dividend payments made by the banks and insurance companies located in one area of the country. The total value of these payments was over $3 billion. Later investigations suggested that the tapes were misplaced because of weaknesses in the agency's receipt and control procedures.

The loss of these tapes, and a variety of other problems directly related to the failure of the IRS to comprehend that its new computer system was way behind schedule, meant that the agency that year sent out millions of erroneous dunning notices. Millions of incorrect notices, millions of confused and angry taxpayers, almost certainly hundreds of millions of dollars of taxes paid by people who did not owe them. But no public executions.

There were other telling signs of the agency's 1985 problems. That year, for example, the number of taxpayers who did not receive their refunds within the forty-five-day period required by law increased by 50 percent, 2.2 million in 1985 compared with 1.4 million in 1984. The failure of the IRS to meet this deadline obligated it to pay out $15.5 million more in interest than it had during the previous year.

The lost records, the incorrect dunning notices, the improper levies and liens obviously forced individual and corporate taxpayers to take whatever steps they could to defend themselves against a bureaucracy that suddenly had gone berserk. In January 1985, for example, the IRS ordered the Rohm & Haas Company of Philadelphia to pay a $46,806.37 penalty. The basic charge was that Rohm & Haas had failed to pay a $4,488,112.88 payroll tax deposit. After weeks of negotiations, the IRS finally admitted that it had mislaid the company's $4.5 million check. An angry Thomas C. Friel, Rohm & Haas's manager of corporate taxes, said that straightening out the IRS error had required a good deal of extra work by five corporate accountants, the writing of seven separate letters, and an official visit to an IRS office by several corporate executives.[3]

The 1985 IRS disaster was massive and costly. Because it affected so many millions of taxpayers in such a relatively brief period of time, Congress actually became mildly disturbed. The congressional response was entirely predictable: vote the expenditure of millions of additional tax dollars to fix the breakdown that would never have occurred in the first place if the managers had been doing their job.

This particular IRS failure became a public embarrassment that absolutely had to be fixed because it produced so many casualties so quickly. Because most IRS failures are considerably less dramatic, the agency usually is content to let them fester.

More than twenty years ago, for example, a few concerned officials within the IRS began to understand that a good deal of the tax information the agency was providing citizens was just plain wrong. Despite the growing belief within the inner circle of managers that this incorrect information was hindering its ability to collect taxes, nothing was done. In fact, for a three-year period during the Reagan administration the IRS actually began to drastically reduce the small number of employees assigned to answering the questions of puzzled taxpayers.

The most dramatic evidence of the agency's years of callous indifference came in the summer of 1988, when the General Accounting Office completed a detailed analysis of the 6 million notices and letters that the correspondence offices in the regional service centers had sent to taxpayers in 1987.[4]

The key finding of the study: 48 percent of a sample of these IRS notices and letters were "incorrect, unresponsive, unclear or incomplete."

Of the variously flawed responses, the GAO said that a significant number had "resulted in the assessment of incorrect tax and penalties." Inaccurate assessments, however, were just one harmful product of the IRS's error-prone correspondence. The GAO said a second, even more pervasive, problem was the waste of vast amounts of time and money on the part of the IRS and the taxpayers as both sides attempted to resolve the issues generated by the agency's initial letter.

The 1988 Taxpayers' Bill of Rights established the legal principle that any penalty or addition to tax attributable to incorrect written advice from the IRS will be abated. There are, however, a number of conditions. The wrongful written advice must have been given in response to a specific written request from the taxpayer. The wrongful advice must have been relied on by the taxpayer. The wrongful advice must not have been given by the IRS because the taxpayer failed to provide adequate or accurate information.

As bad as the IRS's accuracy record was, however, the GAO found other serious flaws in the basic product of the service center correspondence officers. Here are a few examples:

- IRS regulations require examiners to acknowledge a taxpayer's letter within seven days of its receipt, even in a situation where a complete response is not possible. In half of the cases where it was called for, however, no such acknowledgment was sent.
- IRS regulations require examiners to apologize when the taxpayer's correspondence involves a situation where an error was committed by the IRS. In 70 percent of the cases where an apology was called for, however, no such letter was sent.
- IRS regulations require examiners always to include a reference to the

date of the taxpayer's inquiry. In half the cases where the date of the inquiry was known, the IRS responses did not include any date or referred to an incorrect date.

(The GAO findings were based on a random sample of letters drawn from all of the correspondence prepared by three of the IRS's ten regional service centers from May 4 to July 31, 1987. The centers selected for the study were located in Fresno, Philadelphia, and Kansas City.)

The IRS record here is very bad. What makes it truly awful is evidence uncovered by the GAO indicating that IRS managers seemed to go out of their way to avoid getting the detailed knowledge that would have allowed them to improve the accuracy and completeness of the agency's correspondence.

It is accepted practice for any large organization to establish a quality assurance unit to sample the product and identify problems so that management can solve them. And indeed, for many years the IRS has had special quality assurance units checking the output of the adjustment and correspondence branches at each of the service centers.

The GAO discovered, however, that clerks assigned to quality assurance had exactly the same salary and training as the clerks whose work they were checking. And in fact, at one of the service centers, a rotation policy had been established whereby clerks in the adjustments and correspondence branch would serve specific terms in quality assurance and then return to their original assignment.

Given these circumstances, it is hardly surprising that the error rate found by quality assurance people who had the same training and experience as those preparing the letters was substantially below that found by the GAO.

But the degree of blindness suffered by the agency is breathtaking. By sheer chance, seventeen of the letters that became part of the GAO's sample survey and were found to contain critical errors or other shortcomings had already been examined by the IRS's quality assurance team. The IRS had given passing grades to every single one of the letters that the GAO found wanting.

In July 1988, Lawrence B. Gibbs, then the commissioner of internal revenue, acknowledged what the agency could no longer continue to deny: There were serious deficiencies in the IRS's correspondence. Testifying before a House subcommittee, the commissioner blamed the agency's failure on three factors. First, he said, severe budget cutbacks had been imposed by Congress at a time when the agency was facing increasing workload demands. Second, all the new tax laws that Congress approved were causing confusion. Finally, "a variety of internal systemic problems" prevented the IRS from delivering "the kind of quality service to our 'customers' that we are committed to providing."

There was a surface plausibility to the commissioner's excuses. Yes, the operating budgets of the IRS were cut in the mid-1980s. Yes, Congress has passed a lot of new tax legislation. Yes, there were "internal systemic problems."

Gibbs's excuses, however, were also misleading. Each year, the commissioner and his lieutenants prepare a budget detailing how they propose to allocate funds to different parts of the agency. Although this budget may be somewhat modified by the White House or Congress, the basic outline of the commissioner's spending plan seldom undergoes major changes.

An examination of its annual budgets proves that, at least until the last year or so, providing the public with accurate and complete tax information always has been a secondary concern of the IRS. The record further proves that IRS managers for many years have chosen to shortchange taxpayer service even though repeated study groups within the agency showed this was a serious problem.

A full five years before the GAO's 1988 study, for example, a senior group of IRS officials completed a never-released report on the quality of the agency's correspondence.

The in-house study group found that the agency spent a good deal of time and money trying to respond to the House, Senate, and presidential aides, but paid little attention to the public. "Only Congressional, White House and Treasury correspondence have extensive visibility and emphasis," it said. "General correspondence is not afforded the same luxury nor is it viewed as a major problem. This, compounded with competing priorities, has obscured any consideration for the resulting impact on taxpayers."

To support the contention that the agency itself has consciously chosen to ignore the issue of taxpayer service, the 1983 in-house study group cited reports on correspondence problems that had been written by at least ten previous IRS groups. The recommendations of all these earlier reports, the 1983 report said, "have not been acted upon to date."

A LEAKY VESSEL

A second area where the IRS has shown considerable nonchalance is in its protection of the confidential information it collects on the financial, medical, and other personal secrets of every taxpayer. The Tax Reform

Act of 1976 sets a high legal standard for the IRS: Personal tax return information is not to be disclosed to any other organization or person except in certain precisely defined situations. The law made it a crime for any IRS employee to violate these rules.

In the age of the computer, one important component of protecting individual privacy obviously must be computer security. Shortly after the passage of the 1976 law, the Office of Management and Budget, an arm of the White House, issued a presidential directive requiring all federal agencies to develop elaborate procedures to protect the personal information about individuals stored in their computers. Then in 1982, Congress approved the Federal Managers' Financial Integrity Act, which required the agencies to report to the president and Congress each year on exactly how well the data held in their computers were protected from loss or theft.

The 1977 report of the Privacy Protection Study Commission, which had been created by Congress in the wake of Watergate, explained this concern. "The fact that tax collection is essential to government justifies an extraordinary intrusion on personal privacy by the IRS," the commission report observed. "But it is also the reason why extraordinary precautions must be taken against misuse of information the Service collects from and about taxpayers."[5]

The unusual sensitivity of tax return information, the mandate of two laws, and several presidential directives all point in one direction: For many years the IRS has had an overwhelming legal and moral responsibility to make sure that the tax information it holds is protected from snoopers.

I know of only one case where an IRS employee, former employee, or outside computer hacker has broken into one of the agency's hundreds of computer data bases. But given the near impossibility of proving such intrusions, and the IRS's known penchant for hiding its failures from outside critics, I do not find the absence of a large number of cases particularly reassuring. My uneasiness is compounded by the agency's casual attitude toward computer security.

Over the years, most of the publicity about IRS computers has focused on the giant machines that the agency maintains at its massive National Computer Center in Martinsburg, West Virginia. It is at this center, protected by armed guards and triple rows of ten-foot-high fences, that the IRS permanently stores most of the detailed information it collects about each taxpayer. Partly because the IRS's West Virginia facility is somewhat obsolete, there is no direct access to the center's prime computers via the telephone. Information about taxpayers is transferred to and from the national center by messengers carrying computer discs. This feature works to improve security because it is physically impossible for electronic intruders to invade the computers from a remote location.

But in eighty-one IRS offices around the country—the national office in Washington, the seven regional offices, the sixty-three district offices, and the ten service centers—the agency has kept up with the times and installed Zilog computers. The Zilog computers help the IRS perform at least eight jobs at these eighty-one offices, many of them highly sensitive. One task handled by the Zilogs, for example, is to keep track of every audit conducted in each of the districts. A second task is to handle the agency's word processing and electronic mail services. In some offices, the Criminal Investigation Division uses a Zilog as an electronic filing cabinet to store the details of its investigations.

Unlike the computers at the national center, the Zilogs are vulnerable to raids by unauthorized persons because they were designed deliberately to allow employees to access them by telephone. The IRS contends it has overcome this access problem by adopting stringent security procedures. It says, for example, that only authorized IRS employees are given the passwords they need to get into the Zilog system. The agency also notes that the system periodically erases all the passwords that IRS employees have been given in the past. This feature is designed to assure that employees who retire or resign or are assigned to new duties cannot continue to inspect tax information they no longer require. The agency further boasts that to gain access to certain categories of unusually sensitive information, authorized employees are required to have two passwords.

It all sounds quite impressive. But a series of confidential investigations by the IRS's own Internal Audit Division indicates that there are many lapses in the agency's security efforts. Consider, for example, the report of Charles F. Combs on computer security in the IRS's Central Region, an area covering Michigan, Indiana, Ohio, West Virginia, and Kentucky. In two of the region's six district offices, he investigated the security provisions adopted to protect the tax information stored in their Zilogs.

Combs found that a total of 425 IRS personnel in the two districts were authorized to enter the Zilog system. Under agency regulations, district managers are responsible for deciding who will be permitted access to the information and for assuring that they have undergone extensive security training. The auditor found that 16 percent of those who had the necessary code words and thus could enter the local computer files of the two districts—sixty-six out of 425—were doing so without the required approval of top management. Almost as important, none of those sixty-six IRS employees had undergone the mandated security training.

One of the basic IRS security provisions requires that, when employees leave the agency or are assigned to new offices, the passwords they have been using to gain access to sensitive data will be eliminated.

Combs found, however, that the IRS did not follow its own procedures. In one test he measured the time it took IRS technicians to remove a departing employee's password from the Zilog so he or she no longer could gain access to its information. In one of the sample districts, the average elapsed time between leaving the agency and erasing the password was eight months. In the other, it was a year and a half.

"As a result," Combs said, "Central Region's Zilog systems were exposed to risks over extended periods of time that separated employees could gain unauthorized remote access from any computer equipped with telecommunication devices." It should be remembered that retired IRS agents frequently go to work for accounting firms or law firms or set up their own tax preparation businesses where inside information about an ongoing audit or criminal investigation can be of enormous value.

The computer security lapses are by no means limited to the IRS Central Region. Thomas Black, another inspector with the Internal Audit Division, looked at a small sample of offices in the Southeast, Southwest, and Midwest regions. Black said his investigation had identified forty-three former employees whose passwords had not been erased as required by agency regulation. He said this failure meant the forty-three former employees could have gained improper access to over twenty-seven thousand data files holding detailed information about current IRS employees, illegal tax protestors, and other matters.

Yet another inspector, Garth Streeper, investigated the security screen protecting a sample of thirty-two microcomputer hard disks. He discovered that 40 percent of the disks, thirteen out of thirty-two, were "without proper security to prevent access to this data." Streeper's report said "we [the investigative team] were able to enter the district office after hours on two occasions, access several microcomputers which contained taxpayer data and were not challenged or questioned by personnel in the general area."

There is no question that a former employee or an outsider who has the correct password can gain access to the Zilog computer. This was proved during the early spring of 1985 when a thirty-two-year-old computer expert named William Van Nest tapped into the Zilog computer located at a suburban IRS office near Washington. Van Nest, working from his home computer, somehow had obtained the system's "super user password"—in this case *Zeus*—which allowed him to tap into the IRS computer via the lines of the local telephone company.

After gaining access to the Zilog, Van Nest ordered the computer to destroy several administrative files. It was this second action, court records show, that eventually enabled the IRS to track Van Nest to his home telephone. Although these records are skimpy, they indicate that if Van Nest had entered the Zilog merely to obtain information, rather than committing an act of destruction, the IRS would never have detected the penetration.

On April 23, 1986, Van Nest pleaded guilty in federal court in Washington to breaking into the IRS computer and was sentenced to three years on probation and a $7,500 fine.

The reports of the IRS inspectors and the indictment of Van Nest suggest that the masses of confidential tax information stored in the Zilog computers all over the country are not adequately protected. Almost as disturbing, however, is the evidence that senior IRS officials do not consider the security of tax information a primary concern and have sometimes even sabotaged efforts to identify systemwide security problems.

For at least twenty years, computer experts working in government and business and teaching at the universities have preached the importance of adequately protecting the billions of bits of personal information that insurance companies, banks, and agencies like the IRS routinely collect and store. In 1978, the Office of Management and Budget, the White House office that is supposed to help the president direct the operations of the federal government, issued a directive requiring all federal agencies to implement a continuous series of studies aimed at identifying the security weaknesses of their computer installations. The studies were to identify and correct problems before the systems were seriously compromised.

Between 1979 and 1981, the IRS complied with the presidential directive, performing risk analyses at six of its ten service centers. But such studies cost money. In 1981, according to a confidential report by John G. Hofmann, another IRS inspector, agency officials ordered the risk analyses halted "as part of a decentralized approach to security and to save resources."

In 1983, the Office of Management and Budget imposed a new and tougher security audit requirement on all federal agencies, including the IRS. This new mandate specifically stated that the head of each federal organization was personally responsible for monitoring and improving the security of computerized data files.

But Hofmann, the IRS inspector, reported that the new pressure from the White House did not have the desired effect on the agency. The IRS's Information Systems Risk Management Program, he concluded, "does not provide the information necessary to determine the level of vulnerability of its computer system or the adequacy of current or planned controls."

The Internal Audit Division inspector said that IRS managers had created a serious gap in the risk-management program when they ruled that only the security problems of the computer systems in the major processing centers would be studied. Apparently excluded from consideration, for example, were the Zilog computers that other IRS inspectors had found to be vulnerable to penetration. Also excluded, he said, were "new systems, planned modifications and sensitive computer applications."

Hofmann was disturbed by the agency's decision to restrict its security studies to those systems operating in the agency's service centers and not to examine all of its data bases. "With the proliferation of and increasing reliance on computer-based information systems throughout the Service, management has no means of determining to what extent sensitive data is being dispersed among numerous systems," he said.

At the bottom of every page of every Internal Audit Division report are typed the words *Official Use Only.* The IRS's explanation for the warnings is that federal law requires the agency to protect the privacy of taxpayers and the business secrets of companies that might be mentioned.

This explanation, of course, doesn't make much sense because only a small number of all the hundreds of reports I've obtained contain information that conceivably might require protection. It seems to me much more likely that it is the IRS's fervent desire to prevent the public, the press, congressional committees, and even the president's managers at the White House from learning about all their goofy decisions. Senior IRS officials have an abiding interest in protecting their cozy world from the prying eyes of informed critics.

It is understandable that the managers of the IRS would prefer that the public not know about the instances when their flawed management prevented the agency from collecting hundreds of millions of dollars in lawfully owed taxes. Surely we can all identify with their protective instincts when it comes to those reports describing the occasions when they purchased millions of dollars' worth of overpriced and unneeded equipment. Certainly their failure to protect the privacy of the American people is something they would prefer be kept a secret.

THE IRS'S MURKY BOTTOM LINE

But what must cause senior IRS officials genuine, unmitigated, red-faced chagrin is their inability to balance the books of the IRS: This is truly the gang that can't count straight. The IRS, the agency that each year imposes millions of dollars of fines on individuals and corporations who have failed to maintain their account books in an orderly fashion, itself is unable to keep track of its income and expenditures.

A few years ago, for example, the IRS discovered a massive and unexpected surge in the collection of revenue flowing into a special fund maintained for retiring federal employees. The abrupt $1.2 billion increase reported by the IRS led the Labor Department, the federal agency that administers this particular fund, to publish a special study. A few months later, however, Labor reconsidered the IRS data and decided something was fishy about the numbers: They didn't make sense. Labor called IRS and asked for another count.

When the IRS went back to the books, it discovered that several of the agency's own service centers had not classified the tax payments correctly and that these errors had led the IRS to exaggerate the revenue going to the fund.

Actually, the nonexistent $1.2 billion was just one example of a nagging problem that went back to 1984, when the IRS installed the Revenue Accounting Control System (RACS). RACS, as it is generally referred to within the agency, was supposed to assure that the IRS would be able to carry out one of its key responsibilities: accounting for and classifying the hundreds of billions of dollars of tax revenues it collects each year. RACS is also important for keeping track of agency refunds, disbursements, and other related financial transactions.

The IRS, however, had not followed through on its original intention to automate fully its revenue-accounting procedures, thus enabling a large number of inaccurate and incorrectly classified collection numbers to be introduced into the IRS's books. When the General Accounting Office got around to looking at the problem in late 1988, it concluded that the IRS's basic accounting system for all the tax revenues of the United States was "inefficient and susceptible to error."[6]

In the last few years, the inability of RACS to function properly has been highlighted by another little glitch, this one in the inability of the IRS to count accurately the money that taxpayers owe in back taxes. According to the numbers coming out of RACS, the accounts receivable have jumped from $18.4 billion in 1981, to $53.7 billion in 1987. But because of problems in RACS, the IRS itself is not sure whether this increase was the result of population growth, new methods of detecting underreported taxes, or administrative errors by the service centers.

"Let me put it plain and simple," said one senior GAO official. "The problem we found in RACS means the IRS cannot manage its assets. If the rapid growth in accounts receivable number is for real, why isn't the IRS taking all sorts of administrative measures to collect the missing revenue? If the reported increase is phony, the product of a poorly designed adding machine, then why can't the IRS count straight? Either way you look at it is bad for the IRS."

The IRS demands that every individual and corporate taxpayer accurately estimate the income he or she expects to earn in the next tax year. Fines are imposed on those whose estimates are repeatedly wrong. But from 1978 to 1986, the IRS's own annual estimates of the additional taxes the agency would claim that taxpayers owed the government in the upcoming year have been consistently less than the additional taxes that the agency ended up claiming. On the average, the annual underestimate of the IRS was 28 percent off the mark, ranging from $100 million in 1978 to $3.8 billion in 1986.[7]

There are lots of other examples of sloppy IRS bookkeeping. Some go back a long way. Just about thirty years ago, for example, the White House's Office of Management and Budget completed a study of the casual financial-management practices of the IRS. One example of this easygoing attitude toward bookkeeping, the study said, was the agency's habit of spending appropriated funds as it saw fit, with little regard for the intent of either Congress or the White House. The study mentioned one occasion when the agency spent $1.1 million for the special promotion of favored employees, "although no funds had been appropriated for that purpose."

Despite all the evidence to the contrary, IRS officials continue to boast about their sophisticated and totally rational management of the tax collection business. To support their claims, they often point to the Taxpayer Compliance Measurement Program, the massive national survey designed to tell the IRS what kinds of taxpayers are not paying the taxes they owe and how they are thwarting the tax laws. One obvious purpose of the TCMP is to provide IRS managers with the intelligence needed to direct enforcement efforts toward the most serious problems.

A few years ago, however, Susan B. Long, the persistent tax researcher mentioned previously, decided to test the thesis that IRS operations were based on intelligence obtained by the TCMP, that the agency methodically shifted its enforcement efforts from the geographic areas and income groups with the highest compliance to cover those with the least compliance.

Long loaded the IRS computer tapes with the results from the TCMP surveys completed in 1964, 1966, 1970, 1972, 1974, 1977, and 1980 into the computer at Syracuse University. On these tapes were recorded millions of bits of information documenting the shifting hot spots of the sixteen-year period covered by the surveys. Then she loaded tapes showing where the IRS had assigned its auditors by geographic region and kind of taxpayer.

Long's astonishing conclusion: "In general, the introduction of TCMP compliance data did not bring about any dramatic restructuring in audit coverage—even when it disclosed regions or return classes receiving far less audit attention than compliant groups." In other words, IRS managers have failed to redeploy their troops in response to the intelligence developed by their very expensive surveys.

THE CORPORATE BIAS OF THE IRS

Almost by definition, acts of omission are harder to identify and describe than are acts of commission. One of the agency's most interesting acts of omission goes back more than ten years. In September 1976, a House subcommittee headed by the late Representative Benjamin S. Rosenthal of New York issued a report concluding that there was only one sensible way for the IRS to track down tax cheats in a country as large as the United States. The recommended approach: develop computers to compare the information contained on the millions of income documents sent to the IRS by employers, banks, publishers, real-estate agents, and many other institutions with the data individual and corporate taxpayers provide on their annual tax returns.

The subcommittee's theory was quite simple. If taxpayers knew that the IRS knew about all the income they were receiving, the taxpayers would "voluntarily" pay more of their taxes. The trick was to devise a reasonable way to collect this information.

During the late 1960s and early 1970s, the computer provided the answer. Computerized personnel and payroll records were adopted by major employers. If a corporation decided to harness computers to process the routine payments it was making its employees, why not also use the machine to send out dividend checks to its stockholders? Banks, government agencies, insurance companies, publishing houses. The speed of the revolution was astonishing.

The 1976 report by the Rosenthal subcommittee recommended that the IRS establish a 1980 target date for the matching of all the income tax returns and the income reports. At first, the IRS resisted the proposed initiative. The agency, for example, did not enforce the existing legal requirement that all banks, corporations, and other organizations notify it about the dividends, interest, consulting fees, and other such payments. In 1979, three years after the first Rosenthal report, the General Accounting Office informed Congress that 60 percent of the nation's small- and medium-size corporations were not filing 1099 information returns. A year later, surprisingly enough, the GAO found that five major government agencies, including the IRS itself, also were not fully complying with the payment-reporting requirements. One reason for the lapses, the investigators found, was that the "IRS has given little attention to enforcing this filing requirement."

Slowly, however, the IRS's interest in matching tax returns with information returns began to blossom, and by the mid-1980s the agency had become an enthusiastic supporter of what had developed into one of its most effective investigative techniques. That year, for example, the agency actually matched four out of five of the hundreds of millions of different information returns against every tax return filed by an individual.

It was about this time that the General Accounting Office and Congress discovered an amazing act of omission: Although the IRS in 1986 had the technology and the procedures to compare the information contained on about 107 million *individual* tax returns with the information on almost 800 million *individual* income reports, the agency had not developed parallel procedures to undertake the systematic computer matching of the various payments made to the nation's 1.3 million *businesses*.

For more than a decade, the IRS had exempted more than 1 million of the nation's richest taxpayers from a computerized investigative technique that has proved highly effective in identifying individual taxpayers who had failed either to report all of their income or to file any return at all.

The whistle was blown by Jennie S. Stathis, an official in the General Accounting Office. During the previous ten years, Stathis said, the IRS had come to regard its massive program comparing income reports with individual tax returns as "an extremely important enforcement tool." In fact, she added, the latest available statistics showed that the program was generating $17 in assessments for every $1 it cost the government to operate. With the collection of $2.4 billion attributed to individual matching during the 1982 tax year, the ten-year drive to extend the computerized reach of the IRS was hardly a nickel-and-dime operation.

But, Stathis said, the IRS had not developed a parallel program to match the reports about interest and dividend payments going to business organizations with the income tax returns of these organizations. "Because the IRS's Information Returns Program for individual taxpayers has become an important enforcement tool, and because IRS's latest estimates show business non-compliance is increasing, some level of matching of business information returns should be considered," she testified to the House Government Operations Subcommittee.

Representative Douglas Barnard, the new chairman of the House subcommittee that in 1976 had recommended systematic matching of all taxpayers, was surprised by the IRS's omission. "Given the highly sophisticated matching program that already is in place for individuals, the minimal audit coverage of business taxpayers and the huge amount of interest, dividends and consulting fees paid to them each year, the burden of proof is on the IRS to justify its failure to extend the information return program to business taxpayers," Barnard said at the hearing.

"That burden would appear to be a good deal heavier today in view of the year-long investigation by the General Accounting Office that found substantial numbers of business taxpayers are underreporting a significant percentage of their third-party income," he added.

According to an analysis presented by the IRS itself, the initiation of business matching by the IRS would bring the government an additional $1.7 billion a year from business organizations that failed to report fully interest, dividends, rents, and capital gains. Several surveys by the GAO, however, indicate that the IRS's estimate of corporate underreporting is far too low. Congressional auditors believe that the total tax loss from cheating business organizations may approach $8 billion a year.

Despite the soaring federal budget deficits of the late 1980s, the IRS has not launched a full-scale business matching program. Agency officials contend that such a program is not warranted for a variety of reasons. They say that the GAO has exaggerated the extra income that might be realized and has underestimated the technical difficulties.

Many IRS critics charge that the agency's enforcement programs are biased against the individual and in favor of business. One explanation for this bias, assuming for the moment that it exists, looks to the well-paid corporate lawyers who make going after businesses a lot harder than going after individuals. Some IRS audit statistics appear to support the critics' view of the agency.

The numbers are complicated. First the overview. During the last decade, the overall chance for any kind of audit has steadily declined, even while the total number of IRS employees has increased. The IRS maintains that this decline in the rate of all audits is due to the changes voted into the tax laws by Congress. Everything else being equal, the more complicated the law, the more time it takes a revenue officer to complete a tax audit.

Again considering the last decade, businesses always faced a better chance of being audited than individuals; however, when the decline of audits for businesses is compared with the decline for individuals, it appears that the IRS has allowed businesses to come out way ahead.

In 1976, two out of a thousand individual taxpayers were audited. A bit more than a decade later, in 1987, only about one in a thousand received a visit from the tax man. During the same period, corporate audits went from ten out of a thousand to two out of a thousand. In other words, between 1976 and 1987, audits for corporations have declined five times more than for individuals.

The IRS was asked for an explanation. "Over the past several years our corporate examination program has placed more emphasis on the examination of larger more complex corporations," an agency spokesperson replied in a brief statement. "Since they take more time to examine, fewer can be examined. However, from a yield standpoint, this is a more efficient utilization of our resources." The IRS offered no proof of its assertion.

But what do we know about what might well be the most important measure of the IRS's effectiveness: the quality of the audits that the agency actually conducts? Almost nothing. Of course, individuals and businesses are free to draw conclusions about the knowledge and expertise of the revenue agent who audits them. But as far as I know, no outside organization in recent years has attempted a systematic assessment of the completeness, fairness, and accuracy of the audits completed by the IRS, for either businesses or individuals.

Every once in a while, however, a door will pop open that provides the observer with an insight into this most intimate interaction between the tax agency and the taxed. In this case, our doorman is Peter Stockton, one of the best investigators on Capitol Hill. Stockton is on the staff of the Oversight Subcommittee of the House Energy and Commerce Committee. In the last two decades he has been a lead player in some of the most bruising congressional investigations.

In 1984, the subcommittee obtained information that General Dynamics, at that time the largest defense contractor in the United States, was playing fast and loose with the taxpayers' money. Representative John Dingell, chairman of the subcommittee, ordered Stockton and Arthur

Brouk, an investigator on loan from the General Accounting Office, to investigate the allegations. Some months later, there were explosive public hearings.

During the course of their investigation, however, Stockton and Brouk began to wonder about whether the IRS had any serious interest in the taxes paid by General Dynamics.

"There was a whole lot of funny business going on at General Dynamics," Stockton recalled. "Among many different matters, we came across a large number of fraudulent expense vouchers which General Dynamics had used to support the deductions the company was taking from the federal taxes," he said in an interview. "Hundreds and hundreds of vouchers with no one's name on them. There was one case where one of the executives had submitted vouchers for the expenses he allegedly had racked up while attending more than five hundred business conferences in one year. Of course, vouchers without names on them are not supposed to serve as the basis for a tax deduction and no one can attend five hundred widely scattered business conferences during the 365 days of a single tax year."

After the subcommittee published its General Dynamics hearings, including some of the questionable vouchers, Stockton said he got a call from an IRS employee named Douglas Lindville, who indicated he was the revenue agent assigned to audit the company. "It is hard to believe," Stockton said, "but here was the largest defense contractor in the world and there was one guy from the IRS."

Stockton remembers that Lindville insisted he had never seen the vouchers that he and Brouk had obtained. "Mind you, if some ordinary guy like you or me had submitted those vouchers, the IRS would have been at our throat. But Lindville and his supervisor just kept saying that General Dynamics had shown an overall $3 billion tax loss that year so that denying the deductions claimed on the fraudulent vouchers wouldn't have made any difference. Even if this were so, I never could figure out why the IRS didn't bring criminal fraud cases against both the corporation, which seemed to be using the vouchers in a fraudulent way, and the corporation executives that had submitted them in the first place."

In defense of Lindville, the tax returns and supporting documents of a corporation the size of General Dynamics can easily amount to hundreds of thousands of pages.

Stockton said a second unusual insight provided by the IRS agent concerned the tax year he was then auditing. "What made the whole business totally ridiculous was that Lindville told Art Brouk and me that the General Dynamics books he then was auditing were exactly ten years old," he said. "It was 1984, and here was one tired old IRS bureaucrat looking at the 1974 books of the world's largest defense contractor that we had shown was fiddling with at least some of its numbers. It was pretty sorry."

Although various restrictions limit how far in the past the IRS may conduct its investigations, the agency may lawfully ask a taxpayer to waive these rights. Partly because of fear of precipitous IRS action if they don't, taxpayers usually agree to the requests. Given the rapid turnover of corporate executives and the deterioration of records in most organizations after only two or three years, the question must be asked: What is the value of auditing ten-year-old books?

When I asked the IRS about Stockton's scathing description of the agency's casual approach to auditing General Dynamics, Wilson Fadley, an IRS spokesman, noted that the privacy law prohibited him from commenting on any taxpayer, individual or corporate. "But I can tell you in a general way that for many years the IRS has assigned groups of agents with specialized skills to undertake audits of that class of taxpayer under what we call our large case program," he said.

"These teams, which include a case manager, specialists in major industries, and experts on various areas such as international trade or pensions, conduct the kind of carefully coordinated audit that a company like General Dynamics might expect."

Fadley added that in the case of a large organization with offices in many locations it was possible that a single IRS employee might be working alone in one office. He also said that in the auditing of complex corporate tax transactions it was possible that the agency might be looking at transactions that were a decade old.

Alvin A. Spivak, Washington spokesman for General Dynamics, offered an explanation that partly explained the contrary visions of the IRS presented by Stockton and Fadley.

Spivak, in a 1989 interview, said that the so-called completed contract method of accounting that was in effect at the time of the dispute with Congress provided the company and several other large defense contractors with tax credits that enabled them to avoid paying federal taxes. "I am not saying that this particular method of accounting was good national policy, but under its rules we legitimately did not pay federal taxes for a period of several years, and it made no sense for the IRS to be examining our books. Now, the rules that used to give us these net operating losses have been abolished and we are again paying taxes. And I want to assure you that there currently is a quite extensive group of IRS experts—specialists in international finance, computer experts, and specialists in pensions—looking at our operations."

After all the dust had settled, the federal government did not bring any criminal or tax charges against General Dynamics. In a March 1985 press release, however, the giant corporation advised Congress it would voluntarily reduce by $23 million the $170 million in expense statements it had submitted to the Defense Department for the years 1979 through 1982.

Over the years, IRS officials have frequently defended their relatively friendly approach to the business world, especially the major corporations. The government can pretty well assume the financial affairs of the large corporations are in order, the officials say, because of their association with the Big Eight accounting companies such as Arthur Andersen & Company, Peat Marwick, Main, Deloitte Haskins & Sells, and Arthur Young & Company.

But an examination of the major financial scandals of the United States since the end of World War II involving such well-known companies as General Electric, E. F. Hutton, Penn Square, and General Dynamics itself indicates that the accounting profession has frequently failed in its self-proclaimed role as corporate watchdog.

There are literally scores of documented cases where the most distinguished accounting firms have been named as coconspirators in tax fraud cases involving major corporations. One recent example came to light in 1988; it involved a scheme in which, the IRS alleged, a tax partner of Arthur D. Andersen & Company and more than a dozen senior officials of the Georgia Power Company, one of the nation's leading utilities, conspired to defraud the government of $200 million in federal taxes. Spokesmen for both Georgia Power and Arthur Andersen in August of 1989 denied the still-pending IRS charges.

Further surprising evidence of the poor-quality work performed by many certified public accounting firms emerged in 1989, when the General Accounting Office conducted an intense audit of a sample of eleven savings and loan associations located in the Dallas region that had recently failed. "Based on our evaluation, we believe that for 6 of the 11 S&Ls in our review, CPAs did not properly audit and/or report the S&Ls' financial or internal control problems in accordance with professional standards," the GAO report said.

One of the most outspoken critics of the current ethical standards and practices of the accounting firms is Abraham J. Briloff, the Emanuel Saxe Distinguished Professor of Accountancy at the City University of New York. In testimony before Congress and speeches to professional groups,

Briloff has outlined in excruciating detail how some of the most prestigious accounting firms have closed their eyes while their clients committed a variety of serious economic crimes against the public and their stockholders.

Briloff is outraged by the documented occasions when the nation's leading accounting firms have been involved in swindles or in inadequate audits and is worried about the IRS's assumption that it can rely on their supposed integrity to assure the proper collection of taxes. But he expresses sympathy for the IRS, which he believes has been asked to administer an impossible tax law with totally inadequate resources.

"Given the complexity of the laws, the abilities of the agents that the IRS normally attracts, and the sophistication of the corporate tax men, it seems to me that the IRS is unable to cope with today's business organizations," he said in an interview.

"The role of the IRS is made even more arduous," he continued, "because the books and documents of most of the largest firms are scattered all over the globe, buried in computer programs which even the corporate auditors who are working on the inside have trouble in understanding."

Despite his pessimism about the profound imbalance between the IRS and the corporations, Briloff argues that it remains important to hold the tax agency accountable. "I think we should measure the efficiency of the IRS in the same way we measure the efficiency of the New York City Sanitation Department," he said. "The measure is not only the amount of garbage that the department picks up each day, but the amount of garbage that is left littering the city's streets and parks."

CHAPTER 7

The Zealots

As history students know, the Zealots were a radical Jewish sect that flourished in the first century of the Christian era. The Zealots assured their place in history, and the English language, with an implacable defense of their religious beliefs, the last step of which involved mass suicide.

In more recent times, zealotry has become a less demanding life-style. The seventeenth-century New England patriarchs who accused difficult women of being witches now are regarded as zealots. John Brown, the abolitionist, certainly was a zealot. During the last few years, the late Ayatollah Khomeini and some of his more enthusiastic religious supporters have continued the grand old traditions.

In the minds of a good number of Americans living in the last quarter of the twentieth century, however, zealotry has come to be associated with a single organization, the Internal Revenue Service. This new form of zealotry, of course, has little to do with passionate fanatics and their demands for death to the infidels. Rather, it concerns harassment: sometimes the repeated, petty, and mindless acts of an incompetent bureaucracy; other times the more focused attacks that an agency with the powers of the IRS can bring down on the heads of those who cross it.

Interestingly enough, a confidential IRS survey of its own managers found that a substantial majority of the men and women who direct the agency share some of the public's negative views. In the words of a 1987 report summarizing this internal survey, IRS managers "generally viewed" agency operations "as too authoritarian ('military style,' 'dictatorial,' 'yellers and screamers,' 'rulers'), production oriented at the expense of people, too dependent upon statistics ('rewards those who deliver the plan no matter who or what'), unable to recognize and deal with failure whether involving programs, new ideas, or people ('operates from fear,' 'very defensive'), operating with short term goals, too conservative, and too demanding of conformity ('don't make waves')."

Slightly more than three out of every four managers, the survey found, agreed with the statement that "the IRS is more concerned with the quantity of work than the quality of work." Almost all the managers, 95 percent, felt that the executives above them were "totally task oriented" or "more task oriented than people oriented."[1]

While the victims of the agency's excessive enthusiasms certainly number in the millions, their stories normally are considered as isolated incidents, glitches, and violations of stated policy. This allows the IRS, and the good citizens who have been spared the pleasures of its mindless grip, to avoid a harsh reality: The excesses of the IRS are committed on a regular basis by the troops of a hierarchical organization commanded by a small number of officials. This is not to say that the excesses are a specific goal of the agency—usually they are not—only that excess is often an unavoidable outcome of the policies adopted by the people who run it. Because of the sheer size of the IRS and its assertive command structure, the individual agents who actually commit the acts of zealotry are, at the same time, both monsters and victims.

The excesses rarely seem to stir the consciences of the normal oversight agencies—the White House, congressional committees, or the courts. One explanation for this hear-no-evil, see-no-evil policy toward the IRS is the fear that genuine oversight just might upset the flow of revenue essential to the operation of the government. This conflict of interest has meant that responsible congressional committees and the courts seldom have had the heart to confront directly the IRS and the monstrous ways it sometimes treats the citizens of the United States.

But there are other more subtle reasons why general mechanisms of oversight often fail. Given the nature of the IRS's case selection process, only a very small number of its victims are powerful individuals with quick access to smart lawyers and tough accountants. This quirk means that many routine abuses are not challenged in court. It also means that the powerful and influential people with whom federal judges and members of Congress tend to work and play rarely are the targets of improper IRS enforcement tactics. This guarantees that the judges and lawmakers seldom hear anecdotes of IRS abuse directly from their friends and associates.

Over the years the IRS has been extremely attentive to the judges, congressmen, and White House staff members who were in a position to influence the fortunes of the agency. Until very recently, for example, the IRS routinely provided personal tax advice to any Supreme Court justice, member of Congress, or White House staffer who requested it. One middle-level agency official told me about an occasion several years ago when he was sent up to the Supreme Court to help a sitting justice complete his income tax return. "It somehow wasn't right," he said. "This judge, who each year rules on scores of cases involving the IRS, was getting a unique service that gave him a totally misleading picture of the agency." (Federal court rules, by the way, prohibit judges from accepting anything of value from a person or organization whose case they are considering. A check of several tax cases that reached the Supreme Court indicates that the judge in question never disqualified himself from a case involving the IRS because of the possible conflict.) An IRS spokesman reported that the agency no longer provides personal tax assistance to members of the Supreme Court and the White House staff. He acknowledged, however, that early each spring the IRS still establishes temporary offices in the House and Senate to help members of Congress and their staffs.

It is hardly surprising, therefore, that the inner circle of Washington's influential people looks at the IRS from a somewhat different perspective than many other Americans. Their rosy view could be compared with how a sincere Los Angeles business executive might think about that city's police department after a polite young patrol officer has helped him fix the flat on his Rolls-Royce. How could our wealthy executive help but be somewhat suspicious of the claims of police brutality that he hears from his Spanish-speaking gardener?

The forces of zealotry have many fathers. Often, the outrageous and arbitrary actions of the IRS are the natural product of rigorous production quotas that have for many years been an important part of the agency. On other occasions, they emerge from the IRS's poorly designed or outdated administrative systems. But many times the zealous actions have sprung from a more immediate motive: the desire of an IRS employee to marshal the authoritarian powers of the IRS to commit an act of personal revenge.

One example of vindictive IRS employees getting even with an individual who they had decided was their enemy occurred several years ago in Miami. The victim of this particularly gruesome nightmare was a wealthy lawyer named Daniel Neal Heller. Heller was wrongfully sent to federal prison on charges of income tax evasion as a result of the efforts of an IRS agent who threatened the lawyer's accountant with the possibility of prosecution; the accountant then lied in court about Heller's financial affairs. The accountant's false testimony was the crucial evidence leading to Heller's conviction.[2]

The story, as described in a decision by the Eleventh U.S. Circuit Court of Appeals, began in 1975 when the Criminal Investigation Division set up a loose network of undercover informants to collect intelligence about a group of powerful Miami business executives, politicians, and judges. The network was called Operation Leprechaun.

A few months later, the *Miami Daily News* published a series of critical articles about Operation Leprechaun, charging that the IRS agents running it had improperly collected detailed information about the drinking and sexual habits of dozens of Miami political figures. The key question raised was what connection the drinking habits of an official have with tax collection. Two of the IRS agents who were connected to Leprechaun during this period were Thomas A. Lopez and Lawrence S. Plave. Daniel Heller was the lawyer for the *News*.

The newspaper's sensational stories about the IRS intelligence project generated widespread interest in Miami and other parts of the country. They also prompted investigations by several congressional committees. Although a federal grand jury in Miami later criticized the news accounts, senior IRS officials in Washington also determined that Operation Leprechaun was an improper, out-of-control intelligence operation.

During the course of the various investigations that grew out of this long controversy, Lopez, Plave, and Heller had a number of adversarial meetings about the questionable project. During one meeting with Lopez, the appeals court decision reported, there was "a heated exchange of words in his [Heller's] office."

On June 30, 1982, about six years after the intense argument, Heller was indicted for criminal tax evasion. After a long series of legal disputes, he was convicted in November 1986 and sentenced to three years in prison. The primary IRS investigator and key witness against Heller was

Plave. The IRS supervisor who had assigned him to undertake the criminal investigation was Lopez.

In the fall of 1987, four months after he had begun his prison sentence, the appeals court threw out Heller's conviction. The panel quoted Plave's own testimony stating that on Friday, July 12, 1979, he had threatened the accountant and that the purpose of the threat was to "scare" and "control" him. "It is also undisputed that on the following Monday, July 15, 1979, that accountant's lawyer called Plave to say that the accountant would provide testimony against Heller and that he wanted to be a witness rather than a defendant," the court wrote. "Finally, the record in this case is also clear that the accountant falsely testified against Heller." Thus, the court concluded, the government's "substantial interference" in the case had "deprived Heller of an important defense witness."

In a footnote, the court said that the background of animosity between Heller and the two agents suggested that Plave and Lopez "could have intended to intimidate and frighten the witness into false testimony in revenge against Heller."

The two agents have now retired from the IRS. In separate interviews, both Lopez and Plave insist that the case was handled in a correct manner. On the basis of the evidence, however, the Court of Appeals reversed Heller's conviction. Six months later, a federal district judge in Miami dismissed the entire case against the lawyer.

Shortly thereafter, Heller regained the right to practice law, which he had automatically lost when the jury found him guilty of felony tax violations. In March 1989, the lawyer filed suit against Plave and Lopez, requesting unspecified damages for the violation of his constitutional rights, his legal fees, the loss of his income as a lawyer, and the four months he spent in federal prison. That case is pending. Earlier, Heller won $5 million in damages when his suit against the accountant was settled out of court.

Five million dollars is a lot of money even though Heller's lawyers calculated he lost about $8 million in income during the period between the indictment and the dismissal. But the money seems to have brought little comfort to the prominent lawyer, art collector, and community activist. "While my name and reputation are worth much more to me than $5 million," Heller told the *Miami Herald* at the time, "my wife and I have decided to accept the $5 million from the insurance company rather than waste more time. Another inducement for me to promptly close this chapter in my life is that it enables me to vigorously get back to my first love, namely, devoting my full time and energy to practicing law, going to court and serving clients."

As the Heller case indicates, the dangers of vindictive harassment on the part of the government rapidly increase when IRS agents believe that their targets have questioned the authority and power of the federal government. It is hardly surprising, then, that some of the most serious abuses of the IRS's formidable powers emerge in situations where the agency is ordered to combat people who have been identified as criminals or as somehow helping criminals.

Ronald McKelvey is a lawyer who lives in Yuma, Arizona.[3] During the early 1970s, he represented a number of persons charged with drug offenses. In June 1973, McKelvey filed a civil damage suit against a federal customs agent and a Yuma policeman for a client who claimed he had been abused by the two lawmen in April.

Shortly after the alleged beating, the customs agent informed the IRS that McKelvey had received large legal fees for representing alleged marijuana dealers and suggested an investigation of the lawyer. Despite the fact that the government never claimed that McKelvey was in any way involved in narcotics trafficking, a special Treasury Department committee decided he should be targeted for a special tax investigation.

Revenue Agent E. Joe May was assigned to the case. In August 1973, May called McKelvey and told him that he had been assigned to audit the lawyer's returns. McKelvey gave permission for his personal accountant to give the IRS complete access to his books and records.

In response to inquiries by McKelvey's accountant, Agent May assured the accountant, himself a former revenue agent, "that this was a routine audit," the Ninth Circuit Court of Appeals later said. "In fact, teams of special agents and revenue agents were combing through McKelvey's affairs at that time seeking evidence to use for a criminal indictment."

The appeals court said it fully agreed with the district judge who had originally ruled that the IRS "had obtained evidence from McKelvey and his accountant by deceit and trickery in violation of McKelvey's rights secured by the Fourth Amendment."

But the appeals court said that the district judge's order enjoining "any and all investigation into McKelvey's affairs for 1971" had gone too far. Quoting a 1969 decision of another federal appeals court, the judges pointed to a still unresolved legal question of whether the government is free to use evidence for other purposes, such as civil tax enforcement, that has been declared improper for use in a criminal trial. "Widespread uncertainty is prevalent on the issue of whether evidence, inadmissible in a criminal case, can be used for other purposes, and the Supreme Court has yet to resolve the problem."

But criminal tax charges are not the only weapon available to an angry IRS employee bent on revenge. In March 1987, Richard Jurney, an IRS agent in Denver, requested a local real-estate appraiser named Bob Anderson to place a value on his house. When he went to Jurney's house, Anderson later recalled, the IRS agent had seemed very concerned that he get an appraisal for $110,000, although he indicated that $105,000 would be acceptable.[4]

"It's not unusual to have them [house owners] give us real sales pitches, but Jurney was very insistent about the fact that he knew what the house should be appraised at," Anderson recalled. "Then he asked if I have ever been audited. I didn't answer."

After Anderson had appraised the house for $95,000 to $96,000, Jurney went to Bank Western for a second opinion. When the appraiser for Bank Western valued Jurney's house at $94,000, the IRS agent complained to a bank supervisor named Joe O'Dorisio.

Shortly thereafter, Jurney delivered on the threat implicit in his question to Anderson and his complaint to O'Dorisio when agents of the Denver office of the IRS initiated personal audits of both men. But Jurney apparently was not satisfied. Jurney next persuaded his supervisors in the district office to launch a special project to audit the returns of a large number of appraisers in the Denver area. According to Ron Collins, supervisory appraiser at the Denver office of the Federal Housing Administration, about half of the two hundred appraisers who attended the group's annual meeting in August 1988 said they were being audited.

Months later, on December 23, 1988, Gerald F. Swanson, director of the IRS's Denver district, responded to Representative Patricia Schroeder's inquiry about the questionable audits. Swanson informed the Colorado congresswoman that, because of the serious nature of the charges against Jurney—using his official position to influence who was audited—the agency had decided his "removal from the Service was warranted." The official added, however, that the agent had resigned before he could be fired.

A footnote to the Jurney case demonstrates the tenacity of the IRS. On April 19, 1989, Swanson sent another letter to Schroeder. He said that after all of the returns that appeared to be associated with Jurney's conflict of interest had been eliminated, the IRS had decided the overall effort to audit appraisers in the Denver area was valid. "The project has already had a positive impact on compliance," Swanson said.

It is hardly surprising that Anderson, the appraiser who first offended

Jurney, was upset by what he viewed as the official retribution that had been triggered by his appraisal. "I'm kind of intimidated. I'm to the point that I can't do appraisals for IRS employees anymore."

KIDDIE LAND

When a large faceless organization singles out a person for special treatment, whether for good or evil, it often is hard not to wonder about the organization's motives. Maybe, we sometimes think, the agency is out to get me for my political beliefs. Or maybe the agency gave my neighbor a valuable favor because of his friendship with a particular politician. Either way, we all seem to be more comfortable with the idea that the suspect acts occurred as a result of the conscious decisions of individual bureaucrats. It is hard to remember that the driving force of all large bureaucracies is often incompetence.

Consider the case of Shannon Burns, an industrious ten-year-old fourth-grader who lived in San Jose, California. By early 1987, Shannon had managed to stash away $694 in her personal savings account. Because she was a minor, her account also bore the name of her father. Shannon had earned the money by collecting aluminum cans and by doing chores for neighbors. On January 13, the IRS slapped a lien on Shannon's savings account to help pay the back taxes owed by her father, Kevin Burns, a carpenter who had been unemployed since October 1986 and who owed the IRS $1,000.

After a story about the seizure of the little girl's savings appeared in the *San Jose Mercury News*, a Collection Division agent looked at her bankbook and found there had been no withdrawals from it, evidence that Shannon's father wasn't trying to pull a fast one on the government by siphoning off funds from his daughter's account. The agency decided to lift the lien against the little girl's account. "They're pretty hard-nosed," said IRS spokesman Chips Maurer when asked to explain the initial decision of the Collection Division to seize Shannon's savings. "That's their job."

Six months later in Oregon, the IRS seized $70.76 that nine-year-old Carmin Fisher had been saving in pennies since she was three. This time it was Carmin's grandfather who allegedly owed some back taxes and whose name was on her account. "She didn't owe this debt. She's only 9 years old," Carmin's grandmother told the *Eugene Register Guard*. Once again public disclosure prompted the IRS to back down.

It was about this time that the IRS seized an account containing

$10.35, the savings of Garry D. Keffer, a twelve-year-old from Chesa-peake, Virginia. The seventh-grader got the IRS to rescind the order by the sophisticated tactic of writing a letter to President Reagan and then giving a copy of it to the Associated Press. "I am now feeling distrustful about the United States due to my financial devastation," he wrote. His parents, it turned out, had mailed a check with the final installment of their small debt to the government two days before the IRS ordered the seizure of little Garry's $10.35.

Confronted with the series of embarrassing news stories, the IRS opted for a smidgen of modest reform. From now on, Commissioner Lawrence B. Gibbs ordered grandly, the IRS would make no seizures of amounts under $100 on accounts that bore the name of a person in addition to that of the delinquent taxpayer. Gibbs acknowledged later that some of his friends had read the "horror stories" in the newspapers and had asked him how he could allow such things to happen. He deftly sidestepped the questions raised by his friends. "Some of the stories indicated we are a large, uncaring, insensitive agency, but believe it or not we haven't done this intentionally," he said.

Shannon Burns, Carmin Fisher, and Garry Keffer had several things in common: They all were innocent third parties; they all had guardians who had become entangled with the IRS; they all were subjected to punitive actions by an agency that made no attempt to understand their individual cases. Another change in the basic tax law mandated by the 1988 Taxpay-ers' Bill of Rights may somewhat reduce such abuses. Under the new provision, when the IRS makes this kind of seizure the assets will be held for twenty-one days in a local escrow account rather than being immedi-ately dispatched to one of the IRS service centers. It is hoped that by establishing a system under which local IRS officials maintain control of such seized assets for a three-week period, the agency will have time to sort out the cases where it has acted in an arbitrary fashion before they get sucked into the computerized maw of the agency.

Accurately judging the merits of each case through the working of a massive computer is one of the most difficult challenges facing the mod-ern tax collector, according to John Baldwin, director of the New Jersey tax agency. Baldwin spoke at a 1988 tax conference in Washington.

"Just how is a tax administrator supposed to get into the head of every taxpayer?" he asked. "Has anyone here found some mystical way to determine intent? I don't see how you can determine intent in a comput-erized mass production process. You really need a jury to do this job and there is no way we can provide one."

THE CHECK'S IN THE MAIL?

Baldwin's questions go to the heart of the automated harassment that is dispensed so casually by large, computerized bureaucracies such as the IRS. Although the technicians who run these bureaucracies are seldom conventional zealots, it is hardly surprising that the victims sometimes come to view the multiple injustices of the late twentieth century as exquisitely maddening acts of zealousness. One of these new-age victims is Donald A. Thurow, a fifty-nine-year-old retired postal worker who lives in San Francisco. On July 2, 1986, he wrote his monthly $1,300 mortgage check to California Federal, the bank holding his mortgage, and he mailed it.

But the money never got to its intended destination. Instead, the sealed letter somehow ended up at the IRS's Fresno service center, where the envelope was opened, the check was removed, and the words INTERNAL REVENUE SERVICE were improperly and illegally stamped over the name of the original payee in big black letters. On July 10, 1986, the government's $2 trillion debt was reduced by $1,300 when Thurow's altered check was credited to the account of the Treasurer of the United States.

Donald Thurow did not owe the IRS any money. He got his first inkling of the unannounced seizure of his mortgage check when an official from California Federal, the San Francisco thrift institution, called to ask why he had not paid his mortgage. After a few days of complete confusion, an examination of the markings on the front and back of the canceled mortgage check revealed that it had been hijacked by the IRS.

On October 13, 1986, Thurow and his lawyer filed a refund claim. One month went by with no answer from the IRS. Then a second month slipped by. A third, fourth, fifth, and sixth month passed. The agency's lips were sealed.

Because the IRS had totally ignored his plea for the return of his money, Thurow decided a more forceful approach was required. He filed suit in federal court asking for the return of the $1,300 that the government had so artfully taken from him, plus 10 percent interest, legal fees, and punitive damages of $50,000. No legal action was brought against the bank that had improperly cashed the altered check, in the belief that the bank was under enormous pressure to cooperate with the government and in some ways was a victim too.

"Altering a check is improper and illegal," said Thurow's Oakland lawyer, Montie S. Day. "And Title 18 of the United States Code makes it a felony to open mail in transit and mail is deemed to be in transit if misdirected."

Jay Weill, an assistant U.S. attorney in San Francisco, was not impressed. Returning the $1,300 that the IRS had stolen was one thing. But Weill argued that the rest of the claims were so "frivolous" that the lawyer who filed them should be punished. Weill asked the federal judge to take the unusual step of ordering Thurow's lawyer, Day, to pay the government's legal expenses in responding to Thurow's allegations. (This was the same Jay Weill who defended the IRS when it improperly disclosed personal finance information about Gina and Paul Husby.)

While acknowledging that the government had altered Thurow's check—the markings on it made any other position absurd—Weill asserted that the change had been made by a low-level clerk who had misunderstood her instructions.

Was the Thurow case an aberration, a once-in-a-lifetime accident? Or was the opening of the letter and the altering of the check something worse: the sloppy product of a massive bureaucracy that simply does not have the time or energy to care about the rights and sanity of a few individuals? After reports of the Thurow suit were published in a San Francisco newspaper, Day was approached by a number of other individuals who told him horror stories about the IRS cashing, or attempting to cash, checks that had not been made out to the agency.

One such incident involved Kathleen C. Bregand-Baker, now living in San Jose. She said in her deposition to Day in the Thurow case that in November 1985 the IRS regional service center in Philadelphia had altered and cashed an $89 check she had made out to her Visa account. In another deposition, Robert J. Burns of Clayton, California, said that in October 1986 the IRS office in Ogden, Utah, had altered a $286 check he had made out to City Corporation Savings. A third deposition described the troubles of a San Francisco woman named Amy Adney and a $570 check she had written to Shearson/Lehman Mortgage.

Given the vast number of people sending checks to the IRS and the small number of illicit check-cashing cases that came to Day's attention, the overall problem at first glance would appear to be insignificant. This certainly was the position of Larry Wright, IRS spokesman in San Francisco.

But given the facts that most citizens are reluctant to tangle with the IRS on any subject, that only a small number of people read any given newspaper article, that contacting Day required considerable initiative, and that the individuals who came forward had their checks improperly altered at three widely scattered IRS locations, the first judgment may be wrong; IRS transgressions may be much more frequent than they appear.

Whatever the extent of this exquisitely irritating form of bureaucratic harassment, the reasons for its existence and the IRS response after its disclosure were both revealing and disturbing.

Every year, the Postal Service delivers hundreds of millions of letters to the IRS. The Fresno service center, for example, which is just one of ten such centralized processing locations, last year received more than 32 million pieces of mail. But because the Postal Service has its administrative problems too, 3 percent to 5 percent of the first-class letters dumped off on the IRS loading docks actually are not addressed to the agency. This suggests that at the Fresno center alone as many as sixteen thousand letters a year should have been delivered somewhere else, perhaps even to the California Federal Savings and Loan.

This mass of misdirected mail does give the IRS a genuine problem. Unlike the rest of us, it isn't just a question of glancing at a few letters, noticing that the postman accidentally stuck a neighbor's water bill in the wrong mailbox, and handing it back to the postman the next day. Indeed, at certain times of the year, the IRS has to process hundreds of thousands of letters a day. To handle this problem, as described more fully in Chapter 2, the agency has installed one or two massive machines at each of its service centers to open and sort the daily flood of mail.

ALL IN ALL, I'D RATHER BE IN PHILADELPHIA

Joseph Cloonan, director of the IRS's Philadelphia Service Center, walked briskly through his massive kingdom, a building with floor space equal to four football fields. He was talking about the gigantic job that each year confronts the service center: to process 15 million returns; collect $72 billion; handle tens of millions of other pieces of correspondence, tax delinquency notices, and tax delinquency assessments. "Given our admitted shortcomings in trying to achieve this demanding mission I think the American people are remarkably tolerant," Cloonan said.

A short, ramrod-straight man with a full white beard and mustache, Cloonan is one of the IRS's best managers. He was brought to Philadelphia several years ago after the collapse of the service center's morale, equipment, and overall performance had led to outraged complaints from tens of thousands of citizens and even a few members of Congress.

As we walked through the giant facility, Cloonan frequently stopped to talk with different employees, usually calling to them by name. Finally, we reached the center's receiving department, where each day dozens of Postal Service trucks deliver hundreds of large canvas-sided carts and special wheeled metal frames jammed with tens of thousands of letters. During the busiest period, just before April 15, the crush of mail is even heavier. Cloonan explained that as the clerks remove the letters from the carts and large metal frames they are supposed to check for misdirected letters before directing the flood of envelopes into the receiving end of the giant COMPS sorting machines. "Sometimes, when business is heavy, they miss," Cloonan acknowledged.

After the envelopes have been opened and sorted, they are carried by a gigantic industrial elevator to the floor above, where the "extractors" sit at special round desks, surrounded by stacks of envelopes. The extractors' job is to remove checks and make the first rough check for accuracy. The extractor is armed with a rubber stamp bearing the words: INTERNAL REVENUE SERVICE.

Cloonan said the extractor was authorized to wield the stamp in only three specific situations. "First, if a taxpayer's return says she owed $50.54 and she has written a check for $50.54 that is perfect in every way except that she forgot to write out who was to get the money, the extractor can use the stamp," the official said. "Second, if the taxpayer has written out a perfect check except that she has made it out to the 'IRS,' the extractor can overstamp the initials with the words 'INTERNAL REVENUE SERVICE.' Third, if the taxpayer's return says she owes the federal government $50.54 and her check is made out for the correct amount but has been made payable to a state tax agency, the extractor is authorized to stamp over the state name."

Cloonan said that the IRS carefully trained the extractors about these restrictions on modifying a check. "They are given very definite instruction in this area, both orally and in writing. There definitely should be no slipups."

But the director acknowledged that the system was not perfect. The problem centered on the 3 percent to 5 percent of the letters that are incorrectly sent to the IRS each day, some of which contain checks. "I've had informal chats with some of our good extractors, and they admit that one or two checks are incorrectly stamped each week," he said. During the busiest periods, the incoming mail pouring into each of the ten centers in the United States will go through the hands of hundreds of extractors.

Cloonan was an unusually forthcoming official. First, he frankly had admitted that during the center's busiest periods his extractors may improperly alter a hundred or more checks each week. But then, during our tour of the Philadelphia center, he acknowledged that the IRS had no plans to rectify the problem. The victims were too few, the system too big.

In San Francisco, the outcome of Thurow's suit was equally bleak. True, the IRS finally did return that $1,300 to Thurow. It is also true that the federal judge rejected the prosecutor's request that Montie Day be forced to pay the government's legal fees on the grounds that the damage claim against the IRS was frivolous. At the same time, however, the judge rejected Thurow's request for $50,000 in damages. The claim was turned down because of sovereign immunity, a legal shield that makes it extremely hard for citizens to sue the IRS.

QUOTAS

The improper altering of checks continues to this day partly because the IRS has balanced what it would cost to correct the problem against what the problem costs the public and has made an informed decision to ignore the situation.

Because it is almost impossible to compare the values that the IRS is weighing here, it is hard to know whether the agency's final judgment is right or wrong. We do know, however, that such judgments are heavily influenced by intense congressional pressures to collect the maximum amount of taxes at the least possible cost. Over the years, this continuing pressure has led the IRS to adopt formal and informal production requirements in many parts of the agency that sometimes force employees to act in a zealous, uncaring way.

Quotas are a common part of modern working life. Millions of Americans hold jobs where the organizations paying their wages have set either explicit or implicit production requirements. During my own career, for example, I have worked for three major press organizations, United Press International, *Newsweek*, and *The New York Times*. At each of these institutions, there was a clear understanding among reporters about the number of articles the editors expected them to write: three or four a day at UPI, one major article a week at *Newsweek*, and two or three stories a week at *The New York Times*. (There were indeed individual variations. Because of the explosive impact of many of Seymour Hersh's investigations, for example, the *Times* was delighted to get far fewer of Hersh's blockbusters than it would require from less probing reporters.)

But the polite production expectations imposed on most reporters, the minute-by-minute pressures placed on airline reservation clerks, and the unbending demands of an automobile production line are substantially different from what happens at the IRS. The varied work requirements of the newspaper, the telephone company, and the automaker are mostly aimed at assuring the bosses that a sufficient number of widgets will be produced each week. Although Charlie Chaplin's movie *Modern Times* brilliantly illustrated the brutal effects that such requirements sometimes can have on the individual worker, most people would agree that sensible quotas can provide a necessary spur.

When production requirements are adopted by law enforcement agencies, however, their harmful effects may be greatly magnified, damaging both the enforcers and the subjects of enforcement.

Within the IRS, for example, production pressures sometimes prompt revenue officers and special agents to take inappropriate enforcement actions against taxpayers who in the normal course of events might be treated in a different way. Here is my point: In maintaining pressure to assure that the agency continues to function in a proper way, there is a constant danger that IRS supervisors will push their staff into making unwarranted seizures, levies, or liens.

Allegations that the IRS's enforcement of the tax laws sometimes has been improperly driven by production requirements go back a long, long way. So do the official denials. More than sixty years ago, on March 14, 1924, a staff member of the Select Senate Committee on Investigation of the Bureau of Internal Revenue was questioning C. R. Nash, the assistant to the commissioner. The question turned on whether or not it was the toughest agents who were first promoted to higher-paying jobs. "I frequently hear the rumor that agents and other men are rated on the amount of additional tax they turn up," the staff member said during a committee hearing. "In other words, that their promotion depends upon finding error in favor of the government."

Nash responded in the same world-weary tone that IRS officials would adopt in the years ahead on those rare occasions when they were asked about reports that the agency had secret production quotas. "I believe that a few years ago there was some system—or I would not say there was a system, but the efficiency of a revenue agent was rated to some extent on the amount of additional tax that he reported. That policy has been discarded and today a revenue agent is not rated on the additional tax which he reports but on the general quantity and quality of his work, whether it involves refunds or additional tax."

But the questions about tax enforcement quotas would not go away. On February 27, 1973, Senator Joseph Montoya's Appropriations Subcommittee on the Department of Treasury heard considerable testimony from a number of agents about the IRS's extensive production requirements and how the most aggressive agents almost always were the first to win promotion.

Then IRS Commissioner Johnnie M. Walters was given his turn. Montoya prefaced his questions with the statement that he assumed Walters would not admit the existence of IRS quotas.

"Mr. Chairman, you are absolutely right," Walters replied. "I am not going to admit that. I am going to state flatly that it is not correct."[5]

But the delicate problem of how to prod agents into collecting taxes without turning them into storm troopers remains a genuine challenge. In the spring of 1987, IRS Commissioner Lawrence B. Gibbs joined the long list of his predecessors going back to at least 1924 by insisting that agency policies prohibited the promotion of agents on the basis of numbers of seizures and collections. The forum was a hearing by a Senate Finance Subcommittee.

Senator David Pryor did not buy Gibbs's assurances. Instead, he introduced a memorandum written on February 17, 1987, from Wilbur E. McKean, a Baltimore branch chief, to one of his group managers. McKean was not happy with his managers. "I am sure each of you has analyzed and evaluated the January report for your group," he wrote. "Personally, for a five week period, it is a sorry report. Not one manager has come forward to explain the poor performance statistical indicators. It appears the fewer cases that revenue officers have assigned to them, the less work they do. Revenue officers that are performing above a satisfactory level will be rewarded, and the ones that are not will be documented with corrective action taken. . . . You will be evaluated on your accomplishments or lack of accomplishments. Need I say more?"

Like any supervisor, McKean of course had an obligation to make sure his lieutenants were performing the work the government paid them for. But McKean was talking numbers: the number of seizures that had been performed, the number of investigations closed, the number of criminal tax cases that had been uncovered, and how those on the top of his production charts would be rewarded.

An IRS spokesman responded directly to the questions raised by the McKean memo. "The IRS forbids use of enforcement statistics to rate the performance of its managers or employees," he said. "It is clear the memo that was released today by the subcommittee is in violation of this policy. We feel the branch chief misunderstood the guidelines."

Robert M. Tobias, president of the National Treasury Employees Union, the group that represents many of the IRS's 123,000 employees, however, disagreed with the assertions by both Gibbs and the spokesman that harmful quota systems did not exist because they were prohibited by agency policy. "Most, if not all, of the seemingly irrational IRS actions with regard to taxpayers—especially the unwarranted seizures and levies—are traceable directly to production pressures and the ethos of statistics worship fostered by IRS management," the union chief contended.

A few weeks after Gibbs and Tobias offered the subcommittee their conflicting views of the inner workings of the IRS, the subcommittee held another hearing during which five experienced IRS revenue officers were allowed to speak. For most of their careers, which together totaled one hundred years, the five employees had been assigned to collecting back taxes.

One of the witnesses, John Pepping, worked in the IRS office in Los Angeles. He told the subcommittee about the sign that had been taped on the door of a supervisor: "Seizure Fever—Catch It." More interesting was Pepping's report that his office rewarded agents who had racked up the best weekly performance record in terms of seizures and other aggressive techniques with one-hour increments of leave time. Another witness was Robert Miller, a revenue officer stationed in Wheaton, Maryland. "It's now considered a quality error" if an agent does not seize the property of a delinquent taxpayer, he testified. This mindless pressure to make seizures hurts both the government and the taxpayer, Miller contended, because taxes more often can be collected with less draconian actions.

It thus appears that for many years production requirements have remained a frequently denied part of the IRS. Given the unpleasant nature of many of the agency's jobs and the natural human tendency to avoid pain, it may well be that such reward systems are a necessary evil. Perhaps if the managers of the agency admitted to the reality that is known to everyone who has ever worked for the IRS, and to most of the taxpayers who do business with it, they could develop ways to tame the quota systems and use them to the benefit of all. But the disingenuous denials have led to widespread cynicism and the inescapable conclusion that the managers either are lying or are seriously misinformed.

TRAFFIC COPS AND TAX AGENTS

Sometimes problems become clearer when looked at from a different perspective. Think for a moment about the New York Police Department and the IRS. At first glance, these two giant agencies appear to have few similarities. How, after all, can you compare a police officer chasing a dangerous felon down the street with a revenue officer examining the books of a company?

But arresting the felon who has held up a bank or mugged a woman is a very small part of a police officer's life. Outside of Hollywood studios, the men and women of the New York Police Department spend most of their time enforcing the law in situations where there is no immediate victim. These situations center on society's efforts to control narcotics, prostitution, gambling, and vehicular traffic. Here, both in New York and in most other city and state police agencies, quotas are set requiring the officers to issue so many traffic summonses a week or to make so many arrests a month.

Although usually well intended, police quotas create many harmful effects. For the public, of course, the most obvious problem is arbitrary enforcement. Sydney C. Cooper, a distinguished former senior commander in the New York Police Department, remembers when many years ago he was the precinct captain in the Sheepshead Bay area of Brooklyn. "There was pressure from headquarters to cut down on traffic accidents so we passed on the word from the bosses at Centre Street that each cop in the precinct was going to have to write so many moving violation tickets a month," Cooper explained.

"What happened, of course, was that once a month those jokers would remember the chart and go out and knock off ten cars that didn't come to a complete and total halt at an obscure stop sign in the precinct. I am sure that some of the drivers understood the tickets were not kosher and were understandably offended."

Cooper added, however, that the quotas had a second equally negative impact: They tended to lead the police in the wrong direction. The police goal, after all, was not to hand out so many tickets a month; it was to prevent serious accidents. The specific reason headquarters had demanded an increased number of tickets, Cooper explained, was that there had been a sudden increase in traffic fatalities. "I finally took a careful look at the police reports on these fatals and discovered that almost all of them were happening at three in the morning on one of the major highways that ran through the precinct. The stop sign tickets generated by the quotas were almost totally irrelevant to the fatalities."

In New York City during the late 1960s, Police Commissioner Howard Leary laid down a rule that every narcotics detective had to make a certain number of felony arrests each month if he wanted to keep his highly valued position. This felony arrest quota was not an impossible goal for the narcotics detectives. But an element of uncertainty had been introduced into the game. For many years, department policy was to be extremely stingy about giving detectives "buy money," the funds they used to make undercover purchases of heroin from the small-time dealers so that the dealers could then be arrested for dealing. To reduce the uncertainties of meeting Leary's new quotas, many detectives developed their own secret methods of guaranteeing the required number of arrests. First, the detectives would steal heroin from street addicts. Then they would pass the stolen heroin to other addicts for tips that would help them make the required number of "felony collars."

In the end, the arrest quotas, combined with poor training and very little direct supervision, led to a situation where the Narcotics Division may actually have become one of the major distributors of heroin in New York City.

With all their problems, however, police administrators still think that quotas are an essential management tool. "Given the lack of immediate supervision inherent in this kind of police work, how else can you make sure that everyone is pulling their load?" asked Sydney Cooper, the retired New York police official. But he added that, without very thoughtful application, quota systems easily turn into monsters that lead to abusive, unfair, and ineffective police work.

The nagging management problems that confront the police in one part of their daily responsibilities—the enforcement of traffic, gambling, prostitution, and narcotics laws—also face the IRS field supervisors. The traffic cop, the narcotics detective, and the IRS agent have all been ordered to undertake the difficult task of enforcing laws that are not universally accepted by the public. Many drivers want to speed. Substantial numbers of people desire marijuana, cocaine, heroin, and crack. Most taxpayers would prefer to pay fewer taxes. And in all three situations, there is no immediate victim demanding the arrest of the "criminal" as there usually is in the case of a mugging or burglary. Because neither cops nor IRS agents are automatons, they understandably lean toward postponing the often difficult moment when they stop a speeding motorist or seize the assets of a delinquent taxpayer. To counter this natural reluctance, managers fall back on quota systems, which often produce the acts of mindless, arbitrary law enforcement that so enrage the public and fail to accomplish the desired goal.

The IRS goal is not to make ten jillion seizures a month; the aim is to persuade citizens to pay the taxes they owe with as little fuss as possible. The memo of Wilbur McKean, the IRS branch chief in Baltimore, is a perfect example of this problem. It may well have led the agents he commanded to complete a few more seizures, but it is extremely unlikely that the secret production quotas worked to encourage the taxpayers of Maryland to send their checks to the federal government on a voluntary basis.

Over the years, most of the stories about IRS quota systems have come from the employees assigned to the Collection Division, the part of the agency directly responsible for the hard grungy business of extracting money from taxpayers who don't want to part with it. The more elite parts of the IRS, such as the Criminal Investigation Division, have always seemed immune from the pernicious effects that inevitably follow when arbitrary demands are imposed upon government functionaries with considerable power.

This is not to say, however, that the special agents entrusted with the most far-reaching powers of the IRS are exempt from improper production quotas, even to the extent that they are pressed to prosecute a case without the necessary evidence.

ON A JET PLANE

Omni International Corporation is not a neighborhood bodega. The corporation, with headquarters in suburban Washington, D.C., is in the jet-airline trading business. It has handled planes for scores of the nation's largest corporations and even for a few Arab sheiks. Celebrities like Elvis Presley, Frank Sinatra, and Kenny Rogers have also used its services.

In the spring of 1984, a federal grand jury in Baltimore indicted Omni, three of its top executives, and its outside lawyer and tax adviser on tax fraud charges. The indictment said the company had been illegally channeling millions of dollars a year of its income to a Bermuda subsidiary. The corporation and its executives, the government charged, "willfully and knowingly combined, conspired, confederated and agreed together and with each other to defraud the United States by impeding, obstructing and defeating" the IRS's attempts to collect the taxes owed by the company.

Indictments in complex tax cases require a great deal of sophisticated investigative work. In the Omni case, the investigation had gone on for more than three years and had spanned three continents before senior officials in the IRS and the Justice Department agreed to allow Elizabeth H. Trimble, an assistant U.S. attorney in Baltimore, to present the information to a grand jury.

On the surface, the case against Omni seemed routine. But as a later set of special court hearings would bring out, the Justice Department initially had serious doubts about the case that Trimble and the two IRS investigators working with her—Donald Temple and Paul Mitchell—had developed. In fact, at a routine meeting on October 31, 1983, a Justice Department official in Washington had questioned whether the assistant U.S. attorney and the two IRS agents had gathered sufficient evidence to prove their case against one of the key targets of the alleged conspiracy.

In an effort to meet these highly embarrassing last-minute questions, Temple and Mitchell, with the approval of Trimble, launched a new round of additional investigations. On November 22, 1983, the two agents went to the home of Sandra Poe Wilkins, a former secretary of one of the defendants. "The agents arrived unannounced, presented a grand jury subpoena to Wilkins, and offered Wilkins, in lieu of appearing before the grand jury, an opportunity to talk directly with the agents," federal judge Walter E. Black later wrote in his 1986 opinion on the case. "Wilkins consented and the agents interrogated her for at least five hours."[6]

Following the interview with Wilkins, Judge Black noted, the two agents wrote a memorandum claiming that the secretary had given them important new information incriminating her former boss.

Both the Temple-Mitchell memorandum of the November 1983 interview and the complex series of events that occurred after it was written turned out to be genuine disasters for the government's case against Omni and for the professional reputations of Trimble and the two agents. They also led to the dramatic disclosure of how the government sometimes becomes possessed by a zealous need to win its case, no matter what the cost.

Elizabeth Trimble comes from the right side of the tracks. Her great-great-grandfather, Isaac Ridgeway Trimble, was the highest-ranking Marylander in the Confederate army. Her father, Dr. I. Ridgeway Trimble, was a leading surgeon of Baltimore, a key figure in the development of the bulletproof vest, and an active participant in a broad range of community projects. In the summer of 1965, the year before Elizabeth graduated from one of Baltimore's most exclusive private schools, she traveled to Europe with her family. The highlight of the trip, as recounted on the society page of the *Baltimore Sun,* was a swim and a picnic lunch with Prince Rainier and Princess Grace of Monaco.

"Pretty young Princess Caroline, who apparently is a bit of a tomboy, was in the pool when they arrived, emerging to meet them," the paper reported. "Before lunch, daiquiris were served, and the children were given Cokes, each with a stalk of real straw in it rather than a sipper, a touch that intrigued the American youngsters. There were two tables on the terrace for lunch, one for the adults and one for the children. Two palace waiters served each table. The menu included jellied eggs, American-styled grilled chicken, an artichoke salad, cheese and desserts and strawberries from the woods."

Elizabeth Trimble graduated from Wellesley College in 1970 and from the University of Virginia Law School in 1973. After several years as a congressional legislative assistant in Washington, she joined Baltimore's most distinguished law firm, Venable, Baetjer & Howard. But Trimble was driven. In 1978, she became an assistant U.S. attorney.

There had been very few disappointments in the life of this tall young woman as she moved from the comfortable, elegant, and privileged world of one of Baltimore's leading families to the rough-and-tumble battlefield of the federal court. Then came the October 1983 meeting when the senior Justice Department tax lawyer expressed doubts that there was sufficient evidence to proceed against one of the key defendants in the Omni case. Something had to be done to strengthen the attack or three years of IRS investigations could go down the drain.

The investigators held a strategy meeting. The weak point might be Sandra Poe Wilkins, former secretary of the accountant-lawyer who served as Omni's tax adviser and outside counsel. The approach was made, Wilkins was persuaded to talk, and Donald Temple and Paul Mitchell wrote their memorandum of the conversation. Several weeks later, with Washington's doubts apparently resolved, Trimble presented the case to a federal grand jury in Baltimore, and it indicted Omni, three of its executives, and the company's outside lawyer and tax adviser.

But then, with the expert help of some of Washington's toughest and highest-paid legal talent, the roof began to cave in on Trimble and her IRS investigators. A great deal was at stake for Omni. Money. Reputation. Even possible jail sentences. This was no time to economize. An unusually aggressive lawyer from one of Washington's most expensive law firms, Williams & Connolly, was hired. His name was Brendan V. Sullivan, Jr. Relatively unknown at that time, Sullivan a few years later would help marine colonel Oliver North through his political and legal troubles on charges that he lied to Congress about the Reagan administration's secret assistance to the Contras.

The Omni legal team immediately filed a motion to dismiss the charges. At the same time, as is routine in such cases, lawyers representing Omni were granted access to many of the underlying documents prepared during the government's investigation. What they found was shocking. So shocking, in fact, that after twenty-eight days of hearings that took place over a ten-month period, Judge Black threw out of court all of the government's charges against the company and all four men.

The defense lawyers launched a two-pronged attack against Trimble and the two IRS investigators. First, mostly on the basis of the five-hour interview of Sandra Poe Wilkins, the secretary, the Omni lawyers charged that the government had deliberately set out to breach the attorney-client privilege.

But then, as the defense attorneys started to examine the documents provided by the government in response to their request for discovery, the second, even more serious charge emerged: The two IRS agents, with the full knowledge of Trimble, had created, altered, and suppressed key documents and then all of them had lied under oath about what they had done.

It was an astounding allegation. Of course all ambitious young prosecutors want to win their cases. But at the same time, as suggested by its name, the Justice Department has a special obligation to live within the rule of law. The government is not supposed to go around forging documents. But the defense lawyers, with the help of a nationally respected document expert, provided the court with absolute evidence that the government had secretly altered three typewritten documents summarizing evidence, that it added a line to the handwritten interview notes of the crucial interview with Sandra Poe Wilkins, and that it prepared nine or ten additional memos many months after the time when the government claimed they had been written. "Such conduct is wrong and strikes at the heart of the fundamental values in our adversary system of justice," Judge Black wrote. The judge was equally shocked that the three members of the government team had provided the court "a continuous stream of incorrect, misleading and false testimony."

The unshakable witness for the defense was Lyndal L. Shaneyfelt, a retired FBI agent with more than twenty-five years of experience as an expert document examiner. Shaneyfelt discovered, for example, that at least nine of the documents the government claimed had been prepared in 1983 actually were typed on government paper that was not physically in existence until 1984. Other evidence proved that the handwritten notes jotted down at the time of the IRS's interview with Sandra Poe Wilkins were later altered by the addition of a brief phrase intended to prove that the two agents were concerned about avoiding questions that might violate attorney-client privilege.

J. Frederick Motz, the U.S. attorney in Baltimore, was in a difficult position. The federal prosecutor conceded that it was wrong to prepare memoranda in the way that was done in the Omni case. But he was incensed by the attack on Elizabeth Trimble, the belle of Baltimore's legal world. The anger actually led one of Motz's assistants to charge in open court that Brendan Sullivan and a colleague, Barry Simon, were acting like organized-crime hit men. "The government, as it already has indicated, believes that intimidation is the only purpose," said Ty Cobb, an assistant U.S. attorney, in a last-ditch defense of Trimble. "As such, when tactics become personal, and not legal and not factual, [they] are no less chilling on the willingness and ability of federal prosecutors to pursue major white-collar crime cases, than are the death threats routinely received in major narcotic cases. Their message is clear, if you mess with us you will be burned."

Hyperbolic rhetoric was not the only weapon rolled out in a desperate effort to defend the reputation of Trimble and the U.S. Attorney's Office. A second heavy gun was a supporting brief submitted by former Attorney General Benjamin R. Civiletti, who both before and after his stint as the senior law enforcement official of the United States was a partner in Venable, Baetjer & Howard, the establishment law firm where Trimble worked before she became a federal prosecutor.

In his brief defending Trimble, Civiletti said that the cornerstone of the arguments against her was that she and the two IRS agents were engaged in a conspiracy to save the government's case and to further their careers. "Aside from the ludicrous nature of this idea, the defendants have no facts to support the theory. This is not a person engaged in a criminal cover-up; it is a human being trying her best to remember facts, some of which have little obvious importance at the time they occurred. She may have been wrong in some of her recollection, but any mistakes were innocent ones which pale in comparison to her candor and good faith."

Judge Black supported the company and its lawyers and rejected the passionate high-level pleas on behalf of Elizabeth Trimble. "Factually, the misconduct here is not isolated, but longstanding," he declared in his opinion. "Indeed, untrue testimony and a lack of candor permeated the entire ten-month hearing. The government did not proffer the truth about the creation and alteration of the documents during all that time."

On the basis that Trimble, Temple, and Mitchell had engaged in "flagrant and repeated" instances of misconduct, Judge Black dismissed the charges against Omni and the four defendants. Significantly, the government did not appeal this decision.

Omni had won, although at considerable cost. Legal fees are not among those subjects publicly advertised by lawyers and corporations. But Washington attorneys familiar with the world of Brendan Sullivan and the other defense attorneys hired by the company estimate that Omni's legal fees almost certainly were well over $500,000.

Four years later, during a coffee break at a public meeting of senior IRS officials, I fell into a casual conversation with a senior manager in the

Criminal Investigation Division. As we stood in a corner of the room, I asked him why the Omni case had gone wrong. "Okay, I happen to know the characters involved," he told me. "The two investigators are competent men. They started working on Omni and it got more and more complicated. But their supervisor, the chief of CID in Baltimore, kept pushing and pushing them, demanding that they close the case. Under a lot of pressure, they agreed to ask the Tax Division in Justice to go for a prosecution before they had all the evidence they needed. Then, when the case began to fall apart, they and that dumb assistant United States attorney tried to cover their ass."

There is a disturbing footnote about the Omni case and about many other occasions when the IRS has crossed the line in its zealous enforcement of the tax laws: Agency officials involved in questionable activities are seldom punished. Although Judge Black said he did not believe Elizabeth Trimble was guilty of perjury and obstruction of justice, he held that she had indeed taken part in the alteration of government documents and that the testimony she had given "certainly was untrue and wrong in certain places."

Three years later, despite the unchallenged findings of Judge Black about the questionable handling of the Omni case, the Justice Department's Office of Professional Responsibility closed its investigation of the matter after deciding there had been no criminal violation by the prosecutor and the two IRS agents. Shortly thereafter, Elizabeth Trimble resigned. According to a close friend of Temple and Mitchell, the IRS followed the example of the Justice Department and did not take any disciplinary action against the two agents who had worked with her on the Omni case.

Practicing lawyers who have actually read Judge Black's Omni opinion have one of two reactions. A few contend that the excesses of Trimble, Temple, and Mitchell are a genuinely unusual aberration. Many lawyers, however, are worried, convinced that the zealous, anything-to-win tactics are more and more becoming the accepted practice of the government.

Tax criminals cannot be ignored by society. The whole tax system might well collapse if the IRS somehow was bullied into closing its eyes to the minority of citizens who knowingly attempt to cheat their government.

But the American people believe, and the U.S. Constitution guarantees, that the fight will be fair, even if this means that some of the offenders escape.

Two hundred years ago, Madison, Jefferson, Washington, and a few other clever men sat down in Philadelphia and devised what really are a set of ethical rules to guide the new government in the conduct of its business. The assembled statesmen, politicians, and merchants were a tough-minded lot who understood the general fallibility of all men. Their cool acceptance of human imperfection is the principal reason why the Constitution is both a monument to healthy skepticism and an effective check on abusive government.

Congress was to pass no laws concerning the establishment of religion or the control of the press. Executive branch agencies were to make no searches of a citizen's house unless they had good reason to believe the citizen had committed a crime and had persuaded a judge to give them a warrant. The courts were required to bring accused criminals to trial promptly. Because of the danger of torture and more subtle forms of coercion, citizens were never to be forced to give testimony against themselves.

Finally, because the constitutional fathers had no illusions that a good set of rules, standing alone, was sufficient to assure goodness, they devised a governing mechanism that has become known as the separation of powers. Congress and the courts were given general supervisory authority over the executive branch. Specifically in regard to taxation, all tax laws must originate in the House of Representatives, then viewed as the branch of government closest to the voters. Shortly after the new government began to function, the courts successfully asserted their power to rule on the constitutionality of both the laws of Congress and the actions of the executive branch.

Because of the absolute demand for federal revenue, however, the Congress and the courts have chosen to exempt the IRS from many of these checks and balances. This means that in a large proportion of tax cases, the IRS serves at the same time as policeman, prosecutor, judge, and executioner. The conflicts of interest inherent in this arrangement are extreme.

In testimony shortly before he resigned as IRS commissioner, Lawrence B. Gibbs described the challenge inherent in the agency's nearly impossible mission. "While each IRS representative appropriately approaches his or her job with the objective of protecting the government's interest," he said, "the true interest of the government is the impartial enforcement of the tax laws. And this requires that the treatment of taxpayers not be biased in the government's favor."

With an agency as large, complicated, and secretive as the IRS, it is impossible to define with any kind of precision how frequently overzealous agents abuse individual taxpayers. With no precise measure, it is even easy to deny that problems exist. But an examination of a number of specific cases suggests that parts of the agency have become infected with an attitude of self-righteous zealotry. The conclusion that the known cases of overzealous enforcement are not simply the work of rogue agents is reinforced by a careful analysis of the legal and administrative framework in which the agency operates.

Daniel Heller of Miami. Ronald McKelvey of Yuma. Bob Anderson and Joe O'Dorisio of Denver. Shannon Burns of San Jose. Donald Thurow of San Francisco. The executives of the Omni Corporation in Maryland. These are just a few of the recent victims of the zealotry of the IRS. When looked at as a whole, their experiences present us with strong evidence of just how important, and difficult, it is to assure that the nation's most powerful agency does its job in an evenhanded way that targets the guilty without damaging the innocent.

CHAPTER 8

Bribes, Boodle, and Buyoffs

By the spring of 1984, Stanley D. Welli, George Ecola, and Ron Koperniak, three middle-level IRS officials in the agency's Inspection Division office in Chicago, had become so concerned about the behavior of their immediate boss that they decided they had to act.

Welli, Ecola, and Koperniak were part of a special IRS investigating unit with the mission of combating corruption and mismanagement within the agency. What so disturbed them was evidence that their supervisor, Frank V. Santella, the assistant chief of inspection in the IRS's Midwest Region, was doing improper tax favors for Chicago businessmen who were doing favors for Santella.[1]

Fellow IRS workers had told the three men, for example, that Santella had provided agency tax information to a businessman friend who at the time owed the government about $400,000 in unpaid employment taxes. They also had evidence indicating that Santella was associating with disreputable persons, including one man who had been on an FBI list of Chicago area organized-crime figures. In return for the agency's improper assistance, Santella had indiscreetly informed some of his IRS colleagues, the businessmen had given him a number of gratuities. These included free lunches and dinners at a restaurant favored by organized crime, free theater tickets, invitations to important Democratic political affairs, and, on one occasion, "a huge package of steaks, chops and roasts" for his freezer.

Welli, Ecola, and Koperniak were shocked that any IRS employee would place himself in such a compromising position. But for a top official specifically responsible for maintaining the integrity and efficiency of all IRS employees in a nine-state area of the Midwest stretching from Illinois and Wisconsin in the east to Montana in the west, Santella's actions were unthinkable.

In May 1984, the three officials decided that Santella's special assistance to favored businessmen was so serious a breach of agency rules and practices, and perhaps even the law, that they felt compelled to act. At a confidential meeting with Joe Jech, the regional inspector for the IRS's Midwest Region, who also was Santella's immediate boss, the whistle-blowers formally informed the IRS of their allegations.

Jech did not forward the charges to Washington, even though this was required by IRS regulations. Instead, he privately advised Santella that his actions had created an "appearance" of impropriety. Almost a year went by. In April 1985, despairing that Jech would ever act and convinced that Santella's behavior had grown even more improper, Welli, Ecola, and Koperniak decided their only choice was to contact Washington directly. They dispatched a written report summarizing their charges to Robert L. Rebein, then the top IRS inspection official for the entire United States.

The news that the three Chicago-area men had blown the whistle on their boss immediately became widely known within the ranks of the Inspection Division. It was not well received. In fact, the whistle-blowers were viewed as traitors. All three became the targets of a continuing campaign of verbal abuse by Inspection Division officials from different parts of the country. On one occasion, for example, a regional inspector based in Atlanta warned the three inspectors during an IRS meeting that "the organization will get you, you whores."

Some time later, Jech and Santella began working on an unusual reorganization plan for the Midwest Region. The plan they began to push through the IRS's massive bureaucracy would have had a curiously narrow impact: One of the three whistle-blowers would lose his management position, the second would be demoted, and the third would face the possibility of a downgrade.

In Washington, meanwhile, eleven months after Welli, Ecola, and Koperniak had first filed their complaint with Jech, the IRS initiated a tardy investigation of Santella. A few weeks later, in a report dated June 21, 1985, the national office investigators confirmed that Santella had been associating with disreputable persons, accepting gratuities, and ordering IRS employees to conduct improper tax research for at least six different taxpayers. The Treasury Department inspector general concluded in his own analysis that the IRS investigation showed that Santella had clearly violated the rules of the IRS and criminal provisions of the Federal Code. Despite these seemingly serious findings, however, Santella's immediate boss, Joe Jech, decided that only a comparatively mild punishment was called for: Santella was given a twelve-day suspension without pay.

The decision to discipline Santella at all irritated the senior officials of the Inspection Division. They were sufficiently annoyed, in fact, that two regional inspectors and seven assistant regional inspectors thumbed their noses at the IRS by chipping in at least $820 to a solidarity fund intended to make up some of the salary lost by Santella during his brief suspension.

Surprisingly, the report that Santella had violated a number of important IRS regulations and that his supervisor, Jech, had failed to deal with the problem promptly, did not result in either of the officials losing their management jobs. From these quite senior positions, Santella and Jech continued to urge approval of the reorganization plan that, if adopted, initially would have affected the careers of the three men who had criticized them.

Washington approved the reorganization in November of 1988. Welli was told his management position would be abolished. Koperniak was informed that he could either transfer to Kansas City or be demoted. Ecola, who was known to have medical problems that made it difficult for him to move from Chicago, also was told he must make the Kansas City move or face a downgrade. The first step in an exquisite little bit of bureaucratic torture had been taken.

Further negotiations went nowhere, and Welli filed a formal grievance. On May 21, 1987, the IRS ruled there was no evidence of retaliation. Welli appealed the ruling and, as required by agency regulation, an independent grievance examiner with no knowledge of the individuals or events involved began yet another review of the case.

On November 10, 1987, the examiner ruled that it was "quite evident that retaliation took place and continues to exist. My recommendation is that all retaliation be stopped. Those individuals responsible [for the harassment] must be made accountable so that future retaliation does not take place."

The IRS still refused to admit error. When it appeared that the agency was going to sit on the grievance examiner's embarrassing report, the persistent whistle-blowers decided that they had to go outside the agency for protection. They prepared an eighteen-page single-spaced report describing Santella's improper activities, the agency's reluctance to deal with these problems, and the personal harassment they had undergone since bringing the charges to the attention of the IRS. On February 24, 1988, they sent the letter to several key members of Congress, with a copy to the commissioner.

Shortly thereafter, apparently fearful of possible congressional interest, the IRS offered Welli an extraordinary deal, a proposal that certainly bore some of the appearances of a bribe. The agency still refused to rescind the punitive reorganization plan. But it said it would settle Welli's grievance by providing him with a comfortable private office and reimbursing him for his legal fees. All Welli had to do in return was to promise he would never talk about the deal. Welli refused the offer, demanding instead that he be restored to his original position, that both Jech and Santella be removed from the Inspection Division, and that the IRS reimburse him for his legal expenses.

The IRS rejected Welli's counterproposal, and on March 18, 1988, it issued a decision formally rejecting the grievance examiner's conclusions and recommendations. One month later, however, Teddy Kern was chosen to be the new head of the Inspection Division. On April 25, he flew to Chicago and restored the three men to their original jobs.

Joe Jech, the executive who refused to send the original allegations against Santella to Washington, insisted during a telephone interview in the summer of 1988 that he had handled the matter in a proper manner. Shortly after our conversation, however, Jech was removed from his executive position in Chicago and assigned to a less prestigious staff position in Washington. Although no criminal charges were brought against Santella, the official quietly resigned from the IRS and took an inspections job with another federal agency. Once again, the IRS had avoided taking any serious disciplinary actions against two of its senior executives who had broken the agency's rules.

Even if the failure to promptly investigate Santella and the subsequent harassment of the three whistle-blowers had been isolated events, they would have been disturbing. First, a senior executive of the Inspection Division had been corrupted. Second, the Inspection Division had turned on the men who had reported the problem and had sought to prevent an investigation of it. Third, the Inspection official who tried to suppress the investigation was never disciplined.

There is considerable evidence, however, that the underlying agency problems suggested by the IRS's flawed handling of the Santella affair and the subsequent harassment of the whistle-blowers are not all that unusual; that attempts to corrupt the IRS are far more common than is believed; and that the agency's anticorruption efforts have long been marred by serious underfunding, favoritism, incompetence, and secret efforts by the IRS to block public knowledge of such flaws.

LOS ANGELES

Ronald Saranow was the head of the Criminal Investigation Division in Los Angeles for more than a decade, from 1977 until his retirement in 1988. For most of that time, he was considered the smartest and toughest chief of the best-run criminal investigating unit in the IRS.

Saranow had first joined the IRS in 1962. Five years later, he quit the agency to become an officer with the Elmhurst Liquor Company in Chicago. When Saranow returned to the IRS in December 1971, he told me in a 1988 interview, he was investigated by the agency for alleged connections with organized crime. The investigation, he said, had been triggered by his attempts to help an old childhood friend who was a hoodlum. Saranow said that in the end no evidence had been found that substantiated the suspicions about him held by some IRS officials in Washington.

Overcoming this somewhat shaky start to his second hitch in the IRS, Saranow almost immediately was determined to be a star. Five years after his return to the IRS he was appointed the assistant chief of the Criminal Investigation Division in Los Angeles. Shortly thereafter, he became the head of what was then the largest such unit in the nation.[2]

For a long time, Saranow retained his reputation as one of the most effective managers in the IRS. But by almost all accounts he was arrogant and strong-willed, and all along, especially after 1985, some special agents in Los Angeles found his use of IRS power questionable.

On November 16, 1987, an investigative reporter named Richard Behar wrote an article in *Forbes* magazine charging that a flamboyant Los Angeles clothing company named Guess? Inc. had improperly influenced Saranow in an effort to damage the reputation and financial standing of its major commercial competitor in New York. Behar's charges against Guess? and Saranow were investigated by the House Commerce, Consumer, and Monetary Affairs Subcommittee. On July 25, 1989, the congressional investigators presented the findings of their year-and-a-half-long probe to the subcommittee's members.

Their conclusion: Saranow had "used his reputation as one of the most powerful Criminal Investigation Division chiefs in the country to encourage two criminal investigations against the 'enemies' " of a company that had offered him a high-paying job.

Almost as disturbing as the criticism of Saranow, however, were the findings of the subcommittee's investigators about how the IRS responded to the alarms raised by Behar, which concerned both agents within the IRS and a man named Octavio Pena. Pena, a security consultant, worked for Jordache, the New York competitor of Guess? that had become the target of the questionable IRS raid.

"When individuals both inside and outside of the IRS finally raised serious questions about the legality and propriety of Mr. Saranow's conduct, the Service initiated what can only be described as untimely and inept internal investigations," the House investigators said.

The ineffectiveness of the IRS's investigations of Saranow, the report continued, "can be traced to the overly close relationship between the Los Angeles Inspection and Criminal Investigation Divisions; the refusal of the National Office to follow the advice of its own chief inspector that only high officials in Washington, D.C., could properly manage the probe; and the IRS's institutional mindset that disclosure of serious wrongdoing by its senior managers would be an unacceptable black mark on its public image."

Guess? officials have repeatedly denied any wrongdoing. In a statement issued on the first day of the House hearings, they said the findings of the subcommittee's investigators were "untrue and irresponsible." The officials also flatly denied ever offering Saranow a job. In the same statement, the company attacked Peter Barash, the subcommittee's staff director, suggesting he had a personal dispute with the IRS. About one week before the often postponed hearings were finally held, the subcommittee invited Guess? executives to present publicly their side of the dispute. Guess? lawyers informed the subcommittee that previously arranged vacation plans made such an appearance impossible.

In response to an inquiry from me after the hearing, Marshall B. Grossman, a leading Guess? lawyer, again denied that Saranow ever had been offered a job. He added that the preliminary discussions between the company and the IRS official about his possible employment had occurred after the IRS had raided the New York office of Jordache. "It is, therefore, absurd for anyone to suggest that any discussion of employment with or indeed offer of employment to Mr. Saranow in 1986 could have had any influence or impact whatsoever on the investigation in New York."

Grossman also said that the investigation by the subcommittee "was frankly sloppy and one-sided" and had ignored judicial findings in several related cases that supported his contention that Guess? had been victimized by Jordache and its chief investigator, Octavio Pena, rather than the other way around. He concluded that members of the press, including myself, had been "badly misled."

Saranow, in his 1988 interview with me, admitted that the situation with Guess? looked "suspicious." He contended, however, that "there was absolutely nothing improper in my activities." The former IRS official was not called to testify by the subcommittee after his lawyer informed the staff that Saranow would invoke his Fifth Amendment privilege against possible self-incrimination and would not answer any questions.

The report noted that on May 23, 1989, the Washington attorney for Guess? had informed Representative Doug Barnard, Jr., the chairman, that the company had maintained "an arm's-length relationship with Saranow." The report challenged this assertion, noting that during an internal interview by the IRS Saranow himself had said he was a "front man" for the company. In addition, the report said that evidence from depositions, sworn testimony, IRS files, and subcommittee interviews clearly showed that Saranow met with the brothers who owned Guess? "over 20 times between April 1985 and December 1986. At least 14 of these meetings can be described as social contacts—lunches, dinners, parties, weddings—where various subjects, such as Saranow's future employment with Guess?, were discussed."

The report said that there was strong evidence that Saranow began negotiating with Guess? for a job in late 1985. One senior IRS official testified to the subcommittee staff that Saranow had told him that he (Saranow) was talking about receiving a "six figure salary" from Guess? This statement was buttressed by a former assistant director of the Los Angeles office of the IRS who also testified that Saranow had told him that he was going to work for Guess?. Saranow himself, in later sworn testimony to the IRS, said that he had had lunch with one of the company's executives on March 26, 1986, at which time a job was offered, complete with salary, company car, and bonus.

During the time when, several subcommittee witnesses said, Saranow was negotiating for a job with Guess? the Los Angeles official was urging the New York office of the Criminal Investigation Division to go after Jordache. The two companies were then engaged in a massive contractual dispute involving hundreds of million of dollars.

At 8:30 A.M. on January 28, 1986, fifty IRS and U.S. customs agents burst into the New York headquarters of Jordache. After two days of rummaging through the company's files, they carted off more than 1 million documents. Three and a half years later, the grand jury has yet to indict anyone.

At the time of this writing, the Justice Department has convened a second grand jury in New York to reexamine how and why the original investigation was ever started. This new investigation was launched even though the IRS on March 24, 1988, wrote to Rudolph Giuliani, then the U.S. Attorney in New York, assuring him that the handling of the case by Saranow involved "no evidence of wrongdoing." (The subcommittee called the IRS's letter to Giuliani another cover-up by the agency.)

The Saranow case raises one key question: Who is actually running the Criminal Investigation Division? Are the vast investigative powers of the IRS directed by independent and professional officials seeking to enforce the tax laws in a firm and evenhanded way? Or is an important part of the agency actually directed by the professional investigators hired by combative companies that seek to use the government's power to destroy their competitors?

WASHINGTON, D.C.

From 1986 to 1988 Anthony V. Langone was the man nominally in charge of all criminal investigations conducted by the IRS. Langone, among the most senior IRS officials in the nation, very much appreciated the perks of his office. But there were many in the IRS who did not appreciate him and his imperious ways, especially with women. One of those was his secretary. On September 9, 1986, according to the subcommittee investigators, she informed the head of the Inspection Division that Langone was improperly charging the IRS for air travel to Atlanta to visit a female friend. Without examining Langone's travel vouchers to determine the truth or falsity of the secretary's charges, the head of the Inspection Division decided that no action was warranted.[3]

In November 1986, a second warning about Langone came to the assistant commissioner for inspection, this time from a senior technical adviser in the Criminal Investigation Division named Chuck Wey. He too was worried about the circuitous routes traveled by Langone to see his friend, noting in particular a trip from Seattle to Washington, D.C., via Atlanta. Once again the Inspection Division did not initiate an investigation.

The third notice about Langone's abusive travel habits was made to the Inspection Division on April 23, 1987. The assistant commissioner for inspection later told investigators for the House Government Operations

Subcommittee on Commerce, Consumer, and Monetary Affairs that he consulted with the second-most-senior official in the IRS about how the matter should be handled. The subcommittee found this consultation disturbing because it provided evidence suggesting that the Inspection Division was dominated by the senior executives of the IRS.

The joint decision of the deputy commissioner and the head of the Inspection Division was to handle Langone's indiscretions in an administrative way without a formal investigation. On July 1, 1987, the acting associate commissioner for IRS Operations met with Langone to warn him that his travel arrangements were under scrutiny. Langone denied making any improper trips. For the third time, the matter was dropped.

By that time, the IRS later determined, Langone had made eighteen trips through Atlanta as head of the Criminal Investigation Division. Nine of these trips were made for personal reasons but were paid for by the IRS.

Despite the July warning, the subcommittee investigators said, Langone continued his old ways. On Saturday, February 13, 1988, for example, Langone traveled to San Juan, Puerto Rico, on an unlikely travel extension added to an official round trip between Washington, D.C., and Los Angeles. Because Monday was a holiday and Langone took a day of leave on Tuesday, the official enjoyed a pleasant three-day escape from the nastiness of Washington's February weather. Langone, the House subcommittee later reported, "did not reimburse the government for the additional $294 for air fare expenses incurred as a result of his extended travel itinerary. Interestingly, his female friend was on official travel in Puerto Rico at the same time."

In March 1988, Langone retired to set up a private detective company with Criminal Investigation chiefs in Newark, Dallas, and Los Angeles without reimbursing the government for about $2,000 worth of personal travel that he had charged to the IRS. (One of his partners in the new venture was Ron Sarenow, whose hopes of becoming a Guess? executive had gone awry.)

The Langone matter would have ended there except for the fact that on May 26, 1988, during my preparation of this book, I interviewed the new assistant commissioner for inspection, Teddy R. Kern. During the course of our talk I asked Kern about angry allegations I had heard from IRS agents that Langone had used government resources for personal benefit. Pleading the restrictions of the Privacy Act, Kern declined to make any comment on Langone. But on June 2, a little more than a week after the interview, Inspection opened an investigation of the just-retired official. Without my knowledge, my name was placed on the complaint. About four months later, on October 14, a report charging Langone with improperly billing the IRS for $2,000 worth of travel and several other offenses was forwarded to the Justice Department. The question: Were criminal charges warranted? As of July 1989, the matter was still pending.

In an interview with me after the House hearings that described these events, Langone denied any wrongdoing and insisted his claims for official travel expenses were proper. Langone also said that the presentation of the subcommittee's report had violated his civil liberties. Leonard Bernard, one of the subcommittee's investigators, said that Langone had refused to be interviewed about the handling of his travel expenses. Langone insisted, however, that he had wanted to talk with the subcommittee staff. He said arrangements for the interview had fallen apart because of a dispute over whether his attorney could sit in on the session.

Representative Barnard said at the July 1989 hearing of his subcommittee that the handling of the Langone and Santella cases, along with several others, showed how the IRS actively sought to avoid if at all possible the investigation of senior agency officials.

"Our investigation indicates that there are serious integrity problems among senior managers at the IRS; inadequate internal investigation and punishment of senior-level misconduct; a pervasive fear at all levels of the IRS over retaliation for the reporting of such conduct; and a driving concern that publicly exposing wrongdoing by senior managers will tarnish the agency's image and make its tax enforcement responsibilities more difficult," Barnard said.

CINCINNATI

It must surely be embarrassing to the IRS to have the public learn about cases where it failed to investigate senior agency officials who take gratuities from influential people or cheat the government on their travel expenses. But it must be even more embarrassing when the public gets wind of a high-level IRS manager who appears to have cheated on his taxes for a number of years without being spotted by the agency. After all, catching tax cheats is supposed to be the IRS's job.

John E. McManus became an upper-level manager in the IRS's Central Region Inspection Division in 1971. The Central Region is a five-state area embracing Michigan, Ohio, Indiana, Kentucky, and West Virginia. McManus and his wife had three sons and a daughter, and neighbors describe them as a wonderful all-American family. When the boys were young, for example, the IRS manager was an active coach in the Little League.

McManus also seemed to be a model employee, rapidly moving up the chain of command within the Inspection Division during his twenty-five years with the agency. By dint of a lot of hard work, he was named the top inspector of the region on January 4, 1987. McManus was confident enough of his position within the IRS to praise openly the work of the Inspection Division. In the upside-down world of the IRS, even talking about the Inspection Division was regarded as mildly risky because it implicitly acknowledged the possibility of corruption and poor management. "It is important for Americans to have confidence in their government," he once told a reporter. "It only seems logical that we [in Inspection] should monitor an agency for its honesty and efficiency when it is paid for by the people of America."[4]

When McManus spoke these words, it is unlikely that he saw himself as the target for such monitoring. But sometime in late 1985 or early 1986, Cliff Hargrove, a special IRS agent in Memphis, Tennessee, was given a very sensitive assignment: investigate charges that McManus was engaged in criminal tax fraud. Hargrove went to work on the case, collecting a great deal of incriminating evidence.

In the summer of 1987, IRS records show, the forty-seven-year-old McManus quietly arranged to retire from the agency, his pension intact. On the surface, it was a routine departure. But documents from the U.S. Tax Court and interviews with one current and two former IRS officials indicate otherwise. In fact, just a few months before McManus retired, the Justice Department decided not to act on an IRS recommendation that he be indicted on criminal tax charges. As is normal in tax cases where the option of criminal prosecution is declined by the Justice Department, the evidence concerning McManus's tax-paying habits was referred to another part of the IRS for consideration as a civil case.

On April 15, 1988, the director of the IRS office in Nashville sent John and Alice McManus a letter of deficiency charging them with fraudulently failing to pay all the taxes they owed in 1984. Several weeks later, the couple received a second letter making the same charges for the 1980, 1983, and 1985 tax years. The IRS said that the grand total of their debt to the government was $64,484.14—$37,083.12 in back taxes and $27,-401.02 in fraud penalties and interest. Letters such as those charging McManus and his wife with civil tax fraud are confidential documents that are usually never disclosed to anyone other than the taxpayer and the taxpayer's tax advisers. They become public documents, however, when that taxpayer challenges the IRS in court. The McManuses took this step on May 9, 1988. Through their lawyer, the couple denied most of the agency's charges.

As is normal in such situations, the IRS responded to the McManuses' claim of innocence with a formal answer that also became part of the public file. The IRS commentary about John McManus was pointed. "As a result of his training and education as well as the positions which John E. McManus has held with the Internal Revenue Service, Mr. McManus has a better than average knowledge of Federal tax laws and related matters and, as an employee, he was regularly reminded of his obligation to file timely and accurate tax returns," said Elsie Hall, an IRS litigation specialist, on October 3, 1988.

Despite this special knowledge and responsibility, Hall continued, "almost every item on petitioners' returns for the taxable years 1983, 1984 and 1985 has a proposed adjustment. Petitioner John E. McManus omitted taxable income from dividends, interest, capital gains and medical reimbursements and he intentionally overstated deductions for numerous business expenses, overstated his Schedule A itemized deductions, and claimed false business losses and investment tax credits. The cumulative effect of these false entries was the understatement of taxable income and income taxes on the returns filed for the years 1983 through 1985, inclusive, and the understatement of income tax for 1980 as a result of the carryback of the false investment tax credits from 1983."

To the outsider it would appear that the system had worked, that the IRS had moved against McManus in a straightforward way. But the appearances may be deceptive in at least two important ways.

First, according to the House Government Operations Subcommittee, one of the disturbing aspects of the McManus case is that its review of the financial disclosure statements that the official was routinely required to file with the IRS on an annual basis "indicated that behavior related to the alleged tax fraud began a number of years before he was investigated." Why, the subcommittee asked, given the questions raised by the information in the financial disclosure forms, had the agency waited so long to investigate McManus, an official holding a highly sensitive IRS post?

The second question relates to whether McManus should have faced criminal tax charges rather than civil ones. According to interviews with Ellen Murphy, head of the IRS public affairs office, and Vernon Acree, head of the Inspection Division from 1952 to 1973, the agency sent the Justice Department a recommendation that McManus be indicted for criminal tax fraud, a far more serious matter. During the debate within the Justice Department about this recommendation, McManus was represented by Sheldon Cohen, the IRS commissioner during the Johnson administration. According to both Acree and Murphy, Cohen's effort was

successful and no criminal charges were brought against the former regional inspector. Cohen was reluctant to talk about the McManus case,
limiting himself to one brief comment. "The question was whether this
was a foolish young man or a criminal young man," the former commissioner said from the vantage point of his sixty-two years.

Four IRS agents who were shown the civil charges that were brought
against McManus were more judgmental: They unanimously agreed that
McManus's avoidance of criminal prosecution was highly unusual. "In
most parts of the country, with the possible exceptions of maybe New
York City, Miami, and Los Angeles, any citizen or low-level IRS employee
who did what McManus has been accused of doing almost certainly would
have been indicted on criminal tax charges," said one of the members of
my expert IRS jury.

Except for the denials of wrongdoing included in McManus's Tax
Court filings, the former IRS official, speaking through his Cincinnati
lawyer, Kenneth R. Hughes, declined to comment on his tax problems
and how they had been handled by the IRS. As of September 1989, the
civil tax charges were still pending against McManus.

Chicago, Los Angeles, Washington, and Cincinnati. Four cases. Four
situations where the IRS's determination to confront the questionable
behavior of its senior executives seemed to collapse. But are these matters
isolated events or are they part of a larger problem that infected the entire
agency?

When IRS commissioners and their deputies speak to the public about
this question they always emphasize that corruption within the agency is
a rare event that should not be used to detract from its overall integrity.

In private forums, however, they sing a somewhat different song. In
January 1989, faced by an impending congressional investigation, the top
managers of the IRS acknowledged the breadth of their concern about
the corruption problem. The occasion was the decision of the IRS to
launch a "strategic initiative" to improve its handling of corruption
throughout the agency.[5]

In a brief summary document, the IRS said that the management
failures identified by the congressional investigators were one reason for
the new initiative. A second factor, however, was a never-announced study
conducted by the IRS itself that seemed to confirm the fears of the
harshest congressional critics.

The study's conclusion: There was "a compelling need to address both
systematic shortfalls in the effectiveness of our integrity training and

instruction, and individual failures to identify and report integrity breaches" once they had occurred.

There are many explanations for the acknowledged inadequacy of the IRS's attack on corruption. But one of the most important is the attitude of the senior managers toward what is surely one of the oldest and most persistent problems of any enforcement agency. Corruption, they inevitably argue, is the product of the ubiquitous "rotten apple in the barrel." The bad apple is a comforting symbol for all officials because it distracts public attention from the far more disturbing thought that the rottenness may lie in the barrel, not in the apple.

Corruption does indeed involve the moral collapse of isolated individuals. Each case of corruption, however, is also prima facie evidence of pervasive poor management. It is a sign of ineffective leadership at the top, inadequate supervision in the middle, and poor recruiting and training at the bottom. Certainly the evidence that has emerged during the recent spate of IRS corruption cases strongly suggests that the real problem was not the lapse of individual agents from the normal standards of good behavior, but rather the failure of leadership in the agency's national, regional, and district offices.

Effectively managing a large government agency like the IRS is probably one of the most difficult jobs in the world. It is hard to select the right people as supervisors. It is difficult to maintain the morale of an agency whose basic mission is not generally popular with the public. It is an extraordinary challenge to encourage low-paid employees to do their work while at the same time respecting the rights of citizens. But fighting corruption may well be the most challenging task of all.

The job of assuring the integrity of the IRS currently rests on the shoulders of Teddy R. Kern, a serious man, a trained accountant, and a highly regarded IRS official. At the time we met in May 1988, Kern had just been appointed as the new assistant commissioner for inspections. During a long interview, Kern told me that he and the other senior managers of the IRS fully understood that there was almost nothing as important as maintaining the integrity of the IRS. In fact, Kern said, because citizen cooperation was essential to tax collection, citizen belief in the fundamental integrity of the IRS actually was essential to the survival of the nation.

Although Kern appeared to be completely sincere in his views, there is considerable evidence that at least for the last few years the top managers of the IRS have not fully shared his convictions about integrity.

In response to one of my questions, for example, Kern provided me with figures showing that management had in the past ten years allowed the size of its anticorruption forces to decline gradually in relation to the overall size of the agency. In fiscal year 1979, for example, 1,102 of the agency's 81,505 employees were assigned to the Inspection Division. In fiscal year 1988, the number of Inspection Division employees was virtually unchanged, 1,202, but the agency had grown to 123,000. This means that the responsibility of each individual working in Inspection had expanded from 74 agency employees in 1979 to 102 in 1988.

Along with the decline in the relative size of the Inspection Division has come an apparent drop in the agency's investigative curiosity about bribery. At least this is one conclusion that can be drawn from a series of IRS reports describing the agency's use of secret recording devices to investigate all kinds of tax crimes. In this case, the devices, usually worn under the clothing of a person who is cooperating with the IRS, are designed to record the comments of an unwary investigative target. The reports show a sharp 96 percent increase in the use of these devices for all kinds of investigations during a recent six-year period. In fiscal year 1983, for example, the IRS mobilized body mikes in 519 cases. In fiscal year 1985, it reported 944 such cases. In 1987, there were 1,016.

The same reports showed, however, that the IRS was far less enthusiastic when it came to using body mikes for one sensitive group of cases: bribery. In this category, during the same six-year period, the secret surveillance increased by only 11 percent—349 in fiscal year 1983, 389 in fiscal year 1987.

Not surprisingly, the gradual decline in the relative size of the Inspection Division and the cooling of its investigative ardor appear to have resulted in steadily smaller harvests. In 1985, for example, Inspection Division investigations resulted in corruption charges against 291 individuals. That figure dropped to 235 in 1986 and 199 in 1987. As already noted, of course, during the period when the number of corruption cases was declining by about 30 percent, the total number of IRS employees was increasing by about 10 percent.

Kern and I talked about yet another small sign of the IRS's lukewarm interest in corruption. In an agency as powerful and decentralized as the IRS, the investigations conducted by the anticorruption agents clearly should not be limited to low-level tax collectors. Obviously, any serious program to control corruption must also include serious investigations of possible problems among the thousands of middle- and senior-level managers who direct the daily operation of the agency.

The IRS recognized this vulnerability in 1952, when it created a little-known unit within national headquarters in Washington called the Inspection Branch (IB). The function of the IB is to investigate possible corruption among the IRS's managers and top officials.

But the IB is a charade. Even Kern acknowledged as much when he told me that this elite IRS unit now has a grand total of eight investigators. "Clearly, if you just look at the number of investigators in the IB, you would draw the conclusion, considering what they are responsible for, that they cannot do it," Kern said. The assistant commissioner contended, however, that such a conclusion was not valid because the eight investigators were able to obtain help from other offices of the IRS when such assistance was needed.

In very different ways, Frank Santella in Chicago, Ronald Saranow in Los Angeles, Anthony Langone in Washington, D.C., John McManus in Cincinnati, and Teddy Kern in Washington tell us that the IRS effort to control corruption within its ranks has been withering. Serious cases have been sloughed off or ignored, and the agency's anticorruption forces have been gradually undermined.

But the insights into the Inspection Division provided by these four case studies and Kern's interview don't answer two related questions: How often do American taxpayers try to bribe IRS agents? How frequently do IRS agents succumb to these corrupt offers? The answers, of course, depend somewhat on where you look.

In the fall of 1986, a federal judge in Philadelphia sentenced an accountant named William Kale to ten years in prison. Kale had been convicted of accepting a series of bribes totaling $105,000 in return for his part in helping a thriving Philadelphia investment company largely owned by Robert and Sam Saligman to avoid paying at least $8 million in federal taxes. For most of his working life, the sixty-one-year-old Philadelphian had been a trusted agent of the IRS.

Kale was one of ten IRS employees and former employees and ten wealthy business executives from the Philadelphia area who in 1985 and 1986 were convicted for their involvement in a large number of different bribery schemes. Benjamin J. Redmond, head of all inspection activities in the agency's Mid-Atlantic region, contends that the successful investigation of Kale and the nineteen other assorted grafters in one brief two-year period proves the effectiveness and dedication of the IRS's war against corruption.

Redmond admitted, however, that the evidence presented during the Kale trial alone showed that it had taken the IRS more than twenty-five years to discover that representatives of the Saligman family who had regularly been bribing Kale during the first part of the 1980s had also been handing out boodle to a long string of agents during most of the 1960s and the 1970s. The testimony and handwritten notes of the corporate accountant who had actually paid most of the bribes for the corporate entity of this single Philadelphia family indicated that the illegal payments totaled well over $500,000.

The failure of the IRS to detect a corruption case of such massive and systematic proportions for more than a quarter of a century suggests unpleasant answers to the questions about the willingness of American taxpayers and IRS agents to offer and to accept bribes. The case also reinforces the conclusion that the agency's ability to fight corruption within its ranks is inadequate.

Let's begin the Saligman story in 1946, the year that Israel Saligman died. Saligman, creator and president of the Queen Knitting Mills, was survived by his wife; three sons, Robert, Martin, and Samuel; and a stepson. His estate was valued at a modest $50,000.

The postwar boom years, however, brought great wealth to the Saligmans. A real-estate company, Cynwyd Investments, was formed and prospered mightily. One sign of the family's increasing importance in the community came in June 1957 when the board of directors of the respected Albert Einstein Medical Center voted to bring Robert Saligman into the fold. Robert was by then living at a prestigious address on Rittenhouse Square. His brother Samuel had recently bought "Brookwood," a seven-acre suburban estate that he loyally renamed "Queen Acres," apparently in honor of the thriving garment factory developed by his father. The value of some Atlantic City real estate, purchased for $1.5 million by a syndicate headed by Robert Saligman, quadrupled after New Jersey voters approved legalized gambling there. In October 1974, Alice Saligman, wife of Robert, was named the general chairwoman of the Harvest Ball Benefit Dance for the Albert Einstein Medical Center. Alice Saligman's social raised $60,000, then a record for that event. By the early 1980s the family's holdings were valued at approximately $40 million.

Although the family obviously had flourished, there were some early signs of possible financial irregularities. In 1962, for example, the Pennsylvania Department of Revenue announced an investigation of whether or not sufficient taxes had been paid by Robert Saligman in connection with his purchase of a shopping center for $4.2 million.

At about the same time, another event occurred that eventually would come to haunt the Saligman family. By 1965 the business of Cynwyd Investments had become sufficiently complex that it was decided that an in-house professional was needed to keep track of its finances. The family-owned company selected an ambitious young accountant named Charles Toll to handle the complex bookkeeping required for its joint ventures. Fifteen years later, in 1980, the family rewarded Toll for his faithful service by making him Cynwyd's chief operating officer. According to Harry Jaffe, an experienced *Philadelphia* magazine reporter, during this period Toll gradually became an important social figure in his own right. "He went to all the right parties and fund raising events. He also had become chairman of the Moss Rehabilitation Hospital, an important Jewish charity," Jaffe recounted.[6]

But the world was about to unravel for Toll and the family he had served so long. On May 15, 1984, IRS investigators subpoenaed all the books of Cynwyd Investments. The ledgers suggested that Toll had embezzled millions of dollars from the Saligman family. From at least 1968 to 1984, he appeared to have underreported the company's income, overcharged expenses, and siphoned off a substantial stream of cash to a secret bank account. Altogether, Toll later admitted, he probably had skimmed off at least $3 million for himself.

Toll immediately knew he was in serious trouble, and he hired one of Philadelphia's best criminal lawyers to help him minimize the time in prison he almost certainly faced. While the evidence against Toll was extremely damaging—a thirty-year prison sentence was possible—the government had other, more pressing interests. For several years, the federal prosecutor in charge of the investigation, an assistant U.S. attorney named Terri Marinari, had been handling a string of cases in which wealthy Philadelphia businessmen had been found to be bribing IRS agents. When Marinari was ready to ask the grand jury to indict Toll, she approached his lawyer to see if Toll would cooperate with the government. A deal was cut. Toll would plead guilty to charges of bribery, tax evasion, and mail fraud. Marinari would ask the judge to give Toll a thirty-month sentence.

In return, Toll would tell a federal jury everything he knew about corruption within the IRS, and that, it turned out, was a great deal. His successful efforts to undermine the fair enforcement of the tax laws, he later would testify, went back almost thirty years and resulted in the payment of secret bribes to at least a dozen different agents.

Toll's testimony was unusually valuable because over the years an uncanny protective instinct had led him to keep handwritten notes about many of his bribes. These records tended to support Toll's testimony, making it almost impossible for the defense to argue that he had fabricated the mammoth IRS conspiracy in an effort to save his neck.

HARD EVIDENCE

The trial of William Kale, with Charles Toll as the principal witness for the prosecution, began in a federal courtroom in Philadelphia on Tuesday, July 8, 1986. With assistant U.S. attorney Terri Marinari asking the questions, the fifty-four-year-old certified public accountant spent much of his first day in court quietly recounting a seemingly endless series of corrupt arrangements he had worked out with a long list of IRS agents.

Toll testified that he had initially become aware of the Saligman family practice of paying bribes shortly after graduating from Temple University in the mid-1950s. One of his first jobs was with an independent accounting firm that the Saligmans had hired to prepare their taxes. "Okay, there was [IRS agent] Vincent Maurelli who was paid a bribe for 1957" of "between one and two thousand dollars," Toll recalled.

The accountant told the jury, however, that even within the bureaucracy of the IRS the competitive spirit of the free-enterprise system was always a factor. "Then there was Frank O'Neal," Toll said. "There was a conflict between Frank O'Neal and Maurelli for control of the examination [of the Saligman returns]. Payments were made to both."

Toll recalled other lessons he had learned in the first years of his career. "It was a very common practice for accountants who handled bribes [for the taxpayer] to keep a portion of the money."

"When you say this is a common practice, what do you mean?" Marinari asked.

"I am referring to if an internal revenue agent was going to be bribed to overlook certain transactions and not collect the proper amount of tax, an accountant was taking a great deal of exposure in making the payments. So generally he would tell his client that if he were paying a bribe of $6,000 that he actually was paying $10,000 and keep $4,000 cash for himself as compensation for taking the exposure."

Marinari asked Toll who had taught him this particular lesson. "I learned this practice from year one, as a junior accountant when I first came into accounting by talking with other junior accountants. Evidently, the practice was widespread." He added he also was advised of the protocol of bribery by his first boss, a successful Philadelphia accountant named Sam Needleman.

Toll was very clear about the product he was buying from the IRS agents: "By paying the bribe, we were able to avoid paying substantial taxes."

The accountant added that with very little additional effort IRS examiners could easily have uncovered the fraudulent nature of the Saligman family's books. But Toll worked hard to make sure that this extra effort was not made. "I paid IRS agents not to dig so that I would not have to disclose information about what was going on in our business."

Over the years, Toll said, IRS agents offered his clients a wide range of specific services in return for the illegal payments. Emanuel Leoff, for example, was "employed by the Treasury Department or the Internal Revenue Service as an estate examiner to handle the estate of Robert Saligman's brother-in-law. Robert Saligman and I had a meeting with Manny Leoff at which $2,000 was given by Robert Saligman. The purpose was to save taxes, to save estate or inheritance taxes."

In 1974, Toll said, he paid a $66,000 bribe to an IRS agent named Joseph Berkowitz. "The tax issue involved at Queen Knitting Mills was an inventory understatement in excess of $2,000,000," he testified. "Robert Saligman's personal yacht, 'Queenie,' on the books of Queen Knitting Mills; some travel and entertainment expenses on the books of Queen Knitting Mills. All of these items, if the agent assessed them, would have cost Queen Knitting Mills substantial dollars."

One improper expense item charged to the business account was the $100,036 in legal fees that Robert Saligman paid when he purchased his personal Florida residence. Then there was a $1,500 item for cleaning his boat. A third item carried as a necessary business expense was Robert Saligman's professional yacht skipper. "We paid a salary to the boat captain in Florida," Toll said. "The boat captain did work around the house and maintained Robert Saligman's personal yacht. We took tax deductions for it. It served no business purpose."

The yacht, however, was in fact used to help generate the hard-to-trace greenbacks needed for the long series of IRS bribery payments, an expense hardly likely to be approved in a legitimate audit. "The Saligmans were having difficulty raising the cash [needed for making the bribes] and were complaining about the dollar amounts of the payoffs," Toll informed the jury.

To resolve this problem, the family made a large deposit in a bank in the Bahamas to generate cash interest payments. These were secretly ferried to Florida on the boat.

Then the cash was moved to Philadelphia. "Robert Saligman has a safe in his—in a closet in his bathroom. I had a key to that safe and the combination. We kept an envelope and other records in the safe pertaining to the payoffs." In the case of the money being paid to Kale by the Saligman family, Toll continued, a separate record was maintained. "We kept a record on the envelope, on which we indicated the amount of the bribe, the $105,000 bribe. I also indicated the dates that I made the payments and the amount of the installment payments."

Unfortunately for Kale and the Saligman clan, Toll thought the damaging information he recorded on the envelope in the safe might someday prove useful. "I made a copy to protect myself," the accountant said. "I had been participating in illegal schemes, and I felt that if I was—if we were ever caught, that I would have evidence that I was acting on behalf of other people, that I was not the only one involved."

The copy of the envelope placed in the record of the trial indicated that Toll had made cash payments to Kale on April 3, May 5, June 2, and October 10, 1980. Toll's office calendar indicated that he had appointments with Kale on the same dates that were mentioned on the envelope. The envelope and the calendar provided powerful corroboration of Toll's testimony against Kale.

In the perverted financial world of Charles Toll, the logic of the honest taxpayer was sometimes turned upside down, as, for example, when Toll actually asked the IRS agent he had bribed to expand his audit into additional tax years. This was an excellent, if somewhat surprising, defensive move because it was unheard of for another agent to start investigating a case that was being worked on by one of his colleagues. "We did not want to have the tax returns examined by an agent we did not know and were not paying off," he explained.

Another way the family avoided taxes was to inflate grossly its charitable deductions. Toll informed the jury about one occasion when the Saligmans were thinking of giving Temple University in Philadelphia the Traylor Building, a small rundown structure that was actually worth about $500,000. "We were contemplating a charitable deduction on our tax returns of $2,200,000, which was a substantial benefit to us," the Saligman family official testified.

Toll said that it was in the middle of working out the grossly exaggerated charitable contribution when Kale, the regular recipient of Saligman bribes, decided to retire from the IRS. "At this point, I got very upset, extremely upset. We had already made arrangements and were just about to conclude the transaction with Temple University for the donation of the building."

But Kale told him to calm down, that he already had arranged for the matter to be controlled by one of his colleagues, a middle-level IRS official named Irving Suval. After several negotiating sessions, an agreement was reached that involved an initial payment to Suval of $65,000, followed by a sweetener of $50,000. In return, Kale's friend Suval agreed to assist the Saligmans obtain the IRS's seal of good housekeeping on the spurious value of the building they were giving to Temple.

"Did Mr. Suval explain to you how he was going to get this through the IRS, this deduction?" Marinari asked.

"At that point he did not, but later he did," Toll replied. "He told me he had to submit it to engineering. He was able to submit the situation—the problem—to the Engineering Department at a time when they were very busy. So that one of the engineers signed a form that said, 'Too busy to'—I don't know, I can't repeat the exact words, but it said something to the effect that the Engineering Department was too busy to examine this particular transaction."

Toll said that between November 1981 and April 1983 he paid Suval $115,000 in bribes from the Saligman family, pocketing an additional $15,000 for himself.

Suval, fifty-nine, was the second major witness against Kale. Suval's deep involvement in the long-standing corruption scheme was significant because he was an IRS supervisor, working at various times as a group manager, chief of the district conference staff, and staff analyst in the IRS's national office in Washington. Suval's most sensitive assignment, however, was as chief of the Joint Committee Section of the Philadelphia district's review staff. The Joint Committee Section is a small semiautonomous unit that operates in each of the IRS's sixty-three districts. Its function is to assure the Joint Tax Committee of Congress about the basic fiscal integrity of the tax collection system by reviewing all major refund claims.

Suval's testimony was devastating to Kale and damaging to one of the most important review systems of the entire IRS. "While I was on the review staff, Mr. Kale came to me and asked me if I could make sure that certain returns flowed through the review system as quickly as possible," Suval testified. "And he indicated to me that he was going to be paid money, $65,000 in all, and that he would pay me $6,500."

Suval kept his word. The particular problem in this case involved a set of "fiduciary returns" that had been prepared to report the income earned by separate trust funds set up for five of the Saligman children. "I went to the reviewer after I had assured myself that the returns were in review and I would say to whomever, would you please review these and get them on their way."

Bribery and corruption were an essential part of Charles Toll's working life. According to his testimony, and the handwritten notes he often made, the accountant passed large amounts of cash to a series of IRS agents for at least a quarter of a century. Two particular agents—William Kale and Irving Suval—appear to have been the major beneficiaries of Toll's twisted generosity, together receiving more than $200,000. For much of this period, the benefits he purchased flowed to his employer, Cynwyd Investments.

The rewards, at least for a while, were considerable. Charles Toll was handsomely paid, lived very well, and was a respected member of his community. The Saligman family lived even more lavishly, with many of the millions of dollars of unpaid taxes diverted for such luxuries as a Florida vacation home and a yacht with a full-time skipper. The agents received significant amounts of untaxed cash. The only loser was the public.

Curiously enough, although the testimony of Toll and Suval was more than sufficient to convict Kale, the recipient of the Saligman bribes, the government never brought criminal charges against any member of the Saligman family for paying them. Terri Marinari declined to explain the legal reasons for this inaction. All criminal indictments, of course, become public. If a taxpayer does not contest a civil IRS effort to obtain back taxes, interest, and penalties, however, the assessment remains confidential. It therefore is possible that the Saligmans have paid all or part of the millions of dollars of taxes that the witnesses in the Kale trial said the family had evaded through bribery. At the time of Kale's trial, representatives of the Saligmans denied any involvement in the bribery of IRS agents. In response to a letter of inquiry from me on April 14, 1989, Herbert Kurtz, the chief financial officer of Cynwyd Investments, said he had talked with the Saligman family lawyer and that the family would not grant me an interview.

It would be comforting to report that the Saligmans were alone in their greed, that the story told in federal court was an isolated series of events. Unfortunately, however, the evidence from Philadelphia and from many other cities in the United States suggests that this is not the case.

One of the most difficult questions to answer about any single event, especially one that many people want to hide, is whether it was an isolated occurrence or part of a broad pattern of behavior. In Philadelphia, this question was not so hard to answer because the crimes of William Kale, Charles Toll, and Irving Suval were uncovered during a much larger corruption investigation that so far has resulted in the convictions and imprisonment of ten current and former IRS agents and ten wealthy businessmen.

Perhaps the best known of the businessmen is Albert Nipon, the internationally acclaimed fashion designer who runs full-page advertisements in *The New Yorker* and sometimes sells to celebrities like Nancy Reagan, Rosalyn Carter, and Barbara Walters. In February 1985 Nipon pleaded guilty to paying $200,000 in bribes to two IRS agents to avoid nearly $800,000 in taxes. He was sentenced to three years in federal prison.

Terri Marinari, the assistant U.S. attorney, and Ben Redmond, the IRS regional inspector for the Philadelphia area, have little doubt that a large number of the older IRS agents in Philadelphia had become highly tolerant of corruption.

The actual number of agents who have been convicted, the active role played by some supervisors, the extended periods of time involved in several of the conspiracies, and the manner in which corrupt schemes were continued when a particular agent was reassigned or retired, Marinari said, provided strong if indirect evidence of systemic corruption throughout the Philadelphia area.

A small but revealing example of the self-deceptive thought process that can occur within the mind of an agent when the culture of corruption becomes accepted was inadvertently disclosed by Irving Suval during his testimony against William Kale. Employing the standard tactic of a prosecutor relying on the testimony of a witness who himself has engaged in illegal activities, Marinari asked Suval whether he previously had admitted participating in criminal activities other than those involving the Saligmans.

"Yes, that's correct," Suval replied. "I was involved in at least 11 or 12 other instances of bribery, and I have received fees ranging from as low as $400 up to the Cynwyd Group, which is $115,000."

Professional fees for services rendered, Suval seemed to be saying. Marinari would not indulge him.

"You referred to fees. What did you mean, sir?"

"Bribes, I'm sorry," he replied.

Partly because of this curiously tolerant attitude about some kinds of bribery by both government agents and the public, corruption remains one of the most difficult of all crimes to detect. This is because corruption usually involves a consensual agreement between two or more participants. Even though the American people are the victims of thousands of burglaries each day that never are solved, burglary is a far riskier business than is graft. The burglar, after all, must penetrate a locked or guarded place, carry off a physical object of value, and sell it to a fence. Each act is inherently dangerous. While breaking into a store or home, the burglar sometimes is spotted by either the victim or a neighbor. While carrying the stolen object back to his base, the burglar sometimes is spotted by a passing police officer. While negotiating with the receiver of stolen goods, the burglar can be betrayed.

Contrast these hazards with those faced by a corrupt IRS agent who receives totally negotiable cash in return for not performing a usually obscure act within a massive bureaucracy that has assigned a very small number of guards to protect itself. Although corruption sometimes involves an element of extortion, the different parties making such arrangements usually expect to benefit by them.

Another factor improves the odds that the corrupt IRS agent will not be caught. The homeowner who loses her television set or diamond ring to a burglar genuinely wants her property back. But because the "goods" stolen by the corrupt agent are intangible—one cannot see or hold or taste the effective enforcement of the tax laws—the rage that drives the homeowner seldom is found in the hearts of the agency's top managers. In fact, partly because the intangible goods being stolen by the corrupt agent almost always remain invisible to the public, top IRS officials sometimes have been reluctant to expose corruption.

In Philadelphia, the IRS principal investigator in charge of handling the Kale case was Ben Redmond, a canny man who was named the regional inspector of the Mid-Atlantic Region in 1976. Redmond's turf includes Philadelphia, the rest of Pennsylvania, and all of New Jersey, Maryland, Delaware, Virginia, the District of Columbia, and overseas employees of the IRS. In one recent year, individuals and corporations located in his region filed more than 26 million tax returns.

In addition to worrying about corruption, Redmond's small team is also responsible for supervising most of the management audits designed to measure and ultimately improve the general quality of service provided by the Mid-Atlantic Region. Finally, he is in charge of investigating all incidents where taxpayers attack or threaten to attack IRS agents.

It is not very likely that a secretary typing letters while sitting in an IRS office or a clerk feeding a computer in a regional processing center will ever be offered a bribe. So in measuring the potential size of the corruption problem in the Mid-Atlantic Region, office workers who have infrequent contact with the public can be generally ignored. But the number of "front line" IRS troops with day-to-day contact with the public is not insignificant.

"I would say that the Mid-Atlantic Region employs at least twenty thousand examiners, auditors, investigators, and collection people who hold potentially vulnerable jobs," Redmond said.

"Tax collection is a high-risk business at best and investigating corruption in this area is extremely difficult. You need corroboration, you need a living body, you need someone inside."

But even when the IRS identifies an insider who is willing to work as an undercover operator, corruption investigations are extremely labor intensive. "When an undercover informant has a meeting with a potential target, we often must mobilize six investigators and technicians to capture the evidence on hidden cameras and other kinds of recording devices," Redmond said.

In the face of the sheer mass of the hazard, the complexity of the tax laws, and the time-consuming process of penetrating just one conspiracy, the size of Redmond's inspection unit seems puny, even absurd. Is it not ridiculous to think that the 150 inspectors, technicians, statisticians, supervisors, and secretaries assigned to the Inspection Division in the Mid-Atlantic Region of the IRS can come close to achieving their mission? The relative dimensions of the corruption potential and the corruption fighters are essentially the same in the IRS's six other regions.

To penetrate the secretive underground world of William Kale and Charles Toll and Irving Suval and Robert Saligman and Albert Nipon, Marinari and Redmond needed luck, a great deal of luck. The big break came on November 19, 1980, when a nice young IRS agent named Jude Dougherty was negotiating with an accountant named Victor Gottfried about the tax problems of one of Gottfried's clients. Dougherty's initial examination had led him to believe that the client owed the government additional taxes. But Gottfried had different ideas. In the classically vague terms of an initial bribe offer, Gottfried indicated to Dougherty that he would be "satisfied" if the problem could be resolved.

Dougherty followed what is supposed to be the IRS standard procedure in such situations. He told Gottfried he'd think it over. Then he reported the incident to Redmond. Dougherty was asked to wear a small concealed device to record his next conversations with Gottfried and the reluctant taxpayer. It turned out that Gottfried was a gabby fellow who dropped the names of several other IRS agents who were allegedly "friendly." Redmond and his team reached into the massive computerized files of the IRS and identified Gottfried's other clients. With further checks, the investigators developed a list of potential suspects. Irving Suval was at the top of the list.

But there was the question of proof. With some reluctance, Dougherty agreed to become the bait that would draw the "friendly" agents, hungry accountants, and greedy taxpayers of Philadelphia within range of Redmond's secret recording devices and tiny hidden cameras. From 1980 to 1984, Jude Dougherty was a double agent. With careful coaching, Dougherty began acting like an IRS agent who had more of the good things in life than could be purchased on his modest government salary. He traded in the Thunderbird he was driving for a Mercedes. He took lawyers to lunch at one of Philadelphia's most expensive restaurants.

Incredibly, Terri Marinari and Ben Redmond's luck held. In the spring of 1982, Dougherty agreed to take a $150,000 bribe in return for apparently helping a manufacturer named Herbert Orlowitz avoid $1.8 million in income taxes. The first two payments were completed in an office where the events could be recorded but not photographed. But then, early one July morning, Orlowitz handed a brown paper bag to Dougherty while they were standing in the middle of a deserted parking lot. Opening the bag, the undercover agent pulled out a thick stack of $100 bills and fanned them in a way that looked like he was just checking to make sure they all were of the same denomination. From a window of an apartment located across the street and twelve stories above the parking lot, the telephoto lens of an IRS video camera also noted the denomination of the bills.

Marinari, Redmond, and his investigators were ecstatic. But following the tested and tedious tactics of serious corruption investigators, they did not run down the twelve flights of stairs and arrest Orlowitz. Although an arrest would have been satisfying, it also would have sent a violent warning signal through the network of agents and businessmen that was corrupting the federal tax laws in Philadelphia.

Three months later two special investigators for the IRS intercepted Orlowitz on his way to his office. They asked him to accompany them to another office in the same building. There, the executive was given a special viewing of a short piece of video tape in which he was the star. Faced with the documentary evidence of his bribe, Orlowitz almost immediately agreed to the government's offer to go easy on him if he would cooperate. Orlowitz's office was transformed into a secret television studio equipped with three concealed video cameras and six microphones.

Irving Suval, the IRS supervisor who later would describe his bribes as "fees," passed his first film test with flying colors while meeting with Orlowitz in December 1983. After some small talk about Orlowitz's health, the two men got down to business. As Suval shuffled a large stack of financial documents, he described the special services he could offer his client. "What I am about to do, Herb, is as follows," Suval said. "I am going to conveniently lose a lot of these pages. You're getting a refund of a million in tax plus the interest."

The IRS agent appeared to be subtly suggesting that Orlowitz consider increasing the bribe. "You know what? Most of that money is not yours.

I just want you to know that million dollars you're getting back in tax from those back years, you're not entitled to it. Legally, you're not entitled to one penny."

The tactic of "losing" the key documents was dangerous, Suval said. Maybe the service was worth more than the "buck and a half" that Orlowitz had agreed to pay. A "buck and a half," in Suval's fast-moving world, was $150,000.

In March 1984, the investigators ordered Orlowitz to telephone Suval with the good news that the $1 million refund had arrived. A few days later, Suval stopped by Orlowitz's office to complete the transaction. Instead of Orlowitz, Suval found Jude Dougherty, the IRS agent who had been pretending to be corrupt for more than three years. Dougherty handed Suval $50,000 in cash, far less than the agreed-upon bribe, but plenty for the immediate purposes of the government.

At that moment, according to the game plan worked out by the investigators, four armed special IRS agents were supposed to sweep into the office. But somehow the door they planned to burst through was locked. Improvising quickly, one of the agents knocked.

"Who is it?" Suval asked.

The investigator was really swift. "It's Mike," he replied, dropping the name of Orlowitz's son. With the $50,000 in one hand, Suval turned the lock and opened the door to the four agents. His world crumbled.

Suval, like Orlowitz, was asked to cooperate in return for a promise from Marinari to ask for a lighter sentence. He too became a double agent. The biggest and most complex payoff scheme that Suval disclosed to the investigators involved Charles Toll, Cynwyd Investments, and all the other companies controlled by Robert Saligman.

But Suval turned out to be ineffective as an undercover agent, unable to disguise his underlying nervousness. Toll appeared to smell trouble immediately. "I don't know what you're talking about," Toll said to Suval and the IRS's secret recording device, when asked about the $65,000 bribe the company had paid Kale and Suval.

It was Toll's extremely sensitive early warning system that triggered what became the final step in Marinari and Redmond's investigation: the May 1985 seizure of Cynwyd Investments' books, the discovery of Toll's embezzlement, and Toll's forced decision to testify about his thirty-year involvement in a highly successful effort to thwart the lawful collection of taxes.

The series of bribery trials and convictions that developed out of the undercover work of Jude Dougherty represents the largest wave of corruption to sweep over a major office of the IRS in the last few years. The scandal, however, was far from unique. In fact, about ten years before Benjamin Redmond led the successful investigation in Philadelphia, he uncovered almost as extensive a ring of corruption within the IRS office in Pittsburgh.

In the Pittsburgh case, one of America's largest and best-known corporations, Gulf Oil, was accused of showering hundreds of expensive gratuities for more than three years on approximately thirty IRS employees, including the man who supervised Gulf's federal tax audits. As a result of the investigation, the supervisor was convicted and sentenced to six months in prison, five IRS agents were dismissed and twenty-seven others received punishments including demotions in rank and suspensions without pay.

Cyril J. Niederberger, the man in charge of the tax agency's examinations of the giant corporation, told IRS investigators that he had accepted hundreds of meals, drinks, golf outings, airline tickets, lodgings, and other gifts from Gulf during the eight-year period between 1967 and 1975.

Although the gratuities that Gulf gave Niederberger were considerably smaller than most of the bribes uncovered in Philadelphia a decade later, the potential corporate benefits were massive. According to assistant U.S. attorney Craig R. McKay, one key ruling was Niederberger's decision that an illegal $12 million political slush fund was not subject to taxation. "On March 28, 1974, he turned over his report," McKay told the federal jury. "He found no evidence that Gulf should pay taxes on these funds and that no fraud was involved. On that same day he was booked for a week at Pebble Beach."

The evidence showed that Niederberger and his family received four other no-cost vacations from Gulf in such locations as Miami, Pompano Beach, and Las Vegas. One indication of just how hard the corporation was courting the IRS official was that Gulf's two top tax executives, Fred W. Stadefer, vice president for tax administration, and Joseph F. Fitzgerald, manager of federal tax compliance, accompanied Niederberger on all the trips.

The case provided several fascinating morsels for the connoisseur of corruption. One tasty trifle brought out in a later trial of one of Gulf's lawyers was that Niederberger did very little work for all his gratuities. The lawyer, Thomas D. Wright, said he actually wrote the three-page memorandum exonerating Gulf on the slush-fund charges that the IRS supervisor then submitted as his conclusion. "The actual writing of it was done by me, typed in my office," Wright testified.

Another interesting tidbit concerned the way the payments were discovered. During the trial, an IRS inspector named Alan E. Hobron told the court that the entire investigation began when the IRS belatedly noticed that Gulf was deducting from its taxes sums it was using to entertain Niederberger and the entire IRS team supposedly monitoring the corporation's taxes. The bribes to the IRS were openly reported and deducted as necessary business expenses. No Sherlock Holmes sleuthing here.

Hobron's disclosure that Gulf viewed the payments to the IRS as such an acceptable practice that it routinely informed the government about them raises serious questions about the ethical standards of the corporation and the IRS. At the time of the indictment of Gulf and two of its executives, U.S. Attorney Blair A. Griffith disclosed that during his investigation he had uncovered evidence that a large number of other Pittsburgh corporations had also routinely provided cash gratuities to IRS employees.

Although the Pittsburgh investigation at that time generated a good deal of unpleasant publicity for the IRS and Gulf, the ultimate sanctions were minimal. Niederberger was sentenced to six months in prison; Gulf pleaded guilty to providing the trips and was fined a grand total of $36,000.

Before his successful corruption investigations in Philadelphia and Pittsburgh, Redmond had been assigned to New York City, whose residents have long been portrayed as quick to offer a bribe. If you want an apartment, you pay a little bribe. If you need special police attention, you pay a little bribe. If you want to win a government contract, you pay a little bribe. In an environment like that it would be naive to think that any agency could escape contagion. The IRS was not immune.

During his assignment in New York, Redmond investigated many different conspiracies. In one cast of his net, Redmond came up with twenty-two agents, four former agents, and one certified public accountant. The January 1968 indictments, announced in Manhattan by U.S. Attorney Robert M. Morgenthau, were the product of a two-year investigation that bore the code name of Project W.

Only three years before, the same prosecutor had put together yet another IRS corruption case involving an even larger cast: sixty-five agency auditors and eighty-two accountants and lawyers.

Despite the continued investigations and the steady stream of indictments, corruption did not appear to subside in the New York area. In 1970, for example, an IRS inspector named Barnard T. Smyth completed Project S, an investigation that led to the indictment of ten current and former special agents for taking bribes from organized-crime leaders. Project S shocked the top leadership of the IRS because the men who were charged with corruption were from the ranks of the agency's elite investigating unit, what was then known as the Intelligence Division.

Six years later, in March 1976, Andrew Jackson, the former chief collection officer in the IRS's Long Island office, was convicted of receiving more than $60,000 in bribes. Charged with playing a role in Jackson's conspiracy were one recently retired group supervisor, a still active mid-level IRS official, and a revenue officer.

While the numbers of New York indictments seem high, the official charges brought by the U.S. attorneys in Manhattan and Brooklyn come nowhere near reflecting the day-to-day corruption problem within the IRS at that time. In 1970, for example, Andrew J. Maloney, then an assistant U.S. attorney, reported that in addition to the one hundred agents who had been convicted by his office in New York, another forty had been forced to resign. (Maloney is now the U.S. attorney in Brooklyn.)

But investigators in the New York and Brooklyn districts tell tantalizing and suggestive stories of the many sharks who got away. One such yarn involved a senior IRS investigator who was known to operate a ring of approximately six corrupt agents. The gang arranged for the payment of bribes by having an allied outside attorney, usually a former special agent, approach the attorneys of the taxpayers they were investigating. The bribe thus was made from attorney to attorney. The money then was passed to the IRS supervisor who operated the ring. He would extract his cut and pass the balance on to the agent handling the specific case in question.

By the time this particular conspiracy was revealed by one of the original members of the ring, the supervisor had retired from the IRS and had accepted a management position with a major New York corporation. Although many of the participants were subpoenaed to testify, the grand jury never indicted anyone because of a lack of evidence. In this case, however, the failure to indict does not necessarily mean that the original information was incorrect. When the ringleader was brought in to the grand jury to be questioned about the allegations, he chose to invoke his Fifth Amendment right not to incriminate himself. Shortly thereafter, the corporation requested his resignation.

While it thus is clear that an unknown number of bribe-hungry agents escaped the anticorruption campaigns of Benjamin Redmond and Terri Marinari in Philadelphia and their counterparts in New York, the occasional conviction of a William Kale or a Irving Suval or a Cyril Niederberger surely serves as a warning to at least the most timid of the agents. But what happens when the leadership ducks? What happens when the determined foes of the corruption have no real support? What happens when powerful political forces in a city or in the upper reaches of the

Justice Department decide that determined assistant U.S. attorneys like Terri Marinari should spend their time on other matters?

Is extensive corruption inevitable within the IRS? Given the high stakes involved, isn't it ridiculous to think that the competitive owners of Guess? are not going to try to influence powerful men like Ron Saranow? Given the powerful attraction of money, do we expect too much of ambitious businessmen like Robert Saligman if we assume they will not offer substantial bribes to avoid paying far more in federal taxes? Given the go-go ethic of capitalist America, are we naive to believe that middle-level government officials like Irving Suval are not going to begin thinking of these offers as almost legitimate "fees"? Given the ambiguity of "legal tax shelters" and other accepted forms of tax avoidance, is it ridiculous to hope that the driven executive, the high-powered lawyer, and the relatively low-paid IRS examiner will be able to define the line between correct and incorrect behavior?

Vernon Acree, the man who headed the Inspection Division for more than two decades, told me a story a while ago that suggests the naivete of the public at large and, in this case, Mortimer Caplin, the brilliant University of Virginia law professor who had just been named to head the IRS by President Kennedy.

"Mort was desperate that he didn't want a corruption scandal during his watch," Acree said. "One day after a lot of people had been indicted in New York we had a meeting up there with fifty or sixty New York supervisors. He gave them a real heavy lecture about all the corruption he had heard about in New York. Then he dropped what he thought would be a real bomb. 'From my conversations,' Morty told them, 'I think as many as 50 percent of the agents doing office and field audits are involved in bribery.' He stopped for effect. There was a long silence. Not one of the sixty supervisors looked shocked or amazed. Finally, Mort called on a guy in the front row and asked him what he thought about his estimate. 'Well,' this supervisor replied, 'I would think the percentage of corruption might be higher.' "

"Tax collection is a high-risk business," said Ben Redmond, regional inspector in Philadelphia. And after twenty years of fighting corruption in the IRS, who should know better? "There was a long run of serious problems in New York, the situation in Pittsburgh, and then we found the mess in Philadelphia. People want to believe New York and Philadelphia are unique. I say baloney. I say corruption happens in other parts of the country too."

CHAPTER 9

Influence at the Top

Donald C. Alexander has been a brilliant and combative Washington tax lawyer all his working life. In 1973, Alexander reached the pinnacle of his professional career when he was chosen to be the commissioner of the IRS. Early one cool autumn morning in 1988, from the vantage point of his sixty-six years, Alexander looked back on his long career in the law and his four years at the IRS.

"Let's talk about something that made an indelible impression on me when I was just starting out as a tax lawyer, a brand-new player," Alexander said. "I was working for Covington & Burling here in Washington and thought I was pretty good. There came a time when we couldn't get a tax ruling from the IRS and Treasury on a matter that was very important to a couple of our clients. So my bosses decided to call in the politicians."

Alexander said that as the junior lawyer on the case he was instructed to write a simple one-page summary of the proposed tax rule that the client was trying to get the IRS to approve. This one-page memo, he went on, was given to Maxwell O'Rell Truitt, the son-in-law of Truman's vice president, Alben W. Barkley. Truitt, a Washington lawyer and lobbyist, had been the counsel for the Reconstruction Finance Corporation and the Maritime Commission. In 1938 he was appointed a member of the commission to fill the seat vacated by Joseph P. Kennedy, who had been appointed the U.S. ambassador in London. In 1941, Truitt quit and began practicing law and serving as a lobbyist for such clients as Francisco Franco, the dictator of Spain, and Standard Oil.

Partly because of his father-in-law, Alexander said, Truitt was politically well connected with high officials in the Truman administration and was able to arrange a lunch with Treasury Secretary John W. Snyder, the Truman administration cabinet member then in charge of the tax agency.

The lunch, which Alexander said he did not attend, took place at the Metropolitan Club, to this day one of the most prestigious gathering spots for the powerful of Washington. On the curious grounds that the Metropolitan is a place for cultivated conversations among old friends, one of the club's rules actually prohibits members from transacting any business while they are on its premises. But according to Alexander, what took place during that lunch shortly after the end of World War II involved a payment of $25,000.

"The cost of that little lunch was $25,000, not counting the food," Alexander told me, swiftly calculating that, given the subsequent inflation of the prices, the bribe today might be worth about $400,000.

Alexander said that the $25,000 was paid to Truitt. "Not bad money for one day's work," he said. "The ruling we wanted was issued by the government the next day and, of course, was totally favorable to our cause. So I went to my boss and said I was going to quit the practice of law, that this was crooked, and I wanted no part of it. He explained to me that the people in charge [of the Treasury Department] at that time were dishonest, but that most people were honest and that I shouldn't leave the system because of it."

After considerable thought, Alexander said, "I decided that my boss at that time, Paul Shorb, was right, probably right. And anyway, let's not leave the tax law, let's not abandon it."

Alexander said that none of the lawyers now at Covington & Burling would have knowledge of the bribe. He then declined to provide any additional details about the transaction, such as precisely how he knew his law firm paid Truitt $25,000 and who the clients were who had benefited from the favorable tax ruling. All the men he identified as having attended the lunch—Treasury Secretary Snyder, Max Truitt, and Paul E. Shorb—are now dead.

Did the payment violate federal bribery laws and the ethical rules of the law profession? "I have no idea," he replied, abruptly cutting off the conversation.

John W. Snyder was treasury secretary from 1946 until 1953. While he was in office, there were repeated investigations by the House Ways and Means Committee of allegations that he, the top tax official in the Justice Department, and several IRS officials had arranged for valuable tax favors worth tens of millions of dollars to be given to politically connected corporations and at least one wealthy family. Snyder acknowledged helping such companies as Universal Pictures, whose Washington representative was his son-in-law, and a family whose lawyer said he obtained a favorable ruling from the IRS after making a $30,000 contribution to the Democratic National Committee. But he always insisted that his interventions were only intended to improve the efficiency of the agency.

The $25,000 payment to Truitt—in return for his assistance in winning a ruling from the IRS—occurred at a time when reports of extensive graft within the IRS had prompted Snyder to repeatedly denounce the evil of corruption in the collection of federal taxes. "It is the devoted purpose of every one of us, of the president, of myself as Secretary of Treasury, of the Commissioner of Internal Revenue and the whole rank and file of the service, to discover and throw out every remaining malefactor," he told a New York City veterans' organization in 1951. Snyder's repeated promises to weed out what he called "the unfaithful few" came after a House committee had initiated an investigation that eventually led to the resignations and indictments of scores of senior tax officials all over the United States.

Snyder, who was never indicted, left the Treasury in 1953 to become the vice president in charge of finance for a now defunct auto company, Willys-Overland Motors, Inc. He died at the age of ninety in 1985. The Associated Press obituary described the former secretary as one of President Truman's closest advisers. It noted that he was the founder of the Harry S. Truman Scholarship Foundation, which provides grants to college students planning careers in public service.

Some tax experts contend that the corruption scandals that swept the tax system in the early 1950s were unique; that since the reorganization of the IRS in the wake of those scandals the agency has been largely isolated from improper and illegal pressures to help the well-connected. But cases of bribery, fixes, and other questionable arrangements have occurred during even the most puritanical administrations and under the noses of the most highly regarded administrators. And as we shall see, they also have occurred during less admirable administrations.

More than a quarter of a century after that expensive little lunch at Washington's Metropolitan Club, six former executives of Frito-Lay, Inc., entered a federal courtroom in Dallas and pleaded guilty to charges of income tax evasion. It was the spring of 1980. The six men had been brought to justice by an unusual team of private and public investigators. A good deal of the initial evidence had been collected by Octavio G. Pena, a respected private security specialist who had been hired by Pepsico, Inc., the owner of Frito-Lay. Pepsico had retained Pena and his team of investigators to look into rumors that Frito-Lay was being looted by some of its executives. As is often the case in such matters, after Pena's investigation uncovered evidence that some Frito-Lay executives were taking under-the-table kickbacks, the information was passed to federal enforcement officers, in this case George De Los Santos of the IRS and George Clow of the FBI.

After the Frito-Lay officials had been sentenced on criminal tax charges—the executives had failed to report the kickbacks as income—the chief of the IRS's criminal investigating unit in Dallas sent Pena a congratulatory letter. The IRS praised the private security consultant for his high professionalism and commended him and his staff for initiating the Frito-Lay investigation and "assisting the IRS in bringing these cases to a successful conclusion. Your involvement was an integral segment in the successful prosecutions."

Pena, De Los Santos, and Clow were rightfully pleased that their investigation of kickbacks received by the six Frito-Lay executives had led to guilty pleas for tax evasion. But during their investigation, the three men had uncovered indications of an even more serious crime, a conspiracy to corner the world market in peanut oil. The new leads included an admission by one of the company's most senior officers and long-distance telephone records indicating a suspicious patterns of conversations. Most tantalizing to the three investigators were telephone records suggesting that President Carter's brother, Billy, might have been a part of the conspiracy.

Pena, De Los Santos, Clow, and an assistant U.S. attorney named Dan Guthrie were excited by the new leads. Information about the manipulation of the peanut oil market actually was presented to a grand jury. But according to Pena and De Los Santos, the peanut case was suddenly halted by orders from Washington. A third person directly involved in the government's investigation of the case said that members of the grand jury were upset when the jury's hearings were aborted.

It is unlikely, however, that the federal grand jury in Texas was given the explanation for the cancellation that was offered by George De Los

Santos, now a retired IRS agent. "I was told the White House was taking over," he said in an interview. "Shortly thereafter I was promoted to a good policy-level job. I was very pleased because I think I was the first Hispanic American to reach that level in the IRS's Southwest Region." Interestingly enough, at about the same time Clow too was promoted to a good new job. The Frito-Lay investigation was never reopened.

According to the textbooks, the policies and actions of the IRS are guided by the tax laws passed by Congress and the published rules and regulations adopted by the agency.

As the chapter on bribery demonstrated, however, unscrupulous people have other ways to influence the decisions of the IRS. The bribe is a simple transaction. Here the corporate executive, the lawyer, or the accountant gives the agent something of value in return for a special benefit that under normal circumstances would not be available. The bribe is paid by the person desiring the favor. The favor is granted by the person receiving the bribe. This was the modus operandi, for example, of the Saligman family in Philadelphia.

But there are a host of other more subtle ways to influence tax enforcement. One is the fix. Most commonly, fixes involve situations where the person desiring a special service gives something of value to an influential person in government with the understanding that he or she will arrange for the service to be delivered by someone else. This was what happened when Treasury Secretary Snyder accepted a payment in return for pressuring the IRS to issue a desired ruling.

Within the world of the IRS, the middleman in the tax fix can be an influential official in the agency, in the Treasury Department, or at the White House. It is not unheard-of, however, for a middleman to be a member of Congress or a powerful individual in one of the political parties. A fix can be a straightforward commercial transaction or a political arrangement or a combination of both.

All such transactions can cause the loss of tax revenue. Sometimes these losses are minimal, sometimes they are gigantic. But because the fix, by definition, engages at least three people, it frequently generates a second kind of loss that may be more significant than the disappearing tax dollars. This second loss is not subject to precise measurement because it involves a corrosive cynicism that has come to infect the attitudes of many individuals within the agency. During my reporting on this book, I have talked with dozens of IRS employees—a public affairs officer in New York, a revenue agent in Oklahoma, a special agent in Los Angeles—

whose personal integrity seemed beyond question. At the same time, however, many of these same employees expressed such despair about the ability of the agency to function in a fair way that their will to perform a decent day's work appeared to have been seriously undermined.

If a presidential assistant can assure special tax benefits for the favored few with under-the-table pressure on the IRS, if a top-level Treasury Department official can prevent the investigation of a particular illegal tax transaction that has benefited either himself or his friends, if a Justice Department tax official intervenes in a case being handled by a law firm that subsequently gives the official a job, what difference does it make if an individual IRS employee shirks his or her responsibilities? That is a question that constantly undermines the will of many rank-and-file agents.

Another insidious aspect of tax fixes is that there really is no unit within the IRS that has the specific mission to combat them. The Inspections Division, undermanned and overwhelmed, is so hard pressed to combat conventional forms of bribery it simply has almost no chance of detecting fixes and other questionable arrangements. Who in the IRS, for example, was in a position to question why Treasury Secretary Snyder suddenly pressed the IRS to issue the tax ruling desired by the clients of Covington & Burling? How could De Los Santos, the Inspection Division, or anyone else in the IRS actually determine whether or not the criminal investigation of President Carter's brother was suddenly halted because of political concerns in the White House?

Because IRS tax decisions can involve hundreds of millions, even billions, of dollars, efforts to influence the outcome frequently are extraordinarily intense affairs where all possible tactics are considered. In addition to the vast fortunes that may be lost or gained by a single decision, however, a number of other factors combine to create a uniquely fertile field for questionable deal making. Not infrequently, for example, officials in a position to influence key IRS decisions have direct or indirect interests that might be affected by their decisions. Further contributing to this environment is the secrecy that surrounds most tax arrangements and a web of laws so complicated it is almost beyond challenge.

The only effective institutional checks against high-level fixes and other improper pressures on the IRS's tax decisions are a commissioner and a treasury secretary who have proven their independence and integrity. George Shultz was such a man. During his time as treasury secretary under President Nixon, for example, Shultz successfully blocked several efforts to use the IRS for improper purposes by threatening to go public with the requests and then quit his job. Jerome Kurtz, the commissioner under President Carter, was another such official.

"In the almost four years I was there, I never had a telephone call from the White House, not from anyone, never," Kurtz told me during a long talk in his sunny Washington office. "No, wait a minute, there was one exception. One time a low-level guy called and asked me about a taxpayer case and I said you may not know about the rules but this call is being reported and will be made a matter of public record. And he said, well, forget it. Nor did I ever hear from the secretary of the treasury on any particular case."

What about the investigation of Billy Carter? Kurtz, responding to my specific question about this case, said he had never heard of the case.

Stories, rumors, and whispers of secret, improper, high-level interventions in the administration of the tax law are known to anyone who has worked at the IRS for more than a year or two. Sometimes based on detailed knowledge, sometimes on educated guesses, the stories get passed from employee to employee, over morning coffee, during the tedious drives in the office car pool, while standing in hallways. This underground oral history represents one of the major barriers to genuine IRS reform, an awful legacy that encourages the time-servers, the disenchanted, and the corrupt to engage in their separate secret games.

BIG BARK, NO BITE

Immediately after Donald Alexander was appointed as commissioner in late 1973, he gave a speech to the Cleveland Tax Institute. His words sent a giant shock wave through the financial community, especially among the large brokers and commodity dealers of Wall Street and Chicago. Alexander began his speech by enthusiastically praising a just-published article that had described many tax shelters as "widespread, corrosive, scandalous tax avoidance . . ." that would prove the Achilles' heel of the federal income tax unless promptly controlled.[1]

Alexander told the assembled tax lawyers that he was ready to bite the bullet. Both he and his colleagues in the IRS, Alexander said, "are well aware of these problems. They are not only problems for the taxpayers, but also represent enforcement problems for the IRS. I am not saying that there is anything immoral or questionable about planning your affairs to reduce tax liability. But any investment made with the knowledge that the only profit will result from tax savings, is extremely questionable."

The commissioner concluded by saying that the IRS was committed to ensuring that all promoters and investors in tax shelters were in full compliance with the law. "On the general policy level, it is important to our self assessment system that the public retain its confidence that every taxpayer is paying his proper share. To the extent that upper income taxpayers appear to be avoiding taxes by purchasing shelter investment, public confidence is eroded."

Commissioner Alexander did not keep his bold promises of strict enforcement. In fact, despite these brave words, the IRS mostly continued to ignore what swiftly was becoming one of the most serious fiscal drains in the history of the United States. With any problem as large and complicated as the rapidly developing abuse of tax shelters during the 1970s and early 1980s, there are almost always a number of explanations for official inaction. But certainly one element that worked against Alexander's promise was the hostile attitude of the IRS commissioner's immediate boss, Treasury Secretary William Simon. As is shown by the following comment from *The Wall Street Journal* shortly after Alexander and Simon left office, this attitude was well known to tax experts in Washington and New York. "Mr. Kurtz's predecessor, Donald Alexander, had proposed daring steps on tax shelters and other touchy tax issues but hadn't been able to get them by Treasury Secretary William Simon," the *Journal* reported.

"That is true, that is true in part," Alexander replied when I asked him about Simon's responses to his proposed shelter program. "One example of what happened under Bill Simon involves a regulation that I proposed in December of 1976 that would have attacked one aspect of shelter abuse. This rule turned out to be the shortest-lived regulation in the history of the Treasury Department. I signed it one day and exactly seven hours later Secretary Simon killed it. Secretary Simon, an admirable guy in many ways, heard about it on a beach in Hawaii and immediately telephoned halfway round the world to rescind it."

Alexander's memory of this long-ago but still momentous event is backed up by two items in the dusty pages of the Federal Register, the always tardy official reporter of all administrative actions and proposed actions of the U.S. government. As required by law, the commissioner's proposal to close a loophole in the control of tax shelters had been approved by the Treasury Department tax policy experts in late 1976. Then, beginning on page 1038 of the January 5, 1977, edition of the Federal Register, the proposal was printed. Two days later, the brief notice of withdrawal, actually signed by Simon, was printed on page 1498.

No public debate in Congress. No change in the tax law. No legislation providing appropriations for a special enforcement program. Just two official announcements by appointed bureaucrats. The first announcement proposed a plan to begin an attack on a widely recognized problem of startling dimensions. The second announcement halted the attack.

Simon's rescission required less than thirty words: "In order to permit consideration of certain aspects of the notice of proposed rulemaking in the Federal Register for January 5, 1977 (42 FR 1038), said notice is hereby withdrawn. William E. Simon, Secretary of the Treasury."

According to estimates by the IRS, "abusive tax shelters" at that time were allowing wealthy investors to avoid paying approximately $3.6 billion a year in taxes in what responsible critics have called an outrageous kind of tax avoidance.

Why, I asked Alexander, had Simon blocked his attempts to curb tax shelters? "Well, Simon, Secretary Simon, is an admirable guy and on the whole was a darn good secretary," the former IRS commissioner replied. "Simon would never do that for his own personal interest, but he doesn't like the tax system very much. He didn't and he doesn't."

There is no question that Simon has a personal aversion to paying taxes. Several years ago, for example, he became involved in a financial dispute with several business associates. In an effort to defend himself against their accusations, Simon decided it was necessary to show that his personal situation was such that he had no need to be on the lookout for any additional tax shelters. To prove this point, Simon and his former tax accountant, John Pretto, went to *The Wall Street Journal*. The former secretary, they said, "had enough shelters and deductions so that he didn't pay any federal income tax from 1977 to 1982 and in 1984."[2]

Another small but clear indication of Simon's friendly attitude toward tax shelters came to light in September 1979, when the former treasury secretary became a member of the board of the New York Commodity Exchange (Comex). This association was revealing because for many years Comex had been a leading seedbed for tax arrangements widely regarded as among the most questionable forms of tax shelters. Five months after joining the Comex board, Simon quietly resigned after the collapse of Bunker Hunt's notorious attempt to control the price of all the silver bought and sold in the world. Hunt was a major Comex trader.

Simon strongly defends his performance as treasury secretary. "I have never supported special privileges for some taxpayers at the expense of others nor have I advocated tax shelters, loopholes, or other special exemptions," he told me. "This is perfectly consistent with my general philosophy that the tax system exists to raise revenues for legitimate government purposes, and not to achieve various secondary social purposes, such as the redistribution of income or the targeting of resources into one or another sector of the economy."

Simon also said that he had recommended in testimony and in supporting reports to Congress that "tax shelters and other special exemptions should be eliminated from the tax code." He said that one such specific plan was called the Limitation on Artificial Losses. The financier further said that, although Congress failed to act on his proposals at the time, he and other senior Treasury Department officials "made an honest effort to curb abusive tax shelters."

Simon added that his personal tax situation was irrelevant to his tax policy decisions while he was treasury secretary. "I never acted, nor did my colleagues at the Treasury Department, out of motives of personal gain," he said.

Concerning his decision to kill the 1976 proposal, Simon accused Alexander and the IRS of attempting to sneak far-reaching regulations onto the books in a highly suspicious manner. He said that during his time in office he had "numerous face-offs" because the agency was constantly issuing rules that exceeded its authority.

THE SILVER BUTTERFLY

William Simon's summary execution of Donald Alexander's proposed regulations provides a vivid glimpse of how billion-dollar enforcement decisions sometimes are made at the very top of the IRS. But during the same period, the agency's handling of a specific illegal tax avoidance scheme provides a perspective from the trenches. The dubious scheme was marketed under a wonderfully poetic name, the silver butterfly.

The silver butterfly gained its name because when diagramed on paper it somewhat resembles that delicate short-lived creature. As the experts designed it in the mid-1960s, the butterfly was a special kind of commodity transaction in which the broker simultaneously placed his customer on both the buy and the sell sides of the silver-futures market. Then the broker would "unwind" the positions in two different tax years.

This complex transaction gave the customer an intentional short-term trading loss that was used to offset short-term gains that otherwise would have been subject to taxes. At the same time, the comparable gains were rolled over into the next tax year, where they qualified for much-reduced, longer-term capital tax treatment or could be offset by a whole new tax straddle. With a good broker, successful investors could avoid or postpone paying their income taxes with almost no risk. Because of high interest rates, the simple postponement of a large tax payment was in effect interest-free money that gave the savvy customer a big advantage in the money-making business.

The silver butterfly apparently took wing in the late 1960s as a special form of speculation mostly designed to create make-believe losses that could be balanced against real profits so that the speculator could avoid paying federal taxes. The designers of this particular technique were a handful of sophisticated commodity traders who worked at some of Wall Street's biggest firms, such as E. F. Hutton and Merrill Lynch.

Trading in the future prices of commodities is an old and accepted investment practice. But for nearly half a century, a few government agencies have been aware that investors sometimes resorted to such trading techniques for the plain and simple purpose of tax avoidance. As far back as 1947, for example, the agency then responsible for regulating the markets, the Commodity Exchange Authority, expressed this concern: "There is evidence of large use of futures trading for the purposes of postponing, reducing or even completely avoiding payment of income tax." Two years later, the secretary of agriculture voiced the same concern, this time in a letter directed to the head of what was then called the Internal Revenue Bureau.[3]

Commodity experts believe that the bureau's initial sin of omission probably had only a limited impact on the overall revenue of the nation. This is because in its earliest stages the commodity tax straddle was a device known only to a relatively small circle of commodity brokers and a handful of their super-rich clients. At the beginning, the use of the commodity straddle as an amazingly effective way to avoid paying taxes was not available to just any run-of-the-mill millionaire and thus had only a limited national impact.

The picture began to change in the mid-1960s when a handful of Wall Street brokerage firms began marketing the commodity-straddle device to a far wider range of clients. The whole story would be funny, except that it is ludicrous.

As one experienced tax expert said: "The commodity tax straddle became a device which allowed a large number of rich folks to avoid paying any federal taxes at all. Maybe this explains why so few of them ever got worried about laws which on their face called for the government to take up to 80 percent of their income. The truth is, very few were ever in danger of paying."

According to an authoritative *Wall Street Journal* study in 1978, the marketing of the silver butterfly and other similar transactions was generating a gigantic loss to the federal government that already had topped

$1 billion a year in what were then regarded as highly questionable tax dodges.

The IRS was serenely supine. Ignorance of the law has never been a good defense for the criminal. But for a law enforcement agency, ignorance of the crime is just plain ridiculous. And in the case of the IRS's casual approach to commodity straddles, of course, the defense is impossible. It is impossible first because of that irritating 1947 report from the Commodity Exchange Authority and the follow-up letter from the secretary of agriculture two years later. It is impossible second because beginning in 1973 a New York stockbroker named David Jonsson began an incredible six-year effort to inform a long series of incompetent or lazy IRS officials about how some of the major brokerage houses had knowingly launched a broad campaign to sell what he believed were illegal tax shelters to their customers.

As in the cases of Frank Serpico and the New York Police Department, Karen Silkwood and the Atomic Energy Commission, and Ernest Fitzgerald and the Air Force, the IRS did not seem to want to hear the message of the young New York stockbroker.

The unlikely story of David Jonsson's long fight to persuade the IRS to net the silver butterfly began on October 22, 1971, when Jonsson took a job as a member of the Commodity Tax Straddle Department of Merrill Lynch. He was then twenty-nine, the bright son of a successful corporate executive. His assignment: increase Merrill Lynch's tax-straddle business. One of his first specific tasks was to write a script for an unusual tape-recorded message designed to persuade Merrill Lynch brokers around the country to interest their "high bracket customers" in commodity tax straddles.

The tape-recorded sales pitch Jonsson wrote was narrated by Tom O'Hare, then in charge of Merrill Lynch's tax-straddle department. As O'Hare explained on the tape, he would send the company's brokers no written material about the advantages of straddles because "it's against Merrill Lynch policy to give legal or tax advice." Ignoring company policy, O'Hare's taped voice informed the brokers why he felt that tax straddles made sense. "First, the right kind of taxpayer can often derive substantial tax benefits by doing a tax straddle. Second, you will be well paid in commissions for finding us appropriate business."

But even as Jonsson was preparing O'Hare's paperless sales pitch, he later recalled in an interview, he said he became "convinced that silver butterfly tax straddles were not legitimate."

But it wasn't until he had taken a new job in a different part of Merrill Lynch that the young broker, on June 23, 1973, met with a branch manager and senior vice president of the company and explained why he felt the straddles violated the law. The startled vice president immediately telephoned Jonsson's former boss, O'Hare, and informed him of Jonsson's views. "O'Hare, of course, said I was wrong. A few days later, the executive called me in and said he had checked with the experts in Merrill Lynch. He assured me that tax straddles were okay." The summer of 1973 was an extraordinary time in the history of the United States and, as it developed, in the personal career of David Jonsson. In Washington, the Nixon administration was slowly collapsing as witness after witness came before Senator Sam Ervin and testified about his role in Watergate. "Partly because of my emotional response to the hearings, and partly because I thought Merrill Lynch was going ahead with a particular $7 million silver straddle which I felt was improper, I decided I had to talk with someone in the Internal Revenue Service."

Jonsson first presented his case against the legality of selling straddles on July 23, 1973, during a forty-five-minute meeting in the IRS's New York office at 120 Church Street in downtown Manhattan with a special agent named David Rundlett. "I gave him a detailed statement about the particular operation I was worried about," Jonsson later wrote in a diary he kept. "Rundlett said he would get back to me within a week. When he didn't, I phoned him in late August and was informed that he had been transferred." Jonsson said he then was naive enough about the IRS and the power of his information that he was not particularly concerned. His false expectations were nourished by Wall Street rumors that an IRS investigation of tax straddles had actually been launched in New York and Chicago. He also had read news reports about the speech in Cleveland in which IRS Commissioner Alexander had made sweeping promises to close down illegal and improper tax shelters. As we already know, however, Alexander was unable to deliver on his promises.

On October 13, 1976, more than three years after his initial approach to the IRS, Jonsson got a letter asking for help from two IRS agents named Dixon and Moscowitz. A week later, on October 22, Jonsson met with the two agents and was told, according to his diary, that "not only had my information not been acted upon, it had inadvertently been misplaced in an unused filing cabinet."

Jonsson, who admits to sharing some of the winsome characteristics of Don Quixote, said that this second interview with IRS agents revived his hopes about the agency's intentions. On February 23, 1977, five months after the meeting with Dixon and Moscowitz, IRS Special Agent Ron Nowicki stopped by Jonsson's house and left a card asking him to telephone the next day. After several preliminary conversations, the broker met with Nowicki and an assistant U.S. attorney named Paul Vizcarrando for about two hours. Jonsson brought his father along as a witness. "They said that they had initiated a criminal investigation of tax straddles and needed my assistance," Jonsson remembers. "I gave them a copy of my straddle file, with the script of O'Hare's tape, a lot of detailed inside information, everything." He also met with three investigators from the Commodity Futures Trading Commission.

On May 12, 1977, Jonsson appeared before a federal grand jury in Manhattan. In September of 1977 he initiated a number of telephone calls trying to determine what had happened. "There were no indictments, and no explanations," he said. "It was about this time I left Merrill Lynch, angry and disillusioned."

It was also about this time that Simon left Treasury and that the IRS began to move against questionable tax shelters. After overlooking the problem for at least three decades, the agency published a regulation that prohibited taxpayers from using the losses from tax straddles as tax deductions on the grounds that the taxpayer's "dominant purpose" was "to create an artificial short term capital loss . . . while insuring that no real economic effect resulted from such transactions." It appears that the IRS officials in Washington had published this new regulation, Revenue Rule 77–185, without knowing that Jonsson had been giving inside information about the practice to IRS agents in New York for the past four years. The agency's 1977 action apparently was triggered by an IRS agent in California who independently had audited the returns of four taxpayers, Herbert and Ruth Jacobson and Harry Lee and Patricia Ann Smith, and discovered that in 1973 they had claimed tax losses as a result of commodity tax straddles. The broker for the taxpayers was Merrill Lynch.

David Jonsson was unaware of the IRS's first limited enforcement efforts against the Jacobsons and the Smiths. Not sympathetic with the fact that criminal tax cases require a great deal of time to prepare as they make their way through both the IRS and the Justice Department, Jonsson became frustrated because the federal grand jury in Manhattan had not yet issued an indictment. He decided to try a different strategy. His chosen instrument was Shirley Jackewicz, an unusually bright and aggressive young reporter with *The Wall Street Journal* in New York. "She latched onto the story immediately and began interviewing everyone on the Street," Jonsson said. He also decided it was time to go to the top of the IRS. On April 13, 1978, the persistent whistle-blower wrote a letter to Jerome Kurtz, the IRS commissioner appointed by President Carter. Once again, he described the silver butterfly and why he believed it violated the tax law. He also complained about how in his view IRS agents in New York had repeatedly dropped the ball. After a number of weeks, he got a polite noncommittal note from one of Kurtz's assistants.

On June 6, 1978, Jackewicz's clearly written story about the silver butterfly was published on the front page of the *Journal.* "For the first time, the incredible but complicated story of this particular scheme was described in plain English that could be understood by anyone who read it," Jonsson remembers. "For the first time, the intimate role of Merrill Lynch in marketing the straddle was described. This story probably was my major contribution in the long battle to exterminate the silver butterfly."

About a year later, in one of those wonderful small accidents of history, a Washington-based IRS lawyer named Dan Morrison, who had been dispatched to New York to gauge the national implications of the tax straddle problem, was given Jonsson's name during a Manhattan cocktail party. Morrison immediately called Jonsson. "We hit it off right away," Jonsson said. "We met in a restaurant for about three hours, during which time we discussed my Merrill Lynch files, the 1977 grand jury hearing, the later investigation, none of which he was aware of. I also gave him a copy of the tax-straddle marketing tape."

Jonsson and Morrison began a long and ultimately unsuccessful effort to rewrite Revenue Ruling 77–185. Both men felt the existing rule, while well intentioned, was seriously flawed because it was drafted in such a way that the intent of the taxpayer to avoid paying taxes had to be proven by the IRS in each individual case.

As the two men continued to discuss how to devise an effective rule to prevent the use of commodity trading for tax avoidance purposes, the IRS asked David Jonsson whether he would help prosecute a tax-straddle case. This time, the agency wondered whether he would be willing to testify in the long-delayed silver butterfly trial of the Jacobsons and the Smiths.

Although the government's case was weak, Merrill Lynch, the broker for the two couples, was distinctly unhappy about the details of its silver butterfly offerings being discussed in an open courtroom. In November 1980, the clumsy effort by the company to prevent such discussions backfired when a Tax Court judge handed down an unprecedented decision refusing to let the two couples admit the error of their ways and pay the $57,000 that the IRS said they owed the government.

The judge issued his unusual decision after the lawyer for the IRS charged that Merrill Lynch had bought off the couples with an agreement to pay them $114,000—twice as much as they owed in taxes—to settle the case before trial.

The November 1980 disclosure of the Merrill Lynch effort to smother the case turned out to be somewhat embarrassing for Donald T. Regan. Regan, after all, was the aggressive head of Merrill Lynch during the period when the company made millions of dollars marketing tax straddles. And it was only a few weeks later that President-elect Ronald Reagan selected Regan to be his secretary of the treasury. It was the department that Regan was about to take over that for the last several years had been attacking commodity tax straddles as an illegal tax avoidance scheme that had cost the government $3 to $4 billion a year in lost revenue.

Upon becoming secretary, Regan announced that he would disqualify himself from making any decisions about the tax-straddle issue. In Congress, New York Democrats Senator Daniel Patrick Moynihan and the late Representative Benjamin S. Rosenthal had introduced legislation to curb what they called one of the biggest and most flagrant loopholes in the tax law. Behind the scenes, staff members for the two New York legislators were receiving tactical advice from Jonsson on Wall Street and from Morrison at the IRS.

Five months later, on April 10, 1981, Jonsson testified at the tax trial of the Jacobsons and the Smiths. During the trial, the government asserted that in a recent year only one of Merrill Lynch's 103 tax-straddle customers actually made a profit; all the others established what were defined as "tax losses" for income tax purposes. Thomas O'Hare, head of the Merrill Lynch tax straddle department, said under questioning that one purpose of the department's activities was to generate tax losses but that Merrill Lynch also hoped to make profits for its customers. In the end, the judge ruled that the two California couples did not aim to make profits so they could not deduct their losses. But he rejected the IRS contention that the transactions were a sham.

Despite these and other tactical victories, the war was far from over. Powerful industry groups spent a great deal of money lobbying Congress not to pass a law permanently choking off the use of tax straddles. The counterattack was led by Representative Dan Rostenkowski, the Illinois Democrat who is chairman of the House Ways and Means Committee, and Senator Robert Dole of Kansas, who was then the Senate majority leader. At a last-minute House-Senate conference on the Deficit Reduction Act of 1984, Rostenkowski and Dole added a killer amendment that ultimately allowed a broad range of straddlers to avoid paying the government $1.5 billion in taxes.

It is an incredible story about a high-finance world where few of us live. It is a story that might prompt the skeptic to question David Jonsson's credibility. But there is a fascinating footnote to the story that proves that in the end even the IRS came to accept the views of this incredibly persistent whistle-blower.

For many years, the IRS has had a program under which it gives cash awards to citizens who provide the agency with useful information leading to the successful prosecution of tax cases. Between 1975 and 1984, the IRS made an average of 527 awards each year. The program appears to be effective. With a total annual cost of only $456,000, the IRS calculates that the awards were responsible for the recovery of $16.4 million.

The promise of an award is one of the easiest and cheapest ways an IRS agent has to encourage a citizen to provide information. Almost every time that David Jonsson met with the IRS, the agents assured him that he would receive an award. The assurances were good tactics because the agents wanted the information. The assurances became more and more important to Jonsson because, as the brokerage industry came to realize that he was helping the government, his personal stock began to plummet. At the suggestion of the IRS agent he had initially approached, Jonsson filed his first Form 211 request for a "Reward for Original Information" in July 1973. He was to have a very long wait.

Dan Morrison, the IRS attorney in Washington who had also become obsessed with the straddle problem, went to bat for Jonsson in February 1981, collecting documents and writing memos proving that the broker had provided information leading to the disallowance of at least $42 million in phony tax losses. But the bureaucracy would not be moved. Worried that the IRS did not intend to keep its promises to provide him financial assistance, Jonsson began writing a series of personal letters asking IRS officials for help. "The reason I ask is that I feel like I'm working on borrowed time because of my participation in exposing commodity tax straddles. It is absolutely imperative, given my exposed position, that I emerge from all of this as financially secure as possible. I'm sure you and the IRS understand this concern and will act accordingly on my behalf," Jonsson wrote Howard V. Walsh, an IRS official in New York.

Jonsson had left Merrill Lynch in October 1977. He then took a number of different jobs with New York area financial companies, including one with what now is called Prudential-Bache Securities. During this period he continued filing new requests with the IRS. They were not successful. On August 12, 1982, the broker wrote to IRS Commissioner Roscoe Egger. "I am proud of what I did, and proud that the IRS, after making a very slow and shaky start towards dealing with the admittedly complex tax straddle issue, had the courage to withstand the intense political pressure brought to bear upon it by the potent brokerage industry lobby. Unfortunately, as a result of my public testimony in the Smith Jacobson tax court case, I am understandably a marked man in the close-knit brokerage community where I earn my livelihood as a securities analyst. It therefore is absolutely imperative that the IRS follow through on its promises to me so my family will have the necessary financial security to withstand the wrath being directed at me by the brokerage industry."

Three weeks later, Jonsson got a telephone call from Morrison in Washington. In a note to himself after the call, the broker wrote that Morrison had told him that "IRS bigs in a panic over my case—worried about Congressional investigation re how they mishandled tax straddles & my information." In a recent interview, Morrison recalled that at the time of his telephone call the agency was privately considering handing Jonsson a $500,000 award. Because the grand total of IRS awards to helpful taxpayers all over the country then amounted to only about $450,000 a year, the possibility of the agency handing $500,000 to a single individual was surprising.

But the stall continued. On October 11, 1982, Jonsson hired on a contingency-fee basis a Washington attorney named Mitchell Rogovin to represent him. Rogovin had been a top tax official himself during the Kennedy administration and was well known to the IRS. On September 30, 1983, Jonsson received a brief letter from P. J. Medina, the IRS district director in New York. "Your claim for a reward has been allowed. You will receive a check soon for the amount shown above." The amount typed into the blank space was not $500,000. But it was probably the largest single award in the history of the IRS: $220,659.

Although old-timers in the IRS have hundreds of different horror stories they love to tell, one of their all-time favorites concerns the secret revenue ruling issued on October 21, 1969, to the Nixon administration's favorite multinational, the International Telephone and Telegraph Corporation (ITT).

The circumstances under which ITT won this unusual tax ruling weave an astonishing story. And then there is the additional fillip of the long stubborn drive by Ralph Nader and two of his colleagues to get the ruling reversed and how their efforts achieved success only at the very last moment. And finally, twelve years after it all began, there is the sad, ironic coda in which ITT managed to win the war even though it had lost the battle.

Certainly one of the most fascinating episodes in this long and incredibly complex story of how the Nixon administration helped ITT must be the disclosure on March 3, 1972, of a memo allegedly written by Dita A. Beard, a Washington lobbyist for the giant corporation. In her memo, some aspects of which subsequently were denied, Beard discussed the promise of ITT President Harold S. Geneen to provide the Nixon team $400,000 support for the 1972 Republican convention. After complaining that some ITT officials seemed to be violating the understanding that there was to be absolutely no discussion of the $400,000 promised, Beard said she was convinced "our noble commitment has gone a long way toward our negotiations on the mergers coming out as Hal [Geneen] wants them." She concluded that "certainly the President has told [Attorney General John] Mitchell to see things come out fairly."[4]

Following publication of the explosive memo by the syndicated columnist Jack Anderson, ITT President Geneen and Representative Bob Wilson, an influential Republican who arranged the deal, confirmed that a corporate campaign pledge had been discussed, although Geneen insisted it was for $200,000, rather than the $400,000 mentioned by Beard and Wilson.

But in testimony to the Senate Judiciary Committee shortly after publication of the Beard memo, Geneen swore under oath that "there was absolutely no connection" between ITT's pledge to the Republican National Convention and the Justice Department's settlement of three antitrust suits against the company.[5]

Congressional doubts about Geneen's claim of corporate innocence, however, were enhanced two years later when former Attorney General Richard G. Kleindienst was given a suspended sentence in federal court for misleading a Senate committee that was investigating ITT. The key misleading answer that led to Kleindienst's sentence involved his insistence that he had not been "pressured" by the White House, even though independent evidence showed that President Nixon had telephoned him and ordered him to drop a Justice Department appeal of a separate ITT antitrust case.[6]

No hard evidence ever emerged, however, that proved Nixon's political operatives had leaned on the IRS to give ITT the favorable tax ruling. In fact, on August 25, 1975, the special team of Watergate investigators assigned to the ITT affair concluded that "there was no evidence that the rulings were in any way influenced by pressure from outside the Internal Revenue Service or that the individuals responsible for them were subject to pressure to reach any result."

However, the long-secret report, obtained with the help of a Freedom of Information Act request to the National Archives, shows that even as the investigators completed their case they still had doubts about some aspects of its handling. Richard S. Davis, the special prosecutor who wrote the ITT report, said that the team questioned one explanation offered by the IRS about why it had not been more skeptical of the ITT presentation to the agency. "It should be remembered that ITT submitted the contract and a full explanation of its terms to IRS, and their failure to adequately analyze it arguably amounts to negligence," the report said.

In sum, Davis wrote, his investigative team had concluded that it could file no criminal case in this area, against either ITT or individuals. Davis then added that "the investigation did not leave us feeling comfortable." At least one of Davis's specific examples of this discomfort had been deleted by the National Archives for reasons of privacy.[7]

Although the details of ITT's intimate dealings with the Nixon administration were known to only a handful of top White House and CIA officials in the late 1960s and early 1970s, it certainly was no secret in Washington that ITT was well regarded by the new administration. It is in this connection that the IRS's 1969 ITT ruling and the extraordinary manner in which it was proffered have become a classic story in the folklore of the IRS.

Washington reporter Joseph C. Goulden is one of those who spent a lot of time investigating the ITT ruling. "In studying a revenue ruling," he wrote in the May 1974 issue of *Washingtonian* magazine, "you look for three things: Did the IRS follow its normal procedures and routines? Was the ruling consistent with earlier holdings? And did the IRS and the taxpayer try to shove the whole deal off in the shadows where it wouldn't be noticed? If you have the wrong answers to these three questions, you start looking for skullduggery or favoritism."

The precipitating event of the whole complicated affair was ITT's desire to buy the Hartford Fire Insurance Company. To understand its importance, remember that at that time the transaction represented nothing less than the single largest corporate merger in the history of the United States.

The effect of the ruling was to allow ITT to go ahead with its plan to take over the Hartford Fire Insurance Company on a tax-free basis. Without the ruling, according to some estimates, the consummation of the takeover would have made the stockholders of Hartford liable for as much as $100 million in taxes. (After the 1969 ruling later became controversial, ITT announced that it would assume responsibility for paying any of the taxes that the Hartford stockholders would have to pay should the case ultimately be lost in the courts.)

The IRS received ITT's request for the key ruling on October 14, 1969. Exactly one week later, on October 21, a middle-level official named John F. Bogaard signed a Revenue Ruling.[8] The speed of the agency's response was more than surprising; it was probably unprecedented. So was the substance of Bogaard's ruling. "The way things normally work you couldn't get the IRS to type a revenue ruling in seven days, much less decide such a complex case," said Reuben Robertson in an interview. In the early seventies, Robertson was a lawyer on the Ralph Nader team who played a key role in ultimately getting the IRS opinion reversed.

Boris L. Bitker, Yale Law School's preeminent tax scholar, was astonished by the ruling's substance. In a letter to the IRS after the ITT controversy became public, Bitker asserted that every expert tax lawyer of his acquaintance thought the ruling had no precedent. Robert A. Klayman, an attorney with the leading Washington law firm of Caplin & Drysdale, agreed with Bitker's analysis.

There were other factors that raised questions about the IRS's ITT decision. When a revenue ruling changes IRS policy, the agency normally publishes it with the names of the interested parties removed. This way other taxpayers can learn about significant new tax policies. Although the ITT ruling concerned a matter of major importance, the IRS decided not to publish it.

With the 1969 help of the IRS, ITT's acquisition of the Hartford Fire Insurance Company had been consummated. But word of the transaction soon reached Ralph Nader, who asked Reuben Robertson, a persistent young lawyer on his team, to dig into the case. In March 1970, Robertson recalled in an interview, the Nader team brought suit in a Connecticut court challenging the state insurance commission's approval of the merger. During the discovery proceedings that grew out of this suit, Robertson obtained a copy of the previously secret IRS ruling when ITT handed the young lawyer a large stack of confusing documents. Although Robertson, Nader, and a third colleague, Alan Morrison, were not tax lawyers, and the transaction was astonishingly complex, the papers further whetted their interest. Robertson then filed additional legal challenges to the merger in federal district court and the Securities and Exchange Commission (SEC), which yielded additional documents.

Meanwhile, *The Wall Street Journal* published a skeptical story about the ITT transaction that caught the eye of Albert Fink, a level-headed middle-echelon examiner in the New York office of the IRS. In early 1973, Fink pulled out ITT's corporate tax returns. Then he traveled to Washington and examined the documents obtained by the SEC during its investigation of the merger. In April 1973, Fink completed a 110-page report charging that the transaction that the IRS had approved had been a sham, that Bogaard's 1969 ruling should be revoked, and that ITT owed $150 million in back taxes.

The period in which the agency could bring tax charges against ITT was about to expire, and in theory, at least, no one except a handful of people in the IRS knew about Fink's report. Maybe the whole thing would blow over?

The Fink report was deposited in the highly secure files of the IRS's national office in Washington and might have never seen the light of day except for Michael Barrett, then a brassy young lawyer working for the investigating subcommittee of what is now known as the House Energy and Commerce Committee. Washington is a small city, and when Reuben Robertson picked up faint rumors of a mysterious report in the files of the IRS, it didn't take him very long to knock on the door of the inquisitive Mike Barrett.

Soon the chairman of Barrett's subcommittee, Representative J. J. Pickle, began writing mean letters to Donald C. Alexander, who had been named commissioner of the IRS in May 1973. "Evidence mounts each day that favors were given to ITT on a quid pro quo basis," the subcommittee chairman said. "Was your agency, and is your agency, part of this sad story?"

The leadership of the IRS, citing privacy concerns, responded with bland generalities. So in early 1974 Barrett and a colleague decided to launch a direct attack by making an unannounced trip to the IRS's New York office and demanding an interview with the author of the mysterious ITT report. "Fink was a nice, smart, cautious middle-level guy in the IRS, a GS 9 or 11, and as soon as we asked about his ITT report he disappeared," Barrett recalled recently.

"After he disappeared, we sat there in his dingy little office, wondering what to do," Barrett continued. "About forty-five minutes later, we were summoned to the much jazzier office of the director of the IRS's New York district. The director was terrifically nervous. I'll never forget it. He was wearing a suit jacket and the room was normal temperature, even a little bit cool. But the director was sweating so hard that the armpits of his jacket were soaked through with large black rings of sweat. Fink sat there very calmly, with a smile like the proverbial cat."

Barrett said that the timing of the visit to the New York office had been critical. "The statute of limitations was about to run on the ITT case, but now the IRS knew that we knew about Fink's report. The New York director was surrounded by all his senior people. Everyone was very nervous except Fink. After a certain amount of baloney, the director told us he could not discuss the report, that the only way he could discuss a matter involving an individual taxpayer was with a full vote of the House of Representatives."

But the deal was too questionable and the pressure was too great. Shortly after the New York confrontation, on March 6, 1974, the IRS revoked its 1969 ITT ruling. The doubts of four separate men with very little direct power had worked something of a miracle. The initial suspicions of Ralph Nader, the lengthy investigations of his associate Reuben Robertson, the independent toughness of Al Fink, the brash aggressiveness of Mike Barrett together had undone the improper secret decision.

Now it was ITT's turn: It tried to revoke the IRS's revocation or at least lessen its impact. Lawyers for the corporation began filing a new round of legal challenges. Twelve years after the IRS's initial 1969 decision, seven years after it was reversed at the last possible moment, the IRS and ITT agreed to settle.

Despite the extraordinary history of the case, the final agreement got almost no attention in the press. ITT paid the government a grand total of $17.8 million in taxes its stockholders owed as a result of its purchase of Hartford. This is a good deal of money. But as noted in a May 1981 ITT press release, the settlement relieved the corporation of paying the government five times more, "an estimated possible liability of $100 million."

Who was the winner? The question is difficult to answer. But it certainly does not appear to be the public, who arguably might have been entitled to the benefits of $100 million in federal revenue. It also does not seem to be the IRS, whose reputation was further tarnished.

Were the winners actually ITT and Harold Geneen? ITT, of course, did have to cough up the $17.8 million tax payment. Then there were all those legal fees. But the IRS's improper tax ruling allowed ITT to obtain the financing needed to complete the massive merger with the Hartford Fire Insurance Company. The transaction that at that time represented the largest corporate merger in U.S. history was not disturbed.

There was another curious winner: Ralph Nader and his Center for Responsive Law. On March 31, 1982, citing the information it had developed about the tax implications of the questionable ITT transaction, the Center applied to the IRS for an award. After recounting the work of Reuben Robertson, Nader said the Center was entitled to a payment "for the information and analysis which was provided and which led to the collection of this $17.8 million in back taxes."

At first, Nader's application was rejected out of hand. But after several appeals, the IRS changed its mind. In December 1984, the IRS paid the Center $92,875 for its contribution in forcing the agency to reverse its own highly questionable ruling.

The Nixon White House received a good deal of criticism for its association with ITT. But many other presidents have mobilized their power over the IRS for improper purposes. In 1942, for example, the IRS began a routine examination of the books of Brown & Root, Inc., a large Texas contractor. What had caught the attention of the local IRS agents were some puzzling payments—bonuses that the company had given its own executives and some hard-to-explain "attorney's fees." Brown & Root had deducted the bonuses and fees as routine business expenses. But the auditors believed the money actually had been diverted for political purposes. Campaign contributions, of course, were not deductible. The IRS further believed that the recipient of these illegal campaign contributions was an ambitious young Texas congressman named Lyndon Baines Johnson.

The story of this sensitive investigation, both its beginning and abrupt end, was first told in 1956 by Washington columnist Drew Pearson. In 1982, in the first volume of his biography of Johnson, Robert A. Caro added significant details to Pearson's account. In the same year, Ronnie Dugger also discussed the case in his book about Johnson.[9]

The agent in charge of the Brown & Root investigation, Case No. S.I. 19267–F, was Elmer C. Werner. The investigation, which at times involved as many as six agents, went on for more than eighteen months. During this entire period, Representative Johnson and his allies made repeated efforts to persuade the White House to order the IRS to drop the investigation. Johnson, for example, convinced James H. Rowe, then a White House staffer, that the IRS investigation had been inspired by Democratic enemies of the New Deal in Texas. Rowe sent President Roosevelt a memo urging that the investigation be halted and also approached Treasury Secretary Henry Morgenthau about the matter.

But at least for a while, IRS investigators refused to be deflected. By January 1944, with many matters still open, Werner and his colleagues calculated that Brown & Root owed the government a lot of money: $1,099,944 in back taxes, plus a fraud penalty of $549,972. Penalties for criminal tax fraud also can include jail.

An enormous amount was at stake for both the executives of Brown & Root and the young congressman they had so generously supported. This case just had to be fixed. At 11:50 A.M. on January 13, 1944, Lyndon Johnson played his trump card: He met with Roosevelt in the White House. Four hours later, Elmer Irey, head of the IRS's criminal division in Washington and Werner's boss, telephoned Texas. Irey said he had just been ordered to brief the president on the Brown & Root investigation at ten the next morning. Irey asked Werner to send him "detailed information on political payments made by Brown & Root, Inc., to the Lyndon Johnson 1941 senatorial campaign."[10]

Werner's report was transmitted to Washington by government teletype. But the detailed evidence collected by Werner and his team during their eighteen-month investigation was of little importance to the political calculations of the president. Two days after Irey's meeting with Roosevelt, an IRS agent was dispatched from Atlanta to look over Werner's material. It is hardly surprising that this agent found the evidence insufficient for criminal prosecution. After lengthy negotiations, the IRS decided that criminal charges were not called for. No indictment. No trial. No messy publicity. The only obligation was that Brown & Root had to pay $372,000 in back taxes in a civil proceeding that by law was confidential.

Lyndon Johnson, with the help of that man in the White House, had avoided a public scandal that almost certainly would have short-circuited his political career.

The stark clarity of Lyndon Johnson's pressure on the White House and President Roosevelt's response to it is unusual. But the government's extreme sensitivity to confronting the improper tax activities of powerful politicians is common.

In 1966, for example, the chief of the IRS's criminal investigation unit in Los Angeles launched an investigation of some questionable political contributions being made in his district.

The story of the Los Angeles investigation of illegal corporate campaign contributions—and its suspiciously quiet demise a short time later—was first told almost ten years later during a congressional hearing in 1975. One witness was Robert K. Lund, a former head of what is now called the Criminal Investigation Division.

In 1966, he said, while he was head of the division's Los Angeles office, his investigators had received "certain information that political contributions were being made by corporations and were being charged off as business expenses." If Lund knew how eerily close his words came to describing the aborted Brown & Root investigation he gave no indication. "Fictitious entries were made. We made quite a study out there. As I recall, we catalogued some $2 million worth of contributions within Los Angeles County just to see what the pattern was," he told a House Government Operations subcommittee. Lund said he informed IRS headquarters in Washington about five or six different methods the corporations were using to disguise their illegal contributions. "The national office took this up and instituted a test of selected cities throughout the country."

Lund indicated to the subcommittee that in his view the IRS had obtained sufficient evidence to support indictments, "but there was a determination made not to prosecute generally for the tax violation." At that point another former head of the Criminal Investigation Division, John J. Olszewski, who had also been asked to appear before the subcommittee, said that the decision not to bring criminal tax charges had been made by the Justice Department.

Shortly before this exchange, however, Lund informed the subcommittee that the IRS commissioner at the time of the investigations had also been aware of them. "As a result of this—at least this was what I was told by the then commissioner, Sheldon Cohen—he took this information to the head of both parties and said, 'This is what the Revenue Service has discovered. Cut it out.' "

Then a third former Criminal Investigation chief, William A. Kolar, entered the discussion. He testified that the IRS had become "somewhat discouraged because of all the cases investigated, none of them to my knowledge—maybe a few did—went forward as tax prosecutions." Instead, Kolar added, the Justice Department "decided to take guilty pleas under the Corrupt Practices Act which gave them a slap on the wrist and that was that. As a result, I think the Intelligence Division [Criminal Investigation] lost interest in pursuing this kind of case because of the attitude of the Justice Department against prosecution [for tax violations]; and second, I think that business felt that it was not a terrible crime if all they were going to get was a small fine for a guilty plea."

Lund, Olszewski, and Kolar told their tales, almost in passing, after the late Representative Benjamin S. Rosenthal had asked them why the corporations that made illegal contributions to President Richard Nixon before the 1972 reelection campaign had not understood there would be trouble. Underlying Rosenthal's question was the assumption that the enormous surplus of cash flowing into Republican coffers later contributed to many of the Watergate outrages.

"Why weren't these most sophisticated leaders of industry scared off?" Rosenthal asked. "If the Intelligence Division were [sic] doing an effective job [in the late sixties] and the corporate community was aware of that," he asked, "would not that have scared them off in 1972?"

"It would have made a difference if we had a number of prosecutions out of our . . . investigations in Los Angeles and other cities," Lund replied. "But there was a determination made not to prosecute generally for the tax violation. I do personally believe that if the government had followed through and continued these earlier investigations that you wouldn't have had Watergate." Cohen, asked about the account of the three officials, said he couldn't recall the precise details but he believed they had mixed up several different cases.

CHAPTER 10

Presidents, Politics, and the IRS

The Great Depression had struck the nation. Sullen dispossessed farmers drifted off the land. Despairing unemployed workers stood in bread lines. Scattered troops of articulate, well-educated city people flirted with radical political solutions and challenged the policies of the man in the White House.

But the brickbats being thrown at President Herbert Hoover were not coming from the Left alone. In fact, one of the noisiest sources of presidential criticism was the Navy League, a powerful organization whose members included right-wing superpatriots, retired naval officers, and senior executives from the shipbuilding and munitions industries.

The reason for their anger was President Hoover's 1931 proposal to balance the federal budget. The League members were upset by Hoover's budget-cutting plan because it included a drastic reduction in the navy's shipbuilding program. To make their opposition perfectly clear, the League published a sixteen-page brochure entitled "The President and the Navy." It accused Hoover of "abysmal ignorance" about world affairs and suggested that his plan to curtail the construction of American warships was part of a secret, almost traitorous agreement with British Prime Minister Ramsey MacDonald.[1]

President Hoover and his immediate staff apparently were furious about the critical blast from the arms industry. Although the available records give no indication that the administration had reason to believe the League had violated any federal law, the White House ordered an investigation of the politically offensive organization. This response was not entirely out of character. Several historical studies have found evidence that the White House staff under President Hoover maintained an informal blacklist of Hoover's critics, aggressively investigated unwanted leaks to the press, and collected derogatory information on the personal and professional lives of Democratic officials.[2]

The agency chosen to investigate the Navy League was the Federal Bureau of Investigation. Setting the pattern that would become his modus operandi for the next forty years, young J. Edgar Hoover was suitably sensitive to the whims of the White House. During the fall of 1931, the director of the FBI wrote President Hoover's secretary, Lawrence Richey, a series of five confidential letters describing various aspects of the bureau's investigation of the Navy League. The urgency of the White House interest and the desire of the FBI to please are suggested by the fact that the FBI director wrote three of the letters on a single day, October 30, one on October 31, and the last on November 2, 1931.

The job turned out to be more difficult than expected. Publicly available biographical details about the League's principal members were rushed to the White House. So was the news that several leading American figures, such as Henry Cabot Lodge and Ogden Mills Reid, were major contributors and that the League had a total of about 4,500 members. The FBI, J. Edgar Hoover bragged, had obtained this information by undertaking a number of "pretext" interviews in which top officials of the League, including its president, William H. Gardiner, were questioned in such a manner that they were not "cognizant of the Bureau's interest."

Partly because the investigators had been unable to obtain a list with the names and addresses of all the League's members, however, neither the White House nor the FBI was satisfied. In an effort to get additional intelligence, the young FBI director decided to tap the income tax records maintained by the Internal Revenue Bureau.

Income tax files were a relatively new source of information about the activities of the American people. It was only in 1913, less than twenty years before, that the constitutional amendment authorizing the collection of a federal income tax had been approved. In fact, as far as is known, this was the first occasion that federal investigators working for an angry president had ever used the tax records for intelligence purposes.

On this occasion, however, the tax returns were not helpful. "A search of the records of the Bureau of Internal Revenue indicates that no income tax returns were filed [by the Navy League] in the Washington district during the period 1927 to date," J. Edgar Hoover told Richey in October 1931. "Under present laws some organizations which do not operate for benefit are exempted from making income tax returns. This is accomplished by a letter addressed to them by the Bureau of Internal Revenue. No such letter was addressed to the Navy League, as far back as 1923. The search for income tax returns is being extended to all districts in the United States. So far no return has been found in any district, including New York City."[3]

The surprising thing is that the FBI's secret examination of tax information for the White House was not illegal. In fact, the confused drafting of a vaguely worded amendment added to an appropriations act in 1910 actually authorized presidents to use tax records any way they saw fit. This 1910 amendment, which remained the controlling law until after the Watergate scandals of the mid-1970s, stated that tax records were to be open for inspection "only upon the order of the President under rules and regulations to be prescribed by the Secretary of the Treasury and approved by the president."

Partly because of the curious wording of what really was an open records law, few Americans have understood that, from 1910 until 1976, the IRS routinely made tax information available to almost any federal or state agency that requested it. "Given the prevalence of the belief that tax returns are confidential, distribution to government agencies seems anomalous. Most likely, it [the casual sharing of tax records] has been permitted because it occurred without any public debate," one authoritative study concluded.[4]

Although many Americans believe that President Nixon's White House was uniquely active in this regard, almost every administration since the end of World War I has one way or another used the selective enforcement of the tax laws and the information contained in tax records for improper political purposes. Confidential government documents prove, for example, that Franklin Delano Roosevelt and the officials around him did not hesitate to mobilize the tax agency in efforts to destroy the careers of individuals they had decided were enemies. The records even show that on one occasion an inquiry from Eleanor Roosevelt prompted Treasury Secretary Morgenthau to order a tax investigation of a conservative newspaper publisher who had become one of the Roosevelt administration's leading critics.

Probably the single most brazen display of the Roosevelt administration's willingness to use the tax agency for political purposes was its attack on Andrew Mellon, the millionaire capitalist who served as the Republican secretary of the treasury from 1921 to 1932. No document has yet emerged that directly links Roosevelt to the decision to go after Mellon. But Elmer L. Irey, the first director of what is now called the Criminal Investigation Division, acknowledged that Treasury Secretary Henry Morgenthau, Jr., ordered him to develop serious tax charges against Mellon even though he knew that the just-retired treasury secretary was innocent.[5] It seems unlikely that Morgenthau would have mounted such a campaign without the approval of FDR.

"The Roosevelt Administration made me go after Andy Mellon," Irey wrote in his autobiography, explaining that his marching orders had come directly from Morgenthau. The chief of criminal intelligence said that he was so uncomfortable with the order that he went directly to Morgenthau to express his objections. But Morgenthau brushed Irey's concerns aside. " 'Irey, you can't be 99 2/3 percent on that job. Investigate Mellon. I order it,' " the official recalled Morgenthau telling him.

In his autobiography, Irey did not say when his unusual conversation with Morgenthau actually took place, and more than fifty years after the Mellon affair the exact chronology is not clear. The available record also leaves unclear the actual criminal charges that the Roosevelt administration tried to bring against Mellon before it attempted to punish the former treasury secretary by other means.

Roosevelt had won the election in November 1932 and had taken over the reins of government on March 4, 1933. Morgenthau had assumed de facto control of Treasury on November 17, 1933, when he was named acting secretary. He succeeded to the secretaryship itself on January 1, 1934. A Justice Department memorandum written about the case in early 1934 adopts the same view as Irey: The charges that the Roosevelt administration wanted to lodge against Mellon were either invalid or could not be proved. The memo also noted, however, that Acting Secretary Morgenthau had informed Justice on December 10 of his intent to charge Mellon.[6]

On March 11, 1934, ignoring the expert views of Irey and the two Justice Department lawyers, the Roosevelt administration announced it would seek criminal tax evasion charges against the former secretary.[7] The initiation of any kind of tax case against a person with so much power and so many lawyers is extremely rare; the lodging of criminal tax charges was then, and remains today, almost unprecedented. In the Mellon case, the department alleged that the financier owed the government additional taxes of $1,319,080.90, plus a 50 percent fraud penalty of $659,540.45. The government said the grounds for its charges were that certain transfers of his stock to a bank and to a corporation controlled by his daughter, for the purpose of establishing a loss, were not legitimate.

"Later the Bureau of Internal Revenue, bent upon what its former chief [Mellon] called 'political prosecution,' increased its claimed deficiency to $3,089,261.24," a historian would write some years later.[8] At the time, Mellon also denounced the charges as "impertinent, scandalous and improper." He added that in 1931—the year covered by the government's charges—he had actually overpaid his federal taxes.

The government immediately ran into serious trouble with its attack. First, a balky federal grand jury in Pittsburgh, Mellon's hometown, took the highly unusual action of ignoring the recommendation of the prosecutor. It refused to indict Mellon on any charge. Some historians have speculated that the powerful millionaire secretly influenced that decision. But the social backgrounds of the jury members—five laborers, two mechanics, two farmers, two clerks, two engineers, one carpenter, one plumber, one writer, one lumber dealer, and only a single banker—argue against this proposition.

The bitter case then moved to a new battleground, the Board of Tax Appeals in Washington. At that time, the Tax Board theoretically functioned as an independent agency. But it was housed within the executive branch, a bureaucratic arrangement that tended to encourage the members to view tax cases brought by the government in a favorable light.

But even the relatively compliant Tax Board refused to accept most of the Roosevelt administration's hoked-up charges against Mellon. After developing a hearing record of more than 10,000 pages and reading voluminous legal briefs, the board on December 7, 1937, issued a ruling that rejected the most significant aspects of the charges. Mellon's intentions in setting up the charitable foundation, the board concluded, were truly charitable and not a tax dodge. While the former treasury secretary was found to owe $485,809—about one sixth of the government's original claim—the board totally dismissed all the criminal and civil fraud penalties that the Roosevelt administration had brought against him.

CASTING FOR THE KINGFISH

The Mellon case was hardly the only occasion on which the Roosevelt administration mobilized the tax agency for political purposes. From his very first moments as the Democratic presidential candidate in 1931, for example, Roosevelt had understood that Huey Long, the mesmerizing Louisiana governor and senator, represented a genuine political threat.

Part of Long's appeal lay in his populist social programs, which had brought to him the support of millions of working-class Americans who were being ravaged by the Great Depression. But Long, known as the Kingfish, was also a brilliant demagogue who would adopt any tactic to increase his power. Long's definitive biographer, Harry Williams, emphasized this unique quality when he observed that, unlike all other American politicians', Long's goal was never "to contain the opposition or to impose certain conditions upon it, but to force it out of existence."[9]

Long was indeed a ruthless politician. But Roosevelt too was a driven man who did not hesitate to adopt questionable tactics to maintain his power.

The administration's deep concern about Long was translated into action exactly three days after Morgenthau became Roosevelt's treasury secretary on January 3, 1934, when Morgenthau ordered Elmer Irey, the man he had instructed to go after Mellon, to launch a second campaign against Long.[10] (Actually, Irey recalled, Herbert Hoover had also been worried about the rapidly growing power of Long and his machine. In July 1932, months before Roosevelt had entered the White House, the bureau had been encouraged to initiate an intensive investigation of the flamboyant politician. Somehow, however, Long, then a senator from Louisiana, managed to get the Hoover administration's investigation stopped in its tracks through secret intervention by Hoover's assistant secretary of the navy, a New Orleans businessman named Ernest L. Jahncke.[11]

The Roosevelt administration's tax investigation of Long was disclosed by the senator himself. In a speech to the Senate on January 7, 1935, Long revealed that the Treasury Department had dispatched a "horde" of 250 agents to check his tax returns and the returns of his lieutenants. "They did not try to put any covering over this thing," he informed his Senate colleagues. It was, he added, a simple drive to put Long, and all the top officials of the Long machine, in prison.

The Roosevelt administration did not publicly respond to Long's disclosure. But a few months later, Irey sent Morgenthau an extraordinary set of confidential memos that provides a revealing glimpse of the hard-nosed tactics that the government had adopted in its investigation of Long and his machine. The memos were written by Irey and two other bureau officials. Directed to Morgenthau, they concerned the progress and tactics of one narrow aspect of the Long investigation that the treasury secretary had ordered.

The first document was a one-page memorandum from Irey dated June 14, 1935. The subject was the Jahncke Service Company of New Orleans and the three Jahncke brothers, Paul, Walter, and Ernest.[12] Irey noted that Paul and Walter had been very helpful in the investigation of Long but that "Ernest has lent little or no assistance." It was Ernest, you will recall, who had managed to stop Irey's first investigation of Long at the very end of the Hoover administration.

Irey began his one-page memo by reminding Morgenthau that the treasury secretary had requested information about the Jahncke brothers. After stating that the two documents attached to his own would answer Morgenthau's questions, the intelligence chief made a somewhat cryptic reference to a favor that he thought the government should bestow on the company, then controlled by Paul and Walter Jahncke. "In so far as the interests of our Service are concerned," Irey wrote, "it would be of considerable value if something could be done to assist the Jahncke Service Company in working out their problems through the Reconstruction Finance Company [RFC]. . . ." Irey did not explain the exact nature of the assistance he was requesting or why it would be in the service's interest to grant it.

The second document sent to Morgenthau was a bit more forthcoming. Written by A. D. Burford, the special agent in charge of the bureau's operations in Dallas, it too concerned the Jahncke family.

For many years, Burford explained, the Jahncke Service Company had been in the business of dredging the rivers and canals of the Mississippi and then selling the sand, gravel, and shells that it recovered to state highway contractors. The company, however, was about to collapse because the Long machine had recently started giving all its business to the Jahnckes' competitors. It is not known whether the withdrawal of state business was related to the decision of the company's executives to help the federal government.

Burford proposed a course of action and the reason why he was recommending it. "It is believed that it would be advisable to assist the Jahncke Service Company in working out their financial program through the Reconstruction Finance Corporation in every possible way to prevent the company's extermination. Paul Jahncke in particular has been very helpful in a confidential way and promises more and complete cooperation."

It appears certain that Burford was suggesting what, in the middle of the Depression, could be considered an official bribe: an RFC loan to the Jahnckes in return for their continued cooperation in the Long investigation. A third document sent to Morgenthau reinforces this interpretation. This document was a report that a special tax agent named Alf Oftedal had prepared after a three-hour interview of Paul Jahncke in January 1935. According to Oftedal's account, Jahncke had spelled out how "Huey P. Long proposes to do what he can to ruin" the Jahncke family. Oftedal also quoted Jahncke as saying he planned to approach Secretary Morgenthau about a loan from the RFC. "He expressed the opinion, in this connection, that with a little aid from such a source that [his] corporation could eventually recover from its difficulties, provided, of course, that Senator Huey P. Long was, as he put it, placed where he belonged. He stated that unless the Federal government succeeded in prosecuting the senator and his associates for their fraudulent practices and their wilful attempts to evade and defeat the income tax, that there was no hope for Jahncke Service, Inc., or any other upright, decent and honorable business organization in the State of Louisiana."

A massive file of dusty index cards deep in the stacks of the National Archives Building in Washington shows that the RFC did in fact provide the Jahncke company the financial assistance mentioned in the documents sent to Morgenthau. But a note typed on the bottom of one of these index cards by some long-retired clerk of the Reconstruction Finance Corporation states that for unexplained reasons the full file containing the details of this particular transaction "cannot be processed for transmittal to National Archives." And indeed, a search of the appropriate storage box at the National Records Center in Suitland, Maryland, found no records explaining the precise nature of the assistance that the index-card notation shows was indeed provided the Jahncke Service Company by the RFC.

The bureau's investigation of Long, apparently enriched by information offered by the grateful Jahncke brothers, now moved into high gear. Just how important the Long case had become to the Roosevelt administration is indicated by the direct involvement of the president in an important last-minute aspect of the effort to crush Long: the selection and recruiting of a lawyer to handle the actual prosecution.

The story of FDR's direct intervention in the case was told by Irey. Bureau agents working the Louisiana investigation, he recalled, had repeatedly picked up reports that Huey Long was not concerned because he believed that no Louisiana jury would ever convict the state's most popular politician. To stand a chance of putting Long in jail, Irey had become convinced that the government had to recruit a special prosecutor who was fearless, honest, and, most important, a Southerner.

"I told this to Secretary Morgenthau and he said, 'Come on with me. I want you to tell it to someone else.' Somebody else was only across the street and I soon found myself explaining the Huey Long situation to Franklin D. Roosevelt," Irey recalled.[13] Shortly after the White House meeting, FDR personally took on the job of persuading Dan Moody, a highly respected former governor of Texas, to become the government's special prosecutor.

The bureau's initial target in its attack on the Long machine was Louisiana State Representative Joseph Fisher. On April 26, 1935, Fisher was found guilty of tax evasion by a federal jury in New Orleans and sentenced to eighteen months in prison. Irey was elated. The first step in the broad attack on Huey Long and his lieutenants had been successful.

But five months later, a brilliant young physician named Carl Austin Weiss gunned down Long in the marble hallways of the Louisiana capitol. He was a passionate liberal, and his motive was probably political. Long was rushed to a nearby hospital, where surgeons attempted to repair the damage from the bullet, which had entered his stomach just under the ribs on his right side. Their efforts were not successful. Early on the morning of September 10, 1935, the Kingfish died.

Not surprisingly, the administration's campaign against the Long machine immediately began to lose its momentum. One month after the assassination, a second Long lieutenant, Abraham Shushan, was brought to trial. He was acquitted of tax evasion charges. In May 1936, the U.S. attorney announced the dismissal of a number of other tax charges against powerful members of the Long machine. It was widely reported at the time that the cases had been dropped in return for a pledge from Long's heirs to support Roosevelt in his bid for a second term.

There seems to be no question but that members of the Long machine were cheating on their taxes. Whether Long himself was not reporting all his income is less clear. Some experts contend that Long was only interested in the exercise of power, not in lining his pockets. Others scoff at this argument. In the case of Andrew Mellon, there appears to be clear evidence that the former treasury secretary was not guilty of criminal tax fraud.

Whatever the underlying facts in these two cases, however, there appears to be no question that the Roosevelt administration's actions were motivated by politics rather than by recovering lost tax revenues. As in the Nixon years, this serious misuse of the tax agency's law enforcement powers created a cynical climate that was destructive to both the agency and the attitude of all taxpayers.

Another political figure of considerable concern to the Roosevelt administration was the Reverend Charles E. Coughlin, a right wing, anti-Semitic Catholic priest who used the Radio League of the Little Flower and the Social Justice Publishing Company to spout his venom. It is worth noting that some months before Long's assassination in 1935, the senator and the priest had met to explore a possible alliance. On September 18, 1940, the bureau sent Secretary Morgenthau a detailed report "for your information" about the tax status of Father Coughlin and his outlets.[14]

For the tax year 1936, the report said, Coughlin received a salary of $4,040. The next year, it dropped to $3,440. In 1938, his salary again was $4,040. In 1939, his salary dropped to $1,440. Income tax paid was $14.54 in 1936, $7.27 in 1937, $17.78 in 1938, and none in 1940.

Ted Morgan, in his 1985 biography of Roosevelt, reports that FDR directly asked Morgenthau to investigate the tax returns of Representative Hamilton Fish, a right-wing Republican whose district included Roosevelt's Hudson River estate and who had met with several Nazi leaders in 1939. An investigation was conducted. "The worst side of [Roosevelt's] self-righteousness, however, was not the perfectly human trait of taking credit when he had achieved so much but the habit of equating all forms of opposition with disloyalty," Morgan concluded.[15]

The Revenue Bureau, Irey, and Morgenthau, however, were not only worried about the fanatic voices of the right. On June 25, 1941, Irey sent his boss a memo about Bernard Ades, a Baltimore lawyer who had become a controversial figure after a Maryland congressman demanded his removal as an auditor for the U.S. Housing Authority.[16] Six years before, Irey informed Morgenthau, Ades had been denied a job in the bureau because, among other actions, "he had run as a communist for President of the Baltimore City Council." The tax official also wrote that, because Ades had severely criticized a judge and a number of public officials while serving as a defense attorney, "the sincerity of his motives is seriously questioned by a large group of prominent business and professional men as well as high officials in the state."

The purpose of the report on Ades is not clear. Although Irey devoted a good deal of attention to the political beliefs and actions of this insignificant left-wing lawyer, the report provided absolutely no information about whether or not Ades was paying his taxes.

A second, far more famous, target whose political persuasion was left-wing was the black singer and actor Paul Robeson. A cover note attached to the Revenue Bureau's report on the investigation of Robeson said it had been undertaken at the request of Morgenthau. There again is no indication why the treasury secretary ordered the probe. But on August 7, 1941, Irey sent Morgenthau a thirteen-page report about Robeson's "communist and communist-front activities, and his expressions concerning communists and Soviet Russia." The report, by Special Agent George H. Allen, was backed up with thirty-seven separate exhibits, mostly articles about the singer that had been carefully clipped from *The New York Times,* the *New York Herald Tribune,* and the *Daily Worker.* Predictably, the report concluded: "It is believed that Paul Robeson is an ardent supporter of Soviet Russia and communism, and that probably he is a member of the Communist Party. His activities in or on behalf of communist and communist front activities have been so constant and widespread, and he has followed the 'party line' so consistently that it appears reasonable to conclude that he is attempting to fulfill the mission of the Communist Party of the United States without reservation."[17]

EVEN ELEANOR

The surviving documents do not always make clear who it was that initiated the major political investigations undertaken by the Internal Revenue Bureau during the Roosevelt years. Circumstantial evidence suggests that at least in the cases of Mellon and Long it was probably the president himself who triggered the probes.

In one case, however, a clear paper trail shows how a casual inquiry from Eleanor Roosevelt prompted Morgenthau to order a tax investigation with significant political overtones. The subject of Mrs. Roosevelt's curiosity was the conservative newspaper publisher Frank Gannett, who at the time was also the vice chairman of the Republican National Committee. The matter that had caught Mrs. Roosevelt's eye was a report in an unpublished manuscript that Gannett had obtained indirect financial support from Cornell University in his drive to enlarge his chain of newspapers. The evidence shows that Mrs. Roosevelt was aware that the Gannett chain's editorials had been highly critical of the Roosevelt administration.

In addition to being a leading publisher and a senior officer of the Republican party, Gannett held a third position of considerable consequence: the chairmanship of Cornell University's Board of Governors. This last connection meant that the tax inquiry prompted by Mrs. Roosevelt's June 7, 1944, note to Morgenthau could have had a major impact on one of the leading educational institutions in the United States, some parts of which were then regarded as important centers of conservative thought hostile to Roosevelt.

Mrs. Roosevelt's interest in Gannett began on June 2, 1944, when Alvin W. Hofer, a New York writer, sent the first lady a typed manuscript of his unpublished book, *The Fork in the Road*. [18] Hofer was concerned about what he believed was a fascist threat to America. One story cited to support his thesis involved an allegation that the trustees of Cornell had used $400,000 of the university's tax-exempt endowment fund to help Gannett purchase the *Binghamton Press* and thus prevented the establishment of a liberal paper in the upstate New York area.

In a brief "Dear Henry" note to the treasury secretary about the manuscript, Mrs. Roosevelt said she was sending him "this voluminous bundle because it seems to be an account of something rather serious which actually happened." She said she was unable to judge the accuracy of the allegations, but that "I thought you might know some one who would look at it and decide whether it was deserving of any attention since it deals with the experimental station at Geneva and the Cornell Agricultural College."

Morgenthau did not waste any time. Within two weeks of receiving the manuscript, two Treasury Department staff members had read the book, undertaken a limited independent investigation, and provided the secretary with a three-page, largely critical review. While rejecting Hofer's overall thesis, that the United States was about to be taken over by the fascists, the two reviewers appeared to accept some of his underlying research about the political activities and affiliations of Cornell University. Frank Gannett, they reported, was the chairman of the executive committee of the Board of Trustees of Cornell. On June 18, 1943, they added, Cornell had bought a building for $400,000, which it then leased to Gannett.

At the bottom of the cover note accompanying the June 16 review, Morgenthau wrote a brief note asking for further investigation and clarification of one sensitive question. "Check whether Cornell used trustee fund to buy newspaper. This if true might endanger their [unclear word] tax status."

An investigation of whether Cornell's activities might affect its tax situation was immediately launched. On June 29, Assistant Treasury Secretary Sullivan sent Morgenthau a note describing the transaction. "The trustees purchased the building in which the newspaper had been published. At the same time, Frank Gannett's company purchased the stock of the Binghamton Press. Title to the building passed to Cornell and the lease of the premises by the University to the newspaper company is duly recorded. The amount of rent is not disclosed." Sullivan concluded with his analysis that the arrangement did not "in any way affect the tax-exempt status of Cornell University."

In the end, based on this opinion, nothing came of Morgenthau's investigation of Gannett and Cornell. On the same day that Morgenthau received Sullivan's assessment, he dispatched a four-page letter to Mrs. Roosevelt sharply criticizing Hofer's analysis of the threat of fascism. Concerning the specific question of the legality of the Gannett contract with Cornell, however, he offered Mrs. Roosevelt no judgment.

WHO RUNS THE IRS?

Given the obvious fact that the IRS is an integral part of the executive branch, it is hardly surprising that over the years many of the narrowly focused political chores undertaken by the agency have been ordered by the president, the White House staff, the secretary of the treasury, and other powerful administration figures. From time to time, however, a member of Congress has gained sufficient authority to bully the IRS into serving his political needs. Such a man was Sam Rayburn, the powerful Speaker of the House of Representatives for a total of sixteen years between 1940 and 1961.

The story of how the Democrat Rayburn forced the Republican-controlled IRS to jump through his hoop was told by Tip O'Neill, the garrulous Massachusetts Democrat who was a well-connected member of the House during most of the Rayburn years. O'Neill himself later served as House Speaker.[19]

The year was 1955. At that time, the city of Albany, New York, was represented in the House by Leo O'Brien, a former radio talk show host. O'Brien had been sent to Washington by the Albany Democratic machine, then controlled by the O'Connell brothers. While the O'Connells were all-powerful in the precincts of Albany, they had a big problem in Washington: The IRS had serious doubts about the accuracy and completeness of their tax returns.

The O'Connells needed help, and through their front man in the House of Representatives they were granted a meeting with Rayburn. "Mr. Speaker," Tip O'Neill would later recall one of the brothers as saying, "they've been holding our case up for years. My wife is in an institution, they're driving us all nuts. We want them to make a decision: let them take it criminal or take it civil. We just want to know which way it will go so we can get this thing behind us and move on."

Rayburn told the O'Connells to come back at five that afternoon. He then called T. Coleman Andrews, the IRS commissioner, and summoned him to the Capitol. When Andrews arrived, Rayburn told him that he wanted to talk about the O'Connell case. The commissioner said he had the matter on his desk.

" 'From what I hear,' " O'Neill remembers Rayburn saying, " 'it's been sitting there for three years. You're driving these people crazy. I want a decision by five o'clock tonight. Either take it criminal or take it civil. Personally, I think you should take it civil because these folks have suffered enough.' "

Like anyone holding the top job in the IRS, the commissioner was a political animal. He didn't have to be told that a request like this from the most powerful Democrat then in office—Eisenhower was in the White House at the time—had to be given serious attention. A half hour before the deadline, the IRS called and the speaker got the word: The case was civil; the proposed fine would be $42,000.

But there was one additional twist to the story. When O'Brien brought the O'Connells back to the speaker's office at five, Rayburn gave them the happy news. In the way of big-city politics, the brothers then promised Rayburn he could have O'Brien's vote anytime he needed it.

" 'That's not how I operate,' " O'Neill recalls Rayburn piously replying. " 'I've never done a quid pro quo in my life. I helped you because I thought the IRS was wrong in the way they treated you. But if you really want to help me out, there's an interesting bill coming up concerning off-shore oil. Most of the northerners want those revenues to go into a special fund for a national education program. But there are many of us who think that money should go back to the states.' "

" 'No problem,' " the O'Connells said. " 'Leo will be delighted to vote with you on that one, won't you, Leo?' "

Speaker Rayburn had used the political power of his office to muscle the Republican-controlled IRS to provide a special service to two powerful Democratic politicians. The politicians, in turn, had muscled their man in the House of Representatives to promise his vote for legislation that his constituents strongly opposed.

In spite of the considerable influence that officials at the top can wield when it comes to a specific sensitive case, a great deal of power is also exercised at the local level. This fact means that it is not only senior officials in Washington who sometimes target a political enemy. Although it clearly is not an everyday experience, IRS agents acknowledge that every one of the IRS's seven regional commissioners and sixty-three district directors have sufficient authority to arrange for the harassment of troublesome taxpayers. But the decentralization of power within the IRS goes much further than that. Even individual tax agents have considerable discretion in the application of their enforcement powers.

Only on very few occasions in the history of the IRS has a taxpayer actually proved in a court of law that a single tax agent had initiated a serious tax case for political purposes. Partly, of course, this is because such actions are rare events. Another explanation for the rarity of such cases, however, is that very few taxpayers have the will and financial resources needed to mount a legal battle against the IRS, even when its enforcement actions are totally unjustified.

FIGHTING BACK

Reuben G. Lenske, an energetic and outspoken Oregon lawyer, waged one of those rare heroic campaigns.

The IRS first brought criminal tax charges against Lenske in 1962. The original indictment charged him with attempting to evade paying $500,-000 in income taxes in 1955, 1957, and 1958 and with filing a false return in 1956. After a lengthy trial in federal district court, Lenske was convicted.

But Lenske took his case to the Ninth Circuit Court of Appeals. On October 5, 1966, a three-judge panel reversed the lawyer's conviction on two grounds. First, the court said, the tax charges leveled against the lawyer were based on factully incorrect information. Second, the whole prosecution was legally suspect because it had been triggered for political reasons having nothing to do with violations of the tax law.

"This court will not place its stamp of approval upon a witch-hunt, a crusade to rid society of unorthodox thinkers and actors by using the federal income tax laws and the courts to put such people in the penitentiary," the judges said.

The Court of Appeals described the IRS investigation and prosecution of Lenske as being "contrary to law," "outrageously unfair," speculative, and astonishingly sloppy. The court found that the IRS agent who prepared the case against Lenske; the prosecutors; and the federal trial judge all contributed to an astonishing miscarriage of justice. But the court came down the hardest on Albert DesChennes, the lead investigator for the IRS.

The crucial moment in the case, according to the court, occurred on June 13, 1961, when DesChennes handed his final investigative report to the director of the IRS office in Portland, Oregon. The report was 37 closely typed pages and was followed by an appendix of 84 pages that listed 468 exhibits and the names and addresses of 315 witnesses should their testimony ever be required.

Impressive as this bulky document seemed, it was the extraordinary political commentary in the first few pages that astonished the appeals court. After noting that Lenske had been born in Russia, the court said, DesChennes's report observed that "representatives of the Federal Bureau of Investigation, Portland, and the Intelligence Division of the Portland Police Department stated that they have reason to believe that Mr. Lenske is a communist. In fact, they each maintain an extensive file on Mr. Lenske."

To support this conclusion, DesChennes included a newspaper clipping of an announcement made by the lawyer and one of the lawyer's colleagues about a forthcoming meeting to form a local chapter of the Lawyers' Guild, a left-leaning organization. The agent noted that the clip had also said that the organizing meeting would be followed by a showing of a controversial documentary film criticizing the tactics of the House Un-American Activities Committee. Another part of the special agent's evidence against Lenske was a letter published in a local newspaper in which the lawyer stated that some of the actions taken by the United States in its relations with Cuba, Laos, and China violated U.S. laws and treaty obligations.

As a result of an IRS appeal, the Court of Appeals issued a second opinion on August 27, 1967. The second decision again reversed Lenske's conviction, but this time only on the grounds that the government had failed to prove that he was a tax cheat. In an additional separate opinion, however, one of the judges returned to the political aspects of the case.

"I regard what I have recited above as a scandal of the first magnitude in the administration of the tax laws of the United States. It discloses nothing less than a witch-hunt, a crusade by the key agent of the United States in this prosecution, to rid our country of unorthodox thinkers and actors by using federal income tax laws and federal courts to put them in the penitentiary. No court should become an accessory to such a project." He added that the investigation of Lenske by Special Agent DesChennes could "only be described as grotesque."

The stated reasons for the IRS's investigation and prosecution of Lenske were bizarre. But according to both the first and second Court of Appeals decisions, almost as curious were the gross inaccuracies of the tax charges brought against the lawyer.

In the court's first decision, for example, the panel observed that as a result of his two-and-a-half-year investigation DesChennes had concluded that for 1955 alone "Lenske had evaded taxes in the amount of $11,465.-74." But during the actual trial, the district court judge determined that the agent's accounting skills were poor and that the extra taxes owed were only $414.78.

The court was not impressed. "The special agent determined Lenske's taxes to be 27 times as much as the court found them to be. On an examination testing his accuracy, the special agent would have scored less than 4 out of a possible 100."

Another unusual aspect of the case cited by the appeals court concerned the government's reaction to the testimony of an expert witness called by Lenske. The witness, the court said, had identified a large number of significant errors in the charges that the government had brought against Lenske. But instead of abandoning its prosecution, the government simply adopted all the corrections in the revised tax charts that the prosecutors subsequently submitted to the trial court.

In its second reversal of Lenske's conviction, the court called the government's handling of the case "outrageously unfair." The panel added that the evidence presented by the government was so speculative and uncertain that the court could not allow the case to stand.

There is no suggestion in the IRS documents cited by the two Court of Appeals decisions that Lenske was the target of a national campaign directed by agency headquarters in Washington. What the record suggests is that DesChennes decided to initiate his tax investigation after federal and local law enforcement officials in the area decided that the lawyer was a politically suspicious person. Perhaps their suspicions were fed by Lenske's letters to the editor and by conspiratorial whispers from the "Red squad" of the Portland Police Department and the local office of the FBI.

But Lenske himself believes that the actual trigger of the IRS investigation was his decision to represent a World War II army veteran named William Mackie. The Immigration and Naturalization Service had begun proceedings to deport Mackie on the grounds that he had been a member of the Communist party. Lenske took the Mackie case to the Supreme Court, where he lost by a five-to-four decision.

"There was another lawyer in Oregon who represented most of the Communists in those days but for one reason or another Mackie came to me. I think the fuss and bother over this case probably is what caught the eye of the IRS," Lenske said in an interview in 1987, more than two decades after his trial.

"I was not and have never been a Communist, but I did represent a citizen who the government wanted to kick out of the United States for political reasons."

The lawyer said that from the very beginning he was convinced he eventually would defeat the IRS. "But the Court of Appeals decision surprised me. I thought I'd have to go to the Supreme Court before my conviction would be turned around."

Even though Lenske did not have to go as high as the Supreme Court, the lawyer's successful battle against the IRS was extraordinarily costly. "You understand, first of all, that with my conviction I automatically lost my right to practice law. It was not until the Court of Appeals reversed my conviction four years later that I could once again earn any income as a working lawyer."

But the loss of a regular source of income was only one part of the devastating effect of the tax prosecution on Lenske's financial situation. He estimates that the actual cost of his defense came to about $100,000. "I was very lucky because I had some resources," he said. "I was able to raise $20,000 to pay the lawyer who represented me at the district level. After Judge Carter sentenced me to two years in federal prison, I talked to my lawyer about an appeal. He said it would cost me another $50,000. But because the Internal Revenue Service had assessed me with $500,000 in unreported income taxes and placed liens against all my properties, I couldn't raise any money for the appeal. I had no choice but to handle the appeal myself."

Lenske, who said he was a strong advocate of the graduated income tax, never received any damages. In fact, partly because of the difficulty of the law, he never even sought them. "I always was more interested in the principle of this case, not the money," he said. Albert DesChennes, now retired from the IRS, at first declined to comment on the case. He did say, however, that the agency did not reprimand him after the court decisions criticizing him.

The prosecution of Reuben Lenske is an example of how an individual agent in some special circumstances can use the powers of the IRS to bludgeon a citizen for political reasons. Often, however, the use of the IRS's power and information for political advantage is far more subtle.

On April 11, 1970, Lawrence F. O'Brien, a former Kennedy administration official who was then chairman of the Democratic National Committee, issued a press release denouncing President Nixon for allowing one of his White House aides to obtain tax information.

"I call upon President Nixon to terminate immediately this illegal access of his personal staff to confidential tax returns of 80 million Americans," O'Brien said. The Democratic official added that, by allowing a former newspaperman named Clark Mollenhoff to examine tax records, President Nixon had violated the federal laws and regulations protecting the privacy of all Americans.

O'Brien said his judgment about the impropriety of the Nixon program was based on a legal memorandum prepared by Mortimer M. Caplin, IRS commissioner during the Kennedy administration, and two other former agency officials.

The 1970 O'Brien denunciation of President Nixon, and Caplin's legal analysis, however, turned out to be an embarrassment to the Democrats.

This is because almost a decade before, on May 23, 1961, Caplin, then serving as Kennedy's brand-new IRS commissioner, had written a long memorandum explaining that a few months before he had allowed Carmine Bellino, a special consultant to President Kennedy, to inspect IRS files "without a written request."

In an interview in the spring of 1989, Vernon (Mike) Acree, an IRS official from the early 1950s through the Nixon years, provided an interesting insight into the secret use of tax information by various presidents. During the Watergate hearings, Acree was identified by John J. Caufield, a Nixon staff member, as the source of tax information for the White House.

"Right after Kennedy was elected, I got called down to Caplin's office," Acree said. "He introduced me to Bellino. Caplin said Bellino was a special assistant to the president and could have anything. One of my assistants set Bellino up in a little office in the IRS headquarters building. I remember that one day during the Kennedy years that my assistant provided Bellino a stack of tax records about ten inches high that had been submitted by *The New York Times*. We weren't told why the White House wanted to see the *Times*'s returns and didn't ask." (Bellino, who has retired to Florida, did not return several telephone calls to his home. James Reston, who was the *Times*'s Washington bureau chief during the period, said in an interview that he had never previously heard that the Kennedy aide was looking at the tax returns of the paper and that he had no idea why the investigation was conducted.)

Acree said that his point was not to criticize Bellino or Kennedy. "The tax information I made available to Kennedy and Nixon was not unusual and did not violate the laws of the period," he said. "Furthermore, I had provided the same service to White House people under Truman, Eisenhower, and Johnson."

It wasn't only President Kennedy who wanted the IRS to open its files to Bellino. In a letter dated less than a week after Kennedy assumed office,

Attorney General Robert Kennedy asked Caplin to give Bellino access to federal tax information in connection with joint investigations by the IRS and the Justice Department. On February 1, Robert Kennedy got his wish.

One of the purposes for the attorney general's request that Bellino be given total access to the nation's tax records was Robert Kennedy's decision to mount an intensive and coordinated attack on organized crime. The seriousness of this drive was indicated about a month after taking office, when Caplin issued an IRS-wide order on February 24, 1961, calling for the saturation treatment of the racketeers' files and the "full use" of "available electronic equipment." (Chapter 5 on criminal tax enforcement described additional details of this drive against organized crime.)

The hypocritical charges from O'Brien and Caplin that the Nixon administration was misusing tax records in a historically unique way enraged Senator John Williams, a tenacious Delaware Republican who had made a successful political career out of giving the IRS a hard time.

One day after the O'Brien-Caplin attack on the Nixon team, Williams went on the floor of the Senate and disclosed the existence of the Caplin order granting Bellino permission to view any kind of records held by the IRS.

Williams and his Republican colleagues in the Senate were deeply annoyed by Lawrence O'Brien and Mortimer Caplin's pious 1970 complaints about the Nixon White House. But they would have been genuinely furious if they had known about the full range of the Kennedy administration's political misuse of the powers of the IRS. Details of the secret Kennedy operations were to remain hidden until after the cumulative weight of the Watergate scandals drove Nixon from the White House.

Because the Kennedy campaign was aimed at smothering a fairly broad political movement, rather than a single political figure such as Secretary Mellon or Senator Long, I have chosen to describe its functioning in chapter 11.

But one interesting case showing how the Kennedys used the power of the IRS for their own political purposes will be discussed here because it involves a single fallen member of the Eisenhower team.

Tax information can be marshaled for political advantage in an almost endless number of ways. Many, of course, involve the disclosure of embarrassing tax information by formal or informal means,. Conversely, even suppressing tax information has been used to political advantage. William Safire, now a conservative and witty columnist at *The New York Times*, told of one such incident in a 1986 column. Before joining the *Times*, Safire was a speechwriter in the Nixon White House and a Republican public-relations man.

The subject of Safire's fascinating November 3, 1986, column was Sherman Adams, who had just died. Adams was the former Republican governor of New Hampshire who had become a powerful White House chief of staff during the Eisenhower administration. He had been forced to quit after congressional Democrats disclosed he had accepted the gift of a vicuña coat from an industrialist named Bernard Goldfine.

Safire reported that shortly after Kennedy took over the White House in January 1961, Sherman Adams's landlady informed the IRS that he had not paid his taxes for a number of years. (Vernon Acree, in his 1989 interview, confirmed that the IRS had conducted an extensive tax investigation of Adams. Acree said that he knew about the investigation because he had conducted it himself. "We found that Adams was depositing large amounts of cash in accounts he maintained all over the country," Acree said. "It seems he would often make the deposits in these banks while flying around the country with President Eisenhower.") Safire said that the IRS investigation found hard evidence that Adams had not reported $300,000 of his income on his tax returns, and the case was then turned over to the Kennedy Justice Department for prosecution. It was a ticklish matter. After a talk with Senate Minority leader Everett Dirksen, White House political assistant Kenneth O'Donnell took the matter up with President Kennedy, who ordered him to see former President Eisenhower.

"Eisenhower thought that his former aide had suffered enough," Safire reported. "Both John and Robert Kennedy saw a good way to get the former President and the minority leader indebted to them and (as Kenny O'Donnell later confirmed to me) the Justice Department informed the IRS that the case was too weak to prosecute."

The Kennedy brothers had turned the decision not to enforce the law to their long-term political advantage. But Safire said the potency of the Adams information was still not spent. Shortly after Kennedy's assassination, he reported, diehards at the IRS decided to renew their efforts to nail Adams. Eisenhower still felt his former colleague had suffered enough and he called President Johnson and complained that the IRS was harassing poor Adams. "President Johnson, too, wanted Ike in his political debt," Safire said, and the White House ordered the IRS to cool down its aggressive tactics. "Prosecution, of course, was out."

There are many insights to be gleaned from Safire's story about the political usefulness of Sherman Adams's indiscretion. One of them is how two willful and powerful presidents sought psychological advantage over a former president by persuading the IRS not to prosecute his former assistant. A second insight is how withholding official sanction sometimes can provide the withholder more clout than applying the penalty.

There were many occasions during Lyndon Johnson's long political career in Washington when he successfully manipulated the IRS for his own purposes. But bureaucracies have a way of getting even.

In September 1965, the powerful wife of one of Washington's most powerful men received a rude computerized notice about some money she allegedly owed the IRS. Carolyn Agger, a leading tax lawyer at the distinguished Washington law firm of Arnold & Porter, knew a great deal about taxes and she was quite positive that the IRS was wrong.

Agger is not shy and she shot off a blistering letter to IRS Commissioner Sheldon Cohen about the "congenital idiots" who had sent her the incorrect notice. Because Agger was one of the nation's leading tax lawyers, she was reasonably confident that her letter to Cohen would not be intercepted by a secretary. But the fact that her husband was Associate Supreme Court Justice Abe Fortas, one of Lyndon Johnson's closest and oldest friends, certainly didn't hurt the chances that Cohen would be personally attentive.

Commissioner Cohen's September 16, 1965, "Dear Carolyn" reply was a model of cheery diplomacy. It also was an early example of what soon would become the government's silly all-purpose excuse for sloppy administrative work: It's not my fault; the computer did it. "In all fairness to the 'congenital idiots' in Baltimore, they actually reside in Philadelphia at our Regional Service Center!" he wrote. "I realize that it is a small comfort to know that your current problem is with our data processing equipment rather than our district employees, but I do want you to understand that we are in the throes of working out the new system and are having a little trouble with some of our credit and billing cycles."

Cohen ended the formal part of his note by expressing his apologies and asking "your indulgence while we wage our battle with the machines." But then the IRS commissioner added a brief handwritten note: "After all we may need Abe's vote one day."

The postscript was a tacky reminder to Agger about who really wore the pants in the family. But it takes on a genuinely ironic undertone when one remembers that just three years later the agency that Cohen still headed would improperly disclose information about Abe Fortas that would destroy his career and reputation.

The distasteful act in the Fortas story began on an October afternoon in 1968, shortly before Lyndon Johnson left the White House, when one of the most successful investigative reporters of that period stopped by the Washington office of a middle-level official of the IRS.

"It was a casual conversation about a lot of different matters," recalled William Lambert, then the senior reporter for *Life* magazine. "But all of a sudden my IRS friend said something like, 'You ought to look into the association between Fortas and Wolfson, between Fortas and the foundation set up by Wolfson.' "

It was an extraordinary lead from the core of the IRS, the key federal agency responsible for keeping track of foundations and how they spend their money. After six months of intensive reporting, on April 30, 1969, Lambert broke the story that Supreme Court Justice Abe Fortas had accepted a $20,000 fee from the Wolfson Foundation. This connection raised serious ethical questions because Wolfson, an ambitious and flamboyant Florida millionaire, was then asking the federal appeals court to reverse his conviction for violating U.S. securities laws. It was true that Fortas had been Wolfson's lawyer before he had joined the Supreme Court, but the arrangement for the $20,000 fee was completed while he was a member of the highest court of the land.

On May 14, just two weeks after publication of Lambert's story and several earnest protests about the innocence of the arrangement, Fortas became the first and only Supreme Court justice ever to submit his resignation while under fire for questionable conduct. One of the Court's most forceful and articulate liberals had been forced to step down as the result of a confidential tip from the files of the IRS. Because of the vast authority of the Court and the guaranteed tenure of its members, Fortas's decision had great political significance. With the unrelated resignation of Chief Justice Earl Warren a few months later, Richard Nixon, who had just been elected president, was able to begin the long slow process of altering the liberal tone and direction of American law.

Almost certainly, the leak was not the result of pressure from the White House. Fortas, after all, was Johnson's man. Almost certainly, the leak was not the result of pressure from the commissioner. Cohen was Johnson's man. Was the middle-level official who violated the law by steering Lambert to the biggest story of his life just a dedicated worker disgusted by the smell of the transaction? Or was the official a right-wing zealot who had become enraged by the decisions of the liberal wing of the Warren court? Or was Lambert being rewarded with what turned out to be a momentous tip in return for his previous favors for the agency? As we shall see in chapter 12, this was not the first time that Lambert was leaked sensitive tax information about a powerful political figure.

Neither we nor Bill Lambert will ever be certain. But during an interview in his house in a quiet village near Philadelphia, he argued against the theories that he was given the Fortas tip as a result of a right-wing conspiracy or as a reward for previous services rendered. "This guy knew me and I think he just was offended by what he saw," Lambert contended.

Thus did tax information that was leaked from the IRS while Lyndon Johnson was in the White House trigger an investigation that destroyed the career of one of his closest friends.

TRICKY DICK

While the question of motive remains an enigma in the Fortas case, there are few doubts about the aggressively political goals of many of the operators who took over control of the federal government when Richard Nixon became president.

Some of these activities had narrow goals such as the destruction of the presidential campaign of George Wallace, the Alabama governor, and will be told here. Other IRS activities were far more ambitious projects aimed at curbing broad social programs. They will be described in chapter 11.

On February 6, 1974, the House of Representatives approved a resolution directing the House Judiciary Committee to investigate whether sufficient grounds existed to impeach President Nixon. So many reports of abuses had appeared in the *Washington Post* and other newspapers that the resolution was approved by a vote of 410 to 4.

The investigative staff of the House Judiciary Committee began collecting evidence. From May 9 to June 21, 1974, the committee met in executive session to consider the evidence against President Nixon on a number of specific subjects, including the Watergate break-in and its aftermath, government favors granted ITT, the use of federal investigative agencies for questionable surveillance activities, and the abuse of the IRS.

On July 27, 29, and 30, 1974, the committee voted to approve three articles of impeachment. Article I concerned President Nixon's illegal efforts to impede and obstruct the investigation of the break-in of the Democratic National Committee. Article III charged Nixon with the willful disobedience of subpoenas of the House for presidential papers and tape recordings.

Article II, which the committee approved by a vote of 28 to 10, charged the president with repeatedly violating the constitutional rights of the American people. The first specific charge in Article II involved the IRS.

"He has, acting personally and through his subordinates and agents, sought to obtain from the Internal Revenue Service, in violation of the constitutional rights of citizens, confidential information contained in income tax returns for purposes not authorized by law, and to cause, in violation of the constitutional rights of citizens, income tax audits or other income tax investigations to be initiated or conducted in a discriminatory manner."[20]

To support its allegations against the president, the committee presented evidence concerning five separate situations, mostly involving the use or attempted use of the IRS for specific political purposes.

In the spring of 1970, for example, George Wallace of Alabama was running against Albert Brewer in the Alabama primary for the Democratic nomination for governor. Nixon political strategists believed a Wallace defeat would be helpful to the president because it would lessen Wallace's appeal in the 1972 presidential election. According to the testimony of Herbert Kalmbach, Mr. Nixon's personal attorney and fundraiser, $400,000 from the president's 1968 campaign fund was secretly passed to the Brewer team.

But the White House team was still uneasy. In early 1970, H. R. Haldeman, White House chief of staff, saw a confidential report that the IRS was investigating George Wallace and his brother Gerald. Haldeman ordered Clark Mollenhoff, a former newspaper reporter who was then a special assistant to Nixon, to obtain a copy of the IRS report. On March 21, 1970, the material was delivered to Haldeman.

"Material contained in the report was later transmitted to columnist Jack Anderson. Portions of it adverse to George Wallace were published nationally on April 13, 1970, several weeks before the primary election," the House Judiciary Committee said.

A second example of the Nixon administration's misuse of the IRS occurred in 1972 after John Ehrlichman, then the executive director of the Domestic Council of the White House, read another confidential IRS investigative report, this one concerning Howard Hughes. The report on the eccentric industrialist caught Ehrlichman's eye because it suggested a connection with the personal finances of Lawrence O'Brien, then chairman of the Democratic National Committee. Ehrlichman ordered Roger Barth, a Nixon political operative then working as an assistant to IRS Commissioner Johnnie Walters, to provide him with detailed information drawn from O'Brien's tax return.

Armed with these tidbits, Ehrlichman told Treasury Secretary George Shultz that O'Brien should be interviewed by the IRS. It was then IRS policy that candidates and other leading political figures would not be audited or questioned during an election year unless the statute of limitations was about to run or there was some other compelling consideration.

Despite this policy, Shultz and IRS Commissioner Walters bent to White House pressure and O'Brien was interviewed on August 17, just eleven weeks before the 1972 election.

In his later testimony to the House Judiciary Committee, Walters said O'Brien was completely cooperative and the IRS decided there was no tax problem.

Ehrlichman was not pleased by the IRS decision. On August 29, Walters recalled in his testimony, the White House counsel expressed his disappointment. "I'm goddamn tired of your foot-dragging tactics," Walters quoted Ehrlichman as saying.

Rejected by Shultz and Walters, Ehrlichman then telephoned Kalmbach, the Nixon associate who had assisted in the secret transfer of funds to Wallace's opponent. "He gave Kalmbach figures on O'Brien's allegedly unreported income and asked Kalmbach to plant the information with Las Vegas newspaperman Hank Greenspun, a friend of Kalmbach. Kalmbach refused to do so, despite subsequent requests by Ehrlichman and Mitchell," the committee reported. John Mitchell had been Nixon's attorney general and chairman of the Committee to Re-elect the President.

Ehrlichman failed in his attempt to force the IRS to bring politically embarrassing charges against the chairman of the opposition party. He also did not succeed in an attempt to leak the information about the investigation to the press. But he successfully undermined the agency's somewhat shaky policy of not initiating politically sensitive investigations that could be safely postponed until after an election.

One unanticipated effect of Ehrlichman's partial success in forcing the IRS to question O'Brien, as we have seen, was O'Brien's counterattack on the unsavory tactics of the Nixon administration, which ultimately led to the disclosure of the Kennedy brothers' casual way with tax returns.

The last specific situation cited by the House Judiciary Committee to support its charges that President Nixon had knowingly and improperly misused the IRS was based on a conversation he had on March 13, 1973, with John Dean, counsel to the president. The talk, which was picked up on the hidden microphones that the president had ordered for his office, concerned the "project to take the offensive" with respect to the Senate Watergate hearings that were then proceeding. The president mentioned an earlier occasion when Secretary Shultz and Commissioner Walters had resisted a White House demand that the agency investigate everyone making contributions to the campaign of the Democratic presidential candidate, George McGovern. The president then asked Dean, "Do you need any IRS [unintelligible] stuff?"

"[T]here is no need at this hour for anything from the IRS, and we have a couple of sources over there that I can go to," Dean replied. "I don't have to fool around with Johnnie Walters or anybody, we can get right in and get what we need."

Dean may have been puffing a bit for his boss, but documents of the period obtained from the National Archives indicate that the White House counsel did indeed have rather casual access to theoretically confidential tax files.

On October 6, 1971, for example, Dean received a brief note from John J. Caulfield, a former New York City police detective hired by Ehrlichman to supervise White House investigations. Caulfield's note was attached to a four-page summary memorandum from the IRS concerning the agency's audit examinations of nine Hollywood stars "who are politically active."

One of the entertainers on the IRS list was John Wayne, who the agency claimed owed the government $237,331 in taxes for the 1966 tax year. The list indicated that Wayne's returns for 1967, 1968, and 1969 were still being actively audited.

Caulfield's note to Dean suggested that the White House had requested the information about the nine Hollywood figures because John Wayne had complained to the White House that the IRS was picking on him for political reasons. "The Wayne complaint when viewed in the attached context does not appear to be strong enough to pursue," Caulfield wrote.

AUDITING RONALD REAGAN

The special IRS list showed that Richard Boone, Sammy Davis, Jr., Jerry Lewis, Peter Lawford, Fred MacMurray, Lucille Ball, Frank Sinatra, and an undistinguished actor named Ronald W. Reagan had all been audited during the same period. The list further showed that each one had been ordered to pay additional taxes, although the individual assessments varied. Jerry Lewis had been ordered to pay an additional $142,718 in 1963 and $94,272 in 1965. But the deficiencies for most of the other actors, given the size of their incomes, were quite small. Reagan, for example, was ordered to pay an additional $3,541 in 1964 and $1,122 in 1965. The list Caulfield provided Dean indicated that Reagan's returns from 1967 to 1970 were still being audited.

The intelligence on these tax problems must have provided Dean and his colleagues excellent material for amusing chatter at Washington's endless dinner parties. But the IRS intelligence was useful for serious political purposes too.

Egil (Bud) Krogh was deputy assistant to the president for domestic affairs and assistant director of the White House Domestic Council. On July 20, 1971, Krogh received a brief note from John Dean. The Nixon team had picked up rumors that the Brookings Institution, a liberal Washington think tank, was planning to issue a report on Vietnam. The White House was not happy.

"I requested that Caulfield obtain the tax returns of the Brookings Institution to determine if there is anything that we might do by way of turning off money or dealing with principals of the Brookings Institution to determine what they are doing and deal with anything that might be adverse to the Administration," Dean wrote to Krogh. "Attached are copies of these tax returns and you will note that Brookings receives a number of large government contracts."

Seven days later, Dean sent Krogh a second note concerning Brookings. "Please note the attached memorandum on what should be done about the large number of government contracts now held by the Brookings Institution. If you want me to 'turn the spigot off' please let me know; otherwise, I will assume you are proceeding on this matter."

The unsigned memo was a detailed analysis of Brookings and one of its important supporters, the Ford Foundation. "In recent years, the Institution has obtained more than $14 million in Ford subsidies, including $175,000 to produce a book called 'Agenda for the Nation' immediately after the 1968 Presidential election," the analysis reported. "The Wall Street Journal called it [the book] a collection of policy papers by 18 writers who 'comprise an honor roll of academicians of the New Frontier and Great Society.'"

The report added that it was clear that Ford and Brookings represented "formidable opposition to the best interests of this Administration. It would appear that an expeditious political response to this challenge would be the simple expedient of applying pressures to have the Internal Revenue Service strictly enforce existing statutes and promulgated regulations designed to threaten the tax exempt status enjoyed by these organizations."

The unknown author of the White House study then complained that top officials in the IRS were not being entirely cooperative. "Commissioner Walters has not yet exercised the firm leadership expected at the time of his appointment. Additionally, there appears to be a reluctance on his part to make discreet politically oriented decisions and to effect major appointments based upon Administration loyalty considerations."

SQUEAKY CLEAN?

There were literally dozens of different ways that the tax-collecting powers of the IRS were marshaled for political purposes during the Nixon years. With accelerating speed after the discovery of the mysterious burglary at the Watergate on June 17, 1972, evidence of the repeated abuse of the powers of government tumbled into public view. A little more than two years later the House Judiciary Committee voted to impeach Richard Nixon.

Although Nixon resigned before an impeachment trial could be scheduled in the Senate, the carefully documented charges of the House Judiciary Committee provided a powerful lesson for both the senior government officials who ran the enforcement agencies and the staffs who managed the White House under Gerald Ford and Jimmy Carter. Suddenly, much more attention was given to managing the CIA, the FBI, and the IRS in a lawful manner for lawful purposes. And Congress soon passed a law establishing for the first time the principle that tax returns must be kept secret except in certain specific circumstances.

As will be discussed in the next chapter, however, there is considerable evidence that some members of the Reagan administration forgot the painful lessons of the Nixon impeachment and the Watergate hearings and once again began to see the IRS as a useful instrument of political control.

CHAPTER 11

Curbing Political Dissent, Maintaining the Official Line, and Suppressing Unpopular Views

Peter K. Bros had a title that would please almost any bureaucrat worthy of the name. He was Chief, Rulings Section Number 2, Exempt Organization Technical Branch, Internal Revenue Service, Department of the Treasury, Washington, D.C. On October 23, 1981, Bros wrote an official letter to the Minnesota Association for the Improvement of Science Education.[1]

Three months before, the association had asked the IRS to grant it tax-exempt status for the general purpose of promoting and defending the teaching of good science. Hardly a matter for lifted eyebrows. More exactly, the association wanted to encourage the continued "teaching of evolution in the public schools as the only recognized scientific theory of the origin of life on earth."

From the angry tone of Bros's letter, it is clear that the IRS official was personally upset with the request. The tax official expressed his concern in words that appeared to align the IRS with the passionate opposition of many fundamentalist Christians to the widely accepted theory of evolution.

"What do you consider to be pseudo-scientific versions of the origin of life on earth?" Bros asked. "When you advocate that 'evolution' should be taught in the schools, state specifically what you mean by 'evolution' or what 'theory of evolution' should be taught. What gives you the standing or the prerogative to deem certain version[s] of the origin of life on earth as pseudo-scientific? Why are you opposed to permitting the granting of equal time in school curricula to the teaching of the theory of creationism?"

Bros also asked the organization to "substantiate your statement that the number of professional biologists and geologists with Ph.D's from accredited universities who believe in creationism is extremely small" and requested copies of the minutes of all of the association's meetings.

Sister Lucy Knoll, a science teacher in the Catholic school system of Minneapolis and the association's secretary, understood the power of the IRS and its individual bureaucrats. Within two weeks, she dispatched a low-keyed six-page response with detailed answers to Bros's questions. "In science, evolution means that the universe and the earth are very old—billions of years old—and that they have been gradually and continually changing over time," she informed the tax man. "The pseudo scientific versions of the origin of life on earth are those that are derived from other than scientific data. Pseudo scientific versions are put forward by . . . numerous groups in our society, especially by religious fundamentalists whose views of what the Bible teaches are contrary to modern science."

Sister Knoll asked Bros two questions. Then she answered them. "What data suggests that the earth was stocked with various life forms by flying saucers, as claimed by the Ancient Astronaut Society? What data suggests that creation took place in six solar days less than 10,000 years ago, as 'scientific creationists' frequently claim? There is none. All that these people can do is object to certain methodologies of science and then claim that their version is correct by default. That is not science."

Sister Knoll's formal response to Bros was relatively straightforward. But the complaint she wrote to Roscoe Egger, commissioner of the IRS during most of the Reagan administration, had a far different tone.

"The letter from Mr. Bros is partisan in the extreme and expresses his hostility toward the scientific view of the origin of life on earth," she told Egger. "The questions he asks are those one might expect from a totalitarian regime."

Sister Knoll demanded that the association's request for tax exemption be assigned to another official. "We certainly would understand being asked to answer questions related to lobbying, fund raising and so forth, but not those which demand that we defend the scientific method and suggest that we have some special 'prerogative.' "

But the nun did not let it go at that. She and the board members of the Minnesota Association for the Improvement of Science Education shot off angry letters to their two senators and congressman.

"To us these questions represent nothing less than the return of the spirit of McCarthyism," wrote John D. Bohlig, the association's attorney. "The inquisitor obviously adheres to the doctrines of 'scientific creationism' and deems it best to use the power of his office to promote his personal religion."

Senators David Durenberger and Rudy Boschwitz and Representative Bruce Vento contacted the IRS. A few months later, the association won its tax-exempt status. In the grand tradition of all great bureaucracies, however, the IRS blandly insisted that it had all been a misunderstanding. Bros's original request, the IRS informed Durenberger, was merely intended to make sure that the association was presenting a "full and fair exposition of the facts" of the case. "We regret that our letter was interpreted as being hostile toward the position espoused by the Association. This certainly was not the intent."

Because of the personal grit of Sister Knoll and her friends, this story had a happy ending.

DOWN WITH SLAVERY ON THE PLANTATION, UP WITH SLAVERY IN THE FAMILY

In too many cases, however, the social and religious views of the administration in power or of the officials who run the IRS have influenced how the agency interpreted the tax laws of the nation. The result: The IRS has long exercised significant power over a range of matters that are far removed from the collection of taxes. The IRS does not just enforce the laws in an evenhanded and uniform way.

Such selective enforcement of the tax laws is not new nor is it unique to the IRS. In 1867, for example, a Massachusetts court ruled on suits brought by heirs to the Phillips fortune, which challenged the decision of Phillips to create two charitable trusts. One trust had been established to support the cause of black people, the second for women. The court held that the trust created to generate public sentiment on behalf of blacks was charitable while the trust to equalize the treatment of women was not. The court justified the distinction on murky grounds: The laws involving slavery would change because of newly created public sentiment—and not by actions of the trustees—while in the case of women's suffrage the trustees would be improperly active.[2]

William J. Lehrfeld, a Washington lawyer with years of experience in the subtle problems of tax exemption, offers another explanation of the court's decision that he finds plausible. "What may have perpetuated one trust over the other was the fact that, at the time, the status quo [in Boston] would not have been affected by anti-slavery sentiment but would be if the suffragettes created sentiment in favor of equal treatment for women."

When Congress writes the nation's tax laws, it often makes explicit decisions to use taxes to influence the behavior of the American people. In 1894, for example, Congress decided to encourage taxpayers to support worthy causes by allowing them to deduct contributions from their federal income tax.[3] More recently, when Congress became concerned about the wasteful consumption of energy, it authorized an exemption for families who spent money improving the insulation of their homes. When done in an open way, the use of tax laws for such purposes is completely appropriate.

But because Congress frequently writes laws that are vague, ambiguous, or open-ended, the IRS itself has functioned as the controlling agent, a largely invisible bureaucracy that has exercised a great deal of influence over many aspects of our daily lives. Sometimes the IRS has exercised its authority through Kafkaesque bullying, bringing serious tax charges against organizations that have fallen out of favor. From the government's point of view, such prosecutions have the advantage of forcing the leaders of the unpopular organizations to exhaust themselves and their financial resources on defending against the allegations of the agency rather than on promoting their unpopular cause.

On many other occasions, the IRS has denied tax exemptions to groups seeking to educate the public on socially taboo subjects, just as the Massachusetts court forbade the creation of a trust to promote the rights of women.

A third way the IRS has exercised its power is by unilaterally lifting the tax-exempt status it previously had granted because the activities of the organizations were no longer viewed as proper.

Over the years, the IRS's actions against unpopular groups and movements have been triggered by pressures from several different sources. There have been occasions when the president or the White House staff was the villain. There have also been a substantial number of cases when the IRS has responded to prodding from a powerful congressional figure.

Most surprising, perhaps, are the numerous instances when middle-level bureaucrats of the IRS itself, offended by some particular movement or organization, have on their own initiative used the powers of their agency for political harassment.

THE IRS's VIEWS ON NICARAGUA
DURING THE REAGAN ERA

The IRS's response to Sister Lucy Knoll and the theory of evolution is one example where an individual IRS official, and not the White House or Congress, appears to have been the source of the implied threat to withhold tax-exempt status. But at about the same time that Bros was launching his quixotic little campaign on behalf of creationism, an IRS agent in New York took an action that may well have been triggered by the Reagan White House.

In February 1982, a New York IRS agent named David S. Levine sent a report to the agency's Washington office asking whether the IRS should yank the tax-exempt status of the North American Congress on Latin America (NACLA), an organization that had repeatedly criticized the policies of the Reagan administration. Levine's report said the organization had been distributing publications that contained a substantial number of "disparaging terms and innuendos." He further argued that the NACLA material did not "attempt to present a full and fair exposition of pertinent facts from which its readers may draw informed, independent conclusions."[4]

Shortly after Levine sent his report to Washington, the IRS agent initiated a formal action against NACLA by mailing a copy of the report to the suspect organization. Because it had long been criticized by President Reagan and other influential figures around the president, NACLA was convinced that Levine's action had been ordered by the White House. In January 1978, for example, long before his election as president, Reagan had twice attacked NACLA by name. This criticism was echoed in a 1981 Heritage Foundation report. At that time, the foundation's report was regarded as the policy wish list of the incoming Reagan administration. The report described NACLA as one of a number of radical organizations that could become "internal security problems" and that "have had influence on federal policy making in recent years." The foundation called upon the Reagan administration to increase government surveillance of NACLA and other such groups.[5]

The few IRS documents available do not answer the question whether the agency's attempt to take away NACLA's tax exemption was directly or indirectly triggered by Reagan or his staff. But Steve Volk, then president of NACLA, is convinced that the move was political and that the administration hoped to achieve more than simply taking away tax-exempt status from a single articulate critic. "With their hit-and-run tactics, it was clear that the IRS was hoping to intimidate dissident organizations," he said in a 1988 interview. "Once the news spread that NACLA or the magazine *Mother Jones* was threatened, other organizations, fearful of losing their exemption, would begin to tone down their criticism."

NACLA strenuously objected to the IRS's proposal, and some months later the organization was informed that its status would not be changed. Volk, now an assistant professor of Latin American history at Oberlin College, said that the IRS allegations had absolutely no basis in law. But he added that putting together the material to respond to the charges had been a painful and time-consuming chore that had seriously reduced the time he could devote to preparing NACLA's reports. "That's where the IRS really hurt us," Volk said.

Other organizations and individuals who had questioned the administration's Central American policy at about the same time came under similar pressures. One such organization was the Quixote Center, another Washington-based tax-exempt organization.

Finally, a number of U.S. citizens who visited Nicaragua as part of a broad effort to educate themselves about Central America have reported being audited by the IRS shortly after they returned home. Because in the mid-1980s, at least five hundred groups around the country opposed the Reagan administration's Central American policy and at least sixty thousand Americans visited Nicaragua, it is not possible to demonstrate that these audits were the product of an articulated policy.

But documents written by many generations of White House, Justice Department, and IRS officials prove that in almost every administration since the IRS's inception the information and power of the tax agency have been mobilized for explicitly political purposes. Because political manipulation certainly violates the spirit of the law—and sometimes its letter too—the use of the agency's authority for nontax purposes normally has remained only a private suspicion of those who were targeted.

One of the rare exceptions to this general rule of secrecy, where the IRS proudly boasted of its unlawful enforcement drive, was the agency's concerted effort to muzzle a number of leftist and communist organizations shortly after World War II.

GETTING THE COMMIES AND THE LEFTISTS

During the 1930s the federal government had routinely granted tax-exempt status to almost anyone who asked, including a few dozen organizations that had not sought to hide their ties to the Soviet Union or to communism. On February 5, 1930, for example, the American Society for Cultural Relations with Russia, Inc., was routinely granted an exemption.

But with the defeat of Germany and Japan, and the growth of the Soviet Union as a world power, a strong wave of anticommunism swept across the United States. To counter allegations that the State Department and other federal agencies had been infiltrated by Communist agents, President Truman in 1947 issued an executive order authorizing the dismissal from government of anyone found to be affiliated with subversive organizations. The Truman order, however, said nothing about tax policy.

This silence did not trouble the IRS. On February 4, 1948, George J. Schoeneman, commissioner of internal revenue, announced a bold, new, and basically dishonest policy concerning tax-exempt organizations. The commissioner's brief, bland statement encompassed a kind of doublethink that might have astonished even George Orwell.

"The tax laws do not contemplate and it has never been our policy to grant tax exemption or other tax privileges to subversive organizations," Schoeneman ruled. "Whenever we discover an organization that obtained exemption by misrepresenting its purposes and activities, we revoke these privileges immediately."

There had been no change in the law under which organizations of every political hue had been granted tax exemption. The IRS had not issued a ruling defining what it meant by "subversive organization." The agency had brought no formal charges against the targeted organizations that would have allowed them to respond. Without the benefit of a single hearing, Schoeneman announced the revocation of exemptions for a small number of organizations, including the National Council of American-Soviet Friendship, Hollywood Writers' Mobilization, Ohio School of Social Science, Samuel Adams School, School of Jewish Studies (New York City) and the Philadelphia School of Social Science and Art.[6]

For a country that repeatedly emphasizes that it is a nation of laws, not men, it is important to remember that the first wave of IRS revocations was carried out under administrative fiat, not law. In fact, almost two years would pass before Congress enacted the Subversive Activities Control Act of 1950, one section of which explicitly stated that no Communist group registered with the Justice Department's Control Board was entitled to tax exemption or was eligible to receive deductible contributions.

Despite the absence of a legal mandate, the political climate was such that none of the six organizations named in Schoeneman's first statement, or the dozens of others that lost their tax-exempt status in subsequent rulings, ever challenged the IRS in court.[7]

The withdrawal of tax exemptions, however, was not the only action that the IRS took in its publicly announced political action campaign against Communists and leftists. On March 23, 1954, two years after Dwight D. Eisenhower had been elected President, IRS agents in New York began auditing the Communist Party of the United States of America (CPUSA). Two years later, the IRS struck when the director of the agency's Lower Manhattan District ruled that the party owed the government $261,050.38 in taxes and $65,262.60 in penalties. The agency filed levies and liens against the party, thus seizing all of its known assets. In addition, the CPUSA's offices in New York, Philadelphia, San Francisco, Los Angeles, and Chicago were padlocked.[8]

The raid came on Passover of 1954, John Abt recalled in an interview more than thirty years later. "I was in my law office, trying to catch up on some of my work. The phone rang and someone from party headquarters said we had been raided by the IRS, that our doors had been chained and padlocked and levies and liens had been placed against us."

Abt, then a party lawyer, said he knew almost nothing about tax law. "I called up a friend to find out what a jeopardy assessment was. In addition to party headquarters, they also had raided the *Daily Worker.* My memory is that the seizure stopped the *Worker* from being published for a short period, maybe a week."

Abt said that because the bank accounts had been seized the party began operating on a cash basis and continued to do so for about ten years. "The party had to carry on all of its operations in cash. We paid our employees in cash, our utilities in cash, everything. When we got our dues, we also took them in cash."

In August 1956 the CPUSA formally denied its liability for the assessed taxes in Tax Court. In one of Abt's pleadings, the lawyer charged that the government had singled out his client "for taxation under the income tax laws while continuing to treat all other political parties as exempt." He added that this action was "arbitrary and discriminatory, denies petitioner due process of law, and violates rights guaranteed to it by the First Amendment." The party and the IRS began what developed into a tortuous, indecisive, and lengthy battle in the courts.

After ten years of legal wrangling, senior IRS and Justice Department officials began to realize that they might well lose the case. This outcome became likely when a federal court of appeals ordered the case back to the trial court because the "plausible claims of discriminatory treatment [against the Communist party] must be explored."

In 1967, Mitchell Rogovin, who at that time was assistant attorney general for tax matters, sent a confidential memorandum to Attorney General Ramsey Clark recommending that the case be settled. Copies of this and several other government documents were made available to me by a former IRS employee indirectly involved in the case.

Rogovin was opposed to further probing in open court because he knew the government had illegally used the tax law to go after the Communist party. The case was a poor one for the government, he secretly warned Clark, because it looked as though some of the judges suspected that the IRS "was using the tax laws to obtain disclosure of financial records to be used against the petitioner or its members in subversive activities cases."

Another official who came to doubt the IRS's case against the CPUSA was Arthur B. White, head of the agency's interpretive division. In a never-released fourteen-page analysis of the case, White said that the essential problem was that the IRS had an extraordinary Alice in Wonderland policy when it came to political parties. He specifically cited a 1947 IRS ruling about the John Hay Republican Association in Philadelphia in which the commissioner had advised the association that "while political organizations were technically not exempt from tax, it would not be the policy of the Bureau to require purely political organizations to file income tax returns."

Given the IRS's long history of totally ignoring political parties, the only way it could have fairly targeted the CPUSA would have been to argue that the party fell into a special category, that it was not really a political organization. Unfortunately, however, the Justice Department had told the court of appeals several years before that the CPUSA did not stand "in a posture generally different from that of any other political party."

Given the hysterical cold-war mood of the United States during the 1950s, it probably is not surprising that the IRS unilaterally withdrew the tax-exempt status from a dozen "subversive" groups and charged the Communist party with failing to pay its taxes. But the utilization of the tax collection powers of the IRS for the clearly political goal of silencing these groups certainly was improper.

Of course, many Americans would argue that the Communist party was trying to overthrow the government of the United States and thus was not entitled to constitutionally protected rights, such as freedom of association and speech. A variation of this is the argument that the unusual enforcement powers that Congress gave to the IRS solely for the purpose of collecting taxes should be employed against individuals who are suspected of being drug dealers or organized-crime figures. It seems likely that a good number of citizens would today forgive the IRS for bending the tax laws when it came to the CPUSA or the Mafia. But would these same citizens also forgive the Internal Revenue Service for subjecting the National Council of Churches (NCC) to a ten-year investigation because of its open political involvement in the battles to end racial segregation and the Vietnam war?

RACISM, JINGOISM, AND THE IRS

A few years ago, the Reverend Dean M. Kelley, director for governmental relations at the National Council of Churches, applied to the Internal Revenue Service for a copy of all the files it maintained on the council. Kelley's request was made under the provisions of the Freedom of Information Act. Months later, the IRS provided the council with a massive stack of documents, reports, and handwritten notes. Sections of many of the hundreds of pages of documents had been deleted or are illegible. But they clearly document the continuous visceral opposition of the IRS to the liberal policies of the Council of Churches under two entirely different administrations, one led by Lyndon Johnson and the other by Richard Nixon.

One neatly typed document turned over to Kelley summarized some of the key dates in the IRS's decade-long investigation of the National Council of Churches. The first entry in the summary was April 1, 1964: "Manhattan District requested by National Office to conduct fact gathering examination of the NCC for National Office."

The summary gives no indication why Washington ordered the investigation, but a brief handwritten note that appears to have been drafted at the same time suggests the conservative mind-set of the agency. The memo said a review of the Manhattan district's existing files "indicates that the NCC sponsors many conferences that turn out to be militant and disruptive." The memo then quoted a staff study of the Alabama Legislative Commission to Preserve Peace. "On June 7, 1963, the NCC set up a Commission on Religion and Race 'to engage the churches more directly in the present racial revolution.' " The IRS memo offers no warning about the racist views of the Alabama legislature of that period.

Also in the IRS's file from that period was page after page of extracts drawn from newspapers all over the country about the council's involvement in various civil rights activities. One clipping, for example, came from the July 2, 1965, issue of the *Chicago Daily News*. It reported that an official of the council had said that Chicago Mayor Richard J. Daley was "childish and immature" when he linked Communist agitators to the civil rights demonstrations against segregation in the Chicago school system.

The language of an internal IRS report suggests that the tax agency remained deeply disturbed about the council's civil rights activities until at least 1969. "Allegations have been made in a number of areas and by a number of people that the general board of the National Council of Churches is an ultra-liberal, Leftist-oriented body of churchmen who have diverted great sums of money through the Inter-Religious Foundation for Community Organizations to extremist, dissident, militant and revolutionary causes," it concluded.

The IRS report then listed some of the causes supported by the council that the agency appeared to find abhorrent. The council, for example, had issued papers supporting the right of citizens to organize nonviolent sit-in demonstrations. The council had also called for the "redistribution of power and opportunity for social and economic betterment in the United States."

In an interview in the Manhattan office of the council, Kelley said that the IRS's investigation of the national organization representing many of the major Protestant church groups appeared to have two very distinct focuses. "The first episode came in the mid-1960s at the time of the civil rights struggles," he said. Kelley added that, although there was no way he could prove it, he was convinced the IRS investigation had been triggered by a particular conservative senator who was disturbed by the council's activities. "After a lot of back and forth, our general counsel, Charles H. Tuttle, asked the staff to make a list of all our activities that could be remotely considered an attempt to influence legislation.

"We scrambled around and pulled everything together," Kelley continued. "When the list was compiled, [former] Judge Tuttle concluded that the council's total legislative effort came to something like two or three percent of our activities and he so notified the IRS. I guess they then felt they had satisfied their obligation to [a leading southern senator] and they sort of disappeared."

Kelley said the second go-around with the IRS began in the late 1960s and was directly focused on the activities of the council relating to the Vietnam war. As a result of the agency's concerns about these activities, it launched a formal, time-consuming audit and nationwide investigation of the council. Government documents show that despite the desires of top IRS officials, however, the agency never was able to obtain sufficient evidence to bring tax charges against the council.

According to handwritten minutes, Commissioner Randolph W. Thrower held a meeting on June 29, 1970, exclusively devoted to the council and an affiliated organization, Clergy and Laymen Concerned about Vietnam. Present at the session, in addition to Thrower, were three senior Justice Department lawyers and Donald Bacon, assistant IRS commissioner for compliance.

The notes indicate that, even though the agency's audit and investigation had not yet commenced, Thrower, President Nixon's first commissioner, wanted the council to know that the IRS wasn't fooling around. "Openly ask for records. If refuse—consider prompt action."

In the margin to the immediate left of the second paragraph of the minutes, the person taking the notes had written the word "commissioner," thus indicating that this paragraph represented Thrower's direct command. Two sentences were heavily underlined. *"Delisting of NCC. Even without resorting to summons."*

Kelley said that initially the agency had been given complete access to the council's books for 1967, 1968, and 1969. But he said that the tax men were asked to leave when the council's lawyer learned about their investigation. The council had just become aware of a new provision of the 1969 Tax Reform Act that expressly prohibited IRS examination of church records.

"So there was a little standoff for about a year," Kelley recalled. "Then the Treasury issued a regulation which eviscerated the amendment prohibiting the IRS from examining the churches and back came the agents."

The IRS investigative team created elaborate flowcharts that illustrated the major sources of income going to Clergy and Laymen Concerned about Vietnam through the council during 1968 and 1969. One of the flowcharts concerned "substantial contributions by individual" while the second focused on "substantial contributions by foundation."

IRS agents from all over the United States appear to have been involved in the investigation. On April 29, 1971, for example, Bob Handley, an agent in Los Angeles, sent a package of documents to one of his colleagues in Washington. "Attached are two photocopies of cancelled checks. The one made payable to American Report is actually the publication of CLERGY AND LAYMEN CONCERNED ABOUT VIETNAM. The one made out to CUBA PROJECT, a radical group, supports Castro's crowd. NOTE both cancelled checks have been endorsed by the NATIONAL COUNCIL OF

CHURCHES. Would you please make this available to Bill Heath, Exempt Org. coordinator on the NATIONAL COUNCIL OF CHURCHES."

The intimidating IRS investigation of the council's activities in connection with the Vietnam war continued until the end of 1972. On December 7 of that year, Peter Persutty, a New York revenue agent, telephoned the office of a midlevel agency official in Washington and left a brief message that signaled the end of Thrower's war.

Persutty had been the lead agent actually examining the council's books at its headquarters on the Upper West Side of Manhattan. The message taken by the secretary in Washington said that Persutty had called to report that only 8 percent of the council's funds had been used for activities that did not fall in the tax-exempt areas and that this percentage was "not enough to affect C-3 [tax] status." At that time, the IRS policy was to keep the legally acceptable percentage secret. The IRS's long campaign against the National Council of Churches was over.

DOWN SOUTH

The evidence is overwhelming that the IRS's interest in the National Council of Churches was first triggered by the agency's gut-level opposition to the council's liberal views about race and was not a legitimate concern about enforcing the tax laws. Even so, if this was the only case where racism appears to have influenced the agency's enforcement of the tax laws, it might be considered an aberration. There are a number of additional cases, however, that suggest that for many years civil rights activities were a major worry of the agency.

In 1954, the liberal Mississippi publisher Hodding Carter took the then daring step for a southern newspaper of endorsing as the law of the land the Supreme Court's school desegregation decision. Almost immediately Carter's newspaper, the *Delta Democrat Times*, became the subject of a long series of annual IRS audits. Like many who are selected for intense IRS attention, the Carter family has never been able to uncover documents that would support their belief that the audits were politically motivated. However, the publisher's son, W. Hodding Carter III, is convinced that the agency's audits were triggered by IRS officials in Mississippi who shared the profound anger felt by the state's political, business, and social leaders toward his father's relatively moderate editorial stance on race.

The Carter family was hardly the only object of special IRS attention as the South moved into this difficult period of social change. In the late 1950s, for example, the IRS and the tax agency of Alabama began auditing Dr. Martin Luther King, Jr.[9] After the auditors raised several questions about some deductions he was unable to document, King settled, paying the IRS $500 in back taxes. He also settled with the state of Alabama, which had at the same time also brought tax charges against him.

Shortly after accepting the settlement in the civil case, however, Alabama had second thoughts. The result: King became the first person ever prosecuted by the state on felony tax charges. Because of his controversial civil rights activities in Alabama, conviction and a long prison sentence seemed almost certain. As a result of this fear, King and his lawyers spent a great deal of time searching every available record. Just before the case went to trial, the lawyers discovered that King had maintained a personal diary that contained detailed contemporaneous notes that proved the Alabama charges were false. The notes were so persuasive, in fact, that on May 28, 1960, an Alabama jury defied the prejudices of those times and found King not guilty.

A few years after the IRS audit of King and Alabama's use of its tax laws to harass the civil rights leader, the IRS again demonstrated its concern about his activities. Sometime in 1964 the Federal Bureau of Investigation labeled the Southern Christian Leadership Conference a "Black Nationalist–Hate Type Organization" and asked the IRS for any information it might have about the group. The IRS gave the FBI the tax returns of King and the conference and a number of its investigative files, according to the Senate Select Committee on Intelligence. The committee did not report what the FBI did with the returns.[10]

The IRS interest in civil rights activists did not end with the National Council of Churches, Hodding Carter, and Martin Luther King. An investigation by Jason Berry, a New Orleans–based reporter, discovered that the agency audited a large number of civil rights activists working in the South. He further discovered the many of these activists were subjected to repeated audits.

Berry disclosed, for example, that in 1973, 1974, and 1975 the IRS had audited at least sixty southern civil rights activists or liberal politicians. They included Julian Bond, then a Georgia state senator; his brother James Bond, an Atlanta city councilman; eight black Atlanta officials; Ben Brown, then with the Democratic National Committee in Washington; and Charles Evers, the mayor of Fayette, Mississippi.

In late 1976, pressed by Representative Charles Rangel, Democrat of New York, the Oversight Subcommittee of the House Ways and Means

Committee ordered the General Accounting Office to investigate Berry's findings concerning the IRS's interest in twenty-eight specific civil rights activists who during the early seventies had done organizing work in Mississippi.

The GAO investigators were thorough. They examined the tax returns, audit case files, and intelligence records of the twenty-eight civil rights workers and interviewed many of the IRS officials who had worked in the state during the period in question. In January 1978, the GAO sent its completed report to Congress. The official investigation found that the twenty-eight activists had been audited at least forty-five times.

Despite the suspicious nature of the repeated audits, the summary statement of investigation rejected Berry's theory that the IRS activities resulted from official policy: "IRS followed normal procedures in initiating, conducting and closing the audits. IRS also followed normal procedures in obtaining limited information on some of the 28 taxpayers through its intelligence-gathering apparatus and in using that information."

A reading of the full report, however, discloses that the GAO investigators were uncertain about their findings. The full report also underlined the near impossibility of developing concrete evidence about the actual motive for a particular audit even when, as in this case, the investigators were given access to normally secret IRS documents.

The GAO report first noted that all over the United States citizens sometimes feel they have been unfairly harassed. "Indeed, it is not unreasonable to assume that an IRS examiner may, on occasion, go beyond the limits of propriety, and contrary to policy, harass a taxpayer," the GAO said. "It would be difficult for any organization with 85,000 employees, like the IRS, to assure proper conduct by its employees all the time. The allegations in this instance, however, did not charge that a particular examiner harassed a particular taxpayer during a particular audit. The allegations charged instead that the IRS, as an organization, purposefully used its audit authority to harass Mississippi civil rights activists. GAO found no evidence to support that allegation."

The GAO thus said that it had found no procedural aberrations or internal documents that proved the audits were the product of a formal policy of harassment but that it had no way of determining whether the racial biases of individual agents or supervisors may have played a role in some or all of the forty-five audits.

THE RIGHT WING GETS ITS TURN

On the other hand, a great deal of concrete evidence does indicate that John F. Kennedy mobilized the legal might of the IRS against an entirely different target: the right-wing fundamentalist ministers who had been so critical of his religion and his brother Robert during his presidential campaign and his first months in the White House.

The first indirect warning of the forthcoming campaign came in a speech by Kennedy on November 18, 1961. The subject of the speech was the difficult cold war with communism and how, "under the strains and frustrations imposed by constant tension and harassment, the discordant voices of extremism are once again heard in the land. Men who are unwilling to face up to the danger from without," Kennedy said, "are convinced that the real danger is from within."

The president then called on the nation to ignore the voices of fear and suspicion. "Let our patriotism be reflected in the creation of confidence in one another, rather than crusades of suspicion." Kennedy did not have to tell his audience that his administration had been the primary target for these critics.

Having defined this new enemy, the president waited a week to suggest how it should be dealt with. The occasion was a question at a news conference seeking his views on the legality of campaign contributions that supported the activities of "right-wing extremist groups."

Kennedy's response began in a statesmanlike way. "As long as they meet the requirements of the tax law, I don't think that the Federal government can interfere or should interfere with the right of any individual to take any position he wants. The only thing we should be concerned about is that it does not represent a diversion of funds which might be taxable to—for nontaxable purposes. But that is another question and I am sure the Internal Revenue system examines that."

At the time Kennedy spoke, in fact, the IRS had an unannounced policy of rarely auditing such groups because such examinations were "difficult and time-consuming" and "rarely were productive of revenue."

But IRS Commissioner Mortimer H. Caplin was a team player. Within a day or two of President Kennedy's November 1961 press conference, the agency launched a test audit of twenty-two "extremist organizations."

The first IRS document providing an overall description of the agency's response to the presidential nudge was written a bit more than a year and a half later. It was a secret memo that Caplin sent to Myer Feldman, deputy special counsel to President Kennedy. The document was dated July 11, 1963.

A copy of the Feldman memo that was retained in the IRS commissioner's files subsequently was made available to me. In the period after the original was sent to the White House, Caplin's secretary jotted down a series of handwritten notes in the margin of the copy describing several crucial events in the history of the IRS's effort to curb right-wing critics of the president. One notation, for example, indicates that on July 20, Caplin met with Attorney General Kennedy to discuss the special IRS investigation. Another brief jotting indicates that on the next day the commissioner "met with Feldman at White House to bring him up to date."

President Kennedy himself took a direct interest in Caplin's project. According to yet another brief note scribbled on the copy of the Feldman memo, the leader of the free world on July 23 informed the commissioner that the IRS was now at liberty to move against the organizations that the agency had identified as possible targets. "President Kennedy called Commissioner re attached," the note reads. "Wants the IRS to go ahead with aggressive program—on both sides of center."

The "both sides of center" reference had crept into the documents shortly after the president first indicated that he would like an investigation focused on the right. The talk about examining both the right and the left was a political cover devised by Caplin to protect the president against the truthful charges that he was using the IRS to mount a vendetta against his political enemies.

The creation of this cover was explicitly acknowledged by Commissioner Caplin in a May 1962 memorandum he sent the under secretary of treasury. "Inasmuch as we are not certain any of these organizations [of the right] or their benefactors are failing to comply with the tax laws, we thought it prudent to avoid any possible charges that the service is giving special attention to a group with a special ideology. In furtherance of this goal, we are planning to examine the returns of a representative group of alleged left-wing organizations."

The left-wing groups included the Anti-Defamation League of B'nai B'rith, the League for Industrial Democracy, Inc., the American Veterans Committee, Inc., and Fair Play for Cuba.

But almost all of Caplin's memo to the under secretary of treasury concerned the other end of the political spectrum. "The activities of so called extremist right-wing political action organizations have recently been given a great deal of publicity by magazines, newspapers and television programs. This publicity, however, has made little mention of the tax status of these organizations or their supporters. Nevertheless, the alleged activities of these groups are such that we plan to determine the extent of their compliance with Federal tax laws. In addition, we propose to ascertain whether contributors to these organizations are deducting their contributions from taxable income."

Caplin then listed twelve organizations that the IRS field offices already had been directed to examine, including the Christian Anti-Communist Crusade, the Life-Line Foundation, the Conservative Society of America, the John Birch Society, and Robert Welch, Inc.

Another indication of the political weight of the Kennedy administration effort against the right is an August 21, 1963, memorandum written by Mitchell Rogovin, who was then an ambitious young special assistant to Commissioner Caplin. The memo concerned the briefings that Rogovin had provided the attorney general and White House assistant Myer Feldman on the political audit program.

Rogovin said that the attorney general offered to have the Justice Department defend the IRS if any of the organizations sued the agency. This offer is revealing because it suggests that Robert Kennedy supported the program even though he recognized that it might be challenged in federal court.

Rogovin also disclosed that Myer Feldman had requested that he call off the IRS investigation of two of the organizations already selected for the special audit program. "In reviewing the organizations listed by the Service, he suggested we delete the DAR [Daughters of the American Revolution] and the Zionist Organization of America," the IRS staffer wrote. Rogovin did not explain the reasons for Feldman's request. Presumably, however, the White House was worried about the backlash that might occur among conservative white women and the Jewish community if the audits of the two groups ever became widely known.

In April 1976, the Senate Select Intelligence Committee, then controlled by the Democrats and headed by the late Senator Frank Church of Idaho, concluded that the Kennedy administration project to mobilize the IRS against the right had led to more extensive political abuses during the Johnson and Nixon years.

"By directing tax audits at individuals and groups solely because of their political beliefs, the Ideological Organizations Audit Project [as the 1961 Kennedy program was known] established a precedent for a far more elaborate program of targeting 'dissidents,' " the committee concluded.[11]

The actual enforcement actions initiated by the IRS when the Kennedy team was in charge were all directed toward the right. According to a 1963 report by Caplin, the agency recommended revoking the exempt status of H. L. Hunt's Life-Line Foundation and of Dr. Fred Schwarz's Christian Anti-Communist Crusade. Similar action was not recommended for the John Birch Society because it did not claim tax exemption. But Caplin informed the White House that the IRS investigations had discovered that some taxpayers contributing to the John Birch Society had improperly claimed business deductions for their subscriptions to *American Opinion* magazine, the society's publication. As for the ten left-wing groups, Caplin reported that nine had been given a clean bill of health and that one "requires further study."

During the Johnson administration, as already noted, the focus of the IRS's never-acknowledged effort at political control swung from the right wing to individuals and organizations concerned with racial matters or with opposing the U.S. presence in Vietnam. Unlike the Kennedy period, no evidence has yet emerged that directly links President Johnson to what became increasingly frenetic efforts by the FBI and the IRS to defang and declaw the critics of his administration.

However, not too much should be made of this lack of documentary evidence. On January 1, 1967, Cartha DeLoach, J. Edgar Hoover's deputy, wrote a memorandum to Hoover stating that the White House had informed him that "the President does not want any record made" that would prove his direct involvement in FBI intelligence operations directed at war critics. DeLoach added that any FBI documents on such sensitive matters were to be directed to a low-level White House staff member who did not have direct contact with Johnson. The stated reason for this policy: Anyone who saw the FBI papers actually going to Johnson would not suspect that "the president had requested such information."[12]

The record contains a great deal of information, however, proving that the IRS, the FBI, and several other federal agencies were involved in a large number of such projects during the years that LBJ occupied the White House.

Between 1957 and 1975, the IRS gave tax information to the Central Intelligence Agency at least thirteen times. Because most of the requests involved CIA investigations of its own employees or were under circumstances proper to its charter, the requests would not have been illegal if they had been made through appropriate channels. The CIA, however, was not comfortable about the transmittal records that are created when working within lawful channels, so the spy agency obtained the tax records in an informal and illegal manner.

But beyond the questionable procedures involved in most of the CIA's penetrations of the IRS, the substance of several of the CIA inquiries was clearly improper.

In late 1966, for example, top officials of the CIA heard rumors that *Ramparts* magazine, a muckraking publication based in San Francisco, was working on a story about secret CIA funding of some of the operations of what was then called the United States National Students Association (USNSA). A preliminary investigation confirmed the rumors.

What to do? On February 1, 1967, a senior CIA agent met with three top officials of the IRS—Thomas Terry, assistant to the commissioner; Leon Green, assistant to the chief of compliance; and John Barber, chief of the rules unit of the IRS's Exempt Organizations Branch.

The day after the meeting, the CIA official wrote a memo describing the session with the IRS. It indicated that the tax agency was willing to tailor its treatment of *Ramparts* according to the concerns of the spy agency. The name of the writer was deleted from the memo, presumably for security reasons, when it subsequently was published by the Senate Select Committee on Intelligence. The CIA official, after telling the IRS about the forthcoming exposé, said that he "impressed upon them the Director's concern and expressed our certainty that this is an attack on the CIA in particular, and the administration in general, which is merely using the USNSA and [deleted name of a foundation] as tools."[13]

The CIA official then got to the serious business. "I suggested that the corporate tax returns of Ramparts, Inc., be examined and that any leads to possible financial supporters be followed up by examination of their individual tax returns," he wrote. "The returns can be called in for review by the Assistant Commissioner for Compliance without causing any particular notice in the respective IRS districts. The proposed examinations would be made by Mr. Green who would advise me if there was any information on the returns worth following up."

Although the IRS officials appeared to have been sympathetic to the CIA's plight, the request to initiate an investigation of a publication that had broken no tax laws made everyone a little nervous. "This matter contains the elements for political repercussions against the Internal Revenue Service as well as this agency and Mr. Terry feels we can make no move until he has briefed the Commissioner. Mr. Terry will brief the Commissioner as soon as possible and contact me when he has done so."

Thomas Terry, now a San Francisco lawyer, remembers the *Ramparts* meeting but says he does not recall what action, if any, the IRS took in response to the CIA request. "I have a vague recollection that the CIA people reported that individuals connected with *Ramparts* were under investigation and I assume they expressed their concern in terms of national security," he said in an interview. Terry added, however, that auditing a magazine because of something it was about to print would not have been "appropriate and we could not have done that."

Follow-up memos, however, suggest otherwise. Two weeks after the February 1 meeting, a second CIA memo dated February 15, 1967, said that the agency had in fact obtained the tax return of Edward Keating and that on the return Keating had reported he was the owner of *Ramparts*. The CIA said that the "statement of ownership, management and circulation published in the January 1967 issue of *Ramparts*, as required by law and postal regulations, lists five stockholders. . . . This is not consistent with the sole ownership of Keating as reported to Revenue as recently as fiscal year 1965. We intend to check this fact and so does Revenue in as much as Keating has been claiming 100 percent losses on his own tax return." A third CIA memo, this one written sometime in May, indicated that the spy agency had come back to the IRS with information from its informants that the CIA summarized as proving that Keating should be officially audited.*

It is not known whether the IRS, in the end, acted on the CIA's information about Keating. Attempts to locate him in the summer of 1989 were not successful. The fact remains, however, that the IRS did conduct an audit of Robert Scheer, then a young reporter with *Ramparts*. At the time, of course, Scheer had no knowledge of the CIA's requests to the IRS. "In some ways, it was pretty funny because I didn't have any money," Scheer recalled during an interview in the spring of 1989. "But it also was pretty scary."

Joseph Ippolito, the San Jose, California, accountant who prepared the tax returns for *Ramparts* and many of its writers and editors, said he was uncertain about what had triggered Scheer's audit. "The guy the IRS sent down from San Francisco had a lot of time in the government and I remember thinking he was kind of heavy for a young kid like Scheer," Ippolito said. "He wasn't a bad guy, though, and we had lunch. While we were eating he told me in passing that Scheer was 'a sensitive tax case.' The IRS guy didn't explain exactly what he meant."

---

*The Senate Select Intelligence Committee only printed the first CIA memo in the transcript of its hearing on the IRS. The second and third memos, however, were mentioned in a front-page story on October 3, 1975, in *The New York Times* that was written by Nicholas M. Horrock. The occasion of Horrock's story was the previous day's hearing by the Select Committee when the 1967 memos were made public. Why the committee did not publish all of the CIA memos that were released to the public at its hearing could not be determined.

On the other hand, the accountant said, Scheer had been traveling all over the country to give speeches to radical college groups and had failed to keep all the receipts he needed to back up his claimed deductions. "His claims were legitimate but because he didn't always have the backup for them, he ended up owing the government a little more money."

Ippolito said that the IRS never audited *Ramparts* itself.

FIGHTING THE WAR CRITICS

Perhaps because the law specifically prohibited the CIA from engaging in most domestic intelligence activities, the spy agency was relatively unimaginative when it came to using the IRS to curb the voices of dissent that swept the country in the late 1960s and early 1970s. Of course, there were no such general restrictions to hobble the FBI. One of the bureau's most devious little operations began on May 31, 1968, when the FBI asked the IRS for the tax returns of six particularly irritating nay-sayers.

One of the six was a professor at a midwestern university. After the Washington office of the FBI had obtained his tax return, it was sent to the local FBI office in the city where he lived. According to a later investigation by the Senate Intelligence Committee, the local FBI office studied the return and decided the professor had some questionable deductions.

On July 18, 1968, the local FBI office sent a memo to bureau headquarters in Washington requesting permission to trigger an IRS audit. The memo said that the professor's tax return showed he had made "a claim for home maintenance deductions when, in fact, he doubtless has only the usual type of study found in many homes rather than actual office space." The ingenious G-men discovered another matter they thought of interest. The professor's contributions to the Student Non-Violent Coordinating Committee, the Students for a Democratic Society, and a third relatively unknown protest group, the local FBI office reported, "may also be productive of embarrassing consequences."

The local FBI office, however, was interested in more than the passive collection of intelligence. It wanted to organize a government strike against the professor. "Most importantly," the memo said, "if IRS contact with [the professor] can be arranged within the next two weeks their demands upon him may be a source of distraction during the critical period when he is engaged in meetings and plans for disruption of the [forthcoming] Democratic National Convention. Any drain upon the time and concentration which [the professor] can bring to bear upon this activity can only accrue to the benefit of the government and general public."

Almost immediately, FBI headquarters in Washington flashed a green light to the local FBI office to initiate its plan. At that point, FBI agents in the midwestern city passed the tips about the professor's possible tax problems to the local IRS office.

The IRS agents immediately initiated the audit desired by the FBI. In the end, however, the FBI's hope that the professor's involvement in the demonstrations at the 1968 Democratic convention would be limited as a result of the IRS action was not fulfilled: The professor took advantage of IRS rules that grant taxpayers the right to request a temporary postponement of an audit. The Senate Intelligence Committee did not disclose the outcome of the professor's audit.

CLAWING BACK AT THE BLACK PANTHERS

A great deal of the pressure on federal law enforcement agencies to move against civil rights activists and critics of the Vietnam war came from President Johnson, President Nixon, FBI Director Hoover, and CIA Director Richard Helms. It is well to remember, however, that powerful members of Congress were also pressing the agencies to act against the dissenters. Especially after the assassination of Dr. Martin Luther King, Jr., in April 1968 and the subsequent riots in Washington, D.C., and a number of other cities, conservative members of Congress repeatedly demanded that the IRS become actively involved in collecting political intelligence.

The details of congressional involvement in encouraging the IRS and other agencies to collect information about a variety of political activists remained secret until after the serious abuses of the Watergate era had been firmly pinned on President Nixon. Subsequent investigations by the Joint Committee on Internal Revenue Taxation and the Senate Judiciary Subcommittee on Constitutional Rights, however, prove that Congress played a leading role in the IRS's decision to become active during this turbulent period.

In September 1968, for example, Philip Manuel, an investigator with the Senate Government Operations Committee, met with IRS officials and demanded more information about black activist groups such as the Student Non-Violent Coordinating Committee and the Congress of Racial Equality. Manuel also wanted intelligence about Students for a Democratic Society. A 1975 staff study by a Senate Finance subcommittee found that Manuel and his colleagues complained to the IRS that the agencies "have not done more in gathering real hard facts."[14]

Two weeks after meeting with Manuel, the IRS informed Senator John McClellan, the conservative Arkansas Democrat who headed the Government Operations Committee, that the agency "would cooperate with the committee's investigation." Washington also ordered IRS district directors in thirteen cities to cooperate.

The pressure from Senator McClellan's staff for more political intelligence from the IRS continued throughout the remaining months of Lyndon Johnson's presidency in 1968 and into the first heady days of the Nixon administration.

The Nixon White House soon showed it was at least as worried about the demonstrations as Senator McClellan and President Johnson. On June 16, 1969, IRS Commissioner Randolph Thrower wrote a memorandum for the record about a meeting he had had that day with Arthur Burns, then head of the White House office of domestic policy. According to Thrower, Burns said that Nixon was concerned "over the fact that tax-exempt funds may be supporting activist groups engaged in stimulating riots both on the campus and within our inner cities."

The record further indicates that two weeks later, on July 1, 1969, another White House staff member expressed interest in IRS efforts to investigate "ideological organizations." We know this because about a year later Tom Charles Huston sent Roger Barth, an assistant to Commissioner Thrower, to request an update on the IRS's "review of the operations of ideological organizations. I would be interested in knowing what progress has been made since July 1, 1969, when we first expressed our interest in this matter."

It was also on July 1 that Donald Bacon, the assistant IRS commissioner for compliance, sent Barth a long note concerning the "recent high level interest shown in the activities of Ideological Organizations. . . ." He explained that his division had been collecting all known facts about "the National Student Association, the Black Panther Party, Students for a Democratic Society, the Progressive Labor Party and the Inter-religious Foundation for Community Organization."

Meanwhile in the IRS's Atlanta office, again on July 1, Special Agent E. D. Hughes filed a travel expense authorization request for a trip to Washington. Hughes's request, which was approved, said, "My presence in Washington, D.C. is necessary to assist the National Office with a report on militant organizations. . . . The report was requested by and will be submitted to the White House."

Two and a half weeks later, Bacon, assistant commissioner for compliance, sent the other IRS assistant commissioners and the agency's chief counsel a confidential statement about the formation of a group to coordinate all IRS activities involving "ideological militant, subversive, radical and similar type organizations."

A few days later, an IRS official, in a memo about the new group's first formal meeting, wrote that the participants were engaged in "an extremely important and sensitive matter in which the highest levels of government are interested." For some reason, this memo did not indicate who had written it.

While boasting about high-level backing, the memo contained an unusual confession: The work of the group had nothing to do with the lawful mission of the IRS and everything to do with the agency's political standing among the power brokers of Washington. "From a strictly revenue standpoint, we may have little reason for establishing this committee or expending the time and effort which may be necessary, but we must do it. We have gotten too much adverse publicity about exempt organizations. . . ."

AN UNFORTUNATE NAME: THE SSS

By the middle of August, Paul H. Wright, IRS manager of what was soon officially named the Special Service Staff, began submitting progress reports. One described the establishment of formal relations with the FBI and the McClellan committee. Another disclosed the rental of a postal box under an assumed name so that the SSS could secretly subscribe to "communist endorsed newspapers" without the knowledge of the publications. By August 20, Wright claimed he had collected data on seven hundred individuals or organizations about whom "there is ample evidence of activities involving arson, fire-bombing, civil disorders, stores of ammunition, printing and distribution of publications advocating revolution against the government of this country."

It was heady stuff.

Donald Bacon, the assistant IRS commissioner under whose wing the SSS was located, appeared to have no doubts about the new project. Using vague phrases that made no reference to possible tax abuses, he asked Hoover to provide the secret new intelligence group with information about "various organizations of predominantly dissident or extremist nature and/or people prominently identified with these organizations." Bacon apparently did not believe it was necessary to define what he meant by a "predominantly dissident or extremist" organization of person. D. J.

Brennan, an FBI intelligence official, recommended that the bureau comply with the request because the SSS would "deal a blow" to "dissident elements."

Among the material the FBI sent along was a list of 2,300 organizations categorized as "Old Left," "New Left," and "Right Wing." The SSS also received about ten thousand names from the Interdivision Information Unit (IDIU), a computerized intelligence file started by Ramsey Clark when he was running the Justice Department for President Johnson.

Once news of the secret IRS political surveillance group became public in a *Time* magazine article in the summer of 1973, the SSS was immediately abolished by Donald Alexander, then the commissioner. The SSS was so improper it simply could not stand the light of day. In the following year, several congressional committees launched investigations. The Senate Judiciary Subcommittee on Constitutional Rights concluded that the establishment of the SSS was not legal and that its operations undermined public faith in the IRS. Finally, it said, the activities of the SSS endangered the constitutionally guaranteed right to free speech.

The Senate Select Committee on Intelligence said that its investigation had determined that thousands of individuals and organizations in the files of the SSS had been targeted "because of their political and ideological beliefs and activities," not "on the basis of probable noncompliance with the tax laws."

In recent years, some Americans have sought to minimize the importance of the domestic intelligence operations of this period by suggesting that little harm was done. The Senate Select Intelligence Committee, however, noted that many of the individuals and organizations whose names were obtained by the SSS "were later subjected to tax audits and some tax fraud investigations."

The names on the SSS lists illustrate the ridiculous problem created by the inability of government officials to define the threat that obsessed them. Selected for special attention were Nobel laureate Linus Pauling, Senators Charles Goodell of New York and Ernest Gruening of Alaska, Representative Charles Diggs of Michigan, journalists Joseph Alsop and Jimmy Breslin, and Mitchell Rogovin, the former IRS official. Organizations ranged from the right-wing John Birch Society to the upper-middle-class good-government lobby Common Cause. Also on the list were the Legal Aid Society, the Associated Catholic Charities, the Carnegie Foundation, *Playboy* magazine, and even one federal agency, the U.S. Civil Rights Commission.

Ever since Richard Nixon resigned as president of the United States, a substantial number of Americans have taken comfort in the false notion that he was a unique monster whose term in office marked the beginning, and the end, of improper activities by the IRS. The record clearly shows that this notion is incorrect.

There thus was and is no single devil who can conveniently be blamed for runaway government of the post–World War II period. The Nixon officials were right when they claimed that Kennedy was guilty too. Of course, they should also have mentioned Herbert Hoover, Franklin Roosevelt, Harry Truman, Dwight Eisenhower, and Lyndon Johnson.

The incremental creation of domestic intelligence programs within the federal government led to a situation where the special talents of many agencies—sometimes to investigate, sometimes to prosecute, and sometimes to subject to such administrative penalties as tax audits—were routinely leveled against those who chose to dissent, whether lawfully or otherwise.

Given the narrow focus of the IRS's mission to collect the nation's taxes, the agency's broad opposition to political dissent sometimes was breathtaking. Consider, for example, Revenue Ruling 75–384, an advisory opinion the agency issued in the mid-1970s at the request of a nonprofit organization that had been formed to promote "peace and disarmament." This organization was unusual because its application for tax-exempt status included an explicit statement that its actions on behalf of peace might involve civil disobedience. The organization asked the IRS whether that might pose a problem.

The answer came in one of the agency's public rulings, a relatively brief advisory opinion designed to provide general guidance. For reasons of privacy, the name of the individual or organization asking the question is deleted from the public version of the ruling.

The IRS said that the peace group couldn't qualify as a tax-exempt charity for several reasons. Under one of the major rules of charity, the agency said, no trust can be created for a purpose that is illegal. The IRS added that a trust would be illegal if it had been established to promote "an object which is in violation of the criminal law, or if the trust tends to induce the commission of a crime, or if the accomplishment of the purpose is otherwise against public policy."

The IRS ruling then held that charitable trusts, and by implication all tax-exempt organizations, "are subject to the requirement that their purposes may not be illegal or contrary to public policy." The IRS was worried about groups that questioned public policy, especially if they expressed their questions through any form of civil disobedience.

THE THREAT OF PUBLIC INTEREST LAW FIRMS

At times, the IRS's opposition to those who challenge its understanding of the status quo has gone far beyond those difficult citizens who exercise their rights to free speech by organizing noisy demonstrations concerning sensitive questions of race and national security. On one occasion, for example, the IRS actually sought to deny tax exemption to a handful of lawyers who sought to use the federal courts as a forum where important questions of social equity could be decided lawfully.

The story goes back a long way. In 1876, the German Society of New York established an office to provide legal aid to the poor. By the beginning of World War I, legal aid societies had been established in forty-one cities. In 1916, another group of citizens established the American Civil Liberties Union (ACLU). And in 1939, the NAACP's Legal Defense Fund was created to undertake court actions to protect the rights of blacks. Thus the accepted role for tax-exempt law groups developed slowly: to look out for the interests of unpopular or disenfranchised minorities.

But as Oliver A. Houck pointed out in his brilliant 1984 analysis in the *Yale Law Journal,* the definition of the appropriate role for public interest law firms was not static.[15] In 1968, for example, a small group of citizens formed the Environmental Defense Fund. A year later, some others created the Center for Law and Social Policy. And in 1970, Ralph Nader held a news conference announcing that a group of lawyers not connected with his organization had asked the IRS to grant them tax-exempt status for what they initially called the Project for Corporate Responsibility. The purpose of all these new groups was to reach out beyond the worthy minorities represented by the NAACP and the ACLU and attempt to represent a larger public on such subjects as protecting the environment from industrial pollution.

Both the IRS and the Nixon White House were worried. Were the new groups charitable? Were they accountable? Did they not offer services that put law firms without tax exemption at a disadvantage?

Again, as persuasively argued by Houck, an associate professor at the Tulane Law School, the new firms did not unbalance the scales of justice. They were, in fact, an attempt to balance them. Under the tax laws and procedures in place before these new firms were created, corporations were allowed to deduct as necessary business expenses the costs of defending their interests in court. The salaries of lawyers representing the immediate interests of government agencies such as the Nuclear Regulatory

Commission were, of course, paid by taxpayers. The only groups not directly or indirectly subsidized by the taxpayers were those representing consumers, environmentalists, and other broadly defined public-interest groups.

The IRS was at first baffled by the new groups, which challenged the performance both of business and of government regulatory agencies. Some requests for tax-exempt status were stalled, some were granted, and others were denied. But on October 9, 1970, an IRS press release announced that it had temporarily suspended the issuance of all new rulings for public interest groups that brought legal actions "for what they determine to be the public good in some chosen field of national interest." Concerning donations to the new firms the agency had already approved, the IRS appeared to execute a retroactive retreat. The IRS, the press release said, was "in no position at this stage to make any judgment about the deductibility of contributions . . . to currently tax exempt firms of the type being studied."

The IRS's clumsy but sweeping suspension of rule making had the effect of once again enlisting the power of the agency against those who challenged the status quo and, in this case, for those large corporations that pollute the air and water of the nation. Unlike many of the protests of the civil rights and anti–Vietnam war groups, however, the new challenge was not mounted on the streets. Instead, the public interest groups made the explicit assumption that they would obtain a fair hearing in the federal courts.

The IRS decision was incomprehensible. So absurd, in fact, that the roof fell in on the agency. Senate hearings were scheduled. Nineteen former Cabinet members joined in writing a letter demanding qualification of the new groups. Even Washington's most prestigious corporate law firms—Arnold & Porter, Caplin & Drysdale, and Wilmer, Cutler & Pickering—joined the chorus of criticism against the IRS.

On November 17, 1970, five weeks after it had announced the suspension and four days before it was scheduled to defend its policy before a Senate committee, the agency totally reversed itself. The IRS said it had completed a study of the problem and would immediately begin issuing tax-exempt rulings to public interest law firms under newly developed guidelines.

While the IRS's open effort to stop these law firms apparently had been defeated, forces within the Nixon White House and the IRS were not yet prepared to give up their war against the young upstarts who sought to challenge corporate America.

CONSPIRACY IN THE IRS

We know this because at the very same time that the IRS was publicly announcing that it was prepared to approve the applications of the public interest law firms, it was privately doing the exact opposite. The case in point involves the Project for Corporate Responsibility, which went through an extraordinary two-and-a-half-year period of IRS delays before the agency finally rejected its application.

The Project for Corporate Responsibility first filed its application for tax-exempt status on September 3, 1970, just one month before the IRS announced its short-lived decision to suspend its consideration of such applications.

Then on April 16, June 2, and August 18, 1971, and August 18, September 27, and October 24, 1972, the IRS asked the project for additional information. Somehow the IRS could not make up its mind. Regularly, through May 1, 1973, lawyers for the project kept asking the IRS for a decision. Finally, on May 2, they filed suit asking the court to order the IRS to rule one way or the other. Two weeks later, senior IRS officials rejected the recommendation of their professional staff and ruled that the project was not entitled to tax-exempt status because it did not meet the definition of a charity. The negative decision, of course, meant the project was not qualified to receive tax-deductible contributions.

The lead lawyer for the group, which now had changed its name to the Center for Corporate Responsibility, was Tom Troyer, a highly respected partner in the well-established Washington law firm of Caplin & Drysdale. With the blessing of the court, Troyer began discovery proceedings in the files of the IRS and the White House. He also received some inadvertent help from John Dean, President Nixon's legal adviser. On June 29, 1973, Dean presented the Senate Watergate Committee with White House memos written in 1970 and 1971 indicating that attempts were being made to force the IRS to take administrative actions against "left wing" and "activist" organizations whose views the White House found offensive.

As Troyer's discovery proceedings continued, he too found more and more indications of political intervention. For example, the center's application had in fact been approved within the IRS. This initial decision was reversed, however, after it was referred to Roger Barth, a former Nixon political operative who had recently been appointed the agency's deputy counsel. (Barth had begun his career in the IRS as the assistant to the commissioner.)

Equally suggestive was a handwritten note Troyer noticed on one of the thousands of pages he had obtained from the IRS. The October 7, 1971, note was written by Richard Cox, then the assistant director of the IRS's Interpretive Division. "Perhaps White House Pressure," Cox scribbled in his clear hand.

On December 12, 1973, Federal Judge Charles R. Richey handed down his decision, one of the rare instances when the agency has been formally convicted of the political manipulations that it so regularly practices.

"A showing of political influence renders the Service's ruling null and void," Judge Richey wrote. "It is outside the law. The court is concerned not only with direct political intervention, but also with the creation of a political atmosphere generated by the White House in the Internal Revenue Service which may have affected the objectivity of those participating in the ruling in the plaintiff's case."

Over the years, the targets of IRS hostility have usually been political activists of one kind or another—right-wing fundamentalist ministers, Communists, civil rights activists, the Ku Klux Klan, public interest lawyers. But sometimes the agency's weapons have been aimed at those whose principal crime seems to have been to offend the sensibilities of an agency bureaucrat. For many Americans, for example, the gradual emergence of gays and lesbians into public life has been one of the most disturbing developments of the last twenty-five years.

IRS v. GAY

Stanley S. Weithorn is a New York lawyer who for many years has specialized in the nuances of tax-exempt law. Weithorn and his wife live on Long Island, and he maintains a large sunny office on the nineteenth floor of a Manhattan office building. Weithorn's clients include a wide range of different, sometimes controversial, philanthropic organizations. So when Aryeh Neier, national director of the American Civil Liberties Union, called and asked him for help, Weithorn immediately understood the case could be contentious.

"Aryeh said he had an important case," Weithorn recalled. "He said it involved a group that had been established to carry out an educational program to acquaint the public about gay life. I met the leaders of the group in late 1974. The purpose of the proposed organization was to collect and disseminate factual information about the role of homosexual men and women in American life in hopes of reducing the prejudices against them. They were serious people with a serious program."

The name of the organization was the Fund for Human Dignity. After several months of preparation, on March 17, 1975, Weithorn submitted an application for tax-exempt status. "If you excluded the word 'homosexual' from the papers, it was a totally routine application that would have been routinely approved at the local level. But as I expected would happen, the matter was immediately referred to Washington."

Then came a long period of administrative hassling by the IRS. On September 15, 1975, Milton Cerny, Chief of Rulings Section Number 2, Exempt Organizations Technical Branch, sent Weithorn a letter with a number of specific questions.

Several questions were revealing. "Will you advocate in any way the position that homosexuality is a mere preference, orientation, or propensity, which is on a par with heterosexuality or should be otherwise regarded as normal?"

The IRS clearly was uneasy about the possibility that the fund might contend that homosexual life was not a perversion. Cerny posed the question long after leading medical authorities, including the American Psychiatric Association and the American Psychological Association, had formally concluded that homosexuality was simply one form of sexual behavior and was not, in itself, a "mental disorder."

Another group of IRS questions was even more revealing of the agency's hostility. "Will you sponsor any social activities? If so, describe these activities. Will these activities be conducted or utilized so as to not encourage or facilitate homosexual practices to a consequential degree?"

It was during this period, Weithorn said, that he got a telephone call from the IRS in Washington. "They told me that they were leaning toward a favorable ruling, but that to get it we would have to accept four specific conditions."

The IRS conditions shocked Weithorn. "The first condition was that we should promise never to issue a statement indicating that homosexuality is not a disease. We didn't have to say it was a sickness but the IRS clearly didn't want us to quote the ruling of the American Psychiatric Association," the lawyer said.

"The second condition was that any discussion panel we formed would have to have what they called 'true balance,' specifically would have to include an avowed enemy of homosexual life. To me this was like telling a peace group that any panel it formed would have to include General Curtis LeMay.

"Third, the IRS said that even though we would be an educational organization, we must agree not to prepare any material for radio and television. The agency's position here seemed to be that such programs might affect the life-styles of children.

"The final condition was that if the fund organized a meeting, there should not be any 'social interchange.' The IRS was a bit vague on this condition. But it appears the bureaucrats thought it might prevent the mass orgies they seemed to think were a normal part of all homosexual meetings."

Weithorn told the IRS that the four conditions were totally unacceptable, which of course meant that the group's request was not approved. In turn, the failure of the fund to obtain tax-exempt status meant that foundations and individuals withheld their contributions, and the planned operations of the organization had to be sharply curtailed. The IRS, at least for a time, appeared to have achieved its actual goal.

Immediately after Jerome Kurtz was appointed IRS commissioner by President Carter, Weithorn appealed for a new hearing on the agency's effort to muzzle the Fund for Human Dignity. Seven weeks later, the IRS gave the fund a favorable ruling.

THE IRS, THE CATHOLIC CHURCH, AND OTHER KINDS OF SEXUAL ACTIVITY

The IRS's initial response to the application of the Fund for Human Dignity is a perfect example of how it sometimes treats an unpopular group that, at the time of the incident, had very little political power. Of course, there are endless examples of the opposite side of this coin: how far the IRS will go to bend the law for groups with genuine political strength.

One of the most blatant and difficult such examples involves the Roman Catholic Church and its use of tax-exempt funds for directly political purposes. A well-established provision of the tax law explicitly states that religious, educational, and charitable groups with tax exemption may not "participate in, or intervene in (including the publishing or distributing of statements), any political campaign on behalf of any candidate for public office."

Toward the end of the Carter administration, Gail Harmon, a Washington lawyer representing the National Abortion Rights Action League, began sending to the IRS scores of documents distributed by church-connected groups located throughout the United States. Harmon contended that the newsletters, leaflets, questionnaires, reports, and articles proved that the Catholic Church in its campaign against abortion had violated the law forbidding tax-exempt groups from direct political activities. There was a newsletter printed by a Catholic Church in Pennsylvania listing the political candidates for state and national elections who "favor life." There were articles written by a Minnesota priest, the "Diocesan Pro-Life Director," endorsing specific candidates. There was a Missouri newspaper article describing how the official newspaper of the local archdiocese refused to sell advertising space to a congressional candidate with a position on abortion that was unacceptable to the Catholic Church. In several letters to Harmon, the IRS acknowledged receiving her material. But it took no public action.

Then, in 1981, a large group of organizations favoring abortion rights brought suit against three parties: the Roman Catholic Church, the IRS, and the agency's boss, Treasury Secretary Donald Regan. The charge against the church was that it had violated the tax exemption law by repeatedly using tax exemption contributions for political purposes. The charge against the IRS and the treasury secretary was that they had "consistently overlooked these violations and failed and refused to do their duty to enforce the Code and the Constitution."

To buttress their court case, the consortium, Abortion Rights Mobilization, quoted extensively from "A Pastoral Plan for Pro-Life Activities," adopted in November 1975 by both the U.S. Catholic Conference and the National Conference of Bishops. One section of the plan called for the creation of congressional pro-life action groups that would "work for qualified candidates who will vote for a constitutional amendment and other pro-life issues."

The suit also cited many specific examples of the church's direct involvement in political campaigns similar to those documented for the IRS by Harmon. In September 1980, for example, Humberto Cardinal Medeiros, Roman Catholic archbishop of Boston, attacked two congressional candidates in a letter sent to 410 parishes a few days before a primary election. The letter was read from many pulpits and published in the official archdiocesan paper.

The pro-choice groups contended that in the case of the Catholic Church the IRS has flagrantly engaged in selective enforcement of the law concerning the use of tax-exempt funds. The result, they say, is that the church is receiving an illegal subsidy from the government to promote its views by open political activities.

Almost a decade later, the suit is still pending and the IRS has still failed to revoke the tax-exempt status of the Catholic Church as clearly required by law. What makes the agency's inaction in this case such an unusually clear example of selective enforcement is its 1964 decision to revoke the tax-exempt status of Christian Echoes, a nonprofit church organized in Oklahoma by Dr. Billy James Hargis, an ordained minister.

The IRS decision was partly based on its finding that Christian Echoes had sought to influence congressional decisions on dozens of social issues: the Nuclear Test Ban Treaty, civil rights legislation, Medicare, and proposals that the United States withdraw from the United Nations. In addition, the agency said that the conservative fundamentalist church had intervened in political campaigns by attacking the likes of John F. Kennedy and William Fulbright and supporting Barry Goldwater and Strom Thurmond.

Dr. Hargis appealed the ruling to the federal courts, contending that it violated the First Amendment guarantee of freedom of religion. The U.S. Court of Appeals in Denver, however, rejected this argument. It said that the revocation was constitutional because, although the exercise of religion was indeed a right that is fully protected by the First Amendment, tax exemption is a separate privilege that is granted by the government under a set of rules established by law.

The suit brought against the Catholic Church by Abortion Rights Mobilization has been before various federal courts since 1981 and could well be there for another decade before it is resolved. In congressional testimony in 1987, however, Commissioner Lawrence B. Gibbs argued that the current tax exemption laws include so many ambiguities and nuances that they had become a "seedbed for taxpayer controversy." He added that some of the recent changes in the statutes had continued a set of problems that "adversely affects our ability to administer the law even-handedly."

After comparing the overtly political pro-life activities of the Catholic Church with the work of Christian Echoes against its enemies, Gibbs's contention does not wash. The problem created by these two cases is not the product of murky law; the problem is that the law has put the IRS in an impossible place. Given the political power of the Roman Catholic Church, it is inconceivable that the IRS would ever revoke its tax-exempt status, no matter what it did. But with a little pressure from an annoyed President Kennedy, the IRS was perfectly willing to begin the process that ultimately would cause Christian Echoes, a far smaller institution, to lose its tax exemption.

What else could the IRS do? Members of the Catholic Church comprise one of the major voting blocs in the United States. President Reagan had repeatedly trumpeted his opposition to abortion and had been elected with the open support of many Catholics. President Kennedy had publicly urged the IRS to enforce the tax laws against fundamentalist right-wing ministers, who at that time were an insignificant political force. But while selective enforcement may be a necessary part of national politics, it is very damaging to the ideal of justice and to the public respect that the IRS must keep if our tax-supported society is to survive.

More important, perhaps, are the difficult underlying questions that are raised by this and dozens of other similar cases. What mechanisms can be put in place to assure the American people that the IRS does not routinely suppress unpopular social views whether expressed by the left or by the right? How can we prevent future presidents from forcing the IRS to attack the political enemies of the administration in power? What is the purpose of tax exemption? Given the complexity of the law and the understandable passions of many of the officials who can influence the agency's actions, is evenhanded tax enforcement possible? Should a federal enforcement agency as powerful as the IRS be given the power to define which causes are worthy of charity and which are not?

CHAPTER 12

Oversight:
Why the Watchdogs
Seldom Bark

On March 12, 1924, Senator James Couzens, in a speech before the Senate, charged that widespread corruption and secret deal making in the federal tax agency were destroying its ability to collect taxes. Shortly thereafter, the Senate voted to create a special committee to undertake a thorough investigation of the Bureau of Internal Revenue. Couzens was named chairman.

The choice of Couzens to head the special committee was not surprising. Eight years earlier, the wealthy Republican industrialist had earned his spurs as a tough-minded reformer by cleaning up the notoriously corrupt Detroit Police Department after his appointment as its commissioner. He was then elected the city's mayor and led a battle to build a municipal rail system that put pressure on the private transit companies to lower their unusually high fares. These successes led to his election to the U.S. Senate.[1]

By the time the committee's investigators had completed their work two years after Couzens's 1924 speech to the Senate, the reputations of the Revenue Bureau, the Revenue commissioner, and Treasury Secretary Andrew W. Mellon would be seriously tarnished.

From the very beginning of Couzens's inquiry, Mellon and many of the other Republicans then running the federal government were worried about the political problems that might be created by the Michigan senator's intense investigation of the tax agency. Their concern was heightened when they learned that one of Couzens's first targets was William Boyce Thompson, a New York millionaire and leading fundraiser for the Republican National Committee. Thompson was targeted because of reports that he had been saved almost $500,000 in federal taxes when top officials in the bureau granted him a favorable tax ruling over the objections of the agency's auditing and engineering experts. What made the ruling even worse was that it had been arranged even though Thompson had refused to provide the tax agency with any documents to support his claimed deductions.

On the morning of March 7, 1925, just one year after the special committee was created, Secretary Mellon was shocked to read a front-page story in the *New York World*—then one of the nation's leading newspapers—about Thompson's tawdry tax ruling. The story was based on evidence filed with the Senate by Senator Couzens.

Something had to be done to head off the investigation. That very afternoon, Internal Revenue Commissioner David H. Blair and one of his assistants personally went to the U.S. Senate and asked for the senator. When Couzens came off the Senate floor, Blair handed him a letter stating that he owed $10,861,131.50 in back taxes.[2]

The senator was furious. He said the tax charge was an act of retaliation triggered by his investigation of the improper administration of the tax laws. Because he had displayed the "temerity to dare criticize a Republican Administration or Republican Cabinet officer," Couzens said, "they proposed immediately to penalize that senator to the extent of ten to eleven million dollars."

Mellon's crude attempt to intimidate Couzens failed.

The awkwardly named Select Committee on Investigation of the Bureau of Internal Revenue had held weeks of tumultuous hearings before the counterattack. The pace certainly did not slacken after it. With the help of a large staff of lawyers, accountants, and other experts, it heard scores of witnesses and examined thousands of pages of documents, memos, and reports concerning hundreds of questionable tax cases.

On January 7, 1926, almost two years after the investigation began, the special committee issued its final, severely critical report. Although the language was somewhat stilted, Senator Couzens and his staff flayed the bureau for the discriminatory way it was collecting federal income and estate taxes. A special target was the large mining, oil, and manufacturing companies and how they "were escaping taxation through tremendous deductions for depletion and amortization of war facilities."

The report was on occasion astonishingly outspoken. It found, for example, that S. M. Greenidge, head of the bureau's Engineering Division, "appears to be ill informed as to the work under his jurisdiction, incompetent and generally unsuited for any position in government service requiring the exercise of engineering ability and sound discretion."

The report also said that there was a "growing tendency" among senior agency officials to set aside the technical findings of the working-level engineers and then to increase the deductions that corporations were allowed to claim. "In the valuation of oil properties there appears to be no systematic adherence to principle and a total absence of competent supervision."

The committee concluded that it "has been the consistent policy of the Commissioner of Internal Revenue to exceed the authority delegated [to him by Congress] to compromise taxes." The evidence gathered during the hearings, the committee said, showed that the bureau established taxes "by bargain rather than principle. The best and most persistent trader gets the lowest tax and gross discrimination is the inevitable result."

The committee report then presented a number of case studies. It said the depletion allowance granted to the New England Lime Company "violates every provision of the law and regulations and every principle governing depletion allowance."

The most sensitive matters uncovered during the Couzens investigation concerned Mellon himself, the Pittsburgh tycoon who had been treasury secretary since 1921 and would continue to hold the post until 1931. One revelation was a memo written to B. L. Wheeler, the agency's chief of engineers, about a tax dispute concerning the Standard Steel Car Company of Butler, Pennsylvania. It suggested that the hidden hand of the secretary might be pulling the levers within the tax agency. "Secretary Mellon is interested in the above company and has requested that the information be compiled as quickly as possible," the memo said.

Then there was the matter of the Gulf Oil Corporation. This was especially nettlesome because of Andrew Mellon's direct conflict of interest in regard to Gulf. Since Mellon was treasury secretary, of course, the Revenue Bureau was under his overall command. And as the founder and principal owner of Gulf, Mellon stood to gain the most from favorable rulings given the company. The report charged that Gulf had received "exorbitant allowances which can not be justified upon any basis." This was long before even the semipermeable "blind trusts" of today's Washington.

The committee said that the bureau had granted excessive oil depletion allowances to the entire oil industry. "But the allowances to the Gulf Oil Corporation are so excessive as to constitute gross discrimination against even the oil industry."

Mellon was imperturbable in the face of accusations that he secretly used his position as secretary to force the bureau to award him and his companies about $7 million in refunds. "The right hand knew not what the left hand did in the Treasury Department," wrote Harvey O'Connor, Mellon's biographer, in a summary statement of the secretary's defense. "The refunds, as a matter of fact, were as much a surprise to him [Mellon], when brought to his attention, as the outside world. As for the mysterious notations which appeared on the files regarding so-called Mellon companies," O'Connor continued, "they were blamed on over-zealous employees who deluded themselves that they could ingratiate themselves with their superior by favoring cases in which he had an interest." So much for the charges of crass corruption.

It is almost always impossible to develop absolute proof about the motives of any person, let alone a gigantic bureaucracy, even in situations as brazen as the counterattack mounted against Couzens. But several historians have no doubt that Treasury Secretary Mellon and Commissioner David H. Blair were engaged in a blatant retaliatory act that they hoped would bully the senator into abandoning his investigation of the agency and the corrupt deals it was cutting.[3]

The conclusion that the tax charges against Couzens were hokum is based in part upon the senator's reputation for absolute integrity and is strongly supported by the final decision of the Board of Tax Appeals.

The tax board did more than reject the government's assertion that Couzens owed millions of dollars in back taxes. It found that the senator had been so responsible about his potential tax liabilities that he had substantially overestimated what he owed the government. The court ordered the Treasury to return to Couzens a grand total of $989,883.

By itself, this first known example of official IRS retaliation against someone who dared to criticize the way it was administering the national tax laws is disturbing. Over the years, however, many other critics both in and out of Congress have found themselves the target of an improper counterattack.

The numerous acts of retaliation by the IRS might be shrugged off as isolated aberrations of little general importance. But because they have often been aimed at individuals who have a constitutional obligation to supervise the agency or to examine its overall performance, the events have discouraged responsible criticism and have thus undermined one of the basic principles of the U.S. Constitution: the theory of checks and balances. To prevent government from becoming too powerful, the founding fathers divided it into three parts, each having the authority to question the actions of the others.

The attempt to force Couzens to back away from his investigation occurred a long time ago. But as recently as the early 1980s, the IRS appears to have brought tax charges against government officials or former officials whose lawful activities or decisions had irritated the agency.

A few years ago, for example, a White House staff official with supervisory authority over one aspect of the administration of the tax laws found himself in a policy dispute with the IRS. After a heated internal debate, the official won his point and the new policy was adopted despite the strong objections of the agency.

A few months later, President Reagan asked this particular official to take on a more important federal job outside the White House. Sometime after his nomination to this new post was announced, the official received an IRS notice informing him that he owed nearly $10,000 in back taxes.

The official immediately called his accountant and was advised that the IRS was wrong and that he did not owe any additional taxes. "But I was about to go into a confirmation hearing in the Senate and the last thing I wanted was a tax dispute that would become public if I took the agency to court. So I decided to cave in and give them the money," the official said.

"There is no way you or I will ever be able to prove what triggered that tax charge, but I am absolutely certain that the claim against me was out-and-out harassment, somebody getting even."

Shortly after this Reagan administration figure told me about his run-in with the IRS, I visited another man who had been a special assistant to an IRS commissioner in a previous administration. During the time that he had held this noncareer job, he too had occasionally tangled with the agency's senior civil servants. He had made some enemies.

Upon leaving the agency, the man became a partner of an established law firm in a major southern city. Then, just a few years ago, the lawyer was asked to join the legal team defending an unpopular organization against which the IRS had brought tax charges.

"Shortly after taking the case, I received an official warning that I was under investigation by the IRS for serious criminal tax violations," the lawyer said. "The whole business was baloney, an attempt to scare me off the case. But before the matter was dropped, the client and my law firm had to spend an awful lot of money preparing my defense. It was a truly shocking display of misused power."

People who have held important positions rarely will publicly discuss incidents of apparent harassment. It must be remembered that, once a civil tax charge is challenged in court, all the details of the matter become a part of the court's public record. And despite the false charges brought against Senator Couzens and a good number of other taxpayers, too many of us assume that where there is smoke there must be fire. Because the government has so much credibility, individuals like the Reagan administration official or the lawyer in the southern city rightfully fear that openly challenging the IRS may well damage their reputations and future earning power.

Very few congressmen doubt that the IRS will strike back in an illegal or improper way if sufficiently provoked. This fear does not rest on the Couzens case alone. In fact, there have been two additional fairly well documented situations in which information leaked by the IRS appears to have short-circuited the careers of senators who headed committees that had dared to criticize the agency.

SENATOR ED LONG GOES DOWN

On the evening of August 6, 1968, Joseph Rosapepe, public affairs director of the IRS, dialed the number of William Lambert, then considered one of the nation's leading investigative reporters. Lambert was an associate editor of *Life* magazine.[4]

After Rosapepe got Lambert on the line, the public affairs officer handed the phone to Sheldon Cohen, who at that time was IRS commissioner. Lambert remembers that Cohen was ecstatic.

"He told me that at the commissioner's meeting that morning everyone agreed that maybe the IRS should give me a ten-year pass on audits," Lambert recalled. "But then the commissioner added that, because that would not be legal, he just wanted to offer me the IRS's congratulations."

Lambert said that the occasion of the congratulatory call from the commissioner was the defeat in a Democratic primary of a now-forgotten senator named Edward V. Long.

There were two reasons why Cohen called to congratulate Lambert on the political demise of Long. First, Long had been a noisy and difficult critic of the IRS and his defeat would remove a thorn from the side of the agency. Second, Long's defeat was the result of a *Life* magazine article written by Lambert that linked the Missouri senator to Teamster President Jimmy Hoffa.

But several questions remain. Who arranged for the embarrassing information about Long's connections with Hoffa to be given to Lambert? Why was it provided? What was the significance of Commissioner Cohen's congratulatory call to the reporter on the day after Long's defeat?

Long had first come to Washington on March 26, 1963, when the wealthy banker, lawyer, and Missouri lieutenant governor was appointed the state's junior senator after the sudden death of the incumbent, Thomas Hennings. Shortly after coming to Washington, Long was named chairman of the Senate Judiciary Subcommittee on Administrative Practice and Procedure, which his predecessor had led. The broad mandate of the subcommittee allowed it to investigate almost any subject that caught its fancy. Long and the subcommittee's chief counsel, Bernard Fensterwald, decided to hold hearings on how several federal enforcement agencies were improperly invading the privacy of American citizens.

Long's hearings during the early and mid-1960s on the use of mail covers, wiretaps, bugs, and peeping devices by a handful of agencies, including the IRS, were given considerable coverage in the press. (One measure of Long's political savvy is that J. Edgar Hoover's FBI—still a formidable power in those pre-Watergate days—was never called before the subcommittee.) In February 1967, Long published *The Intruders*, a short book that mounted a free-swinging attack on government snooping. The disclosures that federal agents had been routinely ignoring government rules in their secret surveillance activities generated concern in the liberal community, including such stalwarts as Hubert H. Humphrey. Humphrey, by that time Lyndon Johnson's vice president, wrote the foreword to Long's book.

But a number of Washington officials were outraged by Long's hearings, especially by the disclosure of the IRS's widespread and improper use of secret wiretaps and bugs. Chief among the outraged were the IRS and Justice Department bureaucrats involved in the bugging.

Although most of the taps and bugs occurred during the Kennedy administration, when Robert Kennedy and Mortimer Caplin were in charge of tax enforcement, it fell upon Sheldon Cohen, the next commissioner, to defend the IRS. The attacks on the agency were sufficiently serious that even President Johnson was drawn into the discussion of how to handle the evidence of electronic eavesdropping presented during the Long hearings.

At 6:52 P.M. on November 30, 1965, Marvin Watson, then chief of the president's White House staff, dictated a short note to Johnson about Cohen's plan for pacifying Long.

Watson said that Cohen was proposing a two-step strategy. First, Cohen would visit Long and report the "actions taken by IRS to correct the things that have been done by the IRS in the past. Second, that you [Johnson] invite Senator Long to the White House to publicly thank him for drawing attention to IRS errors."

Watson's memo then asked the president whether he approved or disapproved the Cohen plan. Directly under Watson's typed question to LBJ were places where the president could check either yes or no. Johnson checked the negative box and added a brief handwritten response for Watson to pass on to Cohen. "Tell him to discuss with [Treasury Secretary] Fowler and [Assistant Secretary] Davis but don't pull us in—L." The "L" in this case of course stood for Lyndon.

The pesky Long would be dealt with in a different way. One year after Cohen's plan was put to LBJ, according to *Life* reporter Lambert, an official in the Justice Department who worked closely with the IRS provided him with a juicy lead about Long. The official, who Lambert said was an old friend, told the newsman he should investigate the connections between Long and Jimmy Hoffa. The bridge between the two men, the informant said, was Morris Shenker, a famous Missouri criminal lawyer with ties to the Teamsters Union.

"I went to St. Louis, talked with people, and did a lot of other reporting," Lambert remembered. "I sort of camped out there for a while. Denny Walsh, an investigative reporter in St. Louis, gave me a lot of help. Then I came back to Washington and began pumping people I knew in the Justice Department."

That's when the *Life* reporter was given the final tip that quickly would lead to the publication of his story: Shenker had once made a $48,000 payment to Long.

Lambert said that, although this second bit of information also came from "someone in Justice," the original source had to be the IRS. Lambert added that he was confident of the source because the agency and the Justice Department then were conducting a joint investigation of the ties of the Teamsters Union to organized crime and because the information about the size of the payment was so exact that it almost certainly had been drawn from a tax file. He emphasized, however, that he was not actually shown a copy of the tax return of either Long or Shenker. (The reporter said that there were later cases in which the IRS provided him information about politicians and he was actually shown their tax returns.)

Lambert's carefully researched article ran in the May 26, 1967, issue of *Life*. There were three main charges. First, Senator Long was strongly influenced to take up the investigation of federal snooping by his friends in the Teamsters Union. Second, Senator Long's hearings on the IRS's improper wiretapping had blunted the government's war against organized crime. Third, although the *B* word never appeared in the article, Lambert implied that the senator may have been bribed. "Senator Long, who says he has not been in active law practice since the mid-1950's, was paid $48,000 for legal services by a close personal friend, the chief counsel for Jimmy Hoffa, during 1963 and 1964. These were the years immediately preceding the opening of the subcommittee hearings."

Long denied any impropriety. He said that Morris Shenker was a distinguished Missouri criminal lawyer with many clients. He indicated that the $48,000 payment was nothing but a legal finder's fee. There was never an allegation that the IRS had found any tax problem regarding the payment. The senator said that he found it strange that the only time innuendos had been raised about his business and legal associations was after he had exposed unlawful activities on the part of government agencies.

The Senate's Select Committee on Standards and Conduct, always loath to criticize fellow senators, later investigated Lambert's charges against Long and found no impropriety. But it is unlikely that the questions raised by the *Life* article will ever be conclusively decided one way or the other. Long, who is now deceased, was a wealthy country banker and lawyer. Would a $48,000 payment spread over two years be a credible bribe for a millionaire? Morris Shenker did indeed have intimate connections with the Teamsters Union. But he was also a leading criminal lawyer and a longtime figure in the state's Democratic party. On the other hand, Long had been an open booster of Hoffa, whom he once described as a dynamic and fighting union president, a man he was proud to support.

Whatever the truth of the association among Long, Hoffa, and Shenker, the *Life* magazine article had a devastating effect on the Missouri senator's career. Fifteen months after its publication, an ambitious young politician named Thomas Eagleton defeated Long in the 1968 Democratic primary and went on to win the general election. Long retired to his 1,600-acre farm.

Commissioner Cohen, who acknowledged congratulating Lambert on the day after Long's primary defeat, denied that the IRS was the instrument of the senator's destruction. His denial, however, was carefully qualified. "As far as I know, we didn't leak the story," he said. "But that doesn't mean that someone in the organization wasn't the leaker."

SENATOR JOE MONTOYA
IS KNOCKED OUT OF THE RING

In December 1972, the director of the IRS district in New Mexico began a search of the agency's files for information about U.S. Senator Joseph M. Montoya, the amiable old-line Democrat who had begun his career as a state legislator almost four decades earlier.[5]

The unannounced IRS record search was launched shortly after Montoya had issued a press release announcing that he planned to hold a series of hearings on the agency's performance. Montoya's release had said that he was particularly interested in the quality of services the agency was providing and called upon any taxpayer with a legitimate grievance to contact his office. As was the case with Couzens in 1924 and Long in 1968, the Senate Finance Committee, the Senate committee with primary responsibility for keeping track of the agency's performance, was not involved. Because Montoya was chairman of the appropriations subcommittee that passed on the IRS's funding, however, the New Mexican senator had a legitimate jurisdictional claim for conducting the proposed oversight hearings.

At about the same time that Montoya announced his forthcoming hearings and the IRS office in New Mexico began rummaging through its old files on the senator, a secret memorandum began circulating in the IRS that purported to be a list of individuals who had been identified as having connections with "various tax protest groups." The memo, a copy of which was obtained by the Senate Select Committee on Intelligence a few years later, said "some members of these groups are capable of violence against IRS personnel." Among the names included in the list of potentially dangerous tax protestors was one "Montoya, Joseph (Sen), New Mexico."

Adding the name of a senator who had just announced oversight hearings to the list of potentially dangerous tax protestors probably was considered a good little bureaucratic joke within the IRS. But the view of Montoya as an enemy appears to have been quite widespread. There is no reason to believe, for example, that IRS officials were pleased to learn that Montoya's original invitation for citizen complaints had led more than thirteen hundred taxpayers to volunteer negative information about problems they had experienced with the agency.

To an agency that had largely escaped any regular congressional oversight, Montoya's words about his investigation may well have sounded like an open declaration of war. And it was, in fact, one of the most difficult moments in the history of the IRS. The staff of the Montoya subcommittee had lined up a number of powerful witnesses who were prepared to present embarrassing evidence that the agency's managers were inept. Other witnesses had been located who denounced the IRS's quota system. Although this was bad enough, the first embarrassing stories about how the Nixon administration had misused the IRS were also just beginning to surface.

By the time the Montoya hearings got under way in Washington, the IRS investigation was rolling along. Agency investigators in New Mexico, for example, had already pulled copies of Montoya's tax returns and had initiated a "source and application of funds" survey to see how the senator earned and spent his money.

Given Montoya's twin roles—chairman of a Senate subcommittee that set the annual funding for the IRS and member of the Senate Watergate Committee—the IRS investigation of the senator raised three extremely sensitive and contradictory political problems. Had the IRS agents in New Mexico kicked off the Montoya investigation in an effort to block the hearings? Should Washington halt it? If the investigation was halted, might that decision later be interpreted as an improper political cave-in?

At one point, Donald C. Alexander, the new IRS commissioner, was reported as being delighted by the Montoya investigation. "Well, you've made my day," Alexander was quoted as saying when first told about it. A few months later, however, Alexander ordered the Southwest regional commissioner to drop the investigation.

In October 1975, Bob Woodward, the *Washington Post*'s leading investigative reporter, published a front-page story in which several officials of the IRS accused Alexander of halting the highly sensitive investigation. The article quoted agency officials as saying they believed Alexander had halted the audit of Montoya because of the senator's influence over the IRS. Because of high sensitivity during the late Nixon years to all questions of secret deals, Alexander's decision was later examined by both the Treasury and the Justice departments. The verdict: Alexander had violated no laws, but his handling of the case left much to be desired.

Unanswered, however, was the more interesting and complicated question that once again illustrates the unusual power of tax information and those who control it. What were the motives of the IRS officials who leaked the story about Alexander's decision to the *Washington Post*? Who actually was the target?

Woodward, in an interview, said he believes "the original tip was innocent. I do not recall picking up an indication that those who talked to me were out to get either Alexander or Montoya. I think the prime motive was that some people in the system were upset by a violation of proper procedure."

Alexander himself believes a key underlying motive was the ethnic hostility some IRS supervisors in the Southwest felt toward Montoya, a leading Hispanic politician.

Yet another possible motive was related to Commissioner Alexander's contentious dispute with the criminal investigators of the IRS who opposed his enforcement policies. During the period when the Montoya case was being pursued, Alexander had embarked on an intense effort to curb the investigative abuses of the Criminal Investigation Division. These efforts had so enraged the division that some agents had begun trying to force Alexander to resign by anonymously passing embarrassing information about the IRS to a small cadre of Washington reporters.

Montoya, however, believed that he, and not Alexander, was the central target of the IRS officials who had talked to Woodward. The senator said that they were upset because of his many hearings on "the way in which IRS agents and employees handle their job."

In a speech on the Senate floor on November 20, 1975, Montoya insisted that his hearings on the IRS were fair. "We sincerely tried to listen to all sides and . . . our goal was to improve taxpayer services, protect taxpayer rights and also to protect necessary and sensible procedures of the IRS. I do not consider myself to be an enemy of the IRS and I do not believe that the subcommittee has given any IRS employee reason to be fearful of our power."

But some IRS employees were fearful, he said, and it appeared that they had decided to strike. "The matter of possible political misuse of the IRS is serious. The matter of 'leaking' IRS tax information by employees of our tax system is serious. It is not only one Senator, or one Senate subcommittee or one individual IRS commissioner which is under attack. It is our tax system, and the confidence of the public which is most seriously affected by unsupported allegations and political misuse of tax information."

Although Woodward's original story had noted that there was no evidence that Montoya had illegally evaded taxes or was aware of or sought special treatment from the IRS, the mere existence of even a preliminary tax investigation was politically damaging. One year later, Harrison H. (Jack) Schmitt, a conservative Republican and former astronaut, unseated Montoya after twelve years in the U.S. Senate.

THE HARVEST OF FEAR,
THE POLITICS OF TAX COLLECTION

The fear of retaliation has had a pernicious effect: Members of Congress have been discouraged from supporting legislative efforts to improve the administration of tax laws that, for one reason or another, are opposed by the IRS.

Senator David Pryor is an Arkansas Democrat with more than a touch of the old-time populist. In 1988, Pryor astonished most Washington insiders by winning approval of the Taxpayers' Bill of Rights, true tax-reform legislation that the IRS opposed as unnecessary. At a breakfast held in the U.S. Capitol to celebrate his unexpected success, Pryor acknowledged that at the beginning of his campaign it had been very hard to find members of Congress who would cosponsor his bill. "I saw real fear of the possible IRS retaliation among many members of the Senate and the House of Representatives," he explained.[6]

Paradoxically, however, while Congress is extremely cautious about altering the basic powers of the IRS, it has become more and more enthusiastic about changing the tax code. Since 1976, for example, Congress has passed 138 bills modifying the federal tax laws. The increasing congressional interest in adding new wrinkles to the tax law and the effect this interest has on the House and Senate tax committees require examination.

The classic explanation for changing the tax laws is that alterations are made necessary by shifts in the financing of public programs. The public finance theory treats taxes as a necessary evil, increased only to finance essential government programs such as national defense. Because government's greatest needs arise in times of war, and because the most tumultuous period of tax change has occurred in the last decade, when the United States was at peace, the public finance theory does not seem to work.

Richard L. Doernberg and Fred S. McChesney, both law professors at Emory University in Atlanta, have developed an alternative theory. They contend that individual members of Congress, especially those assigned to the House Ways and Means Committee and the Senate Finance Committee, sell tax changes to heavily financed special interest groups.

"If tax legislation is a contracting process," Doernberg asked in a recent research paper, "how do legislators get compensated for obtaining favorable legislation or avoiding unfavorable legislation?"* In answering this question, Doernberg noted that in one recent year campaign contributions from political action committees (PACs) to House tax committee members were 31 percent higher than the average received by all House members. Expressed in a different way, members of the tax-writing committees, who made up only 10 percent of Congress in a recent year, garnered about 25 percent of PAC contributions.

One more factor must be considered. The political action committees that give the members of the House and Senate tax committees so much money were mostly established by small groups with narrowly focused interests. Wall Street brokers have PACs. Chicago commodity dealers have PACs. Groups of corporations engaged in the same business have PACs. Doctors and lawyers have PACs. All these PACs share one general interest: They are each seeking to make specific changes in the federal tax law that either give them new tax benefits or protect their existing ones.

One very large and amorphous group of Americans, however, has no PAC to support the political ambitions of members of Congress: the millions and millions of taxpayers who, in one way or another, have been abused by the IRS.

Thus, the dynamic forces working against genuine oversight are powerful. On the one hand, it is essential to Congress as a whole that nothing interfere with the money machine. On the other hand, because the organized PACs have made changes in the tax code so lucrative, the House Ways and Means Committee and the Senate Finance Committee must hold constant hearings to negotiate yet another tax law that inevitably is described as an important new reform.

One other set of forces pushing Congress to adopt more and more complicated tax laws grows from the current rules guiding the budget and tax process. The current budget rules require that any new federal expend-

---

*Doernberg prepared his paper in response to an IRS invitation to be the keynote speaker at the agency's sixth annual tax research conference on November 17, 1988. His title: The Market for Tax Reform: Public Pain for Private Gain. Upon receiving Doernberg's paper, a somewhat simplified version of previous studies that he and Fred McChesney had done for the *New York University Law Review* and the *Minnesota Law Review*, the IRS asked that the names of Representative Dan Rostenkowski, chairman of the House Ways and Means Committee, and Senator Lloyd Bentsen, chairman of the Senate Finance Committee, be removed from his paper. Doernberg believes that the IRS was concerned his paper would offend the members of Congress who theoretically oversee the agency. After Doernberg refused to remove the names of the two powerful chairmen and two other influential members of Congress, the IRS withdrew its invitation for him to attend the conference. The paper was published by *Tax Notes,* an excellent trade weekly, on November 28, 1988, at pp. 965–69.

iture be balanced with a budget saving. The current tax rules require the indexing of the tax code, a procedure that has had the effect of denying Congress an almost invisible annual increase in federal revenues. The result: Because there is very little room to maneuver, Congress increasingly looks to intricate tax laws to meet program demands that cannot be denied.

It is thus not at all surprising that Representative Dan Rostenkowski and Senator Lloyd Bentsen find little time and have precious little interest in conducting detailed oversight of the actual operations of the IRS. It should also surprise no one that Rostenkowski and most of the other members of the Ways and Means Committee initially opposed Senator Pryor's Taxpayers' Bill of Rights to provide modest legal protections to middle-class taxpayers. (The tax establishment's strong opposition to the bill ultimately collapsed after Pryor conducted an almost unprecedented series of hearings featuring a variety of IRS horror stories and at the same time somewhat scaled back his proposals for giving the taxpayer better protection against arbitrary IRS actions.) Finally, it is also completely logical that Rostenkowski and the staff of his committee would lead an active behind-the-scenes campaign to head off an investigation by the House Government Operations Committee of corruption problems in the IRS.

The net effect of these three dynamic forces—the fear of retaliation, the concern about upsetting the money machine, and the demands for special services by the well-financed PACs—is clear. The single most powerful agency in the federal government has been mostly free of tough, informed congressional oversight. Although the two tax committees have for a few brief periods been jarred into undertaking an essential part of their constitutionally mandated mission, most of the time they have not.

"Looking back, I think we should have spent a lot more time investigating the operations of the IRS such as the actual processing of returns," said William A. Kirk, now a Washington lawyer in private practice. "But there are always a lot of competing concerns."

From 1982 through 1985, Kirk was the staff director of the congressional subcommittee that in theory had the single most pressing responsibility to keep track of the IRS. Kirk ran the Oversight Subcommittee of the House Ways and Means Committee.

"The Ways and Means Committee, our parent, always seemed to end up concentrating on what were regarded as the 'big issues' like the trade bill, catastrophic health care, or tax reform. It's not easy to get members to sit down and look at the impact of computerization on individual taxpayers. But if you had a hearing on racial discrimination in tax-exempt schools, or something like that, they'd be hot to trot."

Kirk said that the subcommittee's semipermanent ties to the IRS also contributed to the failure of oversight. "Almost all of the time, we relied on information given to us by the IRS, hardly an unbiased source. Then, as the months go by, you get used to working with the agency's congressional liaison people and you begin to develop institutional and personal ties with them."

Congress is not alone in its routine failure to scrutinize and correct the conduct of this powerful agency. The private institutions of oversight also tend to avert their eyes from the IRS.

For example, the major newspapers of the nation assign reporters to cover the Justice Department and the FBI on a full-time basis, but routinely ignore the massive and occasionally abusive process of tax collection. The handful of Washington reporters with some knowledge of the agency are required to focus almost all of their reporting time on the writing of tax laws by Congress, rather than on how these laws actually are administered. If *The New York Times* tried to cover the functioning of the criminal justice system in New York City by simply analyzing the changes that the state legislature made in the New York criminal code, it would be considered derelict. If *The New York Times* did not assign reporters to examine police department procedures and crime statistics and to investigate the occasional allegations of police brutality and corruption, it would be viewed as seriously failing the citizens of New York. But that is precisely what all the major papers, television networks, and magazines do when it comes to the IRS. There are thousands of stories about all the endless negotiations leading to the adoption of a new tax law, especially when self-serving congressmen give the law a "reform" label, but virtually no interest in the day-to-day operation of the tax collectors.

Even when a member of Congress introduces legislation aimed at curbing occasional IRS abuses, press treatment often is favorable to the agency. In 1985, Representative Andrew Jacobs, Jr., an Indiana Democrat, introduced an amendment to a pending tax bill. The amendment would have allowed federal judges to hold some IRS employees personally liable for the attorney's fees and court costs of taxpayers who have proven that agency auditors had acted in an "arbitrary and capricious" manner.

On February 11, 1986, Anne Swardson, the *Washington Post* reporter then covering taxes, wrote a story that prominently warned readers that the passage of Jacobs's amendment could result "in fewer audits, fewer court cases and less federal revenue." Swardson did not quote Jacobs until the eighth paragraph as asserting that his amendment was designed to protect taxpayers against unreasonable harassment. The *Post*'s headline accurately reflected the unbalanced quality of Swardson's story: "Tax Provision Seen Crippling IRS." Of course, the amendment was killed.

The very definite pro-IRS bias in Swardson's story is not at all unusual, according to several recent surveys of newspaper content conducted by the agency's Research Division. In 1985, the researchers found that the messages implicit in 70 percent of the articles they examined were either positive or neutral. Examples of headlines on typical positive stories were "Help Is Available for Late Filers" and "Tax Reform Will Produce a Fairer and Simpler System." An example of a neutral story summarized IRS rules for how to file a tax return. Stories classified as negative cited IRS statistics showing that agency performance in processing tax refunds had worsened since the previous year.

Very occasionally, an aggressive reporter provides the exception that makes the rule. From 1967 to 1969, a smart young *Reader's Digest* reporter named John Barron wrote a series of extremely tough articles about the IRS. The first one, for example, charged that in the name of collecting taxes the "IRS has bullied, degraded and crushed countless citizens—while unaccountably favoring others." Barron reported about how the IRS harassed waitresses, salesmen, and even a nursing mother for taxes they did not owe while at the same time it was writing off $26 million in back taxes owed by a major New York City real-estate company that had received $67 million in government-insured loans.

The August 1967 *Digest* article infuriated the IRS and, interestingly enough, the agency's friends in Congress. On August 10, the House subcommittee in charge of the IRS's appropriations held a hearing on "charges of abuses by Internal Revenue Service Agents." The hearing was revealing. Subcommittee chairman Tom Steed did not call the dozen individuals whose cases had been cited by Barron. Neither did Steed call the *Reader's Digest.* Instead, the only witness was Sheldon Cohen, then the commissioner.

The hearing was a total whitewash. One of the first matters inserted in the transcript was a seventeen-page agency press release. "An article in the August issue of the Reader's Digest, entitled 'Tyranny in the IRS,' contains too many half truths, distortions, and unsubstantiated conclusions to go unanswered," the release began. At the same time, however, the IRS added that "the misrepresentations in the article are too numerous to be refuted in detail."

(John Barron said in an interview that the *Digest* immediately released a rebuttal denouncing the IRS's seventeen-page press release and standing behind all the charges in his article. He said that the magazine's lawyers, while preparing this rebuttal, were surprised to discover that the press release attacking his report contained a quote from a federal judge that the agency had fabricated. In addition to the rebuttal, the *Digest* published a formal statement in its November 1967 issue in which the editors again stated their confidence in the factual accuracy and balance of Barron's report.)

That the IRS was angry is not surprising. But that one of the most important oversight bodies of Congress would blindly accept the IRS version of the truth without hearing from the taxpayers who believed they had been unfairly treated is a sad commentary on the generally defensive attitude of Congress toward the agency.

Steed's concern for the IRS went beyond giving Cohen a bully pulpit to denounce the magazine. The Oklahoma Democrat said that almost all IRS agents were honest, dedicated individuals whose major desire was to serve the public. Steed added that the article was filled with unjust "innuendo and propaganda." Finally, he asked Cohen whether either *Reader's Digest* or Barron had tax problems that "might be grounds to question their motives"?

Cohen's answer was elegantly devious. "As the chairman knows, the Revenue Code forbids us to discuss the tax affairs of any individual or corporation and therefore whatever knowledge we might have of the tax affairs of these people is not relevant. I won't say there is or I won't say there isn't a motive, but sexy stories sell magazines or newspapers."

The strong IRS bias displayed by Representative Steed and his subcommittee is widespread in the academic community, where writing law review articles on the subtle nuances of tax policy or on the intricacies of tax law is considered much more rewarding than efforts to undertake tough-minded research about how the largest U.S. enforcement agency actually functions.

THE COURTS LOOK THE OTHER WAY

Over and over again, federal judges have found ways either to ignore or actually to legitimize the growing reach of the tax collectors. As in the case of Congress, this pattern of judicial tenderness is partly the product of the natural sympathy that those in power always feel toward the tax collectors. But it is reinforced by a series of laws that give the IRS more protection from citizen suits than any other federal agency has.

Montie S. Day is a large, agile man whose six-foot-four-inch frame filled up the small Washington conference room where we first met. Day was brought up poor. His father was an impoverished lumberjack in the Sierra Nevada mountains of California, and there was a period when young Day and his family actually lived in a tent. After graduating from high school, Day worked his way through college with the help of a football scholarship, playing tackle and defensive end for Fresno State. After a brief stint as a professional football player with the Chicago Bears and the Detroit Lions in the mid-1960s, he became an IRS agent, then a special assistant U.S. attorney in San Francisco, and now a tax lawyer in Oakland, California.

Partly because of his hands-on experience in the IRS and the Justice Department and partly, I think, because of the inborn aggressive quality that one would expect of a serious football player, Day in recent years has become a leading practitioner in a specialized area of the law: representing citizen taxpayers who have been abused by the sometimes arbitrary IRS.

From his years of experience battling with the IRS, however, the California lawyer argues that the game is not being played on a level field. The field has been strongly tilted against the taxpayers, he says, by the combined impact of a well-established principle of common law and three congressional statutes.

The ancient common law doctrine of sovereign immunity holds that the government cannot be sued without the government's consent. But Congress, at least as far back as 1911, recognized that there were situations in which citizens should be allowed to sue the government. The result: the Federal Tort Claims Act. This law defines specific circumstances in which the doctrine of sovereign immunity does not apply. In its wisdom, however, Congress decided that the IRS should not be among these exceptions. A provision of the Tort Claims Act specifically states that the waiver to the doctrine does not apply to "any claim arising in respect of the assessment or collection of any tax or custom duty, or the detention of any goods or merchandise by any officer of customs or excise or any other law enforcement officer."

The result: Until 1988, a citizen could not sue the IRS for damages directly connected to the assessment or collection of taxes, regardless of the wrong or injury. David Pryor's Taxpayers' Bill of Rights opened up a hole in this general prohibition. The new law allows taxpayers to sue for damages resulting from the action of an IRS employee who recklessly or intentionally disregards the law or regulations relating to the collection of taxes. Relief is available only for acts committed after November 10, 1988. Damages are limited to the lesser of $100,000 or the actual and direct economic damages and the cost of the suit. The award is further limited by damages that could have been mitigated by the taxpayer. Before bringing suit, the taxpayer must exhaust all administrative remedies. To prevent what the IRS feared would be a deluge of claims, the law was amended to allow the agency to seek damages against taxpayers who use it in a frivolous manner.

A second key law is the Anti-Injunction Act. Originally, this law provided that the federal courts could not accept citizen suits requesting that the IRS be enjoined from assessing and collecting taxes. Over the 125 years this law has been on the books, the courts have ruled that the prohibition did not apply in only a handful of cases. In general, however, the courts have supported the Anti-Injunction Act, even extending it to the investigative actions and processes that the IRS may have taken before actually assessing any taxes. It almost goes without saying that bringing any suit normally requires the paid services of a lawyer.

Finally, the Declaratory Relief Act establishes the general right of the federal courts to provide relief to citizen complainants against the government "except with respect to Federal taxes."

Except for the limited situations spelled out by the Taxpayers' Bill of Rights, a strong majority in Congress and most federal courts have long agreed with the theory that the waiver of sovereign immunity or a modification of the anti-injunction and declaratory relief acts would cripple the ability of the agency to collect taxes.

Day disputes this. He notes that the FBI, the Secret Service, and other law enforcement agencies made the same argument but that their operations were not crippled when citizens were provided additional remedies against abuses. "I submit that making the IRS more accountable for damages resulting from abuses of its power will make the agency more likely to operate in a lawful fashion," the lawyer said.

Day described two hypothetical cases to illustrate his claim. "Assume you are under audit and somehow you learn that the revenue agent has decided the best way to investigate you is break a window of your office, climb through it, and examine your correspondence," he explained.

"You come to my office for advice, wanting the court to rule that the IRS agent can't conduct his audit in this way. We consider filing a suit for declaratory relief, but then we remember that the court does not have the authority to issue such a declaration of rights in tax matters because of that exception in the declaratory relief act.

"Then we think about requesting a court order to enjoin the agent from conducting his tax investigation by breaking into your office. This approach, of course, cannot be followed because the court is forbidden to even consider such requests under the anti-injunction act.

"In my hypothetical, after the agent has smashed the window and climbed into the office to examine your records, the IRS decides that the evidence it obtains shows there is no tax case and it sends out what is called a 'no change letter.' You now would like to sue the agency in an effort to require it to pay for the repair of the broken window in your office. I sue for damages. Assuming the agent only examined your return after breaking in your office, the government would argue and the judge would be compelled to agree that under the doctrine of sovereign immunity the suit must be dismissed for lack of jurisdiction."

Day's second hypothetical is much simpler. "Assume you are shot by an on-duty federal agent who is drunk. If the agent works for the FBI, it is almost certain that the court will order the government to pay your medical expenses because the agent has been negligent. But if the agent is on the payroll of the IRS, the chances of recovering your expenses are almost nil." (Some experts contend that, because of a fairly recent Supreme Court decision, *Bivens v. Six Unknown Named Agents of the Federal Bureau of Narcotics,* Day's analysis may be a trifle pessimistic.)

The California lawyer said he understands that the two cases may sound ridiculous. "But in reality these powerful bars to liability are very real and have served to shield the IRS from liability and accountability for its misuse of power. As a former IRS agent I know that the IRS needs unusual legal powers to collect taxes. While the IRS must have power to assess and collect taxes, such power must be used in a responsible manner. Power, without accountability, lends itself to abuse. To control frivolous legal action, the courts have the power to require the citizen or lawyer who brings [such a case] to pay the government's costs and attorney's fees. But it is just plain wrong, and I think harmful to the IRS, the tax system, and our government to deny citizens access to the courts."

One other provision of law has developed into an important protective device for the IRS. This is Section 6103 of the Internal Revenue Code, which was approved by Congress in 1976, shortly after the disclosure of the Watergate abuses of the Nixon White House. The important goal of the legislation was to establish the principle that tax information should be kept confidential and only used by the government for legitimate purposes. Before the passage of the provision, for example, a federal prosecutor could obtain an individual's tax records merely by informally asking the IRS to send them over. Since 1976, an assistant U.S. attorney conducting a criminal investigation who wants a tax return must obtain the permission of the attorney general, deputy attorney general, or assistant attorney general and then obtain a court order authorizing the transaction.

The protection of individual tax records from casual snooping was a major achievement of the 1976 law. But in the process of curbing the improper use of information, Congress may have inadvertently made it harder for outsiders to assure themselves that the agency is functioning properly. Tax lawyers like Montie Day charge, for example, that the IRS sometimes marshals Section 6103 to block the legitimate inquiries of citizens who need information to help them prove that their rights have been abused by the agency.

A second unintended effect of the privacy law has been to undermine the ability of the House of Representatives and the Senate to examine the performance of the IRS. One part of Section 6103 establishes that the House Ways and Means Committee and the Senate Finance Committee are the only two committees routinely authorized to see tax returns. The law further provides, however, that with the passage of a resolution by either the House or the Senate, other congressional committees may also gain access to tax records in the course of a formal investigation.

During the spring of 1988, the House Government Operations Subcommittee with the legal mandate to conduct oversight investigation of the IRS obtained information about what appeared to be widespread corruption in the IRS. The subcommittee, headed by Representative Doug Barnard, Jr., began a preliminary inquiry. To fully resolve the merits of the allegations, however, the subcommittee's staff required access to several tax returns. The subcommittee drafted the resolution required by Section 6103.

It was at this point that Ronald A. Pearlman, senior congressional staff official on tax matters, stepped into the picture. Pearlman was chief of staff of the Democratic-controlled Joint Tax Committee and, curiously enough, a former assistant secretary of the treasury in the Reagan administration. For the last few months of 1988, Pearlman worked to prevent Congress from even considering the proposed resolution, approval of which would have led to the first thorough investigation of IRS corruption in more than thirty-five years. The question of why the staff director of the Joint Tax Committee, ruled by Democrat Rostenkowski and Democrat Bentsen, would work to undermine an investigation of corruption in the Republican-ruled IRS is a puzzle.

Part of the answer, it seems certain, was a turf war between the tax committees, which have specific responsibility for tax matters, and the House Government Operations Committee and its subcommittees, which have general responsibility to ensure the efficiency of all federal agencies, including the IRS. But Peter Barash, who has been the staff director of the House Government Operations Subcommittee for fifteen years, is certain that another force may be at work. "Although I have no way of proving it, I am convinced that the resistance of Ron Pearlman and the House Ways and Means Committee was partly because of IRS pressure on them," Barash observed. It should be remembered that except for a brief period immediately following the disclosure of the Watergate abuses in the mid-1970s, the Joint Tax Committee and the Ways and Means Committee have strenuously resisted any serious investigation of the IRS.

The forces working against meaningful oversight are considerable. Citizens are discouraged from seeking legal redress in the courts by an elaborate set of barriers established by Congress. Lawyers are blocked from obtaining information they need to initiate suits challenging genuine IRS abuses as a result of the misapplication of a well-intentioned privacy law. A congressional committee empowered to investigate the IRS is partially blocked from investigating serious allegations of IRS corruption by a tortured application of the same law. The IRS has repeatedly initiated audits, leaked information, or otherwise harassed individual citizens, both in and out of government, who raised valid questions about its performance.

Like all bureaucracies, public and private, the IRS wages a continuous war against all efforts to make it accountable. Over the years, this war against oversight has taken many forms. When Congress passed the Freedom of Information Act in 1966, establishing the broad principle that most government documents are public property, the IRS mounted a determined and continuing campaign to subvert the goal of the law. When in the early seventies Congress sought to increase the role of the General Accounting Office in measuring the performance of agencies of the executive branch, the IRS resisted. When Congress required most of these agencies to establish an independent inspector general, the IRS mounted a successful effort to be exempt from this mandate. When a citizens' taxpayer group in 1974 fought to require the IRS to make its private tax rulings public, the IRS led the battle to maintain a system that gave special advantage to the wealthiest taxpayers with the highest-paid lawyers. When Congress in 1988 approved a law imposing limited new restrictions on computer matching by the federal government, the IRS was exempted from its restrictions.

An unfortunate symmetry emerges when the IRS's active dislike of oversight is compared with Congress's aversion to investigating the workings of the IRS.

But there are exceptions to this dismal litany, occasions when individual citizens have overcome the resistance of the IRS and insisted upon their rights to examine the workings of their government. I have in several places in this book cited the studies of Susan B. Long, currently a professor of quantitative analysis at Syracuse University. Sue and her husband, Philip, are the kind of citizens who stand up to official bullying.

In November 1969, a small family business run by Philip Long in Bellevue, Washington, was audited by the IRS. Two weeks later, at an informal conference, the IRS informed him that he owed a substantial amount of back taxes.

Long explained to the IRS supervisor that he had an excellent accountant, but that he would be delighted to take the matter to court and abide by whatever a jury decided. The supervisor was not amused by what he viewed as Long's impertinence.

" 'Do you know what a jeopardy assessment is?' " Long recalls the supervisor asking. "I replied that I had no idea. He said, 'Well, you just better find out.' " A jeopardy assessment, as I've discussed, is an emergency legal procedure that allows the IRS to seize swiftly the assets of taxpayers it believes may flee the United States. Because almost all of Long's wealth was tied up in real estate, the possibility of a hasty retreat was impossible and the IRS threat spiteful.

Long called in an outside expert, a certified public accountant and former IRS employee who at the time was working for one of the Big Eight accounting firms. "He spent a day going over my accounts and concluded that the IRS was dead wrong," Long continued.

Four months after the initial audit, Long received a notice from the IRS alleging that he owed the government $33,000 in back taxes. Philip and Sue Long felt seriously wronged. Two days after receiving the notice, they flew to Washington, D.C., and requested an interview with the commissioner. After their request was refused, the Longs placed the first of a series of eleven advertisements in the *Washington Post*. The ads explained their plight and requested information from other taxpayers who felt that the IRS had acted in an unconstitutional or unethical manner.

Long also appealed the thirty-three charges that the IRS had brought against him. After the expenditure of tens of thousands of dollars in legal fees to fight the allegations through the IRS's administrative procedures, the Tax Court, and finally the federal court of appeals, every one of the IRS's thirty-three charges against the Longs was dropped. Phil Long was not a tax cheat.

In addition to a great deal of money, the ultimately successful appeals process required many years. As it was proceeding, and with the help of both frustrated taxpayers and IRS employees, the Longs launched an aggressive campaign to collect information about how this theoretically public agency functioned. The IRS was not happy. One of the couple's first requests was for the IRS manual, the massive printed compilation describing the agency's policies and procedures. Under the Freedom of Information Act, each agency was explicitly required to make public "administrative staff manuals and instructions to staff that affect a member of the public."

"Despite the act's clear disclosure requirement, we were told the IRS had no in-house handbooks or manuals," Sue Long said. "Inquiries at the IRS's national office produced the same response. In short, we were greeted with falsehoods. Even our congressman was unable to obtain them from the IRS, just the name of an index to IRS materials. When we tried to visit the IRS reading room, which the law requires be opened to the public, we were informed that the reading room had been closed and the indexes destroyed. Senior IRS officials told us to drop our foolish efforts. An attorney in the IRS's general counsel's office warned that the agency had six hundred lawyers, by which we assumed he meant the agency had sufficient legal power to hound us for the rest of our lives. Even a request for blank IRS forms was refused."

In June 1971, the Longs filed their first suit under the Freedom of Information Act in the federal district court in Seattle. They asked the court to order the IRS to provide them with the manuals, statistics, and forms they had requested in twenty-three separate written requests. On August 9, 1972, the court ruled that the IRS had unlawfully withheld the manuals and the audit statistics from the Longs. The first skirmish in what has become a life-long battle had been won.

When this battle began in 1969 Sue Long was an undergraduate. Now, twenty years later, she has earned a Ph.D. in sociology, with a dual major in quantitative methodology and criminology. More important, she and Philip have continued their quest despite the persistent resistance of the IRS. At the present time, the couple have filed a total of thirteen suits against the IRS under the information act, of which eleven have been completed successfully and two are still pending.

Despite the IRS's continued resistance, Sue Long so far has obtained over 1.3 million pages of statistical data, hundreds of thousands of computer tape records, and dozens of reports and analyses. Today, her carefully documented studies of the IRS have earned her a reputation as one of the agency's best-informed and most thoughtful students.

For most of this campaign, the Longs have been without allies. But in January 1987 a unique event occurred in the history of the U.S. Congress:

For the first time since the Senate Finance Committee was formed the senator appointed to head its IRS Oversight Subcommittee actually believed the problems of the IRS should be aired in public hearings.

In 1987 and 1988, Senator David Pryor, a former Arkansas governor, acted on his beliefs by holding three sets of hearings during which victims of IRS excesses were allowed to tell their stories. Also called were IRS employees who offered testimony about the harmful impact of IRS production quotas. Finally, the subcommittee required IRS Commissioner Lawrence B. Gibbs and other senior executives to explain to the public various administrative problems, including the agency's disastrous handling of the new W4 form for reporting estimated income.

While the hearings were a significant first for the Senate Finance Committee, the subcommittee was unable to investigate many of the shortcomings that existed. This was because under long-standing Finance Committee tradition its subcommittees are not allotted any funds for staffing. This tradition meant that the subcommittee's expenses, mostly the salary of its single staff member, Jeff Trinca, had to be paid out of the budget given to Senator Pryor for representing his Arkansas constituents. Trinca is an intelligent, hardworking, and insightful lawyer. Despite his considerable abilities and the full backing of Senator Pryor, however, the idea that a single staff person can keep track of an agency with more than 100,000 employees is inherently silly.

Pryor is a moderate Democrat of the new South. But he has an old-fashioned populist streak that these days is very much out of style in Washington, especially among members of the congressional tax committees. During the hearings, Pryor decided that the witnesses were describing problems that required a remedy in the law. Working with Trinca, Pryor began drafting what he called the Taxpayers' Bill of Rights.

At first there was very little support, partly, as explained earlier, because many members of Congress genuinely fear the IRS. Slowly, however, as the scope and form of the provisions in the bill were modified, Pryor began to pick up support. Of course the IRS and its allies, most importantly the chairmen of the House Ways and Means and the Senate Finance committees, argued that the proposal would pose a serious threat to the ability of the IRS to collect taxes. As Congress came close to adjournment, however, Senator Lloyd Bentsen of Texas, chairman of the Finance Committee, changed his position. Almost miraculously, in the final hours of the hundredth Congress, the substantially modified Taxpayers' Bill of Rights became law.

Senator Pryor is rightfully proud that Congress passed his bill, noting that it marked the only occasion in the 124-year history of the IRS that the House and Senate have approved a piece of tax legislation "aimed solely at helping the little guy in the tax collection process. For many decades we have continued to strengthen the hand of the IRS with more power and more personnel. This is the first time we have done something to strengthen the hand of the taxpayer in dealing with the IRS," he told me in an interview.

While the new law has important provisions, its actual impact on an agency with the power of the IRS is quite limited. For example, the statute requires the IRS to inform a taxpayer of his rights and obligations prior to beginning an audit or other proceeding and prohibits the IRS from basing pay raises or promotions on the collection statistics of individual revenue officers.

Another section that could prove important is that for the first time ever the Treasury Department inspector general was granted the right to investigate the IRS. During the law's consideration by Congress, of course, the agency strenuously objected to this change.

A third potentially important provision of the Taxpayers' Bill of Rights would allow taxpayers to recover the fees they pay to accountants and attorneys during the administrative proceedings that establish whether the IRS has brought an unreasonable claim. Under past law, taxpayers could only recover such fees incurred in court.

The fourth key provision gives taxpayers the right to sue the IRS if the agency recklessly or intentionally disregarded the Internal Revenue Code in the collection of taxes. The damages would be capped at $100,000. In the past, as explained by California lawyer Montie Day, such suits were almost impossible to win.

Any improvement, however modest, in the right to challenge an agency as large and powerful as the IRS must be regarded as significant. But a handful of suits brought by a tiny fraction of taxpayers who each year are improperly treated by the IRS will not work miracles. To effectively help the agency collect the necessary taxes in a fair and evenhanded manner will require drastic changes in the priorities of the IRS itself and in the attitudes and actions of the committees of Congress, the supervising officials in the White House and Treasury, and the editors and reporters of the great national newspapers. The IRS's mission is too important, its impact too far-reaching, to leave in the hands of a few senior bureaucrats. The watchdogs no longer can afford to remain silent.

CHAPTER 13

Tax Collection
in the Next Decade

The revolution could be just a few years off.

Sometime early in the nineties, according to a feasibility study by the Internal Revenue Service, the IRS could make the first mailings of a special new form to as many as 20 million American taxpayers. On the business part of this document would be printed the exact earnings of the selected taxpayers and precisely how much each owed the government in federal taxes, all calculated by the giant computers of the IRS. If the individual's withholding for the year did not cover the tax that the IRS had decided was due, the form would serve as a bill. If withholding exceeded the individual's legal obligation to the government, the form would serve as a refund notice.

By 1993, the IRS study estimated that up to half of all American taxpayers could choose to let the government take over the tiresome annual chore of figuring out how much they earned and how much they owed the government.

The concept of having the Internal Revenue Service assume responsibility for virtually all aspects of tax collection—including those traditionally undertaken by the individual taxpayer—has been a gleam in the eye of the IRS for more than three decades. That may explain why the agency gave the latest version of this proposal such a modest, positive, and marketable name: the Return-Free Tax System. But for a nation whose politicians have constantly invoked the unique glories of voluntary compliance, the full-scale adoption of the "return-free" process would represent a significant shift in the function of the IRS and an alteration in the basic responsibilities of a U.S. citizen.

Benjamin R. Barber, professor of political science at Rutgers University in New Jersey, has spent a great deal of his academic career writing and thinking about the importance of representative democracy. "If the IRS moves ahead with the return-free system—which seems almost inevitable—we will see a profound change in one of the basic roles of the citizen," he said in an interview.

"The citizen will become even more passive than he is today, the government more active. Instead of the citizen telling the government what taxes he or she owes, the government, like Bloomingdale's, will just submit its bill to the citizen."

Barber noted that the act of filling out the tax form served a positive civic function. "It makes you wonder about your government. Where is the money going? Who are getting the special deductions? You need active, engaged citizens if representative democracy is to survive and flourish. The government's desire to take over a key responsibility of every citizen is just one more step in the continued pacification of the American people."

Interestingly enough, Barber's concerns are partly shared by some officials in the IRS, although they emphasize how the process might affect tax collection rather than representative democracy. In March 1988, tax experts from all over the United States met for several days with Lawrence Gibbs, then the commissioner of the IRS. The members of the commissioner's advisory group had come to Washington for one of their regular policy meetings. During a discussion about possible changes in IRS operations, the conversation turned to the return-free tax system.

"This involves policy questions of genuine significance," Gibbs told the group. "It is important that the individual taxpayer identify with his or her return. If we ever get to the point where taxpayers came to see tax returns as government returns, rather than their returns, it would have vast implications for the whole tax collection process."

Ever since the adoption of the modern income tax just before World War I, government and business leaders have joined in celebrating the American people, who, they claimed, paid the taxes they owed on a voluntary basis. The virtuous nature of the home-grown taxpayer was often compared with the devious nature of French and Italian taxpayers. Never mind that systematic withholding made this patriotic boast a somewhat doubtful proposition. Voluntary compliance has long held an elevated position as one of the small but important myths of the nation.

Whatever the current reality of taxpaying, however, the public acceptance of the return-free tax system would mark an important development in the evolution of the passive citizen. At the same time, the IRS's implementation of the plan would provide concrete evidence that technology could radically alter the shape, purpose, and even power of this tradition-bound agency.

Despite the enthusiastic lip service paid to the spirit of voluntary compliance, the IRS has long yearned for a more intrusive, all-knowing kind of tax system. As far back as July 1953, the agency's planning staff completed work on a secret study "to eliminate the need for filing tax returns by wage earners when tax is withheld by employers." The first benefit of the 1953 proposal, the planning document said, would be to reduce "the burden of the wage earner." But the plan gave equal weight to a second goal: The project would "safeguard the revenue" by "reaching more people for annual tax accounting."

The IRS's 1953 plan to collect sufficient information about the citizenry to enable it to calculate the tax obligations of a large part of the population did not fly, probably because of the impossible bureaucratic burden of handling the necessary paperwork in the precomputer age.

But three decades later, in November 1984, the proposal was resurrected by Donald Regan, then secretary of the treasury, in a report to President Reagan. The report bore the title "Tax Reform for Fairness, Simplicity and Economic Growth." By this time, Regan and the IRS had come up with the catchy soft-sell advertising phrase for their revolutionary plan. "The return-free system" was now possible, the report said, because the IRS's improved information-processing equipment would allow it to calculate the tax liabilities of millions of Americans. As a result, Regan called for the initiation of a system "under which many individual taxpayers will be relieved of the obligation of filing an income tax return." While the 1953 Treasury Department documents show that increasing the IRS's power to collect the revenue was an important factor behind the government's interest in the project, the 1984 report skips this essential element and only mentions the burdens it would lift from the shoulders of the nation's taxpayers.

In late 1984 and 1985, Roscoe L. Egger, Jr., the IRS commissioner at that time, continued to beat the drums for the return-free system, which he called a "very exciting proposal." By 1990, he predicted, two out of three taxpayers "would never have to wrestle with a tax return again."

The Reagan administration's enthusiasm for the return-free system is interesting. Remember, President Reagan was elected partly because of his promise to get the government off the citizen's back. Here his treasury secretary and tax commissioner were boosting a plan that would vastly broaden the supervisory role of government over tens of millions of taxpayers.

Congress has displayed little concern about the system one way or another. While it did not buy the full project as proposed by the Treasury Department, the final version of the 1986 Tax Reform Act contained a brief section authorizing the IRS to initiate an experimental project to test the "return-free" concept. It was under this authorization that the agency completed the 1987 feasibility study suggesting that the return-free system could be operating by 1991.

But the IRS, with no specific authorization from Congress, already had cranked up a smaller computerized tracking operation that in many ways resembles the return-free tax system. In a brief press release handed out in January 1987, the agency said that this more modest operation had two apparently simple goals: to improve the detection of those individuals who didn't file any income tax returns and then to automatically calculate what they owed the government.

Probably because the announced targets of the new system have always been considered to be members of a loathsome class, genus tax cheat, the new IRS plan received almost no public notice.

At first glance, the new Internal Revenue Service operation does seem relatively harmless. But the already functioning "automated assessment system" is of interest because it provides a rough preview of the return-free tax system.

Here is how this increasingly effective process works. First, at relatively little cost to the government, IRS computers have been programed to look through the 1 billion third-party financial reports the agency now routinely receives each year from a large range of private and public organizations. Next, the computers commit all these randomly recorded payments to their memory, eliminate the duplicate names, and prepare a list of everyone in the United States who received a salary from an employer or interest from a bank or alimony from a former husband or dividends from a corporation or a royalty from a publisher or rent from a tenant or a refund from a state tax agency or one of the many other kinds of payments. Then the computers match the list of Americans receiving money from all these sources with the list of those who paid their taxes. The final product: a third list made up of individuals who were on the first list but not on the second, people who reportedly had earned money from one or more sources but then failed to file an individual tax return.

The second step of the automated assessment procedure is equally challenging. The computers take the list of all the miscreants who apparently have failed to file an income tax return, add up all the income they reportedly received during the past year, and prepare an income tax return complete with the taxes they allegedly owe. The machines then mail the returns they have prepared to the individuals who failed to prepare them and dispatches a series of follow-up notices if they are required.

The 1986 start-up of this complex automated detection system by the nation's largest and most powerful civilian agency clearly represented the culmination of a major series of technological advances in the administration of the decades-old federal income tax. At the same time, however, the establishment of this sophisticated computer system targeting a relatively small number of deadbeats was an interim step. First an automated system to calculate the tax for the relatively small number of Americans who don't file any return at all. Then the far more ambitious system designed to calculate the returns of half the taxpayers in the United States.

In the first two and a half years of operation, the IRS automated assessment system identified 827,319 individuals and businesses that apparently failed to file any tax return at all. Furthermore, the system then calculated that these nonfilers owed the government nearly $3 billion in federal taxes. Because mailing a bill is a lot easier than persuading a debtor to cough up the taxes, however, the actual collections for the period, $220,799,000, were far less that the original assessments.

"If the program works the way we want," said William Wauben, assistant IRS commissioner for collection, "the next few years will see a significant drop in the number of people who previously had just walked away from their obligations and paid no taxes. We think the new system will push people toward voluntarily complying with the tax laws."

The system is a technical marvel.

But the system behind the system is just plain astounding. Beginning about fifteen years ago, several congressional committees began to sense that developments in computer technology had moved along to a point where the government could seriously consider launching a tax enforcement technique that it had long dreamed about. Although IRS officials initially disagreed with this judgment, they slowly began to change their minds, eventually becoming committed converts.

The legal requirement that every employer report how much it paid its regular employees and withhold a portion of the paycheck for taxes has been in place since 1943. From the very beginning, IRS statistics show that this reporting and withholding law has guaranteed that most of the country's working stiffs, those who have no source of income other than what they earn from their employers, pretty well meet their federal tax obligations.

But for those who received part or all of their income in the form of dividends, interest, or royalties, it was a different story. It is true that in 1939 Congress had approved a law requiring banks and corporations to report to the government the interest and dividend payments they were making to their customers and stockholders. But except for two very brief periods, Congress has never required the banks and corporations to withhold the federal tax that was due on these kinds of payments.

The law thus has always tended to punish lower-income salaried workers and reward upper-income investors. For without the bite of withholding, the bark of the so-called 1099 reporting forms had minimal impact until the age of the computer. This was because the small number of banks and corporations that bothered to meet their legal requirements initially submitted the 1099 reports on little pieces of paper. And even that massive agency the IRS did not have sufficient funds to hire the thousands of clerks it would have needed to match the hundreds of millions of interest and dividend reports with the correct income tax returns.

But continuing developments in computer technologies have changed that. Now, thirty items of information contained on every one of the 102 million individual tax returns filed each year are immediately transferred to an electronic master file. Now, a significant proportion of all the 1099s and other third-party income reports is submitted to the IRS on tape or computer disk.

This transition from paper to computer has had a significant impact on the IRS's enforcement efforts. In 1986, agency computers compared information found on 818.6 million of the 1 billion third-party reporting documents with information on the 102 million tax returns filed that year by individual taxpayers.

Not only did this ability to read and compare massive amounts of data with extraordinary speed enable the IRS's automated assessment system in one thirty-month period to identify nearly 1 million Americans who did not file any tax return at all. It also allowed the IRS to spot an additional 3.8 million taxpayers who had filed returns but had failed to include one or more of these third-party payments as part of their total income.

Aside from the concerns of Barber and former Commissioner Gibbs about altering the general attitude of the public toward its government, the IRS's headlong rush into the computer age raises many other genuinely serious worries.

GARBAGE IN, GOSPEL OUT

First is the apparently simple question of accuracy.

The massive size of the agency's programs means that a very small problem can very easily result in wrongful government actions against hundreds, and in some cases even millions, of innocent people. One recurring hazard within the IRS, and other large institutions, is the computerized procedures that inadvertently lead to the generation and easy distribution of incorrect information. Depending upon the number of affected taxpayers and the government action actually triggered by the false information, such projects can sometimes lead to serious violations of constitutionally guaranteed rights, such as the Fifth Amendment's fundamental promise of due process.

A few years ago, for example, the IRS sent a notice to a woman in Austin, Texas, asserting that she had failed to report $4,000 of her income and demanding $800 in back taxes, penalties, and interest. It turned out, however, that the IRS's computer-generated assertion was dead wrong. Nor was she the only person who was falsely accused.

The problem began when a local bank purchased some software, or computer instructions, to help it comply with an administrative reporting requirement of the IRS. The new software was supposed to guide the bank's computer through the time-consuming chore of preparing a list of the names and addresses of all the customers who received interest and the amount they had received. The bank then gave the list to the IRS. Because it was on computer tape, and thus did not require error-prone clerks to retype the required information, the list was assumed to be correct. But sad to say, the software was faulty, and the bank had inadvertently informed the IRS that two hundred of its customers had received interest when they had not. These incorrect reports, of course, triggered the IRS's computers to kick out two hundred incorrect dunning notices.

The rash of incorrect notices generated by the faulty software was not discovered by the Austin bank or the IRS but by an enterprising newspaper reporter. The trail, however, did not end with the single Texas bank and its two hundred customers. In fact, further investigation revealed that the faulty list-making software had been sold to at least fifty other companies all over the United States. These companies, in turn, also had sent incorrect income reports to the IRS.

In fact, by the time the computer glitch had been identified, the companies using the faulty software had sent the IRS incorrect income information concerning approximately 1 million Americans. Because of the wide differences in the income levels of the taxpayers incorrectly identified as having received payments, the IRS to this day insists that it is unable to calculate how many wrongful dunning notices were generated as a result of the false information it had been provided.

It seems likely, however, that the agency's bum notices went to a minimum of tens of thousands of mystified citizens. It also seems likely that these tens of thousands of men and women spent hundreds of thousands of hours searching their financial records, made tens of thousands of angry telephone calls, and wrote tens of thousands of confused letters trying to collect the information they needed to rebut the false information in the IRS documents. Finally, it probably can also be assumed that some unknown proportion just went ahead and wrote a check for the additional taxes that the IRS had incorrectly said they owed. After all, a lot of people feel it doesn't make any sense to fight city hall.

(The question of who should be held accountable in such situations actually is one of the more interesting problems of the computer age, a period when a growing number of large bureaucracies seem to be actively involved in more and more of the intimate decisions of each of our lives. Should the company that wrote the bad software be held liable? Or the companies that bought the bad software and sent the incorrect information to the IRS? Or the IRS, which dispatched the inaccurate dunning notices? How can anyone ever be held accountable in this very common kind of mess?)

But when inaccurate information entered into the IRS system triggers more serious enforcement activities such as levying a taxpayer's bank account or seizing a home, even the most obtuse federal judge may begin to worry. The IRS, of course, insists that adequate protection is provided taxpayers by its elaborate notice system. Given the huge numbers of notices involved, the high mobility of the American people, and the somewhat quirky performance of the U.S. Postal Service, however, it is obviously not possible to assume that the notices will always get through.

Because inaccurate records are extremely costly in terms of the efficiency of the agency and the goodwill of citizens, it is nice to hope that the IRS would work very hard to avoid all kinds of errors. A long string of reports by the agency's own internal audit team and Congress's General Accounting Office suggests that such hopes may be naive. The worry that senior IRS administrators view the accuracy of records as a secondary problem is reinforced by the lackadaisical attitude of another large federal agency: the Federal Bureau of Investigation. In 1981, about twenty years after the FBI created a national computerized network to link tens of thousands of local, state, and federal law enforcement agencies, a congressional research office conducted a rigorous first-of-its-kind audit of the computerized entries that the FBI system was zipping about the nation. The finding: 54.1 percent of the entries transmitted were inaccurate, incomplete, or misleading. This was an astonishing finding because of the serious consequences of the flawed records. Innocent people were being arrested, guilty people were being set free, patrol officers were unnecessarily endangered by genuinely dangerous people who were not correctly identified. Individual victims living in Massachusetts, New Jersey, Michigan, Louisiana, and California have brought suits charging that their constitutional rights had been violated when incorrect information in the computers led to their false arrest. Although at least one local police department, Los Angeles, has been ordered to pay damages because of such incorrect information, the FBI has so far managed to avoid any direct liability. The bureau argues that it is not responsible because the inaccurate entries it transmits were created by state and local groups, not by the FBI. By this logic, of course, it certainly would be unfair to hold the IRS accountable for any incorrect information it picks up from other federal agencies, the states, or any other source.

No similar audits of the accuracy and completeness of the data that trigger IRS enforcement actions have ever been made public. But remember the GAO report that almost half of all the official letters the IRS dispatched to taxpayers contained inaccurate or misleading information. This finding is worrisome.

THE COST OF PROGRESS

Hank Philcox is in charge of what the IRS calls information systems development. As part of this overall effort, he and his staff are hard at work on Tax System Redesign (TSR), a twelve-year, multibillion-dollar project intended to fundamentally alter the IRS's tax collection process by the year 1998. It is a massive job, involving the analysis and reorganization of hundreds of different procedures that will affect every taxpayer and IRS employee in the nation. The basic goals of TSR sound prosaic enough. Minimize the IRS's reliance on paper documents. Develop modern data bases through which almost all information collected by the IRS about every taxpayer can be instantly examined by an agent anywhere in the United States. Provide expert systems to help agents better understand tax laws. "We want to modernize the processing and support systems so that IRS employees have the information they need to better serve the public," Philcox said in a lengthy interview.

"With the full-blown system, a tax assister anywhere in the country will be able to look up an account, and say, whoops, there's been a mistake; we've got to get this corrected, and do it right then and there. And the correction would be instantly posted to the national file."

Philcox views in a completely positive way the massive increase in the IRS's computer power, the improved linking of its data bases by secure lines of communication, and the steady growth in the use of computers. More specifically, Philcox believes that the technical revolution he is quietly masterminding will at the same time reduce the cost of collecting taxes, improve the ability of the IRS to investigate tax fraud, and provide the public with better service.

"We're drowning in paper now," he said. "The heart of what we're trying to do is modernize the system so it does not require an excruciating effort for our people to get at the information we routinely collect. We're focusing on the elimination of many of the manual and paper processes we now have so we can avoid a lot of the labor-intensive procedures that are extremely costly and inevitably lead to a certain percentage of errors."

Philcox outlined the complex steps the agency now follows when a revenue agent in one of the IRS's local offices decides it is necessary to obtain detailed information from a taxpayer's return that has not been recorded in the computerized summary statement maintained at the National Computer Center in West Virginia. "The opportunity for error in that process is enormous," the official said. "Right now it's all we can do to make a ten percent error rate."

It is worth noting that Philcox, the official responsible for convincing Congress and the public that the massive new system is needed, is one of the few senior IRS officials who openly discuss the serious inadequacies of current procedures that generate an astonishingly large number of errors.

The IRS's initiation of the Tax System Redesign project in the mid-1980s was not the first time that the agency has sought to systematically enhance its computer operation. More than a decade before, in the early 1970s, the IRS informed Congress that it would require between $750 million and $1 billion for a proposed new computer project called the Tax Administration System (TAS).

But that time, in contrast with the eighties, strong concerns among a number of House and Senate members that the revolutionary new computer system might develop into "a system of harassment, surveillance and political manipulation" led Congress to delay its funding.

The general congressional worry about the potential of TAS to affect the rights of citizens was fueled in part by the rash of disclosures about the various ways the Nixon administration had marshaled the powers of a number of federal agencies, including the IRS, for political purposes. But the specific doubts about TAS were formally articulated by a critical analysis of the system published in March 1977 by the Office of Technology Assessment (OTA), a research arm of Congress. Shortly after a brilliant OTA analyst named Marcia J. MacNaughton completed the critical study of TAS, the incoming Carter administration killed the IRS computer project.

As described by IRS officials today, the computerized procedures envisaged by TSR are very similar to those of TAS. But as the IRS in the last few years has methodically gone about the task of developing the somewhat updated version of TAS, not a single House or Senate member has questioned its potential for mischief. One explanation for this silence may be the general belief that growing federal deficits represent such a serious threat to national security that all questions must be suspended. Another explanation may be that many of the computer applications that together make up the TSR package have already been adopted by a number of large private institutions, such as American Express.

In response to a specific question, Philcox said that the IRS has not developed an overall estimate of what the twelve-year TSR project will cost. "TSR is being constructed in incremental stages during a period of rapid technological change and thus we haven't attempted to estimate the total dollars that will be required."

But in late 1988 the IRS's planning division developed a five-year strategy for only the first half of the 1990s. The plan identified a wish list of fifty-six specific actions that IRS managers said they hoped to accomplish during the period. Twenty-one items were computer and telecommunication projects that appeared to be related to TSR. The estimated cost of the twenty-one items was about $11 billion, ten times more than the TAS system rejected by the Carter administration.

One defense of large government computer programs sometimes offered by technology buffs is that, if many major companies in the private sector have not misused the information they collect, is it fair to be suspicious of agencies like the IRS? Because the IRS has a range of powers unavailable to American Express, TRW, and other major information-hungry companies, the logic behind this argument is obviously specious. On the other hand, it must be acknowledged that such projects as the return-free tax system and TSR do have the potential of providing the American people more efficient, more accurate, and fairer administration of the tax laws.

Another flaw in the "American Express defense" is that the return-free system and TSR are not the only technical changes the agency is developing to discipline society. In fact, both are only small discrete parts of a far broader revolution that affects almost every aspect of our lives.

FRANKENSTEIN'S MONSTER?

Since the 1920s the IRS has provided state tax agencies with various kinds of detailed information about the tax payments made by their citizens to the federal government. The states used the federal information to identify individuals and corporations that might not be paying their state taxes. Then, in the early 1980s, it dawned on the IRS that a great deal of the information held by a variety of state agencies might help its enforcement efforts.

Now, with the gradual computerization of all levels of government, this systematic sharing of information has exploded. In 1988, for example, a Treasury Department report listed more than two hundred systems of records, most of them computerized, that the IRS was regularly sharing with the states.[1] The lists contained an astonishing range of information about hundreds of millions of individual and corporate taxpayers. The same report listed 172 systems of records that various states were routinely sharing with the IRS.

Although the IRS had been giving the states tax information for many decades, it was not until 1976 that Congress passed the first law specifically authorizing what until that time had been an informal process. The law contains some curious provisions. One section, for example, specifically prohibits the IRS from passing the data to the governors of the states. As a matter of state law, of course, governors direct the agencies receiving the tax information that they are excluded from obtaining. One does not have to be overly skeptical to wonder how the directors of many state tax agencies who have been appointed by a governor would respond to a gubernatorial order for a peek at a particular tax return?

Another curious and perhaps well-meaning aspect of the law is the broad power it gives the IRS to establish and enforce the computer security standards of all state tax agencies.

For many years, the IRS has maintained a single office with responsibility for supervising the disclosure of tax information. At the time I was exploring the questions involved in its sharing of federal returns with the states, this office was headed by Arnold Gordon. "The federal tax information is terrifically helpful to the states," Gordon explained. "This is because a large majority of them lag far behind the IRS in income tax enforcement. Some states have no income tax enforcement at all. So our tapes are wonderful for them, really a system of enforcement that doesn't cost them a penny."

Every year, for example, all but one or two states now receive a computer tape containing all the information on the IRS's Individual Master File (IMF). This tape gives state tax agencies more than thirty items of information about every federal-tax payer living in their states, including the taxpayer's name and Social Security number; the number of exemptions claimed; an indication of the child-care credit claimed; total itemized deductions claimed; wages reported; interest income earned; total income tax paid; gross pensions and annuities reported; gross income from small businesses, partnerships, estates, and trusts; and the amount of taxes withheld.

But as we know, that's just one of the more than two hundred tax files that the IRS shares with the states. A second tape is called the Individual Returns Transaction File (IRTF). Among many other matters, it tells the states how the IRS's computer system ranked each individual return for audit potential, the state income tax each individual reported, alimony that has been paid or received, capital gains distributions, employee business expenses, and IRA and Keogh payments.

Then there's the Business Master File (BMF) tape. It includes the receipts, deductions, income, and reported taxes of every business in each state; the number of states to which each business made unemployment insurance contributions; the total income each business withheld from its employees; and all sorts of useful identifying numbers. A second computer file pulled from the agency's Audit Information Management System (AIMS) allows the states to obtain the names and federal identification numbers of out-of-state corporate taxpayers that have operations in a state and have been audited by the IRS.

Another source of information is the Revenue Agent Reports (RARs), summary statements that are completed every time an IRS agent audits an individual or corporation. RARs have for many years been available on paper. Now, they too go to the states on easy-to-match computer tapes.

The details of information sharing are worked out by state tax officials and an IRS district disclosure officer. Because some states have more than one agency that collects taxes, the IRS has completed arrangements with more than ninety different state agencies concerning exactly what information will be shared and how it will be protected.

Over the objections of the IRS, Congress recently passed legislation authorizing the agency to provide federal tax information to New York City. Currently, a number of other large cities desire the same data. Gordon's explanation of why the IRS felt that information should be shared with the states, but not the cities, is less than convincing. It also suggests the flimsy nature of the privacy safeguards ostensibly in place to prevent the misuse of the sensitive information. "We've always been uneasy about the cities because they are so political," he said. "The states, most of them, have long histories of professional tax administration." Everyone knows, of course, how sneaky political calculations never undermine the actions of governors.

Possibly to assure me about the IRS's vigilant concern, Gordon also acknowledged that the IRS had uncovered a number of cases where states have not met the federal security requirements. He declined, however, to name the offending jurisdictions. "In one state," he recalled, "we discovered that all computerized information was stored in a single data base which could be accessed by all of the different agencies of the state. At least in theory, this meant that the state police could have obtained all the tax material that we provided that state." Gordon did not explain how the IRS had allowed the state to even receive the data without spotting such an obvious security problem.

The easy availability of federal tax information, as well as the growing sophistication of computer technology, has encouraged the states to develop programs designed to identify nonfilers and other kinds of potential enforcement targets by comparing names, addresses, and a variety of other information recorded on the computer tapes of a number of different government agencies.

The rapid growth of this investigative technique is illustrated by a research paper presented to the National Association of Tax Administrators by the Pennsylvania Department of Revenue.[2] In 1975, the report said, Pennsylvania ran one match that compared the names of those paying state income taxes with those paying federal income taxes. The goal, of course, was to identify those not paying state taxes. A decade later, Pennsylvania was regularly conducting twenty-six separate matching applications and was planning to start at least a half dozen more.

Pennsylvania's overall effort is indeed impressive. The granddaddy of the state's matching programs, the annual computerized cross-check of all the individuals listed in the federal and state income tax files "results in 140,000 new accounts [investigations] and approximately $700,000 in additional revenue each year." Many of the programs, however, are much more narrowly focused. "Using medicaid payment tracking tapes provided by the Department of Public Welfare, the Department of Revenue has reviewed about 600 physicians, dentists, osteopaths, etc. for income tax compliance. Approximately $163,000 has been collected or billed for three different years."

A pilot program comparing the names of a sample of four hundred licensed attorneys with the state's income tax files "collected about $8,400 in delinquent collections."

Under an old Pennsylvania law, all state contractors, consultants, and vendors are supposed to be in compliance with state tax laws. Before the computer age, it was impossible to enforce this law. The report showed how the times they are a-changing. "In order to determine compliance, we obtained computerized listings of contractors and vendors from the individual agencies. Both letter dunning and field contact of a small group of sample accounts resulted in the collection of $150,000. The extension of this program will result in a procedure to 'set off' delinquent liabilities against current contract amounts."

The IRS, working through the Federation of Tax Administrators, hopes to get a somewhat modified version of the Pennsylvania project going in all the other states that collect income taxes. Under the IRS plan, each state would require any person who provides goods or services to the state or applies for a license to certify under penalty of perjury that the individual has met the state's tax obligations. With this certification system in place, the IRS believes, states could spot their delinquent or nonfiling taxpayers and then make those names available to the federal tax agency for its enforcement efforts. To further enhance the value of the certificates, the IRS hopes to persuade the states to maintain their lists of certifying contractors and license seekers in a uniform computer format that could be easily read by the federal machines.

Sometimes federal agencies having nothing to do with taxation collect information that can be useful to state tax collectors. The Pennsylvania Department of Revenue, for example, obtained aircraft registration tapes from the Federal Aviation Administration in Oklahoma City and compared the names of owners with the list of individuals paying state income taxes. This match "has resulted in collections of about $1.1 million in unpaid Sales and Use taxes over the last year."

Despite the reach of Pennsylvania's current computer-sharing efforts, however, matching in the state is still very much a growth stock. The Revenue Department's report said that it recently had arranged for the Pennsylvania Department of State to redesign the forms that all applicants must fill out either to obtain or to renew a state license. There currently are 600,000 professionals holding various kinds of licenses from Pennsylvania. The new forms will include the Social Security numbers of all such professionals and will allow easy use of the names for a range of other matching projects.

Among those that the Pennsylvania report said would soon be examined on a regular basis were all state employees, licensed insurance brokers, and licensed security brokers. Can barbers be far behind?

In the past, the IRS has tended to look down on state tax agencies, often viewing them as unsophisticated country bumpkins. But in recent years the IRS's attitude has changed as it gradually began to see how it might use all kinds of data, even those gathered by the states, to identify taxpayers who might be trying to bend the law. The agency has not limited its collection efforts to tax information. Just as Pennsylvania has moved to obtain federal data not directly connected to taxes—the tape of licensed aircraft from the Federal Aviation Administration—so the IRS has begun to collect federal, state, and county information concerning matters outside its direct responsibilities.

The IRS's systematic drive to collect additional information from the states and a variety of other institutions was launched in 1984 with the adoption of the agency's 204-page *Strategic Plan.*

One part of the plan, for example, called for the creation of an indexed directory that could help IRS agents access information gathered by the investigative activities of other federal agencies.

"We are aware that the Board of Governors of the Federal Reserve System, the Federal Deposit Insurance Corporation, the Federal Home Loan Bank Board, the National Credit Union Administration and the Office of the Comptroller of the Currency conduct examinations" that warrant "consideration by Service officials for possible tax implications."

Another part of the action plan noted that the agency in the past had relied too much on its own information to spot taxpayers who apparently were not meeting their obligations. The plan called upon the agency's managers to "develop additional resources of information to detect noncompliance through cooperative arrangements with the states."

The federal-state arrangements have not been limited to the process of exchanging computer tapes. As described in part in the chapter on collecting taxes, the IRS has sought to create permanent communication links with a variety of local, state, and private organizations with no obvious connection to tax collection.

IRS offices in several parts of the United States, for example, have developed on-line links with the computerized directories now used by the telephone companies. Although the information in an electronic directory appears to be similar to that in a printed telephone book, the computer has wrought extremely useful, and surprising, changes in the process of locating an individual. Several years ago, Pat Callahan, then an IRS special projects manager, described the benefits of electronic directories to a conference of tax administrators. The specific subject of her talk was called Scantel, a service then offered by Mountain Bell.[3]

"Benefits resulting from Scantel are its increased speed, its increased success rate and the more valuable data it provides," Callahan said. With the new system, IRS agents were two times more likely to locate the individual they were looking for than with the old one. "At the same time, one hour of Scantel work replaces ten hours of city directory reach," she stated.

Callahan said that Scantel, unlike a printed telephone book or reverse directory, was updated on a weekly basis; allowed for on-line access searches by name, specific address or range of addresses, and telephone number; and conducted the searches over a multistate area. One unique feature was a signal that flashed on when the person the IRS was seeking had an unlisted telephone number. While Mountain Bell had a policy of not providing unlisted numbers to the IRS without a warrant, the signal definitely showed that the targeted individual still resided in the region. Another useful feature was Scantel's ability to give IRS investigators the names and telephone numbers of the immediate neighbors of a particular target.

The computer-linking process is a gradual one, with many advances and occasional retreats. The IRS district in Dallas, Texas, for example, was one of the early pioneers in scooping up local records, seeking to establish direct electronic links to the computers of eighty counties within its boundaries. Dallas County, for example, an area with more than 1.6 million residents, was one of the first to sign up. Under this contract, about two thousand IRS agents were currently able to make nearly instantaneous checks about the property owned and the property taxes paid by every person in the county; the names and addresses of all persons with registered vehicles; the make, year, and weight of those vehicles; and the name and address of every registered voter. Marlene Gaysek, at that time an IRS public affairs officer in Dallas, said that the computer links would save the agency about $200,000 a year because lower-paid clerks, rather than field agents, would be able to gather the required information.

Gaysek said that the IRS did not intend to compile new federal lists from county information. "We're not getting this information for general matching programs; we are using the direct access to track specific taxpayers. We need this information when we file a lien against someone or want to check to make sure a taxpayer's financial statement is correct."

On this particular occasion, however, outspoken public opposition forced the IRS to back away from its ambitious plans to form an intricate areawide data base. While officials in Dallas County had welcomed the direct links with the federal government, neighboring Tarrant County, the area around Fort Worth, refused to take part. "This was just another extension by the federal government to increase its power over local government," said B. D. Griffin, then a Tarrant County commissioner. Probably for the first time in Texas history, Tarrant County found itself walking down the same side of the street as the local office of the American Civil Liberties Union. James C. Harrington, an ACLU lawyer in Austin, said that even though the information the IRS was receiving by computer was public, its use of the county data conflicted with one of the prime goals of the Privacy Act, guaranteeing that the information an individual provides for one purpose will not be used for a second purpose without the individual's permission. "We generally oppose this kind of cross-computerization," Harrington said, "because despite what the IRS says, history tells us that information collected by the IRS will be compiled into a giant centralized data base."

The strong negative views expressed by both ends of the political spectrum must have been persuasive because some months later the local office of the IRS actually unplugged some of the computer links to the county data bases.

But the growing intimacy between federal and state tax administrators is not limited to the sharing of income tax information and the imposition of uniform federal security standards on the hundreds of state computers that process federal tax information. On May 7, 1985, the IRS and the National Association of Tax Administrators met to discuss the extent to which fuel suppliers around the country were not paying both federal and state excise taxes. As a result of these discussions, the IRS and five major states—California, Florida, Louisiana, New Jersey, and New York—launched a series of experimental investigations of suspect dealers to test the effectiveness of joint enforcement efforts.

Two years later, the IRS issued a highly favorable report on the experiment. "State results were generally better than the average historical results. IRS results were significantly better than the historical totals." For the states, the primary benefits occurred through an exchange of examination leads and audit results. For the IRS, the advantages included immediate access to the abundance of information contained in state excise tax returns and various state registration and license records.

"While logistical difficulties existed, the consensus was that the joint examinations were highly desirable," the report concluded. One key reason, in addition to the collection of substantially increased revenues, was that the joint audits generally were found to be of higher quality and to take less time to complete than separate audits.

Many are the ties that bind. Joint investigations of suspected tax cheats by the IRS and the state revenue departments. Regular exchanges of IRS and state computer tapes frequently containing highly private information about millions of taxpayers. Systematic development of direct computer links between IRS collection offices and a variety of state and county agencies. Congressional approval of a law requiring the IRS to establish federal computer-security standards for the state tax agencies and then to ensure that the agencies are meeting these standards.

What is one to make of these four developments? One possible conclusion is that federal, state, and local tax agencies, taking advantage of the tide of technology, have improved their ability to identify the individuals and businesses that are not paying their dues to society.

A second conclusion is that the tax laws are today enforced by an increasingly unified army made up of 123,000 federal and more than 60,000 state tax agents. The technology allows it. The revenue needs at every level of government require it. The law-and-order psychology of tax administrators encourages it.

A unified army, of course, is almost always more effective than one that is disorganized. But the Founding Fathers of this nation, aware of the abuses of power that had originally kindled their revolution against England, believed that the agencies of government could have too much unity. As everyone knows, they sought to avoid the hazards of concentrated power by deliberately dividing the new federal government into three competing units; the legislative branch, the executive branch, and the judicial branch. In addition to this horizontal separation of powers at the federal level, the founders also envisaged a strict vertical separation: a society where the federal government was the creature of the states and where powers not explicitly given to the federal government were reserved for the states and the people.

In late 1986, a special panel created by President Reagan's White House Council on Domestic Policy issued a report on the status of federalism in the United States. The panel noted that the founding generations of Americans, and those that followed, were "acutely aware of danger to liberty posed by the concentration of government powers in a central government."[4]

Despite a general awareness of this danger to freedom, the Reagan administration study said, the "framers' vision of a limited government of enumerated powers has gradually given way to a national government with virtually unlimited power to direct the public policy choices of the states in almost any area. The States, once the hub of political activity and the very source of our political tradition, have been reduced—in significant part—to administrative units of the national government, their independent sovereign powers usurped by almost two centuries of centralization."[5]

Over the years, however, the American interest in local control has remained a potent force for at least some parts of government. Consider, for example, our more or less continuous debate about crime. While a long line of presidents and presidential candidates has denounced crime and talked about issues like capital punishment, the Mafia, and drug dealers, it is the locally elected sheriffs and locally appointed police chiefs who remain in command of the war on crime. One product of this consensus on local control has been Congress's explicit decision to limit the jurisdiction of the FBI to a relatively narrow area of crime control. No one, left, right, or middle, openly supports the development of a national police force.

But with almost no public debate, and very little congressional guidance, a somewhat amorphous but still powerful federal/state organization appears to be slowly co-opting the enforcement of the nation's tax laws, thereby undermining the traditional notion of federalism. There is no claim here that the IRS is seeking to assume control of the state tax agencies. Even if this were a secret IRS goal, the tax collectors in such powerful states as California, New York, and Texas are not likely to agree placidly to such an arrangement. What does appear to be emerging, however, is a subtle meshing of federal and state agencies into a unique enforcement alliance with a formidable range of legal powers and resources of information.

Arnold Gordon, in charge of improving the flow of data between the IRS and the states, does not believe this steadily expanding process has reduced the independence of state organizations or diluted the structure of federalism. "The proof of this," Gordon explained, "is that under the law the IRS for many years has had the legal authority to collect and process the income taxes of any state who wanted to use our services. Not one state has picked up on this option. The reason is obvious. Any state that signed up would lose some of its sovereignty. The information sharing we now do increases everyone's efficiency. It has no impact on sovereignty of the states."

Gordon exaggerates. The federal enforcement of computer security requirements on the states obviously has some impact on their sovereignty. So does the steady pressure on the states to store their tax information in forms that are compatible with IRS computers. Because the IRS will naturally be the dominant partner every time the agency and a particular state decide to initiate a joint tax-enforcement project, the balance of power in tax enforcement seems to be gradually drifting from the state capitals to Washington.

There is also the question of legislative oversight, an important part of the checks and balances essential to American representative democracy. How could the House Ways and Means Committee and the Senate Finance Committee which historically have failed to supervise tax collection at the federal level, ever keep track of tax collection managed by a confusing consortium of more than fifty agencies? And how about the tax committees of New York or California? Would the IRS, which often resists answering questions put to it by both the president of the United States and the U.S. Congress, be willing to meet with tax committees in Albany or Sacramento to answer questions about its misuse of state tax data? It seems highly unlikely.

A SUSPECT IN EVERY KITCHEN

In the tax enforcement game, it is not only the lineup of players that seems to be gradually shifting. Also in flux are the basic tactics of the game. During the last two decades, for example, the IRS has been properly engaged in a variety of efforts to identify the fairly small proportion of Americans who seek to avoid any taxes by dropping out of the economy. But in the spring of 1983, Walter E. Bergman, then the agency's deputy assistant commissioner for planning, finance, and research, had an idea that carried to an entirely new level this search for improved techniques for detecting those who do not file tax returns.

Computerized mailing lists are now a major tool of American commerce. Many lists contain far more detailed information about the living habits, political views, and health of the American people than is generally understood.

The first source of information for many lists is the telephone book.

The directory, of course, gives the researcher the names and addresses of most of the people living in a given city. But it can also be the key to other insights.

Several marketing companies, for example, have computer programs that automatically assign each name and address in the directory to the correct census tract, the Census Bureau's basic geographical unit. Because American neighborhoods tend to be homogeneous, this matching allows the researcher to make a well-informed guess about the income, age, race, and family makeup of the individuals who live in a given tract.

Researchers use the telephone directories for a second not-so-obvious purpose. In most cities, directories are published every few years. By checking previous editions, the listmaker determines how long a given family has lived at the same address.

The automobile registration lists maintained by state departments of motor vehicles are another excellent source of information. By combining the information drawn from the telephone directory with that provided by the departments of motor vehicles of thirty-six states, the commercial listmaker learns that the Jones family living at 55 Elm Street has two cars. (Some states for either technical or privacy reasons do not sell the lists.) They also learn the age, type, cost, and model of the two cars. If the Joneses happen to own a recent-model station wagon and a luxury convertible, for example, the marketing company can infer that they are wealthier than a neighboring family which only owns a low-cost hatchback.

State departments of motor vehicles also maintain lists of licensed drivers. From this source, the marketing company can learn the age and race of Mr. and Mrs. Jones and their two teenage children. (In some states, the company may also be able to determine that Mr. Jones has diabetes and that Mrs. Jones wears glasses, two conditions that might affect their driving and also can be useful to advertisers.)

Other computerized public records available in various states allow the marketers to determine whether the Joneses are registered voters, which party they belong to, whether they live in an apartment or a house, the size of their living space, and whether they have a dog or a cat.

On the basis of all this information about the life-style of the Jones family—where they live, how long they have lived there, how many children they have, and what kinds of cars they drive—the marketing company develops a detailed computerized portrait of the family, including an estimate of their annual income.

One of the largest and best listmakers in America is the Donnelley Company. In 1988 the company was merging up-to-date information about 75 million specific families or households. The information was drawn from a number of sources, including 4,700 telephone directories, Postal Service change-of-address cards, and the motor vehicle departments of thirty-six states and the District of Columbia. The telephone information is updated on a daily basis. The automobile-related information is updated once or twice a year.

The managers of the Donnelley Company residential data base try to develop thirty-five sets of information about each of the 75 million families. One of the most interesting sets is called Interest Categories. It shows whether the members of a particular family hold a bank card or a travel card, their level of response to past mailings, and whether they have contributed to religious organizations, politicians, or groups such as the American Cancer Society.

It was this life-style information that Walter Bergman, the IRS researcher, thought might help the government track down people who had not paid their taxes. At first glance, Bergman's surveillance project sounds quite reasonable. Using the agency's computers, the IRS would compare the names and addresses of all taxpayers with the names and addresses of all the households identified by the marketing companies.

"If the cross-check suggests a family hasn't paid," Bergman told me in an interview, "we'll make an inquiry to find out why. This is no big deal."

But the matching project was not so innocuous as Bergman suggested. One of those who saw problems was Robert Ellis Smith, a lawyer and the publisher of a specialized newsletter called the *Privacy Journal.* "The IRS experiment is very troublesome," he said in an interview. "While I am quite sure it does not violate the law, it graphically demonstrates the growing links between government and private computers. National lists of households and their incomes are sufficiently accurate for soliciting business, but that doesn't mean they are precise enough to trigger investigations."

Interestingly, the three major companies that prepare such national lists agreed with Smith's concern. "It is inappropriate for the IRS to use the kind of lists we produce to identify errant taxpayers," said Richard Vincent, then director of marketing for the Donnelley Marketing Service. "This IRS experiment is ill conceived because such lists are not accurate on an individual basis, but only in the aggregate. If a company wants to send a mailer to all American families with incomes over $40,000, we rent it a list for onetime use. Depending somewhat on the group that the company wants to target, we guarantee that 75 to 80 percent of those receiving the material will have the correct characteristics."

Because of these reservations, and concerns that IRS use of the mailing lists might ultimately damage their business, Donnelley and two other companies, R. L. Polk and Metromail, refused to give the agency any names. Several months later, however, a small independent list broker in Washington provided the IRS with a list of 2 million names of households in Brooklyn, New York, Wisconsin, and Indiana, the areas Bergman had selected to test the feasibility of his project.

But the problem of accuracy identified by Robert Ellis Smith and the three major marketing companies is only the first level of concern. Under the American system of law, a policeman may obtain a search warrant from a judge after he has presented evidence that there is "reasonable cause" to begin an investigation. But because of the speed of the computer, this time-honored tradition has been subtly modified.

In fact, the IRS began with its normal assumption that everyone was guilty and the computer allowed it to conduct a general search of the records of every taxpayer in the three districts. Because the courts have held that such records belong to the government, and not to the citizen, they have quite consistently ruled that broad matching projects do not violate the Fourth Amendment prohibition against unreasonable searches. Despite the legal logic of these decisions, however, the steadily growing ability of the IRS to access and compare the computerized files of millions of Americans in hopes of spotting inconsistencies represents a profound change in law-enforcement strategy.

Appropriately enough, Bergman's experimental research project was conducted in the year Orwell made famous, 1984. This time it did not work. Although the IRS never issued a report explaining why, it appears that industry experts were correct: The 1984 version of the marketing lists contained too many inaccuracies to serve as a cost-effective surveillance device.

Some experienced marketing experts, however, think that the project may have failed because of the notoriously inaccurate information contained in IRS files. "Well over 95 percent of the names and addresses on the current lists are accurate," said a senior New York marketing executive with wide experience in using the lists to target customers. "There's no reason why the IRS couldn't use something like the Donnelley list to reduce the U.S. population to mush except that the agency can't control the accuracy of the information in its own files."

However, the improved information technologies resulting from the Tax System Redesign project, parallel developments within the commercial marketing companies, and theoretical work by a number of academics on a computerized analytic technique called "block modeling" suggest that Bergman's dream may well come true in the near future.

Of course, the IRS has already begun to work toward this goal. For more than two decades, the agency's Taxpayer Compliance Measurement Program has collected detailed tax information from a representative sample of taxpayers to develop statistical models predicting the behavior of different groups of taxpayers.

But with the increasing amounts and kinds of information being collected and stored on computers, research to produce far more sophisticated models of expected behavior is inevitable. The possibilities for such research have long fascinated a small circle of law-enforcement officials and academic experts. In December 1981, Roger H. Davis, a special agent in the Behavioral Science Unit at the FBI Academy in Quantico, Virginia, wrote a paper describing how "social network analysis" can be used by police to understand the nature of complex conspiracies, determine the leaders of secret organizations, and ultimately "predict criminal behavior."[6]

Davis described a case where the police in an unnamed western city obtained information about an organized fencing operation that was selling guns to criminals. The operation was being run by the members of a local gang. As the first step in its investigation, the police established a secret surveillance of a tavern known to be popular with the gang. The surveillance was continued for four days.

"From this surveillance, 18 people believed to be connected with the group were identified," Davis reported. "Using social networking techniques, the officers converted their observations of people arriving at and departing from the tavern into a network diagram showing the structure of interpersonal relations within the group. From this picture, police determined connections between group members and began to focus logically on those they considered suspects and who would be most knowledgeable about the crime."

Davis added that social network analysis could be particularly useful for investigating cases involving organized crime, the distribution and sale of illicit narcotics, illegal gambling services, and business fraud.

Although network analysis is hardly routine among either federal or local law-enforcement agencies, its potential has long fascinated a small group of sociologists and mathematicians. In 1975, Scott A. Boorman, then at the University of Pennsylvania; Ronald A. Breiger, then at Harvard University; and Phipps Arabie, then at the University of Minnesota, published a highly technical paper in the *Journal of Mathematical Psychology* describing an advanced method for the hierarchical clustering of relational data that could give researchers a new tool for analyzing the behavior of various groups of individuals. Research for the paper was supported by grants from the National Science Foundation and the National Institute of Mental Health.

On November 20, 1983, after a two-year stint at the IRS, Boorman, by then a professor of sociology at Yale University, and Paul R. Levitt, a research mathematician at Harvard, published a brief article in *The New York Times* about what they now called "block modeling," a computer programing technique to organize various bits of seemingly innocuous data in ways that allow researchers to predict the behavior of individuals with improved accuracy. Boorman and Levitt said that block modeling did not require particularly sensitive information such as medical histories. "Rather, it exploits the unexpected, even uncanny synergy of large masses of 'relational' data buried in organizational files. Examples of relevant data: Whom you talk with in your company, whose phone calls you do not return, whom you eat lunch with, to whom do you send carbon copies of memos." They noted that the increasing use of the computer meant that more and more such data were being routinely collected in ways that made the information readily available for analysis.

The researchers said that the output of block modeling was simple to understand. "As Justice William O. Douglas once observed, a person is defined by the checks he writes. Blocks in block modeling generalize this principle. They are discrete sets of people occupying similar positions in the relational networks, and who thus are likely to behave similarly in ways important to the organization, and be candidates for receiving similar 'treatment.'"

Boorman and Levitt argued that, with proper safeguards, block modeling could provide managers valuable insights about the dynamics of large groups of individuals in a sound, ethical, and constructive way. They warned, however, that "strides in the new 'guilt by association' technologies are easily outstripping the vastly slower evolution of protective legal and administrative responses."

Remember Hank Philcox, the assistant IRS commissioner for Tax System Redesign? Remember Philcox's overall plan to reduce sharply the IRS's reliance on paper? Remember the return-free tax system under which the IRS will calculate the returns for half the taxpayers in the nation? Remember the shared concerns expressed by Benjamin Barber and Commissioner Gibbs about how these new processes might affect the basic role of individual citizens? Remember all the matches with which the IRS is routinely comparing its information against the information in the files of the states? Remember Walter Bergman's 1984 experiment to use commercial marketing lists to spot nonfilers? Remember all the computerized information the IRS is collecting from the states and counties?

Where do these developments take the IRS during the next decade? While no one can predict the future, it is always tempting to try. In 1985, the Office of Technology Assessment, a research arm of Congress, undertook a broad study of how information technology was changing the federal government. In connection with this study, the OTA requested a small Washington research group headed by Joseph F. Coates to extrapolate how five federal agencies would be functioning in the year 1995. One of the agencies was the IRS. Although Coates and his research team assumed full responsibility, the scenarios were all based on interviews with federal officials, and each agency was given an opportunity to comment before the report was published.[7]

The IRS mission in 1995, Coates said, would still be to collect taxes. "Although 'voluntary compliance' will remain the byword, by 1995 the potential for complete internal matching of returns from source information, electronic funds transfer networks, and near complete computerization of even small-scale financial transaction records could make compliance a matter of automatic processing of taxpayer and IRS electronic records rather than a separate voluntary filing."

Electronic filing, return-free filing, optical data storage, and automated examination will have become a routine part of American life. "As these technologies become commonplace they will change the flow of information and responsibility among taxpayer, employer and financial institution and government," Coates continued.

In the government's continuing effort to collect additional taxes, Coates predicted, increasing attention would be focused on tapping the incomes of those who, to various degrees, try to live outside the regular economy. He estimated that by 1989 various illegal entrepreneurs, primarily drug dealers, would be earning as much as $45 billion a year in unreported income.

To capture the tax from this elusive group, Coates foresaw that the government could adopt a drastic law-enforcement strategy with far-reaching implications for the entire society: the printing of machine-readable money. Combined with optical scanners located at every bank, Coates said, such money would enable the IRS to monitor citizen transactions of almost any size.

Legal and technical developments already are carrying the IRS down this road. In 1970, Congress approved legislation requiring banks to report every deposit or withdrawal of more than $10,000 in cash. For many years, this law was largely ignored. Recently, however, computerized record keeping has made compliance less onerous, and in 1987 the banks sent 5.4 million detailed reports to the IRS showing the name, Social Security number, and other details about those involved in large cash transactions. In recent years, IRS reporting requirements have been extended to any-one—a lawyer, auto dealer, or jeweler—who is paid $10,000 or more in cash.

While such reporting requirements obviously are useful to the IRS, Coates believes that they would be far more effective when combined with a monetary system that could constantly monitor the movement of individual bills above a certain denomination in the same fashion as the government now can follow a personal check. During the 1988 celebra-tion of Australia's bicentennial, a special $10 note was issued that might provide the technical answer to how such monitoring might be achieved. The note is printed on a special plastic that includes a hologram portrait of Captain James Cook. While the Reserve Bank of Australia said that this "optically variable device" with Cook's likeness would make counter-feiting almost impossible, Coates said that the experimental bills easily could be adopted for an automated system that tracked cash.

Coates also predicted that as the IRS continued to enlarge its national data bases with new kinds of information the data bases themselves would become increasingly useful to all kinds of institutions, public and private. As their value increased, IRS efforts to protect them would require such stringent security measures as more or less continuous surveillance of all IRS employees, biological identification systems such as voiceprints or retina prints, and increased psychological evaluation and screening.

"The need for privacy and security of IRS data must continually be traded off against the usefulness of that data for non-IRS purposes," Coates observed. "Data sharing can range from the tracking of specific, known criminals, to searching for a small set of suspected child support evaders, to wholesale matching of IRS and Social Security Administration data bases. Data sharing within the government is more restrictive than in the private sector. What is the individual's right to privacy of his own data when that data may help provide information on criminals?" he asked.

Assume, for argument's sake, that we live in a world where every bit of information in every one of the IRS's computers is accurate and that every IRS notice is correct. Do the American people want a world where much of the personal information collected by the IRS is routinely shared with state and local tax agencies? Do the American people want a world where the IRS, to improve its enforcement efforts, has initiated a long-range plan to gain direct access to a broad range of information collected by the states during the registration of automobiles and voters and the licensing of drivers, doctors, and other groups? The American people have long opposed the idea of the federal government creating a single national data base containing a computerized portrait of every citizen. But it is clear that a de facto system is already in place.

Because this growing electronic net is being tossed over the country in the name of such worthy causes as fighting crime and catching tax cheats, the nation's current leaders have not responded to the challenge of men like Professor Emeritus Joseph Weizenbaum of MIT or the late Sam Ervin, the constitutional scholar and Democratic senator from North Carolina. Senator Ervin believed that computer technology threatened to erode liberty and the creative, spontaneous spirit of the American people.

Unless new legislative controls can be devised to limit the reach of the computer and unless federal officials can be persuaded to limit their hunger for more and more information about the activities of the American people, Ervin once warned, individuals will gradually stop exercising "the freedoms that are calculated to make their minds and spirits free. And that, in the long run, the government is going to suffer from the effects of this as much as the citizens are to suffer the loss of their freedom."[8]

Almost 150 years before the worrisome thoughts of Ervin and Coates, a Frenchman named Alexis de Tocqueville came to the United States and expressed some of the same concerns. Tocqueville, of course, celebrated the great American experiment. But he also predicted that the egalitarian spirit of its people might someday lead to the growth of a despotic centralized government. Such a government, Tocqueville wrote in *Democracy in America,* would be very different from the despotisms of old, where the savage power of the emperors was extremely onerous to a few, but largely ignored the many. The despotism of the new democratic nations, he believed, unlike the off-with-their-heads style of the ancients, would be "more extensive and more mild; it would degrade men without tormenting them."[9]

Tocqueville anticipated that the new government's power over its subjects would be minute, regular, and provident. "For their happiness, such a government willingly labors, but it chooses to be the sole agent and only arbiter of that happiness, it provides for their security, foresees and supplies their necessities, facilitates their pleasures, manages their principal concerns, directs their industry, regulates the descent of property, and subdivides their inheritances; what remains but to spare them all the care of thinking and the trouble of living? Thus it every day renders the free exercise of the free agency of man less useful and less frequent, it circumscribes the will within a narrower range and gradually robs a man of all the uses of himself."[10]

Having subverted the individual citizen, the government then extends its arm over the entire community. "It covers the surface of society with a network of small complicated rules, minute and uniform, through which the most original minds and the most energetic characters cannot penetrate, to rise above the crowd. The will of man is not shattered, but softened, bent and guided; men are seldom forced by it to act, but they are constantly restrained from acting. Such a power does not destroy, but it prevents existence; it does not tyrannize but it compresses, enervates, extinguishes, and stupefies a people, till each nation is reduced to nothing better than a flock of timid and industrious animals, of which the government is the shepherd."[11]

CHAPTER 14

The Last Word

A little more than twenty years ago I went to work for *The New York Times*. My first assignment was to cover the New York Police Department. I was on that beat for six years. During the last four years, I have been examining the IRS on pretty much a full-time basis. As I have observed in several other places in this book, the two organizations have a lot of similarities.

Both are among the largest law-enforcement organizations in the world. Both are very old, with institutional histories that go back before the Civil War. Both are led by men with necessarily parochial views because they have spent their working lives within the confines of their separate organizations. Both have thousands of front-line troops vested with the broad legal powers they need to intervene directly in the lives of selected citizens. Both have been handed difficult tasks that often require them to take unpopular actions.

After many years of reporting about the IRS and the NYPD, I have come to believe that they share one other very important quality. This is the pervasive attitude of cynicism that continuously works on the two organizations in the same way that the air from the sea eats away at all the metal objects on an island. The cynicism moves in two equally destructive directions, corroding both the public's perceptions of the IRS and NYPD and the agencies' perceptions of the public.

I remember one Wall Street lawyer asking me why I wrote about police corruption. "There is always going to be corruption in this world," he said. "So why bother trying to document it?" The lawyer thus totally missed the point that there can be more or less corruption in any agency, depending upon the attitude and actions of the managers, and that the cost of corruption is less effective government.

I also remember the comment of a senior official in New York City's politically powerful police union, the Police Benevolent Association. I had to realize, he told me, that corruption never would be reduced in New York because "City Hall" viewed the bribes that police officers were regularly extorting from the public as a secret part of their official pay and benefits.

Then there was the curious complaint from William Federici, a reporter with the *New York Daily News.* Bill was unhappy with a front-page story I had written about the widely accepted practice of "cooping," or sleeping on duty. My story was supported with photographs of snoozing officers in Brooklyn and Manhattan who were supposed to be patrolling the streets. "That wasn't any kind of a goddamn story," he complained furiously. "How can cooping be a story when everyone already knows about it?"

In those days, the Wall Street lawyer, the police union official, the street-smart reporter, and a huge number of their fellow New Yorkers wallowed in their destructive and pervasive cynicism about the cops of their city like pigs in a mud hole.

I believe their attitude of casual cynicism turned out to be mostly incorrect. It is true that yet another study commission was formed. It is also true that Mayor John Lindsay decided that the commission's chairman should be Whitman Knapp, a patrician Wall Street lawyer and former assistant district attorney who on the surface appeared to be totally lacking in the skills and passions of a clever boat-rocker. But under Knapp's courtly veneer was a politically deft and astonishingly intelligent apparatchik. During the brief but flamboyant life of the commission, Knapp helped the city come to understand the real costs of corruption. He also showed New York how key miscalculations by the city's top officials, including Mayor Lindsay and his closest advisors, had contributed to these losses.

At the same time as Knapp was holding his televised seminars on police corruption, a canny former New York City police officer of great integrity, Patrick Murphy, was appointed as the new commissioner of the NYPD. He initiated scores of different steps—some of them big, some of them small—to alter the way the department functioned on the streets of the city. One radical step taken by the commissioner was to order the police not to make gambling arrests unless there was a specific citizen complaint. For as long as anyone could remember, of course, the New York Police Department had regulated gambling in much the same way that the old Civil Aeronautics Board used to regulate the airline industry. (I don't mean to suggest here that the CAB had the same kind of corruption problem as the NYPD, only that both agencies exercised a similar kind of economic control over their respective industries.) This very old arrangement had guaranteed the flow of millions of dollars a year in bribes to a substantial number of New York police officers.

Another of Murphy's moves was to greatly increase the number of supervisors in the Narcotics Division so that arrests would be targeted on more important dealers. Previously, narcotics detectives had worked on an essentially free-lance basis, naturally tending to go after the easy-to-catch small fry. Another, hardly surprising advantage of the relaxed narcotics approach favored in the pre-Murphy era was that the unwatched detectives found themselves showered by huge amounts of cash from dealers who wanted to avoid the fuss and bother of an arrest. Murphy attempted other kinds of changes, altering the way senior police managers were promoted, revising how young police officers were trained, holding the sergeants and captains accountable for the police officers under their command.

The changes brought about by Knapp and Murphy and hundreds of other reform-minded police officers throughout the city were not always successful. Sometimes compromises were made. Occasionally the wrong people were appointed. In several situations, questionable deals were cut. But in the mid-1970s a strong majority of New Yorkers and outside police experts agreed that, for at least a time, real reform was achieved: A better-led and better-directed police force was providing the people of New York somewhat better service.

As is always the case, however, the underlying public outrage, partially created by newspaper stories and the subsequent Knapp Commission hearings, began to fade. The gradual loss of momentum caused by this decline in public interest was accelerated by a second debilitating force; the citywide budget crisis that required all New York agencies to absorb a series of demoralizing cutbacks. Within a decade, the tide of cynicism began to rise and New Yorkers once again were whispering about out-of-control cops dealing drugs and beating prisoners. The reform movement had been partially eclipsed. The cycle was almost complete.

The cynical attitudes of both the police and the public, which made reform so difficult in New York City and in many other cities, have also undermined real reform efforts in the IRS.

The single most obvious sign of the widespread doubt about the integrity of the nation's tax agency was the comment made to me by practically every person I talked with during the writing of this book. At some point in almost every one of these thousands of formal interviews and casual conversations, the person sitting across the desk or on the other side of the dinner table would look over at me with a little laugh and say: "I sure hope you have a good accountant."

The currents of doubt about the tax agency today and the police department of some years ago have infected the thinking of too many Americans. Nothing is on the level, they say, so why bother even thinking about possible changes and improvements?

I ran across another example of this feeling of cynicism in the fall of 1988 when officials from a small group of liberal public interest groups in Washington, D.C., asked me to give them a preview of what I had uncovered while writing this book. I described how the IRS for many years had used the granting and withholding of tax exemption as an instrument of political control, and ended my talk with an appeal. Instead of spending all of their time fighting with the IRS over their day-to-day problems, why didn't the groups consider a much broader question: How could the laws of tax exemption and their administration be reformed? Could not a whole new system be devised to substantially reduce the chances of IRS abuse?

The public interest groups did not pick up on my challenge. Part of their reluctance was their intense preoccupation with the immediate tactical problems they were having with the IRS. But even in this conference room filled with men and women who genuinely thought of themselves as do-gooders, the smell of cynicism was in the air. Although a few individuals were intrigued, the consensus was that no general reform was possible.

Why have the IRS and the NYPD generated so much fear, distrust, and cynicism? Part of the answer, I believe, lies in a curious paradox. At the very same time, many of us look at the agencies in two conflicting ways. At one level we are sure they will fail us. At another level, our hopes for the IRS and the NYPD are so high that they automatically fail us.

Their preordained failure to achieve the incredibly ambitious goals we have assigned to them then leads us to conclude that the lesser hopes we have for the agencies also can never be achieved.

Who in his or her right mind actually thinks that the few thousand police officers who are on duty at any given time in New York City could actually maintain public order among 8 million citizens, most of whom insist on inconveniently working and living in places into which the patroling officers cannot see? Who could imagine that in a country as large and diverse and greedy as the United States the IRS could really persuade all of the American people to regularly give the government a good chunk of their incomes on a voluntary basis and according to a hard-to-understand tax law? In both cases, of course, our impossible hopes must be dashed.

The ambitious leaders of the IRS and the NYPD inadvertently contribute to our sense of hopelessness. In their restless search for bigger budgets and more staff, they repeatedly allow themselves to make promises their agencies cannot keep. The mission of the IRS, for example, is "to collect the proper amount of tax revenues at the least cost to the public, and in a manner that warrants the highest degree of public confidence in our integrity, efficiency and fairness."

But the fact that perfection is beyond their grasp—either in keeping the peace in a fractious city or in collecting the taxes in a massive nation— does not mean that nothing can be done and that nothing is worth doing. In fact, much was done about the New York Police Department. In fact, much can be done about the IRS. In New York, the social fabric of a single great city was at risk. I believe the stakes involved in reforming the federal tax agency may well be far higher.

OVERSIGHT

As in New York City, the first step must be to focus a hundred powerful spotlights on the IRS. All the cases of improper political interference, all the instances of individuals being wrongfully harassed, and all the examples of incompetent management must be brought out and examined in an unbiased and uncompromising way. We cannot allow the secret infections of the IRS to continue to fester. Cleaning up the mess is essential for two quite different reasons. First, the federal government cannot provide the American people the essential services they must have unless the money to pay for these services has been collected. Second, because of the scope of IRS activities, all failures on its part to collect taxes in an evenhanded and constitutional way present a threat to our system of representative government.

Effective oversight is the key to achieving these goals. The House Ways and Means Committee and the Senate Finance Committee must abandon their traditional cheerleader roles. It is absurd to think that any institution with the power and impact of the IRS can operate in a fair and effective way without sustained and forceful oversight. All the great wise men of government—thinkers like Thomas Jefferson, James Madison, and Lord Acton—and all of our direct experiences with government tell us it is dangerous to allow even the best-intentioned institutions to operate without facing regular, tough-minded review.

But for too long Congress has allowed its total obsession with the collection of federal revenue to blind it to the need to examine carefully how this revenue is collected. For too long the campaign funds that can always be extracted from the rich and powerful by simply holding a hearing on yet another proposal to change the tax code have distracted the members of the House and Senate committees from investigating how the agency is actually treating the American people.

The press suffers from a similar kind of blindness, although for different reasons. Despite the IRS's vast size and impact, no major newspaper in the United States currently has a full-time reporter assigned to covering the IRS as a law-enforcement agency. A reporter at the Justice Department, a reporter at the space agency, a reporter at the Securities and Exchange Commission, but no reporter at the IRS. Neither *The New York Times,* the *Washington Post,* the *Los Angeles Times,* nor *The Wall Street Journal* has ever given the agency more than the most casual kind of attention. The only major newspaper in the last fifteen years to make serious periodic efforts to examine the IRS is the *Philadelphia Enquirer.* (The *Enquirer*'s intense coverage of the IRS's near collapse in the mid-1980s was unique.)

Academics must also abandon their infatuation with obscure interpretations of the tax code and throw themselves into tough-minded studies of the real world of tax administration. I will never forget a frustrating interview with one of the leading tax professors at one of the nation's leading law schools. I posed a series of questions about how the IRS actually functioned. The professor had little interest in the concrete. After a fruitless thirty-minute conversation, he pointed to an imposing shelf of dozens of thick and scholarly books he had written on the tax code. "I don't suppose there are more than thirty or forty pages in them about the IRS," the old sage proudly announced. Professors like this are part of the problem.

The studied inattention of Congress, the press, and the academics to the actual process of tax collection means that top IRS managers can be quite certain that most of their worst blunders will escape detection. At the same time, however, the failure of these institutions to examine the day-to-day operations of the tax agency means that the truly innovative efforts that sometimes are undertaken are also not recognized. The recent experience of a handful of states suggests how wrongheaded this myopia may be. While the evidence is somewhat murky, it appears, for example, that when taxpayers believe that their tax administrators are making a genuine attempt to operate in a fair but tough-minded way revenues tend to increase significantly. This is news worth knowing.

WHAT IS THE PURPOSE OF THE IRS?

Partly because of Congress's almost paranoid concern about potential threats to the collection of revenue, almost all senior IRS officials see enforcement as their single most important job. Despite the Internal Revenue *Service*'s name, enforcement is the game. That is why, when push comes to shove in the internal budget battles over how the agency will actually spend its money, enforcement usually comes in first, taxpayer assistance last. Scattered but persuasive evidence suggests that the IRS's seemingly logical emphasis on enforcement may be misguided. The reason: Genuinely helping taxpayers comply with the law appears to increase revenues a lot more effectively than does heavy-handed enforcement. No one believes you should throw away the stick, just that you should offer a lot more carrots.

Various wings of the American Bar Association have been studying the IRS and the problem of tax collection for many years. In July 1987, the ABA's special commission on taxpayer compliance issued one of the more sophisticated and realistic reports about tax collection.[1] The association study concluded that, although Congress and the IRS had gradually increased the agency's various enforcement efforts, expenditure and staffing aimed at improving the taxpayers' ability and willingness to comply with the tax laws had been too limited. The result was that many Americans who wanted to pay their taxes had been frustrated from doing so by poorly written instructions and incorrect advice.

The IRS's heavy emphasis on punishment, the report said, "ignores the role of honest mistakes, embodies an overly narrow view of taxpayers as purely rational calculators who evaluate the potential costs and benefits of noncompliance in making their tax decisions and is based on an overly optimistic view of the potential of law enforcement."[2]

Do the Current Tax Laws
Make the Fair and Equitable Collection
of Taxes Impossible?

Virtually all thoughtful tax experts agree that the tax laws of the United States must be simplified. For too many American taxpayers, accountants, and IRS employees, the current law has grown so complicated that it literally is impossible to understand. In a situation where both the enforcers and the subjects of enforcement are unable to fathom the intent of the law, arbitrary and capricious actions are inevitable. Arbitrary laws are also hard to administer and invite high-level subversion and corruption.

The challenge is very real. It is hard to imagine how reforms can be made within the administrative process until Congress and the public understand that the agency's genuine flaws begin with truly impossible tax laws. One tax lawyer who openly questions the current law and how it is administered is Glenn White, director of taxes for Dow Chemical Company.

What bothers White is the sheer complexity of the tax code. Dow's 1988 tax return, he said, was 3,139 pages long and weighed more than 26 pounds. The company's 1988 return was slightly smaller than the one it filed for 1987, White acknowledged, but not because the tax law had grown more simple or the IRS less demanding. The executive said the reason for the small decline in the size of the return was that the company had sold off a bank and purchased some new computer software that squeezed a bit more information on each page of the supporting documents.

"If we hadn't sold that company and bought the new software, our 1988 return would have been far larger than the 1987 one," he said. "We're convinced that the system is broken."

White said that the tax laws approved by Congress in the last few years seem to authorize anonymous officials in the Treasury Department and the IRS to interpret them any way they see fit. "That's not a good system of law, that's a bad system," he said. "The power the tax committees have handed to the bureaucrats is just a little bit scary."

But tax experts at giant corporations are not the only ones who worry about the long-term effects of ambiguous tax laws, confusing regulations, and escalating penalties. So does Lawrence B. Gibbs, the commissioner during the last few years of the Reagan administration. During a fall 1988 discussion of the philosophy of the system of tax penalties and their application, Gibbs said that as the tax laws become more complex, society's understanding of what is right and what is wrong becomes more fuzzy. "The current situation leads to different standards of enforcement for different classes of taxpayers and that's not good," he said.

Perhaps the greatest confusion is felt by the conscientious IRS agents who come in day-to-day contact with taxpayers. Emil Poggi retired from the IRS a few years ago after serving as a hearing officer on the appellate division staff adjudicating disputes between the agency and angry taxpayers in the New York area and, before that, as a special agent in the Criminal Investigation Division.

"My colleagues and I worked zealously to enforce tax laws passed by Congress," he said, "although many of us were convinced those laws were largely legalized deceptions that encouraged wealthy individuals and corporations to escape with little or no tax payment while the middle class and the poor pay punitive taxes to make up the deficiency. The current laws compel people to think of deception and scheming, they gradually corrode society, and they engender widespread cynicism."

Poggi's diagnosis has obvious merit. But his cure is far easier to prescribe than to swallow. "If every dollar of income, without exception, were to be taxed on a gradually progressive basis, without deductions or loopholes, those who are able to avoid taxes legally would pay a fair share of the tax bill, and the rest of us, the majority, would pay less. The tax form would consist of three lines: total income, applicable percentage and tax due. Period! Additional forms and excruciating schedules would be eliminated."

Would Congress ever eliminate the tax exemption it so long ago provided for a homeowner with a mortgage? Would Congress ever eliminate the $1,950 deduction granted for each child? Not likely.

The absolutely untouchable quality of many such basic exemptions and deductions has created a difficult psychological hurdle for those who would like Congress to take even intermediate steps in this direction. Because the homeowner's mortgage is untouchable, the cynics argue, no other effort to make the tax code simpler and easier to understand is possible.

An entirely new force is at work, however, which may drastically alter the basic political calculus of the tax system. This new force is our current multibillion-dollar deficit. Almost all economists agree that the deficit must be cut. Almost all politicians, on the other hand, are convinced that voting an increase in the federal income tax would be political suicide. The obvious answer: Some new form of tax that would make a serious dent in the deficit while being largely invisible to the taxpayers.

Although substantial increases in the federal excise taxes on alcohol and cigarettes and a brand-new tax on energy are possible, the leading candidate for a secret weapon to attack the deficit appears to be the value-added tax (VAT). Now used in forty-three countries, the VAT is a sales tax with a twist. The widely used retail sales tax is charged only at the final point of sale. The VAT is paid by the supplier of raw materials and the manufacturer and the wholesaler and the retailer and, ultimately, the consumer.

Economists argue that the VAT has several real advantages for society. By making consumption costlier, it should stimulate savings and investments that in recent years have lagged in the United States. By not being aimed at any single part of the economy, the VAT is considered a relatively neutral instrument that would not distort the economy.

One disadvantage of the VAT is that its impact is relatively greater on the poor than on the rich. The regressive quality of the VAT obviously can be offset by a progressive income tax. As Vito Tanzi, a senior official in the International Monetary Fund, observed to a reporter from *Fortune* magazine, "Equity should not be the concern of each individual tax. It should be the concern of tax policy as a whole."

Although many leading business executives support adding the VAT to the federal tax collection process, the Bush administration so far has staunchly opposed any new tax. One major objection specific to the VAT, made by the antigovernment philosophers of both the Bush and the Reagan teams, is that the adoption of the well-proven value tax in the United States might well lead to larger and more aggressive government.

Thus most of the preliminary debate about the VAT has focused on its economic consequences. As is usually the case, the potential impact on the IRS and the tax collection process has been virtually ignored.

One of the big backers of VAT is Don Alexander, the former commissioner. "The VAT would be a lot easier to administer than the income tax law," he said. "That is why they use it as a primary tax in countries that have difficulty in collecting income taxes. When you have different tax rates for different categories of goods it gets a bit more complicated, but the administrative decisions that have to be made under the VAT are child's play compared to the decisions the IRS has to make every day under our present system."

SHOULD THE IRS BE REORGANIZED?

The organization and responsibilities of old institutions like the IRS tend to get set in concrete even though experience shows a particular arrangement is causing real problems. Since the establishment of the income tax just before World War I, for example, the IRS has administered the laws concerning tax-exempt charitable organizations.

The responsibility for deciding who should be granted tax-exempt status and who should lose it often requires the IRS to make complex judgments about some of the most sensitive political, racial, and sexual issues confronting the American people. The IRS's supervision of tax exemption means that for all practical purposes the agency is responsible for governing hundreds of millions of dollars of charitable gifts made each year.

Two former IRS commissioners, Jerome Kurtz and Sheldon Cohen, question whether the public good is served by asking an agency whose key responsibility is tax collection to judge how society exercises its most generous instincts.

In testimony before the Senate Finance Committee in 1973, for example, Cohen said that the IRS's exempt organizations branch had always been considered a stepchild because the agency's major role was tax collection. He added that for this reason the agency's enforcement efforts concerning tax-exempt groups were "generally deficient."

The former commissioner proposed that a National Commission on Philanthropy be created to regulate tax-exempt organizations. The commission would be an independent organization similar to the Securities and Exchange Commission. Members would be appointed by the president and confirmed by the Senate. Although no organizational change can guarantee an end to the abuses that have plagued the IRS, Cohen's proposal would make it more likely that this part of the tax law would be administered more evenhandedly.

Another possible area for organizational change is the IRS's criminal investigating arm. As has been frequently noted, the operation of this division has presented a more or less continuous string of problems for the IRS. No one contends that the tax laws do not have to be enforced. Some have argued, however, that the present structure, where a single organization is responsible for both criminal and civil enforcement activities, creates serious conflict. One suggested remedy would be to remove the Criminal Investigation Division from the IRS and establish it as a separate agency within the Treasury or Justice Department.

WHY DOES THE IRS RESIST REFORM?

Although there are many explanations for the agency's reluctance to change its ways, a 1987 Treasury Department study indicated that one of the most important factors may be the way the IRS selects its senior managers.[3] The department study discovered that almost all the people so promoted have years and years and years of IRS experience. In other words, lifetime devotion is a de facto requirement for advancement. The report said that while there were some advantages in a system that assured that all senior-level officials had worked for the IRS for at least twenty years, there were also some important disadvantages.

"A selection process that is so internally focused does limit the IRS's exposure to ideas and strategies that have emerged from other public and private sector organizations," the report said. "The IRS may have reduced the opportunities for the creative cross-fertilization of ideas that occurs when executives apply in new organizations the solutions that they used while with a previous organization."[4]

The brief Treasury Department study touched upon a profound truth. The men and women who run the IRS are seriously isolated from the American people. One small example of this isolation occurred in 1988 during one of the regular meetings of the IRS's most prestigious outside advisory board. The commissioner's advisory group is composed of about twenty-five experienced tax practitioners, state tax administrators, business executives, and lawyers. One of the participants at this particular meeting was Marjorie J. Joder, a tough-minded Florida accountant who doesn't hesitate to state her opinions. "The inaccuracies routinely found in correspondence from the IRS are undermining the public's opinion of the agency," she bluntly said. "There used to be an impression among most of my customers that if the IRS sent you a notice, it was right. That impression is fading. Now when people come in the office they assume the IRS has made another mistake."

The senior IRS managers present nodded their heads and smiled politely at Joder's warning. But there is little evidence that they acted. Their passive response was in keeping with agency tradition. After all, public complaints about the IRS's frequently inaccurate service have been steadily increasing for at least ten years. Dozens of secret studies done by the IRS itself confirm many of the public complaints. But the same studies show that serious administrative problems routinely have been ignored. The managers who heard Joder's warning have become defensive. They have known about the mistakes for a very long time. And having spent their entire adult lives working in IRS offices and going to IRS parties and traveling with IRS partners to IRS meetings, they could be forgiven for thinking that they knew best. However understandable, the isolated smugness of the agency's managers makes real reform extremely difficult. A massive infusion of new blood is required.

Notes

1. Thinking about Taxes and the Taxman

1. All the documents quoted on the subject of how the federal government should collect taxes after the United States has been attacked with nuclear weapons were obtained as a result of the Freedom of Information Act. Edward Zuckerman, *The Day After World War Three* (New York: Viking Press, 1984). Edward Zuckerman has graciously given me access to his papers.
2. Charles Adams, *Fight, Flight, Fraud: The Story of Taxation* (Curacao: Euro-Dutch Publishers, 1982), p. 9.
3. As quoted by Barbara W. Tuchman, *A Distant Mirror* (New York: Ballantine Books, 1978), p. 15.
4. As quoted by Cedric Sandford, University of Bath, in an article in the British periodical *Accountancy*, June 1986.
5. As quoted by Margaret Levi, *Of Rule and Revenue* (Berkeley: University of California Press, 1988), p. 122.
6. *McCulloch v. Maryland,* 17 U.S. 316 (1819).
7. *Dobson v. Commissioner,* 320 U.S. 489.
8. The story of the strong wave of opposition to the excise tax in Great Britain and how it fed into the first major tax revolt against the United States has been told by many historians. My account is mostly drawn from Thomas P. Slaughter's wonderful book, *The Whiskey Rebellion: Frontier Epilogue to the American Revolution* (New York: Oxford University Press, 1986). I have also drawn upon John C. Chommie's *The Internal Revenue Service* (New York: Praeger Publishers, 1970).
9. Slaughter, *Whiskey Rebellion,* p. 113.
10. As quoted by Chommie, *The Internal Revenue Service,* p. 3
11. Slaughter, *Whiskey Rebellion,* p. 218.
12. Roy G. Blakey and Gladys C. Blakey, *The Federal Income Tax* (New York: Longmans, Green and Co., 1940), p. 4.
13. Chommie, *The Internal Revenue Service,* p. 10.
14. Ibid., p. 11.
15. Blakey and Blakey, *The Federal Income Tax,* p. 559.
16. Randolph E. Paul, *Taxation in the United States* (Boston: Little, Brown and Company, 1954), p. 104.

17. Susan B. Long, *The Internal Revenue Service: Measuring Tax Offenses and Enforcement Response* (Washington, D.C.: National Institute of Justice, 1980), pp. xvi–xvii.
18. Testimony before the Subcommittee on Oversight, House Ways and Means Committee, March 31, 1988, by Johnny C. Finch, Deputy Director, General Government Division, U.S. General Accounting Office.
19. As quoted by Harold Dubroff, *The United States Tax Court: An Historical Analysis* (Chicago: Commerce Clearing House, Albany Law Reviews, 1979), p. 12.
20. Greg Anrig, Jr., "Even Seasoned Pros Are Confused This Year," *Money*, March 1988, pp. 134–143; "The Pros Flunk Our New Tax Return Test," *Money*, March 1989, pp. 110–121.
21. Joel Slemrod and Nikki Sorum, "The Compliance Cost of the U.S. Individual Income Tax System," *National Tax Journal*, vol. 37, no. 4 (December 1984), pp. 461–74.
22. General Accounting Office, "Telephone Assistance to Taxpayers Can Be Improved" (Washington, D.C.: June 10, 1975), p. 22.
23. General Accounting Office, *Tax Administration: Accessibility, Timeliness, and Accuracy of IRS' Telephone Assistance Program* (Washington, D.C., December 1987), p. 11.
24. Graham T. Allison, *The Essence of Decision: Explaining the Cuban Missile Crisis* (Boston: Little, Brown, 1971).

2. First Encounters With the IRS

1. John F. Kennedy Library, Boston, President's Office Files, Box 63.
2. The Ken Cole memo and others concerning the Nixon administration discussion of the political impact of withholding were obtained at the National Archives, Washington, D.C., Treasury Department files, General Government.
3. The Minnesota survey, "The Compliance Cost of the U.S. Individual Income Tax System," was described by Joel Slemrod and Nikki Sorum, *National Tax Journal*, vol. 37, no. 4 (December 1984), pp. 461–74; the Syracuse study was described by Susan B. Long and Judyth A. Swingen, *Tax Notes*, December 19, 1988, pp. 1343–47.
4. *A Report to the Administrative Conference of the United States on Some Administrative Procedures of the Internal Revenue Service*, Washington, D.C., 1975, Principal Consultant, Charles Davenport.
5. IRS *Report on the Role of Sanctions in Tax Compliance*, 1–2 (Sept. 1963), as quoted in Davenport, *A Report to the Administrative Conference*.
6. Karyl A. Kinsey, American Bar Foundation, *The Social Dynamics of Tax Encounters: Perspectives of Practitioners and Officials*, a paper presented at the IRS Research Conference on the Role of the Tax Practitioner in the Tax System, November 1987.
7. Internal Revenue Service, *1988 Annual Report*, Washington, D.C.
8. General Accounting Office, *IRS' Audits of Individual Taxpayers and Its Audit Quality Control System Need to Be Better* (Washington, D.C., August 15, 1979).
9. IRS study cited by Long, *The Internal Revenue Service*, p. 75.
10. David C. Skinner and George Wachendorf, *Defeating the IRS: A Manual of Strategy and Tactics for Attorneys, Accountants, Businessmen and Other Professionals* (Jacksonville, Fla.: Sunbelt Publishing Co., 1981), p. 29.

3. COLLECTING TAXES

1. The production statistics quoted here and elsewhere in this chapter were provided by the IRS. The agency for many years has published an annual report that contains many pages of tabular material about the tax collection process. In addition, however, the IRS develops for its own management purposes even more detailed statistics concerning many matters not covered in the annual reports. For these I am indebted to Professor Susan B. Long of Syracuse University, whose tireless invocation of the Freedom of Information Act during the last fifteen years has won her a cornucopia of statistical data about the agency. For the description of the major collection procedures of the IRS, I am indebted to a large number of IRS officials who patiently gave a good deal of time explaining how the complex process actually functions.
2. General Accounting Office, *Changes to the Appeals Process Could Improve Settlements and Increase Taxpayers' Satisfaction* (Washington, D.C., July 28, 1982), p. 75.
3. IRS Fact Sheet, "Automated Collection System," June 1984.
4. The discussion of penalties is partly based on a lengthy report prepared by the executive task force of the Commissioner's Penalty Study, *Report on Civil Tax Penalties*, February 21, 1989.
5. The story of Sharon Willits and her troubles with the IRS is drawn from a July 18, 1974, decision by the U.S. Court of Appeals, Fifth Circuit, *Sharon Willits v. W. L. Richardson*, 497 F.2d 240 (1974).
6. The story of Thomas L. Treadway and Shirley Lojeski is told in decisions by federal district court judge Charles R. Weiner on January 23, 1985, and by the U.S. Court of Appeals, Third Circuit, on April 22, 1986. The decisions, *Shirley Lojeski v. Richard Boandl*, are 602 F. Supp. 918 (1984) and 788 F.2d 196 (3rd Cir. 1986). In the spring of 1987, Treadway testified before the Oversight Subcommittee of the Senate Finance Committee chaired by Senator David Pryor, Democrat of Arkansas.

4. NAILING THE TAX CRIMINALS

1. The General Accounting Office has completed a number of reports criticizing the effectiveness of various aspects of the IRS's criminal tax-enforcement efforts. One of the first in the series was published on September 1, 1977, and was titled *Internal Revenue Service's Controls Over the Use of Confidential Informants: Recent Improvement Not Adequate*. On November 6, 1979, the GAO published a report titled *Improved Planning for Developing and Selecting Criminal Tax Cases Can Strengthen Enforcement of Federal Tax Laws*. More recently, on April 25, 1988, the GAO published yet another critical report, *Investigating Illegal Income—Success Uncertain, Improvements Needed*.

The Internal Audit Division of the IRS prepares a constant flow of reports criticizing a wide range of agency programs. These reports are not made public. The author, however, has obtained copies of scores of these documents completed by the Audit Division in the last few years. On April 30, 1986, the division published a report titled *Service Programs Are Not Effectively Promoting Taxpayer Compliance*, which criticized Criminal Investigation Division efforts concerning tens of thousands of tax-shelter investors. On June 17, 1986, the division published a report titled *Improvements Are Needed in the Enforcement of Currency Transaction Reporting and the Use of Currency Data in Compliance Programs.* On July 16, 1987, the division published *Review of the Criminal Investigation Division in the Buffalo District.* This report found no evidence of material fraud. It noted, however, that security in the Buffalo office was lax.

2. Concurring opinion of Justice Jackson in *United States v. Kahriger,* 345 U.S. 22, 36 (1952).

3. Drawn from a series of hearings by the Administrative Practices Subcommittee of the Senate Judiciary Committee held in Washington, Pittsburgh, Boston, and San Francisco. The summary information about IRS wiretapping from 1958 to 1965 was presented to the subcommittee on July 12, 1967.

4. The wiretap policy of the United States remained murky and ambiguous until 1968, when Congress approved legislation prohibiting electronic eavesdropping except by law enforcement officials who had obtained a judicial warrant. The legislation was approved by Congress after the Supreme Court ruled in *Katz* that wiretapping violated the Fourth Amendment of the Constitution. The summary of the confused legal situation before the passage of the wiretap law is drawn from an interview with G. Robert Blakey, now a professor at Notre Dame Law School.

5. Directive on Special Racketeer Investigations from Commissioner Caplin to the assistant commissioner (operations), the regional commissioners, and the district directors dated February 15, 1960. The directive was also mentioned in a letter from Caplin to Attorney General Robert Kennedy on the same day. Caplin promised Kennedy his "unstinting cooperation" in the investigation of racketeers.

5. ORGANIZED CRIME IS AN ENEMY IN OUR MIDST

1. The details of the Capone saga are mostly drawn from John Kobler, *Capone: The Life and World of Al Capone* (New York: G. P. Putnam's Sons, 1971), and Elmer L. Irey, *The Tax Dodgers: The Inside Story of the T-Men's War With America's Political and Underworld Hoodlums,* as told to William J. Slocum (New York: Greenberg, 1948).

2. Irey, *The Tax Dodgers,* p. 26.

3. Kobler, *Capone,* p. 316.

4. Irey, *The Tax Dodgers,* p. 62.

5. Victor S. Navasky, *Kennedy Justice* (New York: Atheneum, 1972), p. 56.

6. Ibid., p. 58.

7. The memorandums of the Nixon and Ford administrations about the IRS's drug enforcement policy were printed as part of the November 11, 1975, oversight hearings into the operations of the IRS held by the Commerce, Consumer and Monetary Affairs Subcommittee of the House Committee on Government Operations. On April 25, 1988, the General Accounting Office released a report, *Investigating Illegal Income—Success Uncertain, Improvements Needed,* that found the IRS's special enforcement program was largely ineffective.

6. NEW MATH AT THE IRS: 2 + 2 = 3

1. The Husby story is based on interviews with the couple and their lawyer, Montie Day, interviews with IRS officials and the assistant U.S. attorney who handled the case for the government, Jay Weill, and the decision of Federal District Judge Stanley A. Weigel, *Husby v. United States.*

2. For some years, the IRS's Inspection Division has churned out reports on the administrative failings of the agency. The reports are marked "For Official Use Only" and the agency goes to great lengths to keep them out of the hands of the public. One example of agency concern involved the Office of Management and Budget, the branch of the White House authorized to supervise the operations of the executive branch. When an OMB official with oversight of the agency requested that the IRS start sending him the reports, it simply failed to comply. Despite the IRS's reluctance, I managed to obtain a large number of the internal audit reports through an underground source in the agency.

3. Arthur Howe, *The Philadelphia Enquirer,* March 21, 1985. This was one of a series of ground-breaking articles by Howe and the *Enquirer* on the 1985 collapse of the IRS. Howe's coverage of what was clearly a major national story was unique.

4. General Accounting Office, *Tax Administration: IRS Needs to Improve Handling of Taxpayer Correspondence,* (Washington, D.C., July 1988).

5. Privacy Protection Study Commission, *Personal Privacy in an Information Age* (Washington, D.C.: Government Printing Office, July 1977), p. 537.

6. General Accounting Office, *Internal Revenue Service: Need to Improve the Revenue Accounting Control System,* June 1988.

7. General Accounting Office, *Tax Administration: Difficulties in Accurately Estimating Tax Examination Yield,* August 1988.

7. THE ZEALOTS

1. Internal Revenue Service, ERR-6 Task Force Report, *The Treatment of Managers* (Washington, D.C.: U.S. Government Printing Office, 1987), p. 9.

2. The recent part of the story was told in *U.S. v. Heller,* 830 F.2d 150 (11th Cir. 1987) and several May 1988 stories by Stephen J. Hedges, a reporter with the *Miami Herald.* The early part of the story about Operation Leprechaun is based mostly on December 2, 1975, hearings by the Subcommittee on Oversight of the House Ways and Means Committee.

3. *Ronald McKelvey v. Robert M. McKeever, District Director, Internal Revenue Service,* January 26, 1976.

4. This story was broken in August 1988 by an excellent series of articles by Ann Carnahan of the *Rocky Mountain News.* Following Carnahan's original work, Representative Pat Schroeder and her staff demanded additional confirming details from the IRS.

5. Hearings, Subcommittee of the Department of the Treasury, Senate Committee on Appropriations, Ninety-third Congress, First Session, February 27–March 1, 1973, p. 681.

6. *USA v. Omni International Corp.,* 634 F. Supp. 1414 (1986).

8. BRIBES, BOODLE, AND BUYOFFS

1. The story of Stan Welli, George Ecola, and Ron Koperniak is based on their official complaints to the IRS, the decision of an independent hearing examiner concerning their harassment by the IRS, an interview with Teddy Kern, assistant director for Inspection, interviews with the three men, and their testimony to the House Commerce, Consumer, and Monetary Affairs Subcommittee of the House Government

Operations Committee on July 26, 1989. It also is supported by the sixty-one-page investigative report presented to the subcommittee at those same hearings by subcommittee investigators Leonard Bernard and Richard Stana. Santella himself declined to provide a detailed response to the various charges that had been made about his activities. In a letter to me dated May 17, 1989, two months before the hearing, Santella limited himself to saying that "this situation is very complex" and that I had obtained only "one side of the story."

2. Many of the important elements of the Saranow story were first disclosed on November 16, 1987, by Richard Behar, a superb investigative reporter then working for *Forbes* magazine. Saranow discussed many of the allegations that had been made about him by *Forbes* and other publications in two lengthy telephone interviews he granted me in the summer of 1988. Various aspects of Saranow's career and associates are based on documents obtained from the state of Illinois, the Municipal Court of Orange County, and the Investigation Division of the IRS. A central participant in the investigation of Saranow was Octavio Pena, the president of Lynch International, an international security consulting company with headquarters in New Jersey. He has granted me lengthy interviews. As the result of a civil suit involving two national clothing manufacturers—Jordache and Guess? Jeans—depositions were taken that also provided useful information about Saranow and his relations with Guess? Finally, the case was the subject of a detailed investigation and report by Leonard Bernard and Richard Stana of the Commerce, Consumer and Monetary Affairs Subcommittee of the House Government Operations Committee. As was the case with other parts of their report, this section was made a part of the subcommittee's hearing on July 25, 1989.

3. The Langone story is based on interviews with several IRS agents who requested anonymity, an examination of Langone's travel vouchers obtained from the IRS as the result of a request under the Freedom of Information Act, and the report of Leonard Bernard and Richard Stana presented to the Commerce, Consumer and Monetary Affairs Subcommittee of the House Government Operations Committee on July 25, 1989.

4. The story of John and Alice McManus is based on interviews with several IRS agents who requested anonymity; the legal documents filed in Tax Court by McManus and the IRS; an interview with Vernon Acree, a retired IRS executive; and a brief summary of the case included in the report of Leonard Bernard and Richard Stana to the Commerce, Consumer and Monetary Affairs Subcommittee of the House Government Operations Committee on July 27, 1989.

5. Internal Revenue Service Memorandum, February 22, 1989, *Strategic Initiative ERR-17: Improve Ethics, Integrity and Conduct Awareness.* The memo was directed to all executives and office managers and incorporated the January 23, 1989, decision memo establishing a year-long program designed to improve the agency's corruption prevention efforts.

6. Harry Jaffe, *Philadelphia* magazine, March 1987.

7. Charles Toll's testimony in the Kale trial provided a fascinating portrait of corruption in the IRS. The testimony indicated that, at least in that particular branch of the IRS, corruption had become a systematic and deeply entrenched part of the agency, very similar to what has been repeatedly uncovered in the police departments of New York, Chicago, Miami, and many other big cities. Kale's trial, *United States v. William*

Kale, Number 86-00050, went before a jury in the Eastern District of Pennsylvania on July 8, 1986. Handling the case was Federal District Judge J. William Ditter, Jr.

9. INFLUENCE AT THE TOP

1. Remarks of Donald C. Alexander, Commissioner of Internal Revenue, prepared for delivery before the Cleveland Tax Institute, Internal Revenue Service News Release, IR–1336, November 15, 1973.
2. Edward T. Pound, "Untoward Tips: How William Simon Led Some Friends Astray on Oil Venture," *The Wall Street Journal,* December 22, 1986, page 1.
3. The 1947 Commodity Exchange Commission report and the 1950 letter of the secretary of agriculture were cited in an article by Jerry Knight in *The Washington Post* of July 23, 1981, and in the July 27, 1981, edition of *World Business Weekly.*
4. Text of Dita Beard memo as released by Jack Anderson, the Washington columnist, *The New York Times,* March 3, 1972, p. 20.
5. *The New York Times,* March 16, 1972, p. 1.
6. *The New York Times,* June 8, 1974, p. 1.
7. Memorandum from Richard J. Davis to Henry S. Ruth, head of the Watergate Special Prosecutive Force, *Report of the ITT Task Force,* Washington, August 25, 1975, pp. 115–19.
8. The October 1969 ruling, which was to become the center of so much controversy, eventually became known as Revenue Ruling 72–345. This is because 1972 was the year in which most of what previously had been a private ruling was published as a public document.
9. Robert A. Caro, *The Years of Lyndon Johnson: The Path to Power* (New York: Alfred A. Knopf, 1982), pp. 742–53; Ronnie Dugger, *The Politician: The Life and Times of Lyndon Johnson* (New York: W. W. Norton, 1982), pp. 228–29, 258.
10. During the research for his book on Johnson, Caro explains in his note on sources, Julia Gary, the daughter of IRS agent Elmer C. Werner, gave Caro her father's files on the Brown & Root investigation.

10. PRESIDENTS, POLITICS, AND THE IRS

1. The story about the Navy League's attack on President Hoover and how it prompted the Hoover administration to launch a secret retaliatory investigation by the FBI and what was then called the Internal Revenue Bureau is told by Kenneth O'Reilly, "Herbert Hoover and the FBI," *The Annals of Iowa,* vol. 47, no. 1, summer 1983.
2. One such study is Craig Lloyd, *Aggressive Introvert: A Study of Herbert Hoover and Public Relations Management, 1912–1932* (Columbus, Ohio: Ohio State University Press, 1972).
3. Letter from J. Edgar Hoover to Presidential Secretary Richey, November 2, 1931.
4. "Tax Return Confidentiality: A Report to the Steering Committee for the Internal Revenue Service Project of the Administrative Conference of the United States," Washington, D.C., July 1975, pp. 6–3.
5. Irey, *The Tax Dodgers,* pp. xii–xiii.
6. The Justice Department memo, dated January 17, 1934, was written by J. H. McEvers and H. C. Crowter, two department lawyers. It bore the heading, "In re: Andrew W. Mellon." The seventeen-page single-spaced memo summarizes a number of tax ques-

tions concerning the holdings of Mellon and argues they are without merit. It was kindly provided me by the Mellon family in December 1988.

7. Randolph E. Paul, *Taxation in the United States* (Boston: Little, Brown and Company, 1954) pp. 151–52.

8. Ibid., p. 151.

9. T. Harry Williams, *Huey Long* (New York: Vintage Books, 1981) p. 5.

10. Irey, *The Tax Dodgers*, pp. 88–117.

11. Williams, *Huey Long*, p. 796.

12. Box 369, Confidential Reports About People, 1933, 1934, and 1935, Morgenthau Collection, Franklin D. Roosevelt Library, Hyde Park, N.Y.

13. Irey, *The Tax Dodgers*, p. 97.

14. Box 372, Confidential Reports about People, 1940, Morgenthau Collection, Franklin D. Roosevelt Library, Hyde Park, N.Y.

15. Ted Morgan, *FDR: A Biography* (New York: Simon and Schuster, 1985), p. 554.

16. Elmer Irey memo to Secretary Morgenthau, June 25, 1941, Box 372, Confidential Reports about People, 1941, Morgenthau Collection, Franklin D. Roosevelt Library, Hyde Park, N.Y.

17. Report to the Chief, Intelligence Unit, Bureau of Internal Revenue, Washington, D.C. In re: Paul Robeson, p. 13. Box 372, Confidential Reports about People, 1941, Morgenthau Collection, Franklin D. Roosevelt Library, Hyde Park, N.Y.

18. Box 375, Confidential Reports about People, 1944, Morgenthau Collection, Franklin D. Roosevelt Library, Hyde Park, N.Y.

19. Tip O'Neill with William Novak, *Man of the House*, (New York: Random House, 1987), pp. 132–34.

20. Report of the Committee on the Judiciary, House of Representatives, *Impeachment of Richard M. Nixon, President of the United States*, August 20, 1974, p. 141.

11. CURBING POLITICAL DISSENT, MAINTAINING THE OFFICIAL LINE, AND SUPPRESSING UNPOPULAR VIEWS

1 The correspondence between the IRS and the Minnesota Association for the Improvement of Science Education and the association's subsequent exchanges with Senator David Durenberger and two House members was provided me by John D. Bohlig, a lawyer from New Brighton, Minnesota, who served on the association's board.

2. William J. Lehrfeld, "The Taxation of Ideology," *Catholic University Law Review*, vol. 29, no. 50 (1969), pp. 53–54

3. Bruce R. Hopkins, *The Law of Tax Exempt Organizations*, 5th ed. (New York: John Wiley & Sons, 1987), p. 4. Hopkins explains that the tax exemption applied to the income tax law approved by Congress in 1894 subsequently was declared to be unconstitutional. With the approval of a constitutional amendment and the passage of the Revenue Act of 1913, however, income tax exemption for selected charities again became the law of the land.

4. Levine's report and many other IRS documents were obtained as a result of a request under the Freedom of Information Act made on June 14, 1988, by NACLA's lawyer, Michael Krinsky, who provided them to the author.

5. Charles L. Heatherly, ed., *Mandate for Leadership: Policy Management in a Conservative Administration* (Washington: The Heritage Foundation, 1981), pp. 934–940.
6. 1948 CCH Income Tax Service. Paragraph 6075, P.S.S-613, February 4, 1948.
7. Lehrfeld, "The Taxation of Ideology."
8. Frank J. Donner, *The Age of Surveillance* (New York: Alfred A. Knopf, 1980), p. 326.
9. Taylor Branch, *Parting the Waters: America in the King Years, 1954–63* (New York: Simon and Schuster, 1988), p. 269.
10. U.S. Senate, Select Committee to Study Governmental Operations with Respect to Intelligence Activities, Final Report, *Supplementary Detailed Staff Reports,* Book III, April 1976, p. 847.
11. U.S. Senate, Select Committee to Study Governmental Operations with Respect to Intelligence Activities, Final Report, *Intelligence Activities and the Rights of Americans,* Book II, April 1976, pp. 53–54.
12. U.S. Senate, Select Committee to Study Governmental Operations with Respect to Intelligence Activities, Final Report, Book II, April 26, 1967, p. 229.
13. U.S. Senate, Select Committee to Study Governmental Operations with Respect to Intelligence Activities, Hearings, Volume 3, *Internal Revenue Service,* October 2, 1975, p. 46.
14. Chronology of the Development of the Special Service Staff of the IRS prepared for the chairman of the Senate Subcommittee on Foundations, January 1975.
15. Oliver Houck, "With Charity for All," *The Yale Law Journal,* vol. 93, No. 8 (July 1984), 1419.

12. OVERSIGHT: WHY THE WATCHDOGS SELDOM BARK

1. *The National Cyclopedia of American Biography,* vol. 30 (New York: James T. White & Company, 1943), pp. 32–33.
2. Harvey O'Connor, *Mellon's Millions: The Life and Times of Andrew W. Mellon* (New York: Blue Ribbon Books, 1935), p. 157.
3. The retaliation against Couzens is described by Blakey and Blakey, *The Federal Income Tax,* pp. 552–57; Paul, *Taxation in the United States,* p. 150, and Dubroff, *The United States Tax Court,* p. 26.
4. Both William Lambert and Sheldon Cohen in separate interviews confirmed the congratulatory telephone conversation from the commissioner.
5. The story about the IRS and Senator Montoya is based on interviews with several of the surviving participants, including Bob Woodward of the *Washington Post* and Donald C. Alexander, the IRS commisssioner at the time, on Woodward's story about Montoya that ran in the *Post* October 19, 1975, and on Montoya's statement to the Senate about the affair at page S 20608 of the Congressional Record on November 20, 1975. Some background information about the case also came from a deposition completed for the IRS's Internal Security Division by William B. Orr on March 18, 1976. The subject of this deposition was the information Orr had provided Woodward concerning Montoya.
6. Much of the information concerning Senator Pryor and his tough-minded efforts to disclose the abuses of the IRS was obtained by covering the hearings of the IRS Oversight Subcommittee, which he heads. The senator also granted me several interviews. Jeff Trinca, a lawyer on the senator's staff, and Damon Thompson, his press

secretary, also were extremely generous in the time they found to explain various aspects of the agency and the senator's ultimately successful effort to pass remedial legislation.

13. Tax Collection in the Next Decade

1. Department of Treasury (Internal Revenue Service), Consolidated Listing of Tax Information Exchanged Between State Agencies and the Internal Revenue Service for Tax Administration Purposes, Document 6724 (Rev. 4–88) (Washington, D.C.: Government Printing Office, 1988).
2. National Association of Tax Administrators, Proceedings of the Ninth Annual Workshop, March 22–25, 1987, Willis C. Kartorie, Pennsylvania Department of Revenue, "Pennsylvania's Cross-Matching Initiatives" (Washington, D.C.: Federation of Tax Administrators, 1987), pp. 25–28.
3. National Association of Tax Administrators, Proceedings of the Eighth National Workshop, August 24–27, 1986, Pat Callahan, IRS, "Scantel—A Program for Direct Access to Telephone Records for Locating and Contacting Taxpayers" (Washington, D.C.: Federation of Tax Administrators, 1986), pp. 22–23.
4. Working Group on Federalism, White House Domestic Policy Council, The Status of Federalism in America (Washington, D.C.: Government Printing Office, November 1986), p. 1.
5. Ibid., p. 2.
6. Roger H. Davis, FBI Law Enforcement Bulletin, Federal Bureau of Investigation (Washington, D.C.: U.S. Department of Justice, December 1981).
7. Joseph F. Coates, "Scenarios of Five Federal Agencies (1991–95) as Shaped by Information Technology," a report to the Federal Government Information Technology Project, the Office of Technology Assessment, U.S. Congress, June 1985.
8. David Burnham, The Rise of the Computer State (New York: Random House, 1983), p. 192, from a 1971 hearing by the Administrative Practices Subcommittee, Senate Judiciary Committee.
9. Alexis de Tocqueville, Democracy in America (New York: Vintage, 1945), vol. 2, p. 335.
10. Ibid., p. 336.
11. Ibid., p. 337.

14. The Last Word

1. Report and Recommendations, American Bar Association Commission on Taxpayer Compliance, July 1987.
2. Ibid., page 19.
3. Office of the Assistant Secretary of the Treasury (Management), Department of Treasury, "A Review of the IRS Executive Selection and Development Program" (Washington, D.C., May 1987).
4. Ibid., p. ii.

Selected Bibliography

A great deal has been written about taxes, tax policy, and the tax code. Surprisingly little has been written about the actual operations of the IRS. One source of information is Congress—although as noted elsewhere, the House Ways and Means Committee and the Senate Finance Committee have rarely deigned to seriously examine the workings of the agency. As discussed in greater detail below, the General Accounting Office has done a small number of excellent studies about specific subjects concerning the IRS.

A number of biographies and autobiographies proved valuable. Elmer Irey, a colorful figure in the tax agency during the twenties and thirties, wrote a revealing book about the use of the bureau for political purposes. The first volume of Robert Caro's ground-breaking history of Lyndon B. Johnson contains a fascinating story about Roosevelt's use of the agency to help Johnson.

A number of law journal articles have proved useful.

HOUSE OF REPRESENTATIVES

Hearings, October 3, 1951, and January 22, 23, 24, and 25, 1952, Proposals for Strengthening Tax Administration, Subcommittee on Administration of the Internal Revenue Laws, House Committee on Ways and Means, 1952.

Report, Internal Revenue Investigation, Subcommittee on Administration of the Internal Revenue Laws, House Committee on Ways and Means, 1953.

Hearings, Administration of the Freedom of Information Act, House Subcommittee on Foreign Operations and Government Information, House Committee on Government Operations, April 1972.

Report, Administration of the Freedom of Information Act, Subcommittee on Foreign Operations and Government Information, House Committee on Government Operations, September 20, 1972

Report, Impeachment of Richard M. Nixon, President of the United States, House Committee on the Judiciary, August 20, 1974.

Oversight Hearings into the Operations of the IRS, Subcommittee on Commerce, Consumer, and Monetary Affairs, House Committee on Government Operations, May 14, 22; June 20, 24; July 8, 29, and 31, 1975.

Oversight Hearings into the Operations of the IRS (Operation Tradewinds, Project Have, and Narcotics Traffickers Program), Subcommittee on Commerce, Consumer, and

Monetary Affairs, House Committee on Government Operations, October 6, November 4 and 11, 1975.

Hearings, Operation Leprechaun, Subcommittee on Oversight, House Committee on Ways and Means, December 2, 1975.

SENATE

Hearings, Select Committee on Investigation of the Bureau of Internal Revenue, March 14, 1924 (James E. Watson).

Hearings, Taxpayer Assistance and Compliance Programs, Subcommittee of the Department of Treasury, U.S. Postal Service, and General Appropriations, Senate Committee on Appropriations, February 27 and 28, 1973 (Montoya).

Political Intelligence in the Internal Revenue Service: The Special Service Staff, a documentary analysis prepared by the staff of the Subcommittee on Constitutional Rights, Committee on the Judiciary, December 1974 (Ervin).

Hearings, Federal Tax Return Privacy, Subcommittee on Administration of the Internal Revenue Code, Senate Finance Committee, April 21, 1975 (Haskell).

Hearings, Internal Revenue Service, Select Committee to Study Governmental Operations with Respect to Intelligence Activities, October 2, 1975 (Church).

The Electronic Supervisor: New Technology, New Tensions, Report by the Office of Technology Assessment, United States Congress, September 1987.

OTHER GOVERNMENT PUBLICATIONS

A Report to the Administrative Conference of the United States on Some Administrative Procedures of the Internal Revenue Service, principal consultant, Charles Davenport, October 1975.

Personal Privacy in an Information Society, Report of the Privacy Protection Study Commission, July 1977.

The Internal Revenue Service: Measuring Tax Offenses and Enforcement Response, Susan B. Long, National Institute of Justice, U.S. Department of Justice, 1980.

Revenue Office Job Stress: A Nationwide Assessment of Job Stressors and Their Implications for Health and Organizational Effectiveness, an October 6, 1985, IRS research study by Bronston T. Mayes, California State University, Fullerton, Calif.

Assaults and Threats Against Internal Revenue Service Employees, a September 1986 IRS study by Research Management Associates, Inc., Alexandria, Va.

SPECIAL NOTE

Sometime in 1972 or 1973 the General Accounting Office, an investigative arm of Congress, sought to undertake examinations of the IRS. The IRS strenuously objected. But beginning in 1974 and 1975, the GAO was allowed to study the IRS. Since that time, the GAO has published more than two hundred substantive reports on various aspects of tax agency operations and policy. The quality of these reports has varied. In the first years, 1975 through 1978, many were of top quality. From 1979 through about 1987, many studies were superficial and poorly researched. Beginning about 1988, however, the quality of the GAO investigations improved. The two hundred plus reports are too numerous to list here. The GAO, however, has a computerized list of all its reports touching in any way on the IRS.

The IRS publishes an annual report. In recent years, the reports have contained about forty pages of text, twenty pages of selected statistics about the operations of the IRS, and a few more pages containing an organizational chart, a map showing regional and district boundaries and locations of major offices, and a listing of the names of current senior officials of the agency and all past IRS commissioners. For a student of the IRS, the annual reports sometimes can provide useful information and insights.

Books

Adams, Charles W. *Fight, Flight, Fraud: The Story of Taxation.* Curacao, Netherlands Antilles: Euro-Dutch Publishers, 1982.

Blakey, Roy G., and Gladys C. Blakey. *The Federal Income Tax.* New York: Longmans, Green and Co., 1940.

Branch, Taylor. *Parting the Waters: America in the King Years 1954–63.* New York: Simon and Schuster, 1988.

Caro, Robert A. *The Path to Power.* New York: Alfred A. Knopf, 1982.

Chommie, John C. *The Internal Revenue Service.* New York: Praeger, 1970.

Donner, Frank J. *The Age of Surveillance.* New York: Alfred A. Knopf, 1980.

Dubroff, Harold. *The United States Tax Court: An Historical Analysis.* Chicago: Commerce Clearing House, 1979.

Eisenstein, Louis. *The Ideologies of Taxation.* New York: The Ronald Press Company, 1961.

Frankel, Sandor, and Robert S. Fink. *You Can Protect Yourself from the IRS.* New York: A Fireside Book, Simon & Schuster, 1987.

Garson, Barbara. *The Electronic Sweatshop: How Computers Are Transforming the Office of the Future into the Factory of the Past.* New York: Simon & Schuster, 1988.

Garza, Hedda, ed. *The Watergate Investigation Index: House Judiciary Committee Hearings and Report on Impeachment.* Wilmington: SR Scholarly Resources Inc., 1985.

Irey, Elmer L., as told to William J. Slocum. *The Tax Dodgers: The Inside Story of the T-Man's War With America's Political and Underworld Hoodlums.* New York: Greenberg, 1948.

Kelley, Dean M. *Why Churches Should Not Pay Taxes.* New York: Harper & Row, 1977.

Kobler, John. *Capone: The Life and World of Al Capone.* New York: G. P. Putnam's Sons, 1971.

Kilpatrick, William A. *The Big Tax Lie.* New York: Simon & Schuster, 1986.

Kraemer, Kenneth L., William H. Dutton, and Alana Northrop. *The Management of Information Systems.* New York: Columbia University Press, 1981.

Laudon, Kenneth C., *Dossier Society: Value Choices in the Design of National Information Systems.* New York: Columbia University Press, 1986.

Laudon, Kenneth C., and Jane Price Laudon. *Management Information Systems.* New York: Macmillan Publishing Company, 1988.

Lieberman, Jethro K. *How the Government Breaks the Law.* New York: Stein and Day, 1972.

Long, Edward V. *The Intruders: The Invasion of Privacy by Government and Industry.* New York: Praeger, 1967.

Lowi, Theodore J. *The End of Liberalism: The Second Republic of the United States,* 2nd ed., New York: W. W. Norton & Company, 1979.

Navasky, Victor S. *Kennedy Justice.* New York: Atheneum, 1971.

Nisbet, Robert. *The Present Age: Progress and Anarchy in Modern America.* New York: Harper & Row, 1988.

O'Connor, Harvey. *Mellon's Millions: The Life and Times of Andrew W. Mellon.* New York: Blue Ribbon Books, Inc., 1935.

O'Neill, Tip, with William Novak. *Man of the House.* New York: Random House, 1987.

Oudes, Bruce, ed., *From: The President, Richard Nixon's Secret Files.* New York: Harper & Row, 1989.

Paul, Randolph E. *Taxation in the United States.* Boston: Little, Brown and Company, 1954.

Shogun, Robert. *A Question of Judgment: The Fortas Case and the Struggle for the Supreme Court.* Indianapolis and New York: The Bobbs-Merrill Company, 1972.

Skinner, David C., and George Wachendorf. *Defeating the IRS, A Manual of Strategy and Tactics for Attorneys, Accountants, Businessmen and Other Professionals.* Jacksonville, Fla.: Sunbelt Publishing Company, 1981.

Slaughter, Thomas P. *The Whiskey Rebellion.* New York and Oxford: Oxford University Press, 1986.

Stern, Philip M. *The Rape of the Taxpayer.* New York: Random House, 1972.

Strassels, Paul N., with Robert Wool. *All You Need to Know About the IRS: A Taxpayer's Guide.* New York: Random House, 1979.

Theoharis, Athan G., and John Stuart Cox. *The Boss: J. Edgar Hoover and the Great American Inquisition.* Philadelphia: Temple University Press, 1988.

Tocqueville, Alexis de. *Democracy in America.* New York: Vintage Books, 1945.

Wade, Jack Warren, Jr. *When You Owe the IRS.* New York: Macmillan, 1983.

Webber, Carolyn, and Aaron Wildavsky. *A History of Taxation and Expenditure in the Western World.* New York: Simon and Schuster, 1986.

Williams, T. Harry. *Huey Long.* New York: Alfred A. Knopf, Inc. 1969; Vintage Books, 1981.

Wolfman, Bernard, Jonathan L. F. Silver, Marjorie A. Silver. *Dissent Without Opinion: The Behavior of William O. Douglas in Federal Tax Cases.* Philadelphia: University of Pennsylvania, 1973.

Zuckerman, Edward. *The Day After World War III.* New York: The Viking Press, 1984.

LAW JOURNAL ARTICLES

"Charities, Law-Making, and the Constitution: The Validity of the Restrictions on Influencing Legislation." Thomas A. Troyer. 31st Annual N.Y.U. Institute on Federal Taxation, 1973.

"'Church' in the Internal Revenue Code: The Definitional Problems." Charles M. Whelan. *Fordham Law Review,* vol. 45, 1977.

"Civil Tax Fraud for Failure to File a Return." Stephen E. Silver. *Arizona Law Review,* vol. 13, 1971.

"Civilization at a Discount: The Problem of Tax Evasion." Michael W. Spicer. *National Tax Journal,* vol. 34.

"Constitutionality of Federal Tuition Tax Credits." Leonard J. Henzke, Jr. *Temple Law Quarterly,* vol. 56, no. 4, 1983.

"Effects of the Recent FOIA Decision That IRS Must Publish Its Internal Memoranda." John L. Snyder. *The Journal of Taxation,* June 1980.

"IRS Statistics Show Decline in Prosecuting of Tax Frauds." Alan Kohn. *New York Law Journal,* April 19, 1982.

"IRS Use of Wiretap Evidence in Civil Tax Proceedings in Doubt Despite Recent Case." Stephen E. Silver. *The Journal of Taxation,* May 1982.

"Render Unto Uncle Sam That Which Is Uncle Sam's: The IRS and Tax Protest Evangelism." Ray Walden. *Nebraska Law Review,* vol. 61, 1982.

"Revocation of Tax Exemptions and Tax Deductions for Donations to 501 (c) (3) Organizations on Statutory and Constitutional Grounds." Michael Yaffa. *UCLA Law Review,* vol. 30, 1983.

"Taxation in the People's Republic of China: The System and Its Function." Don R. Castleman. *Albany Law Review,* vol. 46, 1982.

"Terminating the Taxpayer's Taxable Year: How IRS Uses It Against Narcotics Suspects." Stephen E. Silver. *The Journal of Taxation,* February 1974.

"Use of the Freedom of Information Act in Federal Tax Matters." James E. Merritt. 39th Annual N.Y.U. Institute on Federal Taxation, 1979.

"*United States v. Sun Myung Moon*: The Precedent for Tax Fraud Prosecution of Local Pastors." Alfred J. Sciarrino. *Southern Illinois University Law Journal,* vol. 1984, no. 2. 1984–1985.

" 'Voluntary' Self-Assessment? The Unwilling Extraction of Taxpayer Information." Curtis J. Berger. *University of Pittsburgh Law Review,* vol. 42, 1981.

"With Charity for All." Oliver A. Houck. *The Yale Law Journal,* vol. 93, no. 8, July 1984.

Appendix

All bureaucracies are driven to collect statistics about their activities. It is of course entirely predictable that the IRS—the largest and most computerized of all enforcement agencies in the United States—is especially aggressive in attempting to quantify all of its activities.

The IRS's passion for collecting its numbers has both positive and negative consequences. Properly analyzed, the statistics can help the managers of the IRS and the American people to judge the work performed by the men and women who collect their taxes. Properly used, the numbers can raise questions that identify administrative problems. Statistics thus can serve as an important tool of oversight—by the IRS and by the American people through such institutions as Congress, the media, public interest groups, and the academic community.

Improperly analyzed, on the other hand, the statistics can lead Congress to adopt harmful and counterproductive tax collection policies. Improperly used, the numbers can lead unimaginative IRS managers to set arbitrary performance quotas that push the people they command to act like unthinking robots in their dealings with taxpayers.

The following tables were largely drawn from IRS computer tapes and other agency information sources that, in response to her requests under the Freedom of Information Act, were provided to Dr. Susan B. Long, professor of quantitative methods at Syracuse University's School of Management and the director of the Center for Tax Studies. The computer programing to prepare these tables was done by Young Park, a doctoral student at Syracuse University and a research assistant at the Tax Center.

The tables describe key activities of the IRS in each of the agency's seven regions and, where available, each of its sixty-three districts for the years 1986, 1987, and 1988. The statistics in each of the tables concern the rate at which the activities occurred rather than the actual number of events. This allows the reader to compare the activities in one region or district with the activities in another. Variations in the activity rates are influenced by a number of factors, some of which are in the control of the IRS and some of which are not. The number and training level of agency employees working in each area, for example, obviously are important factors determining what the agency accomplishes. But the development of a boom economy in one state and a recession in another also can affect IRS activities. The accompanying map shows the boundaries of these regions and districts.

Table 1 describes the number of individual tax returns that the IRS examined in each region and district in relation to the number of individual tax returns that were filed in each region and district for the three years. A fourth column presents the average adjusted gross income reported on the individual tax returns for the 1987 tax year. These statistics are expressed in terms of the number of examinations conducted by the IRS for every 1,000 individual tax returns.

Table 2 presents the number of first notices that the IRS sent out to both individual and business taxpayers in the three years for each of the seven regions in relation to the number of individual and business tax returns filed in each region. The computer-generated first notices are issued by the IRS to taxpayers believed to be delinquent in paying assessed taxes. Because of the way these notices are generated by the IRS, it is not possible to produce first-notice statistics at the district level. The table also shows the average number of dollars claimed in the first notices of each region. The first-notice statistics are expressed in terms of the number of such notices for every 1,000 individual tax returns.

Table 3 shows the number of Taxpayer Delinquency Accounts (TDAs) in each region in relation to the number of first notices filed in each region for both individuals and businesses. A TDA designation indicates that the IRS considers that a serious delinquency is involved. The table also shows the average dollars claimed for each TDA in each region for both individuals and businesses. The statistics are expressed in terms of the number of TDAs for every 1,000 first notices.

Table 4 gives the number of collection activities of the IRS in relation to the number of TDAs. These activities—where the IRS moves to take control of the assets of a taxpayer—include levies, liens, and actual seizures of such real property as cars. As a result of how levies and liens are created within the IRS, complete district statistics are not available. The number of levies and liens gives an exaggerated impression of the number of taxpayers who receive them. Levies are typically issued to a taxpayer's employer and bank. Liens are usually filed with the county office that maintains the property records where a taxpayer lives or conducts a business. Thus, several levies and liens often are issued on a single taxpayer delinquent account. The collection enforcement activities are expressed in terms of the numbers of levies, liens, and seizures in relation to 1,000 TDAs.

Table 5 describes the number of seizures in each district in relation to the number of TDAs. Seizures, situations where the IRS takes possession of real property, are far less common than levies and liens. This table shows the number of seizures for every 1,000 TDAs.

Table 6 describes the number of installment agreements that each region and district entered into in relation to the number of TDAs that were issued in these areas. Once again, the table shows the number of installment agreements for every 1,000 TDAs.

Table 1

INDIVIDUAL TAX RETURNS EXAMINED PER 1,000 RETURNS FILED

Internal Revenue Service Office						Average
Region	State	District	1986	1987	1988	Income*
UNITED STATES	ALL	ALL	11	11	10	$25,815
NORTH ATLANTIC	ALL	ALL	9	10	9	29,550
	CT	HARTFORD	8	7	6	33,357
	MA	BOSTON	6	6	5	29,500
	ME	AUGUSTA	6	5	5	22,836
	NH	PORTSMOUTH	6	6	5	28,341
	NY	ALL	10	9	8	29,740
		ALBANY	8	7	5	
		BROOKLYN	9	8	7	
		BUFFALO	7	7	6	
		MANHATTAN	15	13	14	
	RI	PROVIDENCE	5	5	8	25,621
	VT	BURLINGTON	8	7	8	23,409
MID-ATLANTIC	ALL	ALL	9	7	7	27,751
	DE	WILMINGTON	9	8	8	26,965
	MD	BALTIMORE	10	8	8	29,186
	NJ	NEWARK	9	6	5	31,067
	PA	ALL	7	7	6	24,746
		PHILADELPHIA	7	7	6	
		PITTSBURGH	7	6	6	
	VA	RICHMOND	8	6	6	27,551
SOUTHEAST	ALL	ALL	10	8	8	23,334
	AL	BIRMINGHAM	9	8	8	22,408
	AR	LITTLE ROCK	8	6	7	20,151
	FL	ALL	9	7	7	25,355
		FT. LAUDERDALE		7	7	
		JACKSONVILLE	9	7	7	
	GA	ATLANTA	10	9	10	24,891
	LA	NEW ORLEANS	12	10	9	21,452
	MS	JACKSON	8	8	9	19,230
	NC	GREENSBORO	7	6	5	23,052
	SC	COLUMBIA	7	6	5	22,051
	TN	NASHVILLE	9	7	7	22,615
CENTRAL	ALL	ALL	7	9	7	24,586
	IN	INDIANAPOLIS	6	8	8	23,885
	KY	LOUISVILLE	5	6	6	21,880
	MI	DETROIT	7	7	6	26,581
	OH	ALL	7	9	6	24,501
		CINCINNATI	7	7	7	
		CLEVELAND	8	11	6	

Table 1 *(Continued)*

Region	State	District	1986	1987	1988	Average Income*
	WV	PARKERSBURG	7	7	6	21,573
MIDWEST	ALL	ALL	9	9	9	24,849
	IA	DES MOINES	7	6	7	22,032
	IL	ALL	9	9	9	27,466
		CHICAGO	9	10	9	
		SPRINGFIELD	7	7	8	
	MN	ST. PAUL	8	9	8	25,216
	MO	ST. LOUIS	7	8	7	24,175
	MT	HELENA	12	12	10	19,129
	ND	FARGO	15	14	11	20,032
	NE	OMAHA	8	9	8	21,887
	SD	ABERDEEN	9	7	7	18,823
	WI	MILWAUKEE	7	6	5	23,880
SOUTHWEST	ALL	ALL	15	16	15	24,041
	AZ	PHOENIX	14	10	9	24,664
	CO	DENVER	11	11	11	25,240
	KS	WICHITA	10	10	8	24,339
	NM	ALBUQUERQUE	9	9	8	20,909
	OK	OKLAHOMA CITY	15	15	13	22,152
	TX	ALL	15	14	12	24,335
		AUSTIN	13	12	11	
		DALLAS	15	12	12	
		HOUSTON	18	19	15	
	UT	SALT LAKE CITY	18	16	11	23,215
	WY	CHEYENNE	18	18	15	22,951
WESTERN	ALL	ALL	16	16	15	27,302
	AK	ANCHORAGE	23	26	15	20,769
	CA	ALL	16	13	12	28,553
		LAGUNA NIGUEL	15	14	13	
		LOS ANGELES	17	12	12	
		SACRAMENTO	13	10	9	
		SAN FRANCISCO	21	18	14	
		SAN JOSE	14	12	12	
	HI	HONOLULU	14	9	7	25,025
	ID	BOISE	13	10	11	20,663
	NV	LAS VEGAS	25	18	19	25,918
	OR	PORTLAND	11	8	7	22,959
	WA	SEATTLE	16	12	9	25,432
INTERNATIONAL	ALL	ALL	12	10	11	15,404

*Average adjusted gross income reported on federal income tax returns filed by individuals for the 1987 tax year.

Table 2

FIRST NOTICES FILED BY IRS PER 1,000 RETURNS FILED

Region	Delinquency Rate (per 1,000)			Average Dollars Delinquent		
	1986	1987	1988	1986	1987	1988
INDIVIDUAL MASTER FILE						
UNITED STATES	74	69	73	$1,703	$1,722	$1,619
NORTH ATLANTIC	69	66	74	1,687	1,846	1,750
MID-ATLANTIC	68	60	67	1,729	1,581	1,461
SOUTHEAST	74	67	72	1,664	1,653	1,550
CENTRAL	52	51	54	1,318	1,396	1,393
MIDWEST	59	56	57	1,442	1,454	1,467
SOUTHWEST	92	84	82	1,732	1,884	1,743
WESTERN	98	93	95	1,996	1,928	1,769
INTERNATIONAL		142	134		1,954	1,893
BUSINESS MASTER FILE						
UNITED STATES	178	170	146	$6,868	$3,130	$3,229
NORTH ATLANTIC	158	172	148	16,155	4,270	3,704
MID-ATLANTIC	171	166	143	7,031	4,050	3,822
SOUTHEAST	168	176	159	2,972	2,053	2,411
CENTRAL	150	159	134	3,796	2,142	2,819
MIDWEST	136	143	120	4,132	3,466	2,970
SOUTHWEST	181	180	154	8,382	3,183	3,381
WESTERN	169	179	153	5,863	2,861	3,188
INTERNATIONAL		313	267		5,578	9,751

Table 3

TAXPAYER DELINQUENCY ACCOUNTS PER 1,000 FIRST NOTICES

Region	Number of Serious Delinquencies (per 1,000 TDAs)			Average Dollars for Serious Delinquencies ($s)		
	1986	1987	1988	1986	1987	1988
INDIVIDUAL MASTER FILE						
UNITED STATES	164	193	198	$5,159	$5,357	$5,410
NORTH ATLANTIC	134	160	153	5,429	5,479	5,518
MID-ATLANTIC	121	132	124	7,121	5,407	5,904
SOUTHEAST	148	174	173	5,125	5,086	5,249
CENTRAL	178	212	218	4,155	4,744	4,548
MIDWEST	108	128	131	4,718	5,044	5,826
SOUTHWEST	218	266	285	4,864	5,158	5,454
WESTERN	197	222	225	5,011	5,654	5,387
INTERNATIONAL		107	118	7,307	15,551	10,649
BUSINESS MASTER FILE						
UNITED STATES	224	234	256	$7,648	$6,924	$6,971
NORTH ATLANTIC	229	239	266	12,411	10,058	8,572
MID-ATLANTIC	222	215	234	10,221	10,006	8,630
SOUTHEAST	192	205	237	5,497	5,202	5,665
CENTRAL	247	265	289	5,743	5,435	5,330
MIDWEST	168	164	179	5,885	5,960	6,094
SOUTHWEST	282	307	339	6,124	6,020	6,705
WESTERN	225	232	245	7,535	6,486	6,977
INTERNATIONAL		391	·366	7,004	4,892	13,023

Table 4

LEVIES, LIENS, AND SEIZURES
PER 1,000 TAXPAYER DELINQUENT ACCOUNTS

Region	1986	1987	1988
RATE OF LEVIES			
UNITED STATES	619	713	718
NORTH ATLANTIC	647	739	714
MID-ATLANTIC	631	664	860
SOUTHEAST	496	576	532
CENTRAL	630	609	714
MIDWEST	661	684	708
SOUTHWEST	560	700	735
WESTERN	738	960	892
INTERNATIONAL		243	215
RATE OF LIENS			
UNITED STATES	294	290	279
NORTH ATLANTIC	261	248	262
MID-ATLANTIC	237	261	289
SOUTHEAST	315	261	282
CENTRAL	278	269	265
MIDWEST	322	317	321
SOUTHWEST	321	331	274
WESTERN	306	326	313
INTERNATIONAL		287	173
SEIZURES			
UNITED STATES	9	7	5
NORTH ATLANTIC	7	5	4
MID-ATLANTIC	9	7	4
SOUTHEAST	10	7	5
CENTRAL	10	7	5
MIDWEST	11	9	5
SOUTHWEST	6	7	6
WESTERN	9	8	5
INTERNATIONAL		4	1
RATE OF LEVIES + LIENS + SEIZURES			
UNITED STATES	921	1,010	1,002
NORTH ATLANTIC	914	993	980
MID-ATLANTIC	877	932	1,154
SOUTHEAST	821	844	819
CENTRAL	918	884	984
MIDWEST	994	1,010	1,034
SOUTHWEST	887	1,039	1,015
WESTERN	1,053	1,294	1,210
INTERNATIONAL		534	388

Table 5

SEIZURES PER 1,000 TAXPAYER DELINQUENT ACCOUNTS

Internal Revenue Service Office					
REGION	**STATE**	**DISTRICT**	1986	1987	1988
UNITED STATES	ALL	ALL	9	7	5
NORTH ATLANTIC	ALL	ALL	7	5	4
	CT	HARTFORD	16	17	13
	MA	BOSTON	3	3	3
	ME	AUGUSTA	6	15	8
	NH	PORTSMOUTH	26	14	8
	NY	ALL	8	5	4
		ALBANY	27	21	17
		BROOKLYN	38	17	19
		BUFFALO	5	3	2
		MANHATTAN	5	4	2
	RI	PROVIDENCE	13	20	6
	VT	BURLINGTON	12	13	5
MID-ATLANTIC	ALL	ALL	9	6	4
	DE	WILMINGTON	12	9	4
	MD	BALTIMORE	10	4	2
	NJ	NEWARK	7	4	2
	PA	ALL	8	6	4
		PHILADELPHIA	6	4	2
		PITTSBURGH	23	32	26
	VA	RICHMOND	36	37	29
SOUTHEAST	ALL	ALL	10	7	5
	AL	BIRMINGHAM	37	30	11
	AR	LITTLE ROCK	30	21	15
	FL	ALL	12	8	5
		FT. LAUDERDALE		57	27
		JACKSONVILLE	12	4	3
	GA	ATLANTA	4	3	2
	LA	NEW ORLEANS	46	27	24
	MS	JACKSON	21	17	16
	NC	GREENSBORO	30	23	16
	SC	COLUMBIA	30	27	13
	TN	NASHVILLE	3	2	1
CENTRAL	ALL	• ALL	10	6	5
	IN	INDIANAPOLIS	6	4	4
	KY	LOUISVILLE	29	28	27
	MI	DETROIT	11	7	4
	OH	ALL	9	6	4
		CINCINNATI	33	21	22
		CLEVELAND	5	4	2

Table 5 (Continued)

Internal Revenue Service Office			1986	1987	1988
REGION	**STATE**	**DISTRICT**			
	WV	PARKERSBURG	26	22	13
MIDWEST	ALL	ALL	11	8	5
	IA	DES MOINES	53	23	15
	IL	ALL	9	7	4
		CHICAGO	8	7	4
		SPRINGFIELD	32	21	14
	MN	ST. PAUL	35	21	18
	MO	ST. LOUIS	7	4	3
	MT	HELENA	11	15	13
	ND	FARGO	14	14	10
	NE	OMAHA	34	28	17
	SD	ABERDEEN	23	8	10
	WI	MILWAUKEE	19	16	12
SOUTHWEST	ALL	ALL	6	7	6
	AZ	PHOENIX	32	24	14
	CO	DENVER	2	2	2
	KS	WICHITA	44	25	26
	NM	ALBUQUERQUE	14	12	15
	OK	OKLAHOMA CITY	28	46	33
	TX	ALL	6	6	6
		AUSTIN	35	41	41
		DALLAS	5	4	4
		HOUSTON	4	4	3
	UT	SALT LAKE CITY	27	21	15
	WY	CHEYENNE	25	34	24
WESTERN	ALL	ALL	9	7	5
	AK	ANCHORAGE	31	29	33
	CA	ALL	10	8	6
		LAGUNA NIGUEL	6	5	3
		LOS ANGELES	38	37	24
		SACRAMENTO	28	21	17
		SAN FRANCISCO	2	2	2
		SAN JOSE	54	29	31
	HI	HONOLULU	51	29	18
	ID	BOISE	31	26	20
	NV	LAS VEGAS	26	43	27
	OR	PORTLAND	26	20	14
	WA	SEATTLE	3	3	2
INTERNATIONAL		OTHER	0	1	0
		PUERTO RICO	4	4	2
		ALL	3	3	1

Table 6

INSTALLMENT AGREEMENTS ENTERED INTO BY IRS PER 1,000 TAXPAYER DELINQUENT ACCOUNTS

Internal Revenue Service Office					
Region	State	District	1986	1987	1988
UNITED STATES	ALL	ALL	119	99	127
NORTH ATLANTIC	ALL	ALL	96	67	68
	CT	HARTFORD	72	49	43
	MA	BOSTON	123	54	57
	ME	AUGUSTA	87	76	71
	NH	PORTSMOUTH	66	24	22
	NY	ALL	86	74	75
		ALBANY	80	64	54
		BROOKLYN	54	36	51
		BUFFALO	120	42	58
		MANHATTAN	73	98	87
	RI	PROVIDENCE	59	39	43
	VT	BURLINGTON	63	56	39
MID-ATLANTIC	ALL	ALL	152	114	95
	DE	WILMINGTON	63	40	39
	MD	BALTIMORE	228	157	116
	NJ	NEWARK	111	116	133
	PA	ALL	142	92	52
		PHILADELPHIA	151	96	53
		PITTSBURGH	32	31	34
	VA	RICHMOND	80	48	52
SOUTHEAST	ALL	ALL	120	90	134
	AL	BIRMINGHAM	97	88	71
	AR	LITTLE ROCK	120	103	87
	FL	ALL	89	64	83
		FT. LAUDERDALE		75	66
		JACKSONVILLE	89	63	84
	GA	ATLANTA	73	72	186
	LA	NEW ORLEANS	56	47	71
	MS	JACKSON	93	73	62
	NC	GREENSBORO	104	88	70
	SC	COLUMBIA	87	70	69
	TN	NASHVILLE	240	168	171
CENTRAL	ALL	ALL	168	157	188
	IN	INDIANAPOLIS	157	159	227
	KY	LOUISVILLE	83	68	66
	MI	DETROIT	186	175	198
	OH	ALL	167	148	160
		CINCINNATI	66	62	64

Table 6 *(Continued)*

Internal Revenue Service Office					
Region	**State**	**District**	**1986**	**1987**	**1988**
		CLEVELAND	181	158	172
	WV	PARKERSBURG	78	48	38
MIDWEST	ALL	ALL	74	57	70
	IA	DES MOINES	113	122	119
	IL	ALL	69	54	65
		CHICAGO	67	53	65
		SPRINGFIELD	102	86	54
	MN	ST. PAUL	62	64	53
	MO	ST. LOUIS	84	55	81
	MT	HELENA	79	57	64
	ND	FARGO	48	49	50
	NE	OMAHA	87	60	67
	SD	ABERDEEN	111	73	77
	WI	MILWAUKEE	74	66	70
SOUTHWEST	ALL	ALL	121	127	158
	AZ	PHOENIX	91	63	74
	CO	DENVER	110	111	160
	KS	WICHITA	109	82	75
	NM	ALBUQUERQUE	44	46	66
	OK	OKLAHOMA CITY	51	59	74
	TX	ALL	133	141	165
		AUSTIN	61	43	53
		DALLAS	128	147	155
		HOUSTON	145	146	190
	UT	SALT LAKE CITY	46	32	30
	WY	CHEYENNE	111	26	43
WESTERN	ALL	ALL	111	81	136
	AK	ANCHORAGE	90	70	97
	CA	ALL	120	85	147
		LAGUNA NIGUEL	130	91	158
		LOS ANGELES	100	62	59
		SACRAMENTO	89	62	68
		SAN FRANCISCO	116	87	163
		SAN JOSE	99	63	72
	HI	HONOLULU	102	71	63
	ID	BOISE	98	74	91
	NV	LAS VEGAS	114	105	100
	OR	PORTLAND	84	69	82
	WA	SEATTLE	88	71	116
INTERNATIONAL		OTHER	18	16	18
		PUERTO RICO	10	4	2
		ALL	12	7	5

Internal Revenue Service
Organization Chart

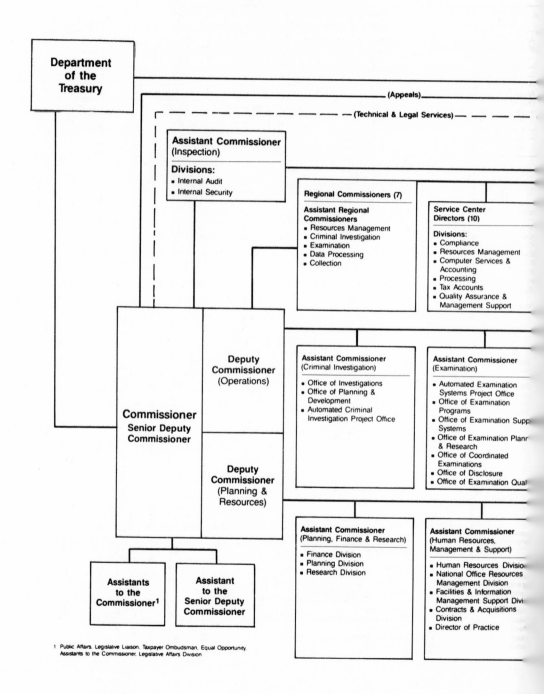

Department of the Treasury

(Appeals)

(Technical & Legal Services)

Assistant Commissioner (Inspection)

Divisions:
- Internal Audit
- Internal Security

Regional Commissioners (7)

Assistant Regional Commissioners
- Resources Management
- Criminal Investigation
- Examination
- Data Processing
- Collection

Service Center Directors (10)

Divisions:
- Compliance
- Resources Management
- Computer Services & Accounting
- Processing
- Tax Accounts
- Quality Assurance & Management Support

Commissioner
Senior Deputy Commissioner

Deputy Commissioner (Operations)

Deputy Commissioner (Planning & Resources)

Assistant Commissioner (Criminal Investigation)
- Office of Investigations
- Office of Planning & Development
- Automated Criminal Investigation Project Office

Assistant Commissioner (Examination)
- Automated Examination Systems Project Office
- Office of Examination Programs
- Office of Examination Supp Systems
- Office of Examination Plann & Research
- Office of Coordinated Examinations
- Office of Disclosure
- Office of Examination Qual

Assistant Commissioner (Planning, Finance & Research)
- Finance Division
- Planning Division
- Research Division

Assistant Commissioner (Human Resources, Management & Support)
- Human Resources Divisio
- National Office Resources Management Division
- Facilities & Information Management Support Divi
- Contracts & Acquisitions Division
- Director of Practice

Assistants to the Commissioner[1]

Assistant to the Senior Deputy Commissioner

1 Public Affairs, Legislative Liaison, Taxpayer Ombudsman, Equal Opportunity, Assistants to the Commissioner, Legislative Affairs Division

Chief Counsel
Deputy Chief Counsel

ociate Chief Counsel
ance and Management)
General Legal Services
Office of Information Systems
Office of Planning & Finance
Office of Human Resources
ociate Chief Counsel
hnical)
Financial Institutions &
Products
Corporate
Passthroughs & Special
Industries

— Income Tax & Accounting
— Employee Benefits &
  Exempt Organizations
• Associate Chief Counsel
  (International)
— Technical
— Litigation & Field Advice
• Associate Chief Counsel
  (Litigation)
— Criminal Tax
— Disclosure Litigation
— General Litigation
— Tax Litigation

• National Director of Appeals
— Office of Training &
  Quality Programs
— Office of Field Services
— Office of Large Case
  Programs
— Office of TEFRA & Tax
  Shelter Programs
— Office of Information
  Management Services
— Office of AES
— Office of Appraisal Services

Regional Counsel (7)
Deputy Regional Counsel

■ Criminal Tax
■ General Litigation
■ Tax Litigation

Assistant Regional Counsel

■ General Legal Services

Regional Director of Appeals

District Counsel

---

ct Directors (63)

ons:
ection
minal Investigation
mination
ployee Plans &
mpt Organizations
ources Management
payer Service

same in all districts

Regional Inspectors (7)
Assistant Regional Inspectors

■ Internal Audit
■ Internal Security

---

stant Commissioner
(ction)

ce of Planning &
nagement
ce of Field Operations
ce of Evaluation &
search

Assistant Commissioner
(Employee Plans & Exempt Organizations)

■ Exempt Organizations
  Technical Division
■ Employee Plans Technical
  and Actuarial Division
■ Employee Plans & Exempt
  Organizations Operations
  Division

Assistant Commissioner
(International)

■ Office of Resources Mgmt.
■ Office of Tax Treaty &
  Technical Services
■ Office of Taxpayer Service
  and Compliance
■ Office of Tax Administration
  Advisory Services
■ Office of International Programs
■ Office of Management,
  Planning & Research
■ Systems Planning & Quality
  Improvement Staff

Assistant Commissioner
(Taxpayer Service & Returns Processing)

■ Office of Legislative &
  Management Support
■ Office of Information Systems
  & Resources
■ Returns Processing &
  Accounting Division
■ Statistics of Income Division
■ Taxpayer Service Division
■ Tax Forms & Publications Div.
  Division

---

stant Commissioner
(mputer Services)

anning, Budgeting &
view Staff
stems Management &
eration Services Division
mpliance Systems Division
x Systems Division
stems Support & Testing
ision
ecommunications Division
troit Computing Center
rtinsburg Computing Center

Assistant Commissioner
(Information Systems Development)

■ Office of Input Processing
■ Office of Departmental
  Systems
■ Office of Corporate Systems
■ Office of Standards & Data
  Administration
■ Office of Planning & Project
  Management
■ Office of Systems Engineering
  & Integration

November 5, 1988

Internal Revenue Service Regions, Districts and Service Centers

WESTERN REGION

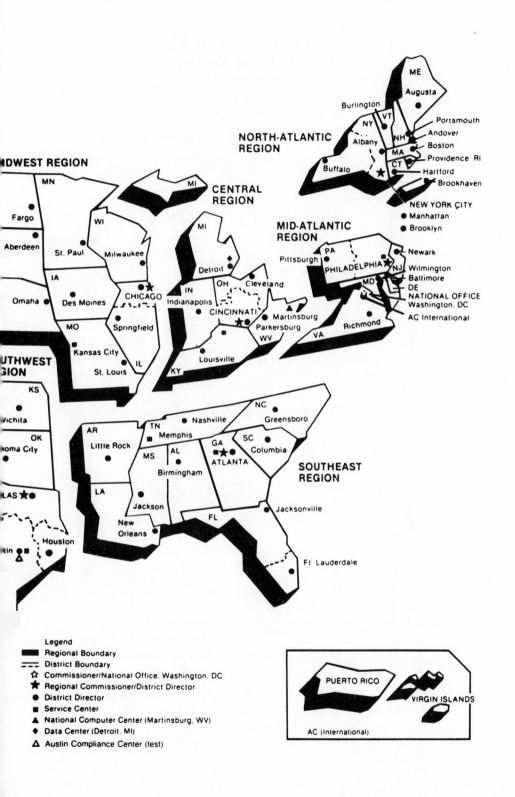

NORTH-ATLANTIC REGION

ME
Augusta
Burlington
NY VT
Portsmouth
Albany
NH
Andover
Boston
MA
Providence RI
CT
Hartford
Buffalo
Brookhaven
NEW YORK CITY
Manhattan
Brooklyn

MIDWEST REGION

CENTRAL REGION

MN
Fargo
WI
Aberdeen
St. Paul
Milwaukee
MI
Detroit
IA
MI
OH
Cleveland
Omaha
Des Moines
CHICAGO
IN
Indianapolis
CINCINNATI
MO
Springfield
Martinsburg
Parkersburg
WV
Kansas City

SOUTHWEST REGION

IL
St. Louis
KY
Louisville

MID-ATLANTIC REGION

PA
Pittsburgh
Newark
PHILADELPHIA
NJ
Wilmington
Baltimore
MD
DE
NATIONAL OFFICE
Washington, DC
AC International
VA
Richmond

KS
Wichita
OK
Oklahoma City
DALLAS

AR
Little Rock
TN
Memphis
Nashville
NC
Greensboro
GA
ATLANTA
SC
Columbia

SOUTHEAST REGION

MS
AL
Birmingham

LA
Jackson
New Orleans
FL
Jacksonville

Austin
Houston
Ft Lauderdale

Legend
▬ Regional Boundary
--- District Boundary
☆ Commissioner/National Office, Washington, DC
★ Regional Commissioner/District Director
● District Director
■ Service Center
▲ National Computer Center (Martinsburg, WV)
♦ Data Center (Detroit, MI)
△ Austin Compliance Center (test)

PUERTO RICO
VIRGIN ISLANDS
AC (International)

Total Number of Returns Filed and Gross Revenues

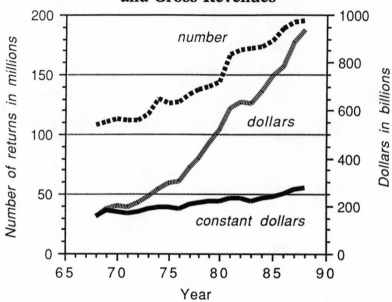

Total Number of IRS Employees and Budget

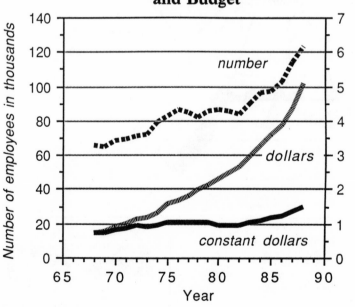

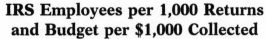

IRS Employees per 1,000 Returns and Budget per $1,000 Collected

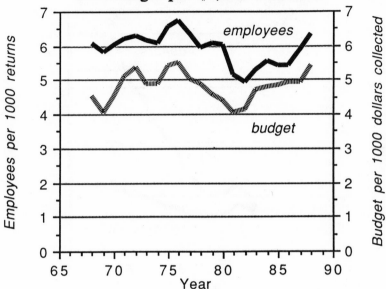

Number and Rate of Audits on All Returns (Individual, Corporate, etc.)

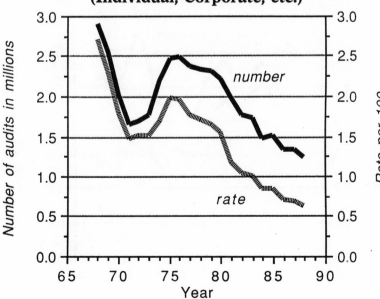

Tax Audits:
Additional Taxes Recommended

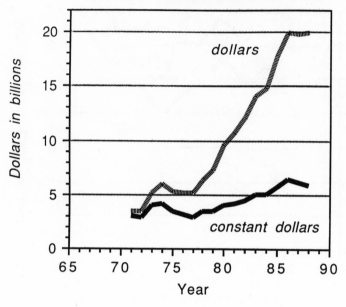

Delinquent Accounts:
Number and Rate

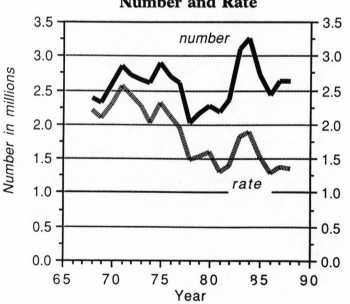

Delinquent Accounts:
Taxes Collected

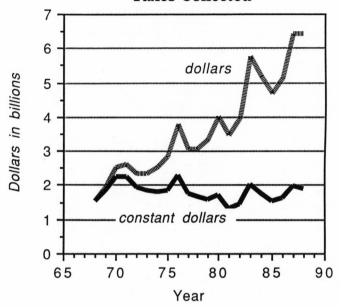

Criminal Tax Indictments:
Number and Rate

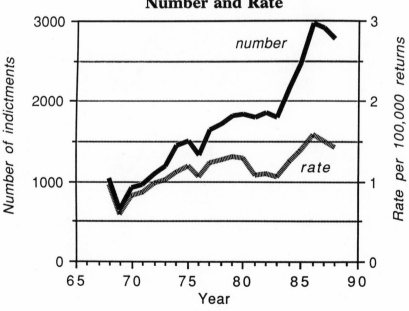

Index

For more than fifteen years, DAVID BURNHAM was an investigative reporter for *The New York Times* in New York and Washington. His reporting, based on information from Frank Serpico and David Durk, led to the creation of the Knapp Commission on police corruption in New York City and far-reaching reforms in its police department. Then, four years before the Three Mile Island incident, he turned his attention to the serious problems plaguing the nation's nuclear industry. Karen Silkwood was on her way to tell him about what was happening at the Kerr-McGee nuclear plant in Oklahoma when she died in a still-disputed car crash.

Before joining the *Times*, Burnham worked for UPI, *Newsweek* and CBS. He has won the George Polk Award for Distinguished Investigative Reporting and a number of Page One awards from the New York Newspaper Guild, the Silurian Society and the New York Press Club. He is also the author of *The Rise of the Computer State,* an investigative book published in 1983 on how the growth of powerful computerized bureaucracies is gradually altering the nature of representative democracy.